ROUTLEDGE LIBRARY EDITIONS: W. B. YEATS

Volume 1

W.B. YEATS

W.B. YEATS
A Census of the Manuscripts

CONRAD A. BALLIET
WITH THE ASSISTANCE OF
CHRISTINE MAWHINNEY

LONDON AND NEW YORK

First published in 1990 by Garland Publishing, Inc.

This edition first published in 2017
by Routledge
2 Park Square, Milton Park, Abingdon, Oxon OX14 4RN

and by Routledge
711 Third Avenue, New York, NY 10017

Routledge is an imprint of the Taylor & Francis Group, an informa business

© 1990 Conrad A. Balliet

All rights reserved. No part of this book may be reprinted or reproduced or utilised in any form or by any electronic, mechanical, or other means, now known or hereafter invented, including photocopying and recording, or in any information storage or retrieval system, without permission in writing from the publishers.

Trademark notice: Product or corporate names may be trademarks or registered trademarks, and are used only for identification and explanation without intent to infringe.

British Library Cataloguing in Publication Data
A catalogue record for this book is available from the British Library

ISBN: 978-1-138-21351-7 (Set)
ISBN: 978-1-315-44820-6 (Set) (ebk)
ISBN: 978-1-138-20120-0 (Volume 1) (hbk)
ISBN: 978-1-138-20122-4 (Volume 1) (pbk)
ISBN: 978-1-315-51241-9 (Volume 1) (ebk)

Publisher's Note
The publisher has gone to great lengths to ensure the quality of this reprint but points out that some imperfections in the original copies may be apparent.

Disclaimer
The publisher has made every effort to trace copyright holders and would welcome correspondence from those they have been unable to trace.

W.B. YEATS
A Census of the Manuscripts

Conrad A. Balliet
with the assistance of
Christine Mawhinney

GARLAND PUBLISHING, INC. • NEW YORK & LONDON
1990

© 1990 Conrad A. Balliet
All rights reserved

Library of Congress Cataloging-in-Publication Data

Balliet, Conrad A., 1927–
   W.B. Yeats: a census of the manuscripts / Conrad A. Balliet.
     p. cm. — (Garland reference library of the humanities ; vol. 772)
   Includes bibliographical references.
   ISBN 0-8240-6629-4 (alk. paper)
   1. Yeats, W.B. (William Butler), 1865–1939—Manuscripts—Union lists. 2. Manuscripts, English—Union lists. I. Title. II. Series..
Z6616.Y43B35 1990
[PR5906]
821'.8—dc20   89-17226
                                                                                             CIP

We acknowledge permission to quote from the poetry and prose of W.B. Yeats by A.P. Watt Ltd., on behalf of Anne Yeats and Michael Yeats, and by Macmillan Publishing Company to quote from the *Variorum Edition of the Poems of W.B. Yeats*, edited by Peter Allt and Russell K. Alspach. Copyright 1916, 1919, 1928 by Macmillan Publishing Company, renewed 1944, 1947, 1956 by Bertha George Yeats. Copyright 1940 by Georgie Yeats, renewed 1968 by Bertha Georgie Yeats, Michael Butler Yeats, and Anne Yeats. We also acknowledge permission to quote from manuscripts in the possession of the Beinecke Rare Book and Manuscript Library, Yale University; The Houghton Library, Harvard University; the Harry Ransom Humanities Research Center, the University of Texas at Austin; the Henry W. and Albert A. Berg Collection, The Astor, Lennox and Tilden Foundations, The New York Public Library; the National Library of Ireland; the Robert W. Woodruff Library, Emory University; the Stanford University Libraries; the University of Arizona; and the University of Kansas.

Printed on acid-free, 250-year-life paper
Manufactured in the United States of America

WITH GRATITUDE
TO MY WIFE MARION
AND OTHER FRIENDS

who have patiently
listened to the chatter
and
put up with the clutter
for all these years

CONTENTS

Preface ix

Acknowledgments xix

List of Abbreviations xxiii

How to Use this *Census* xxiv

MANUSCRIPTS

Books 3

Inscriptions 73

Letters 99

Miscellany
    Diaries and Journals 181
    Documents 187
    Folklore, Myth, and Legend 188
    Irish Academy Material 189
    Lane Material 190
    Lists 191
    Miscellaneous 193

Occult Material	196
Photographs	197
Quoted and Paraphrased Material	198
Reviews	201
Theatre Material	202

Other Authors	205
Plays	223
Poems	243
Poems, Unpublished	335
Prose	357
Speeches	371

LIBRARIES AND OTHER OWNERS	385
APPENDIX	
Alternate and Variant Titles of Poems	449
BIBLIOGRAPHY	457
INDEXES	
Libraries and Other Owners	
Alphabetical	467
Geographical	471
Manuscripts	477

PREFACE

Any scholar who has tried to "edit and annotate the lines" of W.B. Yeats or has set out to do research involving his manuscripts is aware of the difficulty of gathering information. The poet himself, as usual, anticipated the problems in his poem "Where My Books Go":

> All the words that I gather,
> And all the words that I write,
> Must spread out their wings untiring,
> And never rest in their flight.

The search for manuscripts that have taken flight has led scholars to Dublin clubs, Parisian attics, and the Scottish highlands; to India, Texas, and Australia; and, of course, to libraries, archives, and collectors. Some five years ago, I set out on a quest—to find, list, and describe as many manuscripts of W.B. Yeats as possible. Only later did I learn that at least seven people had already started such a search—and given up. My quest led to over ten countries, to more than one hundred and fifty libraries and other owners of manuscripts, and to contacts with many helpful individuals: secretaries, scholars, booksellers, librarians, and other interesting people.

The search involved a lot of work. The effort appears negligible, however, when compared to the effort that W.B. Yeats put into writing all that material—single lines of descriptions here refer to manuscripts of hundreds of pages of WBY's writing—and he did not have a computer. For those interested in technical detail, the information about the manuscripts was entered on a Quo Data program (QDMS) on a

VAX 11/750. The listing has over 3500 titles and names, with descriptions of more than 7000 individual manuscripts, yet the list is no doubt incomplete.

The quest began with the usual library research in reference works and manuscript listings. Then came queries to many libraries, requests for information at Yeats and Irish studies conferences, notices in journals, and personal visits to places with extensive holdings. I spent some time examining directly the manuscripts at The New York Public Library, Harvard University and other Boston libraries, the University of Texas at Austin, the British Museum, the National Library of Ireland (NLI), and the microfilm copies at the State University of New York at Stony Brook (SUNY SB). Some roads seemed not worth following. Although auction catalogues describe manuscripts to be sold, auction houses do not disclose the names of buyers, and the experience of other scholars confirmed my own experience— letters forwarded to purchasers are seldom answered. Booksellers sometimes have manuscripts, but only temporarily, and the manuscripts often disappear into unknown locations. Some roads were detours or dead ends. A number of individuals with significant collections failed to answer queries, and a few librarians were not very helpful. Thus, though I had hoped to locate almost all Yeats manuscripts, I had to compromise by focusing on public and accessible collections.

SOURCES AND METHODS

In a work of this extent and complexity, other compromises were necessary. I was not able to work directly with the material still in possession of the Yeats family. Senator Michael Yeats has an extensive collection of manuscripts: occult material, personal diaries, letters to the family of the poet and to Olivia Shakespear, and other items. The holdings are described in a mimeographed "Partial List of Manuscripts in the Collection of Senator Michael B. Yeats," compiled in 1978 and 1981 by a group of scholars including Mary Fitzgerald

Finneran, Richard J. Finneran, George Mills Harper, John S. Kelly, and Thomas F. Parkinson. Many of the items on the list are now at NLI, with copies of most, but not all, of the manuscripts available at SUNY SB.

These major holdings presented major problems. To make a thorough list, with extensive cross-references, of the manuscripts in the National Library of Ireland and of those still in the possession of the Yeats family, and to integrate that list with the descriptions of the copies at SUNY SB, would require the completion of a task that neither Stony Brook itself nor the National Library of Ireland has yet completed. The *Census* indicates if copies are at SUNY SB and gives box numbers for those items when possible. Unfortunately, because the catalogues and indexes of both NLI and SUNY SB are still incomplete, it has been impossible to identify and describe all the individual items. A missing manuscript number for NLI or box number for SUNY SB indicates that the manuscript is (presumably) at NLI, or the copy is at SUNY SB, but not specifically catalogued or indexed.

The library of W.B. Yeats is in the possession of his daughter, Miss Anne Yeats. Edward O'Shea has details on her collection in *A Descriptive Catalog of W.B. Yeats's Library*. To include all the relevant items from that book would essentially duplicate O'Shea's work; to exclude all would make this *Census* less complete. The compromise here has been to include basic information from O'Shea (and item numbers) on drafts of poems and other writings, on books used as copytexts (with cross-references to individual works), and on inscriptions; but to exclude books with only signatures or marginalia.

On visits to libraries, I worked with the catalogues and with some original manuscripts, but did not make a detailed study of text and variants, provenance, arrangement, or dating. To facilitate such study by other scholars is the goal of this *Census*, but I had neither time nor money for a thorough study. Thus the descriptions are based primarily on information supplied by catalogues, librarians, and other individuals, and the accuracy of this *Census* depends in part upon the accuracy of library records. I am, however, certainly responsible for some mistakes—would that there were errors and omissions insurance available for scholars as there is for real estate and travel agents. The *Census* is intended primarily as a finding aid for manuscripts, not as an authority on dates, quoted material, or content.

Since the systems that libraries use to classify manuscripts vary, and the information received in response to queries was often incomplete, I do not routinely include library call numbers. For libraries with extensive holdings, or where there may be difficulty in locating manuscripts, I have included available shelflist or library call numbers in parentheses at the end of the description. Manuscript numbers are given for the National Library of Ireland; those with numbers in the 30,000 series were formerly in the Yeats family collection, and the last three or four digits represent the "Partial List..." number (Partial List... #104, for example, became NLI Ms 30104; Partial List... #1065 became NLI Ms 31065). For The New York Public Library, the location of items in places other than the Berg Collection is noted. I have included shelflist information for British libraries, relying extensively on the *Location Register of Twentieth-Century English Literary Manuscripts and Letters*, published by The British Library, edited by David C. Sutton of Reading University.

Some terms and data may lack consistency or precision. For example, I use the word "correction" to apply to minor changes, often in proof or fair copies, and "revision" to apply to more significant and extensive changes—but descriptions from libraries may not be completely consistent with that usage. So, too, with dates. Rather than standardize them, I record them as observed or received in the manuscript or in the data from a library, and note if they represent a postmark, a printer's stamp, or a conjecture, when such information is available.

Near the end of the project, in the spring of 1988, I sent printouts of the descriptions to individual libraries for double checking against their listings and for updating; most libraries responded with corrections and information on recent acquisitions. The *Census*, current through the autumn of 1988, has extensive, basic information on many holdings, but is far from complete.

Preface

DEFINITION OF A MANUSCRIPT

The search also required the definition of a manuscript. As used here, the word includes a dictionary definition: "a book, document, or other composition written by hand; handwriting, as opposed to printing." At that simple level, items in the hand of W.B. Yeats are usually easy to identify, even when illegible. But items he may have typed? or dictated? or proofread? Ultimately, I have considered as manuscripts any items that WBY seems to have worked with directly, in the writing, revising, or correcting, with one exception: I have not included mere autographs (in signed editions of his books with 400 copies, for example). My definition of "manuscript" thus includes accounts; contracts; invitations and announcements signed by WBY; marginalia; material copied by him from another source; inscribed photographs; proof and galley sheets; telegrams and postcards as well as letters; and documents WBY may have typed or had typed for him. Photocopied material is not included, with two exceptions. If a library has a copy of a manuscript for which no original is listed, I describe the copy. And, because of the extensive collection of photocopied material at SUNY SB (of originals in the National Library of Ireland, in the Yeats family collection, and elsewhere), the *Census* lists (as noted above) copies at SUNY SB. A Finding Aid is available there.

STYLE AND FORMAT

The computer, the available word processor, and offset printing imposed limitations on typography and format—it was not possible to use italics, underlining, diacritical marks, or some other special characters. Titles of WBY's works appear in ordinary type on the first line of the primary listing; other titles appear with capital letters or quotation marks. In quotations of poetry, the second line begins with a capital letter, but no slash appears before it. Material quoted from manuscripts carries the unique and varied spelling and punctuation of WBY, without the intrusive "sic." Dates are given as they appear in manuscripts or in information from libraries.

ARRANGEMENT

The *Census* is arranged by genre or type (in spite of the difficulties of classification and cross-referencing), since most users will want to know the varied locations of specific manuscripts. A secondary listing is by "Libraries and Other Owners," with abbreviated (QUICK) titles of manuscripts held by them. An appendix lists the alternate and variant titles WBY used in earlier or rejected versions, keyed to the QUICK title used in this *Census*. There are two indexes to the "Libraries and Other Owners" section: one alphabetical, the other geographical. Finally, the major index includes titles, QUICK titles, the type, and the page number where the primary description begins. The primary listing has these types, all arranged alphabetically:

Books: Includes anything WBY wrote or edited and published in book form (with its number from Wade's *Bibliography* if available), with a few exceptions. Items not related to a specific book are included with a generic title: Vision Material; Winding Stair Material; Unpublished Macmillan and Scribner Editions. A few items not published by WBY during his lifetime also appear: *The Speckled Bird, The Rosy Cross,* and *Ye Pleiades.* The basic descriptions of Books inscribed by WBY are repeated in the Inscriptions section. Arranged by title.

Inscriptions: Includes items WBY inscribed, usually in editions he gave to relatives and friends; does not include mere signatures. Arranged by recipient.

Letters: Includes letters, notes, cards, telegrams, invitations, and signed form letters, with basic information on form (ALS, TLS) and number of letters with range of dates, and

Preface   xv

    occasional brief comments on the subject. Arranged by recipient.

Miscellany: Includes material that does not fit elsewhere, in the following subcategories: Diaries and Journals; Documents; Folklore, Myth, and Legend; Irish Academy Material; Lane Material; Lists; Miscellaneous; Occult Material; Photographs; Quoted and Paraphrased Material; Reviews (of plays); and Theatre Material. Arranged by above categories.

Other Authors: Includes items, mostly books, by other authors to which Yeats contributed or in which he wrote (notes, for example, or inscriptions). Arranged by author.

Plays: Includes material related to the plays—those in Alspach's *Variorum Edition*, as well as some not published. Arranged by title.

Poems: Includes published poems, that is, those WBY chose to include in his published collections; based on Allt's *Variorum Edition* and Finneran's *Poems of W.B. Yeats: A New Edition*. Arranged by title.

Poems, Unpublished: Includes poetic material not published in the *Variorum* or Finneran editions. Arranged by title, opening words, or arbitrary subject, with a note indicating if the poem has appeared in print.

Prose: Includes any prose material published in various books and periodicals not covered by the above categories, such as essays and stories, with one section of material that, although not published, seemed intended for publication. Arranged by title.

Speeches: Includes any manuscript material related to the numerous talks and lectures, including radio broadcasts.

    Arranged by title, opening words, or arbitrary subject.

Material related to two or more categories is cross-referenced and may be listed in several places. Inscriptions, for example, are described or listed both under the title of the book in which they are written and the name of the recipient. A copy of *Mosada* inscribed to a Miss Veasey is noted briefly under both Books and Inscriptions. Corrections and revisions of poems in a notebook or galley proof used for a book of poems are listed with the book and cross-referenced to each poem, if possible. In some instances, however, when an entire book has been used as a copytext for a later edition, or when almost the entire Yeats canon appears in galley form (such as the Unpublished Macmillan Edition), the primary entry notes that fact, but individual poems or works are not cross-referenced. Thus the scholar who wishes to be thorough would do well to check a given work in all its manifestations and emanations.

The letters presented some problems. In view of the Oxford edition of *The Collected Letters*, now in progress, it might have been wise simply to omit a listing here. That edition, however, is behind schedule, and will likely be longer than ten years in the making. Though it lists the location of individual letters, it has at this time neither a thorough listing of the letters to individual recipients nor a list of the holdings of any given library. Unfortunately, detailed information on letters to be published in that edition was not available. In order, however, to enable scholars in the interim to find widely scattered letters to some six hundred recipients, and to know what can be found at any given location, this *Census* includes, in limited form, the available information on letters.

Inscriptions presented different problems. They are, perhaps, borderline as manuscripts, scattered more widely than any other items except letters, and often ignored by critics and scholars, yet they are clearly "a form of composition written by hand." Some libraries have no clear catalogue of their holdings, and there are many inscribed books in private hands—thus the listing is, like that of the letters, certainly incomplete. Yet the inscriptions present a rich and largely untapped source of information about dates, friends, opinions, and even the quirks of the poet. The *Census* lists well over one hundred people to whom WBY wrote inscriptions. WBY quoted from some 25 different poems, and inscribed other poems that he never published. Most inscriptions are signed; the presence or absence of a signature is noted, if that information is available. Some have only a date and signature; some discuss a book, some a recipient; many include quotations from WBY's own poetry. The inscriptions provide some new and varied insights.

Speeches presented more problems. WBY often gave the same speech on different occasions, on different dates, in different locations. He sometimes gave a speech under the same title he used earlier for a different speech. As usual, he seldom dated or titled the manuscripts. He often used only notes and fragments as the basis for his speeches. No standard listing or bibliography exists. The speeches, like the inscriptions, invite further study.

LIBRARIES AND OTHER OWNERS

The secondary listing, by "Libraries and Other Owners," has basic information on the address of the owner, with QUICK titles (arranged by type) of the manuscripts held. If a published guide is available, I note that fact and list it in the bibliography. Most libraries will give access to the manuscripts to scholars and others with good reason, and will make copies (usually for a fee) with due respect for copyright law; some expect permission from the literary executor. If I have information about restrictions other than these, I have noted it.

THE INDEXES

The primary index lists the titles of works and the names of individuals for whom there are entries in the listing of manuscripts. It also includes the QUICK title, the "Type" under which the entry can be found (there are listings for Lady Gregory, for example, in the "Inscriptions," "Letters," and "Other Authors" sections), and the page number of the start of the primary listing. The index does not include alternate or variant titles, since manuscripts are listed under their primary or published titles. An appendix lists variant titles. There are two indexes of the "Libraries and Other Owners" section: one alphabetical, one geographical.

CONCLUSION

The project has been a challenge as well as a chore. No doubt it has imperfections; I welcome additional and more accurate information on manuscripts. I hope this *Census* will be a help to those who in the future, like the poet himself in the past, wish to bring "something to perfection," be it "perfection of the life, or of the work," of one of the most prolific and talented of poets.

Conrad A. Balliet
Wittenberg University
Springfield, OH 45501

ACKNOWLEDGMENTS

Fortunately for a work of this magnitude and complexity, the people involved in the study of the writings of W.B. Yeats are friendly and helpful; this *Census* would have been utterly impossible without the cooperation of hundreds of individuals—secretaries, librarians, students, scholars, friends.

Richard Finnernan provided the initial impetus for the project in a talk at a Yeats Symposium at Winthrop College in 1983; since then he has patiently answered queries, helped solve mysteries, read most of the manuscript, and offered many constructive suggestions.

Warwick Gould has shared his knowledge of WBY manuscripts, proofread the copy, clarified confusion, and helped avoid many egregious errors.

Other scholars have also helped with suggestions and read all or parts of this *Census* in manuscript form: George Bornstein, University of Michigan; David Clark, University of Massachusetts, Amherst; William H. O'Donnell, Memphis State University; Ron Schuchard, Emory University.

Wittenberg University has provided support in numerous ways: the sabbatical leave program gave me time to do the research; the Faculty Research Fund Board made possible trips to Austin, Boston, Dublin, London, Long Island, and New York City; the Faculty Development Organization enabled students to work as Faculty Aides: Tom Hilgartner, Patti Hessler, Susan Rafferty, Anne Dolphin, and, for the final three years of the project, Christine Mawhinney, whose patience, concern, and understanding of the unusual combination of W.B. Yeats and the Vax QDMS computer program has contributed extensively to this book. Mary Cox of the Computing Center solved the many problems of organizing and processing vast quantities of information. Other colleagues and staff members also helped: Elizabeth A. Brinkman, Paul W. Miller, Barbara Korn, Verna Parsons.

Senator Michael Yeats and Miss Anne Yeats have made information available on their collections, and have answered numerous queries.

Phyllis Korper and Rita Quintas at Garland helped guide the *Census* from final copy to printed book.

The names of some individuals to whom I owe thanks may have been lost in various folders and letters; those on record include the following: Sherlyn Abdoo, New York University; Martin Antonetti, Mills College; John B. Atteberry, Boston College; Lance J. Bauer, Providence Public Library; Elise Bayley, The Plunkett Foundation; Bruce Berlind, Colgate University; Robert J. Bertholf, SUNY at Buffalo; Giuseppe Bisaccia, Boston Public Library; Beverly D. Bishop, Emory University; Michael Bott, University of Reading Library; Sally Brown, The British Library; Delinda Stephens Buie, University of Louisville; Lucy B. Burgess, Cornell University; Eileen Cahill, The Rosenbach Library; Herbert Cahoon, The Pierpont Morgan Library; Martha Carroll, Dublin; Wayne Chapman, Washington State University; Mary Clapinson, The Bodleian Library; Fiona M. Clark, The Royal Literary Fund; Marion Helen Cobb, Queens University Archives; J. Fraser Cocks III, Colby College; William Crawford, New York City; Lori N. Curtis, University of Tulsa; Daria D'Arienzo, Amherst College Library; Carolyn A. Davis, Syracuse University; Annette Dixon, Yale University; Roger Dixon, Belfast Public Libraries; P.K. Escreet, Glasgow University Library; Catherine Fahy, National Library of Ireland; Stephen Ferguson, Princeton University Library; Barbara Filipac, Brown University Library; Connell B. Gallagher, University of Vermont; K.E. Garay, McMaster University; Jacqueline Genet, Université de Caen; D.S. Goodes, The King's School, Canterbury; Margaret

Acknowledgments

Goostray, Boston University; Rachel Grover, University of Toronto Library; L.A. Hall, The Wellcome Institute for the History of Medicine; M.A. Halls, King's College Library, Cambridge; Tyrus G. Harmsen, Occidental College; George M. Harper, Tallahassee; Cathy Henderson, University of Texas at Austin; T.D. Hobbs, Trinity College, Cambridge; Sara S. Hodson, The Huntington Library; Carolyn Holdsworth, Troy State University, Alabama; K.P.S. Jochum, University of Bamburg; Margaret Kelleher, Boston and Cork; John D. Kendall, University of Massachusettes at Amherst; Mary R. Kent, Connecticut College; Jennifer Knerr, Boulder; Dan Laurence, New York University; Dee Gee Lester, Hendersonville; Marianne Levander, Stockholm; Kenneth A. Lohf, Columbia University Libraries; Richard Londraville, Potsdam; Frank Lorenz, Hamilton College; Leila Luedeking, Washington State University Library; James M. Mahoney, College of the Holy Cross; Angelika G. Malbert, The Fitzwilliam Museum; Charles W. Mann, Pennsylvania State University Libraries; Tony Marshall, State Library of Victoria; Walter Martin, Palo Alto; Anton Masin, University of Notre Dame; Alexandra Mason, University of Kansas; Brian McKenna, National Library of Ireland; Peggy McMullen, SUNY at Stony Brook; S.C. McTernan, Sligo County Library; Diane Menna, Queens; Sylvia V. Metzinger, Tulane University Libraries; Laurie Morton, Dublin; Dorothy Mosakowski, Clark University; William M. Murphy, Schenectady; Maureen Murphy, Hofstra University; Timothy D. Murray, University of Delaware; C. Hoseph Nuesse, Catholic University of America; Annegret Odgen, University of California, Berkeley; Felicity O'Mahony, Trinity College, Dublin; Edward O'Shea, SUNY at Oswego; Mary Y. Osielski, SUNY at Albany; A.E.B. Owen, Cambridge University; M.R. Perkin, University of Liverpool; Sigrid P. Perry, Northwestern University Library; Chris Petter, University of Victoria, B.C.; Jean F. Preston, Princeton University Library; David R. Robrock, University of Arizona; John Rossi, University of Virginia; J.F. Russell, National Library of Scotland; Michael T. Ryan, Stanford University Libraries; Sheila Ryan, Southern Illinois University; Ann Saddlemyer, University of Toronto; Judy

Harvey Sahak, Scripps College; Janet Schroyder, London; P.M. Schute, The Royal Society of Literature; Joan Selby, University of British Columbia; C.D.W. Shepherd, The Brotherton Library; Simon Nowell Smith, Oxford; Colin Smythe, Gerrards Cross; John Sparrow, Oxford; John Stinson, New York Public Library; David C. Sutton, University of Reading; Elizabeth Swaim, Wesleyan University; Saundra Taylor, Indiana University; Robert Tibbets, Ohio State University; Richard Virr, McGill University; Evert Volkercz, SUNY at Stony Brook; Cynthia Wall, The Newberry Library; Jonathan Walters, University of Chicago Library; Stanley Wertheim, New York; Geoffrey Wexler, University of California, San Diego; Robert A. Wright, University of California, Los Angeles; H.M. Young, University of London.

ABBREVIATIONS

A	autograph, handwritten
AL	autograph letter(s)
ALS	autograph letter(s), signed
L	letter(s) (dictated, or form unknown)
LS	letter(s), signed
AMs	autograph manuscript(s)
AMsS	autograph manuscript(s), signed
AN	autograph note(s)
ANS	autograph note(s), signed
T	typewritten
TMs	typewritten manuscript(s)
TMsS	typewritten manuscript(s), signed
nd, ND	no date
n.p.:	no publisher
n.p.	no place of publication
p	page
pp	pages
vol	volume
vols	volumes
NLI	National Library of Ireland
SUNY SB	State University of New York at Stony Brook
WBY	William Butler Yeats (When WBY's actual initials occur in a manuscript, they are listed as W B Y.)

HOW TO USE THIS *CENSUS*

The *Census* has three major sections:
1. A listing of manuscripts, with description and location.
2. A listing of "Libraries and Other Owners," with a brief notation (QUICK title) of manuscripts in their possession.
3. A number of indexes.

The arrangement for the listing of manuscripts is by type (or genre); under each type, titles or names are in alphabetical order (omitting A, An, The). These are the Types:

Books	Plays
Inscriptions	Poems
Letters	Poems, Unpublished
Miscellany	Prose
Other Authors	Speeches

The bases for classifying works, and for inclusion and exclusion, are explained in the "Preface" to this *Census*.

To find the manuscripts for "The Withering of the Boughs" look in the index. "Withering of the Boughs, The" is listed as a Poem, with the QUICK title WITH BOUG, on page 332. In the Poems section of this *Census*, these entries appear:

The Withering of the Boughs   WITH   BOUG
   Copy of LAND HEAR 03 inscribed to COAT FLOR EA with
   two lines beginning "No boughs have withered."
       Indiana University
   Page proof with corrections in POET WORK 06.
       New York Public Library

The first entry notes that some lines from the poem, beginning "No boughs have withered," are inscribed to Florence Earle Coates in a copy of WBY's *The Land of Heart's Desire* (1903 edition) at Indiana University.

The second entry lists page proofs for the poem from *Poetical Works* (1906 edition) at The New York Public Library.

The Books section has similar and sometimes additional information on these entries:

The Land of Heart's Desire (Mosher)   LAND   HEAR 03
   Portland, ME: Mosher, 1903. (Wade 13)
       Copy inscribed to COAT FLOR EA with lines from WITH
BOUG beginning "No boughs have withered because of the wintry
wind," dated Dec. 1903.
       Indiana University

Poetical Works. Vol 1. Lyrical Poems.   POET   WORK 06
   London: Macmillan, 1906. (Wade 65)
      Page proofs with corrections in many poems, including
      the following: ANAS VIJA, BAIL AILL . . . WITH BOUG.
      New York Public Library

A QUICK title in a manuscript entry means there will be one or more entries under that title or name in other sections of the *Census*. A "See . . ." or "See also . . ." entry directs the reader to additional relevant information.

QUICK TITLES

Cross-references as well as the entries in the "Libraries and Other Owners" section use a QUICK title, consisting of the first four letters of the first word (omitting A, An, The), the first four letters of the next significant word (omitting articles, conjunctions, and prepositions), and the first two letters of the third word—except for books, where the last two digits represent the last digits of the date of publication.

Entries cited so far include these:

Full Title			
Poem: The Withering of the Boughs	WITH	BOUG	
Inscription: Coates, Florence Earle	COAT	FLOR	EA
Book: Land of Heart's Desire (pub. 1903)	LAND	HEAR	03

Other examples:

Book: The Unicorn from the Stars (pub. 1908)	UNIC	STAR	08
Play: The Unicorn from the Stars	UNIC	STAR	
Letter: Shakespear, Olivia	SHAK	OLIV	
Prose: The Need for Audacity of Thought	NEED	AUDA	TH
Miscellany: Diaries and Journals	DIAR	JOUR	

Index of Manuscripts

This index lists the titles and names from the manuscript section in alphabetical order, along with the QUICK title, the type, and the page number of the primary description. Thus, with a QUICK title, it is possible to find the type and the full title of a given item. Entries for some items noted above:

Full Title	Quick Title			Type	Page
Coates, Florence Earle	COAT	FLOR	EA	Inscription	74
Need for Audacity of Thought, The	NEED	AUDA	TH	Prose	362
Poems	POEM		99	Book	39
Shakespear, Olivia	SHAK	OLIV		Letter	161
Unicorn from the Stars, The	UNIC	STAR	08	Book	58
Unicorn from the Stars, The	UNIC	STAR		Play	237
Withering of the Boughs, The	WITH	BOUG		Poem	332

Because of the rules used to formulate QUICK titles (omission of articles, prepositions, and conjunctions), QUICK titles will sometimes appear a few places away from their proper alphabetical location, but they can usually be found nearby. The index lists these works:

Player Queen, The	PLAY	QUEE		Play
Players Ask for a Blessing, The	PLAY	ASK	BL	Poem

Alphabetically, in the QUICK list, PLAY ASK should precede the PLAY QUEE, but because the index is alphabetized by title, the QUICK title is slightly out of order.

To avoid duplication or confusion, a few exceptions are made to the rules for QUICK titles. For example, according to the rules, the poems "Her Courage" and "Her Courtesy" would both appear as HER COUR; they appear as HER COUR AG and HER COUR TE.

MANUSCRIPTS

Books

This section includes manuscripts of books WBY wrote or edited, plus a few unpublished items: THE SPECKLED BIRD, the Scribner (Dublin) and Macmillan (Deluxe or Coole) editions, and the homemade volumes of THE ROSY CROSS and YE PLEIADES. Copies inscribed by WBY are also listed here; descriptions are repeated in the Inscriptions section under the name of the person to whom inscribed.

The Augustan Books of English Poetry:
W.B. Yeats   AUGU BOOK 27
  London: Benn, 1927. (Wade 155)
    Copy inscribed to HOWE W.T., dated Dec. 1, 1932.
      New York Public Library

Autobiographies: Reveries over Childhood and
Youth and The Trembling of the Veil   AUTO REVE 26
  London: Macmillan, 1926. (Wade 151)
    AMs and TMs of notes, additions, beginning of section XI, section on John O'Leary, and other parts (Ms 30290, 30293, 30399, 30819, 30843).
      National Library of Ireland
      Copy at SUNY SB   Box 21, 22

    Two inscribed copies: one to EATO NOLA, dated Xmas 1932, the other to FODE GWYN: "to my friend Gwyneth Foden--this book about my friends," dated May 1935.
      University of Victoria

    Copy with note: "George's own copy must not be taken by me W.B.Y.   Oct. 7, 1926" (item 2316a).
      Yeats, Anne

    Copy inscribed to SHAK OLIV, dated Oct 9 1926.
      University of Texas at Austin

    Copy inscribed to HARR FRAN, dated Feb. 27, 1927.
      Crawford, William

Two copies: one inscribed to HOWE W.T., "a good friend to my friends," dated Feb 14 1929; the other to GREG LADY, "from her friend," dated Dec 16, 1926.
    New York Public Library

See also Books: UNPU MACM ED, and individual works in Books: REVE CHIL 15, FOUR YEAR 21, ESTR 26, DEAT SYNG 28, and BOUN SWED 25.

Autobiographies: Reveries over Childhood and Youth and the Trembling of the Veil   AUTO REVE 27
  New York: Macmillan, 1927. (Wade 152)
    Various biographical fragments related to this edition (Ms 30502, 30754).
        National Library of Ireland
        Copy at SUNY SB   Box 21, 22

    AMs drafts in a green notebook (Partial List...#405).
        Yeats, Senator Michael
        Copy at SUNY SB   Box 21, 22

    Copy inscribed to BOGG TOM, dated Jan 19 1933.
        University of Texas at Austin

    Copy "Inscribed for Gladys Baker" (BAKE GLAD).
        University of Delaware

Beltaine   BELT   00
  London: Unicorn, no. 1-3, May 1899-Apr 1900. (Wade 226)
    Copy inscribed to GREG LADY: "To my friend Lady Gregory W B Y" (PN2602.D8.B4).
        Emory University

    Copy inscribed to HORN MISS AN: "Miss Horniman from her friend the editor" (no signature).
        University of Kansas

Bishop Berkeley   BISH BERK 31
  London: Faber, [1931]. (Wade 280)
    Copy of AMs with corrections and additions, in white vellum notebook. See Miscellany: DIAR JOUR (Partial List...#545).
        Location of original unknown
        Copy at SUNY SB   Box 88

Page proofs of the Introduction, with revisions, dated 1931 (Ms 30027); AMs drafts (Ms 30516).
> National Library of Ireland
> Copy at SUNY SB   Box 20, 25

A Book of Irish Verse					BOOK IRIS 95
London: Methuen, 1895. (Wade 225)
Copy with bookplate of SMIT PAME with three lines of verse: "Though leagues asunder..." (THOU LEAG AS), probably inscribed for the occasion (PR 8851 Y4).
> Emory University

Copy inscribed to MACB MAUD GO "from W.B. Yeats March 16th 1896."
> University of Kansas

Copy of second edition with WBY's notes for a new edition that was never made (item 2450).
> Yeats, Anne

Copy inscribed to QUIN JOHN, dated 1904: "John Quinn's book W B Yeats, 1904."
> University of Victoria

Copy inscribed to "Mrs. Shakespear from W B Yeats" (SHAK OLIV).
> University of Texas at Austin

A Book of Irish Verse					BOOK IRIS 00
London: Methuen, 1900. (Wade 225)
Copy inscribed to SAND CAST SC, dated July 1901.
> Indiana University

See also Letters: METH CO.

The Book of the Rhymers' Club				BOOK RHYM 92
London: Matthews, 1892. (Wade 291)
Copy with bookplate of GREG LADY, with the following inscription: "This little book was put together at my suggestion. I suggested it because I wanted to have copies of Dowson's poems. He had read them to us at the Cheshire Cheese. W B Yeats."
> Smith, Simon Nowell

Copy with note: "I got 'the Rhymers' to publish this book because I wanted copies of Dowson's verses." Dated March 1904.
> University of Texas at Austin

The Bounty of Sweden   BOUN SWED 25
   Dublin: Cuala, 1925.
      TMs and galley proofs with corrections (Za Dial).
         Yale University

      TMs (fragment).
         New York Public Library

      Corrected page proofs and AMs note; draft with
      corrections and additions; AMs and TMs; TMs (fragment)
      of early version, with corrections (Ms 30307, 30288,
      30611, 30813).
         National Library of Ireland
         Copy at SUNY SB Box 26

      Copy inscribed to GREG LADY, dated October 20, 1922.
         New York Public Library

      Copy inscribed (to no one) with the line "Only the
      wasteful virtues earn the sun" (from PARD OLD FA).
         University of London Library

      Copy inscribed to SHAK OLIV.
         University of Texas at Austin

      Copy inscribed to HEAL JAME, dated 1938, noting that
      WBY's reference to Lady Gregory as "sinking into the
      infirmety of age" upset her, so he changed it to
      "vigerous old age."
         Stanford University

Broadsides   BROA   35
   Dublin: Cuala, 1935. (Wade 249)
      TMs, corrected, of "Anglo-Irish Ballads," used as
      Introduction (Ms 30279, 30804).
         National Library of Ireland
         Copy at SUNY SB Box 40

Broadsides   BROA   37
   Dublin: Cuala, 1937. (Wade 254)
      AMs of the Introduction (Ms 30396); TMs (5 pp) of
      "Music and Poetry" (Ms 30792).
         National Library of Ireland
         Copy at SUNY SB Box 40

      See also Miscellany: DIAR JOUR (red loose-leaf
      notebook; Ms 30373).

The Cat and the Moon and Certain Poems   CAT MOON 24
   Dublin: Cuala, 1924. (Wade 145)
      Two copies: one inscribed to HEAL JAME, dated 1938:
      "The end of 'the cat and the moon' is feeble in this
      book, but I have improved it & enlarged it, and now it
      plays very well"; another with a verse inscribed on
      margins around bookplate of ROBI LENN: "May-1924- 'Call
      down a blessing on the blossom of the may, Because it
      blows in beauty and in beauty blows away' W B Y" (from
      POET OWEN HA).
         Stanford University

      TMs; notes for this edition, dedicated to GREG LADY (Ms
      30273).
         National Library of Ireland
         Copy at SUNY SB   Box 1

      Page proofs with corrections on pp. 15 and 24
      (PR 5904.37 1924).
         Emory University

      Incomplete page proofs of pp. i-v, numbered 33-42,
      signed and dated Aug. 10, 1924.
         New York Public Library

Cathleen ni Hoolihan   CATH HOOL 02
   London: Bullen, 1902. (Wade 40)
      Galley of note used as proof for a later edition (Ms
      13571).
         National Library of Ireland
         Copy at SUNY SB

      Three copies: one inscribed to GREG ROBE; one with
      lines from COAT; one to GREG LADY, dated Sept 26, 1902.
         New York Public Library

      Number six of eight copies in vellum, inscribed with a
      note: "I never heard of this edition till I knew of it
      from Quinn who owns this book. W.B. Yeats New York
      1904."
         Princeton University Library

      Copy inscribed to "Miss Helen Laird from W B Yeats Nov
      1912" (LAIR HELE).
         University College Dublin

The Celtic Twilight   CELT TWIL 93
   London: Bullen, 1893. (Wade 8)
      AMs; fragment (3 pp; Ms 30436); AMs; list of Contents
      (1 p; Ms 12147).
         National Library of Ireland
         Copy at SUNY SB

      AMs of numerous stories including "A Teller of Tales,"
      "Belief and Unbelief," "A Knight of the Sheep," "The
      Sorcerers," "Regina," "The Untiring Ones," "The Thick
      Skull," "The Religion of a Sailor," "The Eating of
      Precious Stones," "Our Lady of the Hills," "The Golden
      Age" (71 pp; Ms 30366).
         National Library of Ireland
         Copy at SUNY SB   Box 30

      Copy with pencilled annotations and corrections,
      possibly in WBY's hand (Yeats 186).
         Trinity College Dublin

      Inscribed vellum copy with bookplate of GREG LADY, with
      the first stanza of INTO TWIL (PR5904 C4).
         Emory University

      Copy with note (June 1902) about summers in Sligo as
      background: "I like it among the best of my books for I
      got it all in good summer weather" (Ip.Y34.893C).
         Yale University

      Copy 1, author's signed presentation copy, inscribed
      to RUSS GEOR, dated Dec. 1893.
         University of Texas at Austin

      Copy inscribed to O'LE JOHN, dated February 1894.
         University of Victoria

      Copy inscribed to GARN EDWA, dated 1894.
         Princeton University Library

      Copy inscribed to Lionel Johnson (JOHN LION) "from his
      friend W B Yeats Dec 93" (item 2320).
         Yeats, Anne

      Copy inscribed to VYNN NORA "from her friend William
      Butler Yeats Dec 19. 1893."
         University of Louisville

      Copy inscribed to ELLI E.J. (Ellis Collection: 97,934).
         University of Reading Library

Copy inscribed in WBY's hand: "All real stories he[ard] among the people or real incidents but for a little disguise in names & places. W B Yeats 1904."
    Boston Public Library

The Celtic Twilight   CELT TWIL 94
  New York: Macmillan, 1894. (Wade 9)
    Copy inscribed to QUIN JOHN; WBY calls it his first book with "a style," and says it was written for W. E. Henley.
      Wake Forest University Library

The Celtic Twilight   CELT TWIL 02
  London: Bullen, 1902. (Wade 35)
    Three inscribed copies: one to COCK SYDN (1902), one to RUSS GEOR (July 8, 1902), one to POLL GEOR (July 1902).
      University of Texas at Austin

    See also Prose: DUST HATH CL.

The Celtic Twilight   CELT TWIL 05
  Dublin: Maunsel, 1905. (Wade 37)
    Copy inscribed to MEYN ALIC, dated 15 Jan 1905.
      Boston College

The Celtic Twilight   CELT TWIL 12
  London: Bullen, 1912. (Wade 38)
    Copy with corrections and additions used as basis for a later edition, inscribed to BULL A.H., with a note.
      New York Public Library

    Copy inscribed (to no one), dated May 9, 1920.
      Wellesley College

    Fragments of page proofs (Ms 30210).
      National Library of Ireland
      Copy at SUNY SB   Box 30

The Collected Poems   COLL POEM 33
  New York: Macmillan, 1933 (Wade 172).
    Copy inscribed to MOOR STUR "from W.B. Yeats November 1933."
      University of London Library

    Copy with a few revisions, inscribed to YEAT MICH "from W.B. Yeats November 1933."
      Yeats, Senator Michael

    Copy inscribed to YEAT GEOR (item 2323).
      Yeats, Anne

Copy inscribed to TURN W.J. "from W.B. Yeats, June 6, 1935."
   Indiana University

Copy inscribed to YEAT ELIZ: "E.C.Y. from W.B.Y., affectionately. 1933." (Yeats 211).
   Trinity College Dublin

Copy with inscription: "To this book only begetter J Squire from W B Y Dec 1933" (SQUI J; may be bogus).
   University of Texas at Austin

Collected Works in Verse and Prose   8 vols   COLL WORK 08
   Stratford: Shakespeare Head, 1908. (Wade 75)
   Copy with revisions in a number of poems, including ARRO, NEW FACE, OLD MEM, RAGG WOOD; also two unsigned drafts of letters to UNWI T FI (item 2325).
      Yeats, Anne

   Later volumes with revisions and variant lines (none of which appear in later editions) in COUN CATH, DEIR, HOUR GLAS, KING THRE, ON BAIL ST (items 2326, 2327, 2328).
      Yeats, Anne

   Presentation copy of volume 1, with inscription and note to GREG LADY, with autograph copies of various poems; see ALL THIN CA, AT GALW RA, EAST 1916, FRIE ILLN, HIS PHOE, ON THOS TH, QUEE EDAI, SEPT 1913, TO FRIE WH, UPON HOUS SH, WILD SWAN CO.
      New York Public Library

   Copy of Chapman and Hall editon inscribed (to no one) with ANS beginning "The love of God for every soul."
      University of Texas at Austin

   Revised AMs, TMs, and galleys of vols. 3, 4, 8.
      University of Kansas

The Countess Cathleen   COUN CATH 99
   London: n.p., 1899.
   Vellum copy of rare, limited edition inscribed to GREG LADY "from her friend W B Yeats, May 1899" (PR 5904 C6).
      Emory University

The Countess Cathleen   COUN CATH 12
   London: Unwin, 1912. (Wade 93)
   Copy inscribed to VIEL FRAN, dated June 19 1912.
      University of Texas at Austin

Books

    TMs revisions on neatly typed slips pasted in some cases over inked revisions. Copy apparently served as copytext for POEM 13 (item 2334).
        Yeats, Anne

    Copy inscribed to BROW MAUR, dated July 1912.
        Princeton University Library

    Inscribed copy with the bookplate of KIND MARG MA, dated July 1912 (PR5904 C6 1912 cop. 2).
        Emory University

    Copy inscribed to MOOR STUR "from W.B. Yeats, 1912 June 5."
        University of London Library

    Three copies: one with a few corrections and comments; copy inscribed to GREG LADY, dated June 14, 1912 with lines from scene 1 of the play: "This 'unknown thing' that may be nothing--but that's the buyers risk"; another copy with a brief ANS.
        New York Public Library

Countess Cathleen   COUN CATH 29
    London: T. Fisher Unwin, 1929. (Wade 95)
    Copy inscribed (to no one) with line from TOM O'RO "'An aimless joy is a pure joy' W B Yeats July 1932" (item 2335b).
        Yeats, Anne

The Countess Kathleen   COUN KATH 92
    London: Unwin, 1892. (Wade 6)
    AMs of Table of Contents (Ms 30345).
        National Library of Ireland
        Copy at SUNY SB Box 26

    Two sets of page proofs (146 pp each); one labelled "early," the other "later," with a few corrections, possibly by WBY.
        University of Texas at Austin

    Copy inscribed to Katherine Tynan (HINK KATH).
        Colby College Library

    Two copies: one inscribed to QUIN JOHN, dated March 1904 with ANS on Browning (quoted in Wade); another to Bram Stoker (STOK BRAM), dated Sept 1892.
        New York Public Library

Copy with the line "Like the pale waters in their wintry race" pencilled in to replace "More fleeting than the sea's foam-fickle face" (from ROSE WORL).
    Ohio State University

Copy inscribed (to no one): "at Avondale W B Yeats 20-2-03."
    University of California Berkeley

Copy inscribed to ELLI EDWI J. "from his friend W B Y August 30th 1892" (Ellis Collection: 97943).
    University of Reading Library

Copy inscribed to TODH JOHN.
    University of Texas at Austin

Copy (possibly of a later edition) with a few comments and minor corrections.
    Yale University

The Cutting of an Agate   CUTT AGAT 12
  New York: Macmillan, 1912. (Wade 102)
  AMs of Preface; AMs draft in red notebook; galley proof, dated 5 November 1918; TMs list of Contents (Ms 30274, 30411, 30606, 30879).
    National Library of Ireland
    Copy at SUNY SB Box 19

Revisions in pencil in Prefaces to GREG CUCH 07 and GREG GODS 04 in preparing copytext for the "Thoughts on Lady Gregory's Translations" part of this book (item 792).
    Yeats, Anne

Copy inscribed to WADE ALLA "from his friend W B Yeats, Dec 4 1912."
    Indiana University

Copy inscribed to SHAK OLIV, dated Dec 1912.
    University of Texas at Austin

One copy inscribed to GREG LADY, "from her friend," dated Dec 1912; also incomplete galley and page proofs with corrections.
    New York Public Library

The Cutting of an Agate   CUTT AGAT 19
   London: Macmillan and Co. Ltd., 1919.
      Copy inscribed (to no one) with the line from MEDI TIME
      WA: "I knew that one is animate, Mankind inanimate
      phantasy."
         University of London Library

      Copy inscribed (to no one), dated May 3[?] 1920;
      another copy inscribed to "Maud Gonne" (MACB MAUD GO),
      dated April 1919.
         University of Texas at Austin

      Copy inscribed to YEAT ELIZ: "Lolly Yeats from W B
      Yeats April 1919" (Yeats 191).
         Trinity College Dublin

The Death of Synge and Other Passages   DEAT SYNG 28
   Dublin: Cuala, 1928. (Wade 162)
      Page proofs with corrections by L.C. Purser; TMs
      (23 pp; Ms 30205, 30793).
         National Library of Ireland
         Copy at SUNY SB Box 24

      TMs and galley proofs, with corrections, for article in
      the DIAL (April 1928; Za Dial).
         Yale University

      Copy inscribed to GREG LADY, dated 15 June 1928
      (PR5904 D3).
         Emory University

      Copy inscribed to HEAL JAME, dated 1938: "Perhaps my
      best prose book."
         Stanford University

Deirdre   DEIR   07
   London: Bullen, 1907. (Wade 69)
      Copy with moderate AMs revisions, apparently as
      copytext for DEIR 11 (item 2338).
         Yeats, Anne

      Copy inscribed (to no one) with line from WITH BOUG:
      "The boughs are withered because I have told them my
      dreams," dated Dec 1 1905.
         State University of New York at Albany

Copy inscribed to YEAT JACK: "J B Yeats from W B Yeats August 1907."
    New York Public Library

Copy with extensive cancellations and revisions, evidently for the acting edition of 1910 (EC9. Y3455. 907d2).
    Harvard University

Copy inscribed (to no one), dated June 23, 1909; another copy with illegible inscription.
    University of Texas at Austin

Deirdre   DEIR   11
  Stratford: Shakespeare Head, 1911. (Wade 86)
  Copy with revisions, dated June 1911 (item 2340).
      Yeats, Anne

Copy inscribed to GREG LADY, dated May 4 1911.
    New York Public Library

Discoveries: A Volume of Essays   DISC VOLU 07
  Dundrum: Dun Emer, 1907. (Wade 72)
  AMs of various sections, including "Prophet, Priest and King" (Ms 30591); galley proofs of some parts (Ms 30036).
      National Library of Ireland
      Copy at SUNY SB   Box 19

Copy inscribed (to no one) with a note: "The last book to appear with Ben Jonson's old title 'Discoveries.' W.B. Yeats. P.S. Unicorn was drawn by Robert Gregory."
    Dublin City Libraries

Copy inscribed to MACB MAUD GO "from her friend W.B. Yeats."
    Sparrow, John

Copy inscribed to HEAL JAME, dated July 30, 1938, with earlier inscription dated Dec 16 1907: "'banjo' on page 10 is a slip of the pen for 'guitar.'" Added in 1938: "Yes a 'slip' though not of the pen--probably from ignorance...."
    Stanford University

Copy (evidently belonging to YOUN JAME CA) inscribed
with a note about the origin of this order and the
difference it made in his art; dated Dec. 16, 1907
(Ip.y34.907d).
   Yale University

Dramatis Personae   DRAM PERS 35
   Dublin: Cuala, 1935. (Wade 183)
   TMs, with corrections (38 pp).
   Southern Illinois University

   AMs (127 pp; Harvard dates Ms ca 1935; MS Eng 338.5).
   Harvard University

   Copy inscribed to HEAL JAME, dated July 5 1938: "The
   last section of my biography...It will be difficult to
   continue, for I have come to the people who will
   outlive me."
   Stanford University

Dramatis Personae   DRAM PERS 36
   London: Macmillan, 1936. (Wade 187)
   Copy inscribed to "Edmund and Helen" [Blunden], dated
   June 6, 1936 (BLUN EDMU HE); another copy inscribed
   to "Olivia from W.B.Y. June 6, 1936" (SHAK OLIV).
   University of Texas at Austin

   Corrected page proofs; extract corrected by George
   Yeats, perhaps from dictation; and TMs (carbon) of part
   of XI with corrections (Ms 30029, 30058, 30175, 30819).
      National Library of Ireland
      Copy at SUNY SB   Box 24

   Copy inscribed (to no one) with the line from VACI
   "'Animate the trivial days and ram them with the sun'
   W B Yeats" (item 2342).
      Yeats, Anne

Early Poems and Stories (London)   EARL POEM 25
   London: Macmillan, 1925. (Wade 147)
   Incomplete galley proofs (41 pp) with corrections and
   ANS about the Preface. Also a copy inscribed to GREG
   LADY, dated Sept. 23 1925.
      New York Public Library

   AMs and TMs (Ms 30372).
      National Library of Ireland
      Copy at SUNY SB   Box 26

Copy inscribed to Richard and Ashe King (KING RICH), dated September 29, 1925; also a signed presentation copy to SHAK OLIV, and another to Francis and Iseult Stuart (STUA FRAN IS), dated Oct. 7, 1925.
    University of Texas at Austin

See also Books: SECR ROSE 97.

Early Poems and Stories (New York)   EARL POEM 25
  New York: Macmillan, 1925. (Wade 148)
    Copy with a few revisions, inscribed to PRIC FRAN "from W B Yeats Nov 12, 1925" (item 2344).
        Yeats, Anne

    Two signed copies: one to MACB MAUD GO from "her friend," dated Sept 27, 1925; another to ROBI LENN, dated Sept 27, 1925.
        University of Texas at Austin

Easter 1916   EAST   16
  n.p.: Clement Shorter, n.d. (Wade 117)
    Copy inscribed to BOYD ERNE, dated June 22 1917 (Ip.Y34.916g).
        Yale University

    Copy inscribed to GREG LADY, dated May 31, 1917, with fair copy of Poem: EAST 1916 inserted.
        New York Public Library

Eight Poems   EIGH POEM 16
  London: By "Form," [1916]. (Wade 114)
    Inscribed copy with the note "This pamphlet was brought out by a magazine called 'Form' to save my copyright..." (item 2345).
        Yeats, Anne

    Copy inscribed (to no one): "This book was brought out without my leave, and a misunderstanding. It is not a form of publication or decoration that I would have chosen."
        Pennsylvania State University Library

    Copy belonging to HORT WILL inscribed, "I have had nothing to do with the publication of this pretentious pamphlet W B Yeats."
        Harper, George

Two copies: one inscribed to SPAR A.; another with corrections, renumbering of poems, and contents, evidently used in part as the basis for WILD SWAN 17. Latter includes a note: "I am not responsible for this pretentious publication."
    New York Public Library

Two copies inscribed (to no one), dated April 17, 1916.
    University of Texas at Austin

Essays   ESSA   24
  London: Macmillan, 1924. (Wade 141)
  Page proofs, dated 1937 (Ms 30021).
    National Library of Ireland
    Copy at SUNY SB Box 20, 25

  Copy inscribed to GREG LADY, dated May 25 1924.
    New York Public Library

  Copy inscribed to "Lennox Robinson from W.B. Yeats May 26, 1924" (ROBI LENN); another copy to "Iseult & Francis Stuart from W B Yeats 1924" (STUA FRAN IS).
    University of Texas at Austin

Essays by W.B. Yeats, 1931 to 1936   ESSA W.B. 37
  Dublin: Cuala, 1937. (Wade 194)
  AMs of Preface, and corrected page proofs of most of the essays, including (Prose) LOUI LAMB, MAND UPAN, and PARN (MS 30021, 30462).
    National Library of Ireland
    Copy at SUNY SB Box 20, 25

  Copy inscribed to "Helen [Dulac]" (DULA HELE), dated Feb. 1938.
    University of Texas at Austin

  Copy inscribed to HEAL JAME, dated 1938, finding the essays "often difficult, remote from general interest as if I were talking to myself as indeed I was. Of late I have changed & hence forth my friend[s] find me intelligible though more extravagant. Gradually one grows into certainty."
    Stanford University

Estrangement   ESTR   26
   Dublin: Cuala, 1926. (Wade 150)
      AMs of thirteen sections, and of FRIE ILLN (Ms 30350).
      Corrected page proofs, with inscription by WBY dated 17
      May, 1926 (40 pp; Ms 21859). AMs of proposed Preface
      (2 pp; Ms 30291).
            National Library of Ireland
            Copy at SUNY SB   Box 24

      Copy inscribed to "Olivia Shakespear from W B Yeats
      Sept 5 1926" (SHAK OLIV).
            University of Texas at Austin

      Copy inscribed to HEAL JAME, dated 1938: "When I wrote
      these essays I was working at the Abbey Thatre. Fay
      had gone I think & I was over worked or my nerves were.
      That is why there are some sour paragraphs."
            Stanford University

Fairy and Folk Tales of the Irish Peasantry   FAIR FOLK 88
   London: Scott, 1888. (Wade 212)
      Two copies: one inscribed to HINK KATH, dated July 21st
      1889, with corrections; another to GREG LADY, dated
      1901, with a long note.
            New York Public Library

      Two signed presentation copies: one to O'LE ELLE;
      another to POLL HENR, dated May 16, 1889.
            University of Texas at Austin

Four Plays for Dancers   FOUR PLAY 21
   London: Macmillan, 1921. (Wade 129)
      An "Order of contents" and Preface, with typed and
      handwritten additions and an AMs note to the publisher
      (Ms 8773, 30536).
            National Library of Ireland
            Copy at SUNY SB   Box 12

      Proof sheets of Preface and Contents, with title page
      dated 1920; nothing in WBY's hand.
            University of Texas at Austin

      Signed copy, dated Dec. 9 1921, with bookplate
      indicating book was donated to the Bedford College
      War Relief Fund.
            Columbia University

Copy inscribed (to no one) with the lines from HOUR DAWN: "There is no man but cocks his ear To know when Michael's trumpet cries That flesh and blood may disappear."
    University of London Library

Two signed copies: one inscribed to MORR LADY OT; another to SHAK OLIV, dated Oct 1921.
    University of Texas at Austin

See also Plays: ONLY JEAL EM and Books: TWO PLAY 19.

Four Years   FOUR YEAR 21
  Dundrum: Cuala, 1921. (Wade 131)
    Two AMs sections (Ms 30471, 30472); AMs (Ms 30536).
        National Library of Ireland
        Copy at SUNY SB   Box 21, 22

    TMs of second installment as it appeared in the DIAL (Aug 1921; Za Dial).
        Yale University

    Copy inscribed to HEAL JAME, dated July 1938: "The design on the title page was by T. Sturge Moore a distinguished poet & designer & a good friend."
        Stanford University

    Copy inscribed for MORR LADY OT, dated Xmas 1921.
        Pierpont Morgan Library

    Copy inscribed to GREG LADY; WBY notes that people seemed more interested in his memoirs than his poems: "I tried to write first only for after my death but found after writing some hundred of pages that one does not write well for so remote an audience" (PR5906 A55 cop. 2).
        Emory University

    Copy inscribed to SHAK OLIV from "her friend W.B. Yeats."
        University of Texas at Austin

The Golden Helmet   GOLD HELM 08
  New York: John Quinn, 1908.
    Copy no. 21 of 50 copies inscribed (to no one) "From W B Yeats July 1908."
        University of California San Diego

Page and galley proofs with a few corrections, possibly by WBY (in Rare Books and Mss).
    New York Public Library

Copy inscribed to GREG LADY, "from her friend."
    New York Public Library

Copy inscribed to Margaret Collinson (COLL MARG): "The play is a first draft of my play 'The Green Helmet,' which is in verse and I hope a much better play. Please do not judge me by this. W.B. Yeats, Thoor, Ballylee, Aug. 29, 1922."
    Dublin City Libraries

The Green Helmet and Other Poems   GREE HELM 10
  Dundrum: Cuala, 1910. (Wade 84)
    Page proof, signed by WBY in several places, dated May 14, 1924; noted by Lady Gregory as "Imperfect." Also, later page proofs.
    New York Public Library

    Unbound printed pages; nothing in WBY's hand.
    University of Texas at Austin

    Copy inscribed to HEAL JAME, dated July 1938: "The Cuchulain myth was the myth of that time. Standish O'Grady had started it. Padraic Pearse was inspired by it, a fact commemorated by the statue of Cuchulain in the rebuilt Post Office."
    Stanford University

The Green Helmet and Other Poems   GREE HELM 11
  New York: Paget, 1911. (Wade 85)
    Copy with WBY's corrections on pp. 8-9, and printer's instructions for setting up galleys for GREEN HELM 12.
    New York Public Library

The Green Helmet and Other Poems   GREE HELM 12
  New York: Macmillan, 1912. (Wade 101)
    Copy inscribed to MOOR STUR, dated Dec. 1912 with a note: "The cover is the unaided work of the American publisher. He says it is...the kind of cover I like."
    University of London Library

    Copy with revisons, especially of AT GALW RA (item 2355).
    Yeats, Anne

Copy inscribed to MASE JOHN "from W B Yeats, December 1912. This cover was a great effort on the part of the publisher. He describes it as the kind of cover I prefer! W B Y."
Smith, Simon Nowell

Copy inscribed to WADE ALLA, Dec. 1912.
Indiana University

Copy of book with pencilled note about making a selection of poems from this book: "I have left out all poems I want to reserve for the new book," with ticks signifying those to be included (Yeats 194).
Trinity College Dublin

Copy inscribed to GREG LADY, dated Dec 1912: "The cover is a great effort on the part of the publisher, after a vehement letter from me."
New York Public Library

See also Books: GREE HELM 11.

The Herne's Egg: A Stage Play   HERN EGG 38
  London: Macmillan, 1938. (Wade 195)
  Proof sheets, dated 1937, stamped "Second Proof" with corrections and revisions; "for Frank O'Connor" (O'CO FRAN) inscribed on cover sheet (EC 9.Y3455.938 ha).
    Harvard University

  Copy with corrections and revisions (item 2357).
    Yeats, Anne

  Copy inscribed to "Olivia" (SHAK OLIV).
    University of Texas at Austin

The Herne's Egg and Other Plays   HERN OTHE 38
  New York: Macmillan, 1938. (Wade 196)
  TMs, corrected, of Preface (Ms 30304).
    National Library of Ireland
    Copy at SUNY SB   Box 12

The Hour Glass: A Morality   HOUR GLAS 03
  London: Heinemann, 1903. (Wade 51)
  Copy from library of Edmund Gosse inscribed with note quoted in Wade: "Never heard of this edition before. Oct. 13, 1914."
    University of Texas at Austin

The Hour Glass and Other Plays   HOUR GLAS 04
   New York: Macmillan, 1904. (Wade 52)
      Copy with revisions in HOUR GLAS and POT BROT (item 2360).
         Yeats, Anne

      Copy of later edition (1909) inscribed to Josephine Preston Peabody (PEAB JOSE; EC 943455.904 hg).
         Harvard University

      Copy inscribed (to no one) with two notes, both dated April 1906. A long one gives the background for the writing of the play for the Dublin stage and audience; a shorter note pays tribute to Lady Gregory (Ip.Y34.904b).
         Yale University

The Hour-Glass, Cathleen in Houlihan, The Pot
of Broth   HOUR CATH 04
   London: Bullen, 1904. (Wade 53)
      Copy with an alteration in the text (p 77), inscribed with note to QUIN JOHN: "the first copy of the plays," dated March 1904.
         New York Public Library

      Copy of article from NORTH AMERICAN REVIEW (Sept. 1903), with corrections in hand of Lady Gregory, used as copytext for this edition; article later inscribed to GREG LADY, dated April, 1905.
         New York Public Library

      Revised copy; changes mostly in HOUR GLAS and CATH HOUL (item 2362).
         Yeats, Anne

      Copy with letter inscribed (to no one) in front, dated August 31, 1920.
         University of Reading Library

      Copy inscribed to "O Shakespear from her friend the writer. April 1904" (SHAK OLIV).
         University of Texas at Austin

Books

The Hour Glass, Cathleen ni Houlihan, The Pot
of Broth   HOUR CATH 05
   Dublin: Maunsel, 1905. (Wade 54)
      Heavily revised copy (item 2363).
         Yeats, Anne

      Copy inscribed to GREG LADY, "from her friend W B
      Yeats," with inserted sheet with revisions and
      additions to Tramp's speech in "POT BROT" (p. 64).
         New York Public Library

The Hour Glass: A Morality   HOUR GLAS 07
   London: Bullen, 1907. (Wade 67)
      Several copies, heavily revised (items 2361, 2361a,
      2361b, 2361c).
         Yeats, Anne

      Copy with revisions.
         University of Kansas

      Copy with corrections and additions.
         New York Public Library

The Hour Glass   HOUR GLAS 14
   [Dundrun: Cuala, 1914.] (Wade 108)
      Copy inscribed (to no one) with a line from PARD OLD
      FA: "Only the wasteful virtues earn the sun" (EC9
      Y3455.914h).
         Harvard University

      Three copies: two inscribed to GREG LADY (Jan. 30 and
      Aug. 1914); another to QUIN JOHN, dated April 19th.
         New York Public Library

      Copy inscribed to Mrs. Meiklejohn (MEIK MRS.), dated
      March 1914.
         Princeton University Library

      Copy inscribed to MORR LADY OT, dated October 14, 1914.
         Kenyon College Library

      Copy inscribed with the note: "This little book was
      published privately by John Quinn, to save American
      copyright. Since then I have greatly altered the end
      of the play."
         Stanford University

Copy inscribed to QUIN JOHN, dated April 1914.
    University of Texas at Austin

Ideas of Good and Evil   IDEA GOOD 03
    London: Bullen, 1903. (Wade 46)
    Copy inscribed to GREG LADY, "from her friend the
    writer Sept 20th 1903," and a note about WBY's getting
    the title for this book from Blake, dated March 8 1904;
    another note reads: "A golden book--full of the fine
    flowers of a great poet's mind." Another copy
    inscribed to SHAR WILL.
        New York Public Library

    Copy inscribed to YEAT JOHN: "To my father W B Yeats
    May 12 1903" (Yeats 195).
        Trinity College Dublin

    Two inscribed copies: one to "W. Fay from his friend
    the writer" (FAY WILL), dated May, 1903; one to "Mrs.
    Shakespear" (SHAK OLIV).
        University of Texas at Austin

    See also Prose: SYMB PAIN.

Ideas of Good and Evil   IDEA GOOD 04
    New York: Macmillan, 1904. (Wade 47)
    Copy inscribed (to no one) with two lines from TO ROSE
    RO, beginning "To find in all poor foolish things,"
    dated May 1904.
        Mills College Library

If I Were Four-and-twenty   IF I   40
    Dublin: Cuala, 1940. (Wade 205)
    Photocopy of early draft, entitled "If I Were Twenty,"
    dated July 1919, along with some occult writings (Ms
    18750; may be copy of MS 30493).
        National Library of Ireland

    Page proofs; TMs; TMs (carbon; 3 pp); AMs draft; TMs
    (carbon) of alternate ending (6 pp); TMs (fragment) of
    Preface; AMs of early draft (Ms 30212, 30277, 30493,
    30794, 30814).
        National Library of Ireland
        Copy at SUNY SB Box 24

In the Seven Woods (Dundrum)   IN   SEVE 03
   Dundrum: Dun Emer, 1903. (Wade 49)
      Early proofs and three copies of gathering #3, with corrections and revisions; page proofs with corrections (Ms 30073, 30246, 30247); part of corrected proof (Ms 13584).
         National Library of Ireland
         Copy at SUNY SB   Box 1

      Signed page proofs, with notes and revisions (3 pp; MS Eng 338.11).
         Harvard University

      Page proofs with corrections; other incomplete sets of proofs with corrections by WBY and his sister Elizabeth Yeats.
         New York Public Library

      Copy inscribed with two lines from PLAY ASK BL, beginning "The proud and careless notes live on."
         Fiskin, Jeffrey

      Copy inscribed (to no one), dated May 9, 1920.
         Wellesley College

      Copy inscribed (to no one) with two lines from TO ROSE RO beginning, "To find in all poor foolish things"; another (to no one) with the line "How shall we know the dancer from the dance" (from AMON SCHO CH); another inscribed to "Arthur Symons from W B Yeats September 1903" (SYMO ARTH).
         University of Texas at Austin

      Three copies: one inscribed to SHAR WILL with lines from HAPP TOWN; another to GREG LADY, dated May 14, 1924; another with revisions of HAPP TOWN and title page.
         New York Public Library

      Two copies: one with bookplate of QUIN JOHN, with an inscription, dated March 1904: "This is the first book of mine that it is a pleasure to look at--a pleasure whether open or shut." Another, inscribed to HEAL JAME, dated July 1938, complains about the difficulty of getting good hand-made paper.
         Stanford University

In the Seven Woods (New York)　　　　　　　　IN　SEVE 03
  New York: Macmillan, 1903 (Wade 50)
    Copy inscribed to SHAR WILL.
      New York Public Library

Irish Fairy Tales　　　　　　　　　　　　　　IRIS FAIR 92
  New York: Cassell, 1892, ed. W.B. Yeats. (Wade 216)
    Copy inscribed with a line from PARD OLD FA: "'only the
    wasteful virtues earn the sun' W B Yeats, Feb 27, 1931"
    (item 2452).
      Yeats, Anne

Irish Fairy and Folk Tales　　　　　　　　　　IRIS FAIR 95
  New York: Scribner, 1895. (Wade 224)
    Copy inscribed to QUIN JOHN: WBY describes book as
    "good...but my part pretty recklessly & ill written."
      Wake Forest University Library

John Sherman and Dhoya　　　　　　　　　　　　JOHN SHER 91
  London: Unwin, 1891. (Wade 4)
    Two copies: one inscribed to Mr. and Mrs. Mathers (MATH
    MRMS), one to HEAL JAME.
      Colby College Library

    AMs of the "Girl's Song" (Ms 30342). See Poems:
    GIRL SONG JS.
      National Library of Ireland
      Copy at SUNY SB

    Copy inscribed (to no one), dated May 9, 1920.
      Wellesley College

    Sheets of second edition (Unwin) and revised proofs,
    corrected apparently for new edition by Shakespeare
    Head Press (cf. Wade 81), signed and dated November
    1891 (ER136/63).
      Shakespeare Birthplace Trust

    Copy inscribed to RUSS FATH: "from his friend the
    author," with signature in WBY's hand beneath the
    pseudonym of "Ganconagh" (Ip.Y34.891b).
      Yale University

    Copy inscribed to YEAT LILY (1891; 186.q.77 mo. 13).
      Trinity College Dublin

    Copy with AMs note entitled "New Preface," dated
    November 14 1907.
      Kenyon College Library

Books

    Vellum copy inscribed to GREG LADY, dated December 1901, commenting on his belief that none of his Sligo relatives had ever read this story (PR 5904 J5 1891a).
        Emory University

    Copy inscribed to MACB MAUD GO, with eight-line poem beginning, "We poets labour all our days" (TO MAUD GO, related to HE TELL PE), dated September 1, 1891.
        University of Texas at Austin

The King of the Great Clock Tower   KING GREA 34
   Dublin: Cuala, 1934. (Wade 179)
    Proof sheets, with corrections (26 pp).
        Northwestern University Library

    Copy inscribed to HEAL JAME, dated July 5, 1938, with long note about Ninnette Valois who danced in the play and who opened a dance school in Dublin.
        Stanford University

    Inscribed copy with line from PARD OLD FA: "only the wasteful virtues earn the sun W B Yeats."
        Smith, Simon Nowell

The King of the Great Clock Tower   KING GREA 35
   New York: Macmillan, 1935. (Wade 179A)
    Copy inscribed to HIGG F.R., with minor corrections in THRE SONG SA.
        New York Public Library

The King's Threshold   KING THRE 04
   New York: (Privately Printed) 1904. (Wade 55)
    Copy with corrections, deletions, and additions, used for reprinting PLAY PROS 22.
        New York Public Library

    Copy inscribed to WADE ALLA "from W.B. Yeats Jan 24th 1909."
        Indiana University

    Copy inscribed to HEAL JAME "in memory of our friend John Quinn."
        Colby College Library

    Copy inscribed with four-line poem, beginning "The friends that have it I do wrong" (FRIE THAT HA), signed with name and astrological symbols (Ip.u34.904kb).
        Yale University

Two copies: one inscribed to GREG LADY, dated August 1904; another to QUIN JOHN, with fair copies of NEVE GIVE AL and chorus from DEIR.
    New York Public Library

Signed copy with long note beginning, "This was the first play in verse of mine."
    University of Texas at Austin

The King's Threshold & On Baile's Strand   KING BAIL 04
  London: Bullen, 1904. (Wade 56)
    Copy inscribed to GREG LADY, with corrections, deletions, and additions used as copytext for PLAY PROS 22.
    New York Public Library

Copy inscribed to YEAT JOHN: "J B Yeats from W B Yeats March 1904" (Yeats 196).
    Trinity College Dublin

Copy inscribed to WOLL MISS "from W.B. Yeats, March 1904."
    Washington State University

Two copies: one inscribed first to YEAT JOHN, then to RUSS GEOR, dated March, 1904; another to PROK FRED.
    University of Texas at Austin

The King's Threshold   KING THRE 05
  Dublin: Maunsel, 1905. (Wade 57)
    Copy inscribed to GREG LADY.
    New York Public Library

The Lake Isle of Innisfree   LAKE ISLE 24
  n.p.: [Mills College], 1924. (Wade 143)
    Copy inscribed to MOYN THOS KI, dated May 15, 1924.
    University of Texas at Austin

The Land of Heart's Desire (London)   LAND HEAR 94
  London: Unwin, 1894. (Wade 10)
    Copy inscribed to GREG LADY (PR 5904 L3 1894b).
    Emory University

Copy inscribed with lines from the play beginning, "The wind blows out of the gales of day."
    New York Public Library

Copy inscribed to MARK CONS: "Miss Constance Gore Booth with the authors compliments July 18th 1894."
University of British Columbia

Copy belonging to J. Rogers Rees (REES J. RO) with note by WBY: "My uncles old servant Mary Battle, who saw the visions of Queen Maeve said of this poem 'It is so natural. It is just the way it would have happened.' But no I am wrong it was a servant who came while Mary Battle was old that said this."
Indiana University

Two copies: one inscribed to MACB MAUD GO, dated April 20 1894; one with lines beginning, "the years like great black oxen" (from COUN CATH) and a note about his hating his play "Land of Heart's Desire."
University of Texas at Austin

The Land of Heart's Desire (Chicago) LAND HEAR 94
   Chicago: Stone & Kimball, 1894. (Wade 11)
   Copy inscribed to YOUN JAME CA, noting that "this is an edition I have never seen & it strikes me as much better than the English one..." (Ip. Y34. 894b).
      Yale University

   Copy with a note (quoted in Wade) on Wilde.
      New York Public Library

The Land of Heart's Desire (Bibelot) LAND HEAR 03
   Portland, ME: (Privately Printed), 1903. (Wade 12)
   Copy of the Bibelot edition bound for GREG LADY and inscribed to her.
      New York Public Library

The Land of Heart's Desire (Mosher) LAND HEAR 03
   Portland, ME: Mosher, 1903. (Wade 13)
   Copy inscribed to COAT FLOR EA with lines from WITH BOUG beginning, "No boughs have withered because of the wintry wind," dated Dec. 1903.
      Indiana University

   Copy inscribed to GREG LADY.
      New York Public Library

The Land of Heart's Desire   LAND HEAR 12
  London: Unwin, 1912. (Wade 94)
    Copy inscribed to Mabel Dickinson (DICK MABE) "from her
    friend W.B. Yeats, June 22, 1912."
      Indiana University

    Copy inscribed (to no one), dated July 1912 (PR5904 L3
    1912).
      Emory University

The Land of Heart's Desire.....The Countess
Cathleen   LAND HEAR 25
  London: Unwin, 1925. (Wade 95)
    Copy inscribed to ROBI LENN "from his friend the
    writer. W.B. Yeats."
      Indiana University

Last Poems and Two Plays   LAST POEM 39
  Dublin: Cuala, 1939. (Wade 200)
    AMs; holograph Table of Contents (related to Books:
    UNPU MACM ED) tipped in following title page
    (PR5900 A3 1939).
      Emory University

    Page proofs; page proofs, corrected, possibly used as
    printer's copy for 1940 edition; drafts and revisions
    of poems (Ms 13593, 30013, 30206).
      National Library of Ireland
      Copy at SUNY SB   Box 26

    AMs; drafts of poems in brown vellum notebook,
    including COME GATH RO, THRE SONG SA, THRE MARC SO,
    PARN FUNE, and of song for POT BROT (12 pp; Ms 30547).
      National Library of Ireland
      Copy at SUNY SB   Box 26

    See also Miscellany: DIAR JOUR (brown vellum notebook;
    Ms 30546).

Later Poems   LATE POEM 22
  London: Macmillan, 1922. (Wade 134)
    Revisions in this text for various later editions.
    Poems revised include BAIL AILL, DOUB VISI MI, FRIE,
    GREY ROCK, LIVI BEAU, ON BEIN AS, SCHO, SOLO WITC, TO
    YOUN BE (item 2382). Another copy, with the note "Not
    to be given away. Dates written in by George. W B Y"
    (item 2382b).
        Yeats, Anne

Books

    Copy inscribed to GREG LADY, with fair copies of TWO SONG PL and CRAZ JANE KI and a correction in HOUR DAWN.
        New York Public Library

    Copy inscribed to YEAT ELIZ: "To Loll, from Willie. xmas 1922."
        University of Louisville

    Copy of 1917 printing of RESP OTHE 16, with revisions and corrections, used as copytext for this edition (items 2412a, 2412c).
        Yeats, Anne

    Two copies: one inscribed to ROBI LENN, dated Dec 6, 1922; another to SHAK OLIV, dated Dec 7 1922.
        University of Texas at Austin

Later Poems   LATE POEM 24
  New York: Macmillan, 1924. (Wade 135)
    Revisions in this text for various later editions, including changes in PARD OLD FA and three drafts of SCHO (item 2383).
        Yeats, Anne

Later Poems   LATE POEM 26
  London: Macmillan, 1926. (cf Wade 134)
    Copy inscribed to BEND ALBE, dated March 10, 1911.
        Mills College Library

Letters to the New Island   LETT NEW 34
  Cambridge, MA: Harvard, 1934.
    TMs of Preface, with revisions (5 pp; bMS Eng 338.10).
        Harvard University

Michael Robartes and the Dancer   MICH ROBA 20
  Dundrum: Cuala, 1920. (Wade 127)
    Page proofs; AMs and TMs of drafts with revisions, and AMs of Preface (Ms 13588, 30209).
        National Library of Ireland
        Copy at SUNY SB   Box 3

    Page proofs, with corrections by Sir Emery Walker.
        Wesleyan University

    Proof copy with a few editorial markings, for poems as published in the DIAL, November 1920 (Za Dial).
        Yale University

Copy inscribed to HEAL JAME, dated 1938: "I am not proud of the prose parts of this book. They are thoroughly bad, & have been superceded by a book of mine...A Vision."
    Stanford University

Copy inscribed to SHAK OLIV, dated Feb 29, 1920.
    University of Texas at Austin

Mosada   MOSA   86
  Dublin: n.p., 1886. (Wade 1)
    Copy with manuscripts and proofs of TIME WITC VI and ISLA STAT ([1885]; MS3502/4).
      Trinity College Dublin

    AMs notebook and loose sheets of drafts (MS3502/1,3); also galley proofs for the DUBLIN UNIVERSITY REVIEW version (MS3502/4).
      Trinity College Dublin

    Copy inscribed to Miss Veasey (VEAS MISS): "With good wishes for the New Year from her friend the Author."
      State University of New York at Buffalo

    Copy inscribed to O'LE JOHN.
      New York Public Library

    Copy inscribed to POLL HENR: "H.A. Pollexfen from W B Yeats."
      University of California Los Angeles

    Inscribed copy, with note beginning, "The first copy that I have seen in many years," quoted in Wade's description, dated Nov. 10, 1923.
      University of Texas at Austin

New Poems   NEW   POEM 38
  Dublin: Cuala, 1938. (Wade 1978)
    List of contents in a looseleaf notebook with other materials, ca 1938. (Ms 13593, 30362). See also Miscellany: DIAR JOUR (Looseleaf notebook; Ms 30362).
      National Library of Ireland
      Copy at SUNY SB   Box 3

    Page proofs, with corrections by WBY and others; TMs (carbon) corrected (Ms 30008, 30129).
      National Library of Ireland
      Copy at SUNY SB   Box 3, 4

Books

   Copy "Inscribed for my dear friend Dorothy Wellesley,
   W B Yeats July 1938" (WELL DORO), with pencilled
   corrections in MODE LAUR.
      Smith, Simon Nowell

   Copy inscribed with four closing lines of UNDE BEN BU,
   with variant lines.
      Berlind, Bruce

   Copy inscribed to HEAL JAME, dated May 24 [1938], with
   a version of POLI that differs significantly from the
   final one, and a note: "I finished this yesterday if it
   is finished." Book also has a copy of the final
   version laid in. Another copy inscribed to HEAL JAME,
   dated 1938: "Pater told a friend of his that he thought
   his last book Plato and Platonism more natural in its
   style than any other book of his. This is my most
   natural book."
      Stanford University

   Copy inscribed to DULA EDMU, dated May 24 1938.
      Wesleyan University

   See also Miscellany: LIST (Ms 30362).

Nine Poems   NINE POEM 14
   (Privately Printed) 1914. (Wade 109)
      Copy inscribed to MORR LADY OT, dated March 15, 1907.
         Kenyon College Library

   Copy inscribed (to no one) with note beginning "When I
   was in New York" (about WBY's lecture tour), dated
   July 15, 1933; another copy signed and dated April
   1914.
      University of Texas at Austin

Nine Poems   NINE POEM 18
   London: Shorter, 1918. (Wade 122)
      Copy inscribed to GONN ISEU: "Maurice from W B Y. Dec.
      5, 1918"
         Wake Forest University Library

   Copy inscribed to "Lady Ottoline Morrell from W B Yeats
   Mar 16 1932[?]" (MORR LADY OT).
      University of Texas at Austin

October Blast   OCTO BLAS 27
   Dublin: Cuala, 1927. (Wade 156)
   AMs of Contents, and proof sheets with revisions (Ms
   13589).
         National Library of Ireland
         Copy at SUNY SB   Box 4

   Copy inscribed to HEAL JAME, dated 1938: "'The Tower'
   describes my own old Tower in Co Galway Thoor Ballylee
   or rather its neighborhood. Mrs. French lived a couple
   of miles off in the eighteenth century."
         Stanford University

   Copy inscribed to Iseult Stuart (GONN ISEU), dated Sept
   1927.
         University of Texas at Austin

On Baile's Strand   ON   BAIL 05
   Dublin: Maunsel, 1905. (Wade 58)
   Copy inscribed to GREG LADY, "from her friend W B
   Yeats."
         New York Public Library

On the Boiler   ON   BOIL 39
   Dublin: Cuala, 1939. (Wade 202)
   Corrected TMs and copy; printed copy with AMs notes (5
   pp); AMs first draft; early TMsS (18 pp) and heavily
   corrected TMs and AMs; TMs with AMs corrections, dated
   July 1938 (52 pp); TMsS, dated April 1938 (52 pp)
   (Ms 30461,30485, 30486, 30551, 30552, 30553). AMs of
   another section (Ms 30391); proof of preliminary Table
   of Contents (Ms 30154).
         National Library of Ireland
         Copy at SUNY SB   Box 27

   Page proofs with corrections in various poems,
   including CRAZ JANE MO, STAT HOLI, and WHY SHOU NO
   (Add. MS 55881).
         British Library

The Oxford Book of Modern Verse   OXFO BOOK 36
   Oxford: Clarendon, 1936. (Wade 250)
   AMs, TMs, TMs (carbon), and page proofs, with some
   corrections, of Introduction (Ms 30038, 30295, 30522,
   30625, 30797).
         National Library of Ireland
         Copy at SUNY SB   Box 40, 41

Copy with corrections in introductory material and a few poems (item 2454).
    Yeats, Anne

Copy inscribed (on inserted slip) to "Hilda Mattheson from her friend W B Yeats November 1936" (MATT HILD); another copy "Inscribed for my friend Lennox Robinson W B Yeats" (ROBI LENN).
    University of Texas at Austin

A Packet for Ezra Pound   PACK EZRA 29
  Dublin: Cuala, 1929. (Wade 163)
    Copy with revisions and deletions by WBY, J. Manson (compositor) and Thomas Mark (editor) preparatory to its publication in VISI 37 (PR5906 A553 1929).
        Emory University

    Corrected proofs; AMs draft entitled "To Ezra Pound," similar to parts of this edition; TMs (14 pp; Ms 30308, 30495, 30803).
        National Library of Ireland
        Copy at SUNY SB   Box 38

    Copy inscribed to HEAL JAME, dated 1938: "A part of my philosophical book a Vision published in its final form last year."
        Stanford University

Pages from a Diary Written in 1930.   PAGE DIAR 30
  Dublin: Cuala, 1944 (Wade 207).
    Page proofs (Ms 30023); AMs and TMs, corrected with VISI MATE (Ms 30354, 30355).
        National Library of Ireland
        Copy at SUNY SB   Box 87

Per Amica Silentia Lunae (London)   PER AMIC 18
  London: Macmillan, 1918. (Wade 120)
    AMsS, dated Feb 25 1917, with revisions and a note dated May 27 1920 (35 pp). Other pages with notes entitled "Anima Mundi" (50 pp).
        University of Texas at Austin

    AMs; rough draft and fragments of "Anima Hominus" and of "Spiritus Mundi" (over 60 pp; Ms 30368, 30500, 30532).
        National Library of Ireland
        Copy at SUNY SB   Box 20

AMs; note entitled "Personal Equivalent of Anima
Mundi," beginning "An impersonal mirror reflecting all
image" (Ms 30524).
    National Library of Ireland
    Copy at SUNY SB   Box 20

Copy with a few revisions (item 2392).
    Yeats, Anne

Copy inscribed (to no one) with the line from EGO DOMI
TU: "By the help of images I call to my own opposite."
    University of London Library

Per Amica Silentia Lunae (New York)   PER AMIC 18
  New York: Macmillan, 1918. (Wade 121)
    Copy inscribed "To my Friend John Quinn for much
    kindness & good conversation W B Yeats May 26, 1920"
    (QUIN JOHN).
        University of Texas at Austin

Plays and Controversies   PLAY CONT 23
  London: Macmillan, 1923. (Wade 139)
    AMs with corrections of Preface, entitled "A People's
    Theatre," dated Oct. 22. See also Prose: PEOP THEA.
        The Huntington Library

    AMs draft of Preface, dated Dublin Feb. 1923 (3 pp;
    Ms 30190).
        National Library of Ireland
        Copy at SUNY SB   Box 27

    Copy inscribed to SHAK OLIV, dated Dec. 25 1923.
        University of Texas at Austin

    Copy inscribed to ROBI LENN "from his friend," dated
    Feb 27 1924.
        University of Delaware Library

    Copy inscribed to GREG LADY "from W B Yeats Feb 1
    1924."
        New York Public Library

Plays and Controversies   PLAY CONT 24
  New York: Macmillan, 1924. (Wade 140)
    Copy inscribed with line from PARD OLD FA: "only the
    wasteful virtues earn the sun," evidently to AHER KATH,
    after a reading in Hartford.
        University of Louisville

Books   37

Plays for an Irish Theatre   PLAY IRIS 11
  London: Bullen, 1911. (Wade 92)
    Revisions in this text for various later editions.
    Plays revised include CATH HOUL, DEIR, GREE HELM, HOUR
    GLAS, SHAD WATE (item 2397a).
        Yeats, Anne

    Final proof inscribed to GREG LADY, dated Oct. 17,
    1911; also a copy of the book inscribed to her.
        New York Public Library

    Copy with note on 2nd flyleaf: "George's copy. I am not
    to take it whatever the need W B Y" (item 2397).
        Yeats, Anne

    Copy (of 1913 impression) with note about a dream of an
    old woman in a long cloak who was Ireland herself,
    Kathleen ni Houlihan.
        Brown University

    Copy of SHAD WATE 07 with extensive revisions used as
    the copytext for this edition (item 2421).
        Yeats, Anne

    Copy inscribed to SHAK OLIV, dated Xmas 1911.
        University of Texas at Austin

    See also Prose: TRAG THEA and Plays: HOUR GLAS.

Plays in Prose and Verse   PLAY PROS 22
  London: Macmillan, 1922. (Wade 136)
    AMs of Preface (Ms 30482); also printed texts of HOUR
    GLAS and KING THRE and the notes, used as copy for this
    edition (Ms 13571, 30251).
        National Library of Ireland
        Copy at SUNY SB Box 15

    Two copies with notes: "George Yeats (not to be taken
    by me. W B Y)" and "George Yeats her book not to be
    taken by me. W B Yeats." (items 2398, 2398a).
        Yeats, Anne

    Copy inscribed (to no one) with two lines from PRAY
    DAUG, beginning "Ceremony is a name," dated May 16
    1923.
        University of Louisville

Copy inscribed to ROBI LENN, dated Dec. 6 1922.
   Princeton University Library

Copy of KING BAIL 04 with corrections, deletions, and additions, used as copytext for this edition.
   New York Public Library

Copy inscribed to GREG LADY.
   New York Public Library

Copy inscribed to DULA EDMU, dated Dec. 2, 1922; another copy to SHAK OLIV, dated Dec. 6, 1922.
   University of Texas at Austin

Plays in Prose and Verse   PLAY PROS 24
 New York: Macmillan, 1924. (Wade 137)
   Copy inscribed to T. MacGreevy (MACG T.), dated 24 April 1924.
      University of Kansas

   See also Plays: HOUR GLAS.

Poems   POEM   95
 London: Unwin, 1895. (Wade 15)
   Copy inscribed to GARN EDWA, dated 1895.
      Princeton University Library

   Copy inscribed (to no one) with first stanza of LAKE ISLE IN.
      University of Toronto

   Copy inscribed to ROSE EDWA.
      Smith, Simon Nowell

   Copy inscribed (to no one) with two lines from FERG DRUI, beginning "Take if you will this little bag of dreams," dated Nov 1901 (Ip.Y34.C895pb).
      Yale University

   Copy inscribed to HORT WILL "from W B Yeats, January 1898."
      Harper, George

   Copy inscribed ELLI EDWI J., "on August 27th 1895 from W B Yeats" (Ellis Collection: 97940).
      University of Reading Library

Books

> Inscribed vellum copy with bookplate of Lady Gregory with poem O DO NO on first page, with corrections, dated July 12th 1903, noting that the poem was written July 8 and 9; second preliminary page inscribed (to no one) with 12 lines of verse from MAID QUIE entitled "Hanrahan the Red upon his Wanderings"; copies with corrections of VALL BLAC PI, TO HEAR BI, SORR LOVE, PERF BEAU and "The Rose of my Heart" (LOVE TELL RO) tipped in (PR 5900 A3 1895).
> Emory University
>
> Two inscribed copies with corrections: one "To my friend George Russell, on August 26th, 1895" (RUSS GEOR); another "To my friend Mrs. Shakespear, on August 26th, 1895" (SHAK OLIV).
> University of Texas at Austin
>
> Copy of American edition (Boston: Copeland; see Wade 16) inscribed to HOWE W.T., dated Dec. 1, 1932.
> New York Public Library
>
> Copy of American edition inscribed to PROK FRED with line from TOM O'RO: "An aimless joy is a pure joy," dated July 15, 1933.
> University of Texas at Austin

Poems   POEM 99
  London: Unwin, 1899. (Wade 17)
> Copy with corrections in WBY's hand and on inserted typed slips, mostly in COUN KATH (EC9. Y3455.895 pb).
> Harvard University
>
> Copy inscribed to COAT FLOR EA, with a five line inscription from WITH BOUG, with some mistakes and corrections, beginning "No boughs have withered."
> Wake Forest University Library
>
> Copy with extensive corrections.
> The Huntington Library
>
> Copy inscribed to SMIT J. "from W B Yeats."
> Boston College
>
> Copy inscribed to GREG LADY, dated 10 May 1899, with drafts of two unpublished poems: ON CHIL DE and SONG HEFF BL (PR5900 A3 1899).
> Emory University

Poems   POEM   01
   London: Unwin, 1901. (Wade 18)
      Copy inscribed (to no one) with the lines from DOUB
      VISI MI: "For what but eye and ear silence the mind
      With the minute particulars of mankind."
            University of London Library

      Copy (that had belonged to Clifford Bax) with inserted
      letter to FARR FLOR EM and photograph of Maud Gonne
      with note in WBY's hand: "married on Saturday last";
      another copy inscribed to SHAK OLIV, dated 1901.
            University of Texas at Austin

      Copy inscribed to GREG LADY, dated 1901, with first
      draft of APPO, The Three Musicians' songs from DEIR,
      and 24 lines of verse from QUEEN EDAI, beginning "'Why
      is it' queen Edain said" (PR5900 A3 1901 cop.2).
            Emory University

Poems   POEM   04
   London: Unwin, 1904. (Wade 19)
      Vellum copy inscribed to GREG LADY, dated 21 July 1904,
      with draft of second stanza of SORR LOVE (PR5900 A3
      1904a).
            Emory University

      Inscribed copy: "Quinn's book. November twelveth 1904-
      W B Yeats" (QUIN JOHN).
            University of Texas at Austin

Poems   POEM   12
   London: Unwin, 1912. (Wade 99)
      Copy inscribed (to no one) with line from TOM O'RO:
      "An aimless joy is a pure joy."
            University of Kansas

Poems   POEM   13
   London: Unwin, 1913. (Wade 100)
      Inscribed copy, dated October 12, 1923.
            Washington State University

Poems   POEM   22
   London: Unwin, [1922]. (See Wade 100)
      Copy of COUN CATH 12 apparently used as copytext for
      this edition (item 2334).
            Yeats, Anne

Books

    Copy inscribed (to no one) with two lines from FERG DRUI, beginning "Take if you must this little bag of dreams," dated Dec 15 1923.
        University of Massachusetts Amherst

    Copy of 1923 printing with marks and notes about a rearrangement of the poems for a later edition (item 2403a).
        Yeats, Anne

    Copy with bookplate of MOOR STUR with the line from TOM O'RO "'An aimless joy is a pure joy' W B Yeats" (item 2402).
        Yeats, Anne

Poems   POEM   27
   London: Unwin, 1927. (Wade 153)
      AMs of Preface (1 p; Ms 30809).
        National Library of Ireland
        Copy at SUNY SB   Box 4

Poems   POEM   29
   London: Benn, [1929]. (Wade 154)
      Copy with note (printed in Wade) about the financial success of the book (item 2404).
        Yeats, Anne

Poems Written in Discouragement   POEM WRIT 13
   Dundrum: Cuala, 1913. (Wade 107)
      AMs of note on these poems that appeared in RESP POEM 14 (Ms 30314).
        National Library of Ireland
        Copy at SUNY SB   Box 4

    Copy inscribed to GREG LADY, dated Oct 1913.
        New York Public Library

    Copy inscribed to MORR LADY OT "from W.B. Yeats, Dec 20 1921."
        University of Kansas

    Copy inscribed to LANE HUGH, dated Oct 1913; two lines from PAUD beginning, "There cannot be," inscribed on page with TO WEAL MAN.
        Wesleyan University

Copy in collection of HEAL JAME, inscribed with note
about the Lane controversy.
    Stanford University

Copy inscribed to MORR LADY OT, dated Oct. 14, 1914;
another to "John Drinkwater from W B Yeats. April,
1915" (DRIN JOHN).
    University of Texas at Austin

Poems and Ballads of Young Ireland   POEM BALL 88
  Dublin: Gill, 1888. (Wade 289)
    Copy with occasional revisions and corrections
    inscribed to GREG LADY, dated 5 December 1910
    (PR8857 P6).
      Emory University

Poems and Ballads of Young Ireland   POEM BALL 90
  Dublin: Gill, 1890.
    Copy inscribed to JOHN LION.
      Newberry Library

Poems and Translations by John Synge   POEM TRAN 09
  Dundrum: Cuala, 1901. (Wade 243)
    Copy with revisions and corrections in WBY's essay on
    Synge (PR5532 P6).
      Emory University

Poems of Spenser   POEM SPEN 06
  Edinburgh: Jack, [1906]. (Wade 235)
    Page proofs of Introduction, with corrections, stamped
    "Ballantyne Press" and dated June 23, 1906.
      New York Public Library

The Poems of William Blake   POEM WILL 93
  London: Bullen, 1893. (Wade 220)
    Copy inscribed (to no one) with two lines from TOM
    O'RO: "For wisdom is a butterfly And not a gloomy
    bird of prey W B Yeats May 5 1925" (item 208).
      Yeats, Anne

    Drafts and papers relating to WBY's work on Blake (See
    Books: WORK WILL 93).
      University of Reading Library

    Copy inscribed (to no one) with eight lines from REEN
    TIME AF, beginning "Re-engraved time after time, Ever
    in their youthful prime," dated Oct 1901 (Ip.Y34.C893p).
      Yale University

Books   43

Poems, 1899-1905   POEM 1899 06
   London: Bullen, 1906. (Wade 64)
      Incomplete page proofs, dated 24 November 1905 and
      marked "first proof," with parts of SHAD WATE and ON
      BAIL ST (Ms 30017).
            National Library of Ireland
            Copy at SUNY SB   Box 4

      Incomplete galley proofs, with corrections. Also
      revised galley proofs, with corrections in a number of
      Plays: KING THRE, ON BAIL ST; and Poems: ADAM CURS,
      BAIL AILL, HAPP TOWN, OLD AGE QU, OLD MEMO, QUEE EDAI,
      and WITH BOUG.
            New York Public Library

      Copy inscribed to FAY WILL.
            New York Public Library

      Copy inscribed to YEAT JOHN: "To my father. W B Yeats"
      with revisions of ON BAIL ST (item 2400).
            Yeats, Anne

      Copy inscribed to MACB MAUD GO, dated 1906.
            Princeton University Library

      Copy inscribed (to no one) with the line from TOM O'RO:
      "For wisdom is a butterfly."
            University of London Library

Poems: Second Series   POEM SECO 09
   London: Bullen, 1909. (Wade 83)
      Revisions in this text for various later editions.
      Works revised include ADAM CURS, ARRO, BAIL AILL, FOLL
      BEIN CO, RAGG WOOD, SHAD WATE, UNDE MOON (item 2401).
            Yeats, Anne

      Copy inscribed "To Edmund Gosse from W.B. Yeats April
      19, 1910" (GOSS EDMU; may be bogus), possibly with
      corrections by WBY.
            University of Texas at Austin

The Poetical Works. Vol 1. Lyrical Poems.   POET WORK 06
   London: Macmillan, 1906. (Wade 65)
         Copy inscribed (to no one), dated May 9, 1920.
         Wellesley College

AMs of the Preface (Ms 30313).
National Library of Ireland
Copy at SUNY SB   Box 27

Page proofs with corrections in many poems, including
the following: ANAS VIJA, BAIL AILL, BLES, CRAD SONG,
CUCH FIGH SE, DEDI BOOK ST, DREA DEAT, FERG DRUI,
HAPP TOWN, HE HEAR CR, HE MOUR CH, HE REME FO, HE TELL
VA, HE THIN HI, HE THIN TH, INDI GOD, LOVE SPEA HE,
MAN WHO DR, NEVE GIVE AL, OLD AGE QU, QUEE EDAI,
RED HANR SO, TO ROSE RO, TO SOME I, UNDE MOON, WAND
OISI and WITH BOUG.
New York Public Library

Copy inscribed to GREG LADY with drafts of ALL THIN CA
and AT GALW RA, both dated Sept 1908; AMs additions,
marks and cancellations in Table of Contents (PR5900 A3
1906).
Emory University

Poetical Works. Vol. 2. Dramatical Poems   POET WORK 07
   London: Macmillan, 1907. (Wade 71)
   Incomplete page proofs.
   New York Public Library

   AMs of the Preface (Ms 30031)
   National Library of Ireland
   Copy at SUNY SB   Box 27

Poetical Works. Vol 2. Dramatic Poems   POET WORK 12
   New York: Macmillan, 1912. (Wade 98)
   Copy inscribed (to no one), dated May 9, 1920.
   Wellesley College

Poetry and Ireland   POET IREL 08
   Dundrum: Cuala, 1908. (Wade 242)
   Page proof under title of "Poetry and Tradition,"
   signed and dated May 14, 1924.
   New York Public Library

   Copy inscribed to YOUN ELLA "from W B Yeats Xmas 1908."
   The Huntington Library

   Copy inscribed to HEAL JAME, dated July 30 1938, noting
   that the essay by Lionel Johnson was given to the
   National Literary Society in Dublin.
   Stanford University

>   Copy with 10-line ANS, beginning "I like this better
>   than any other essay of mine," dated Jan. 1909.
>   University of Texas at Austin

Representative Irish tales   2 vols   REPR IRIS 91
>   London: G.P. Putnam's Sons [1891]. (Wade 215)
>   First series inscribed to YEAT ELIZ: "Lolly C. Yeats
>   from her brother Willie October 1891-" (Yeats 213,
>   214).
>   Trinity College Dublin
>
>   Copy belonging to QUIN JOHN, with note quoted by Wade,
>   dated March 1904.
>   University of Texas at Austin

Responsibilities and Other Poems   RESP OTHE 16
>   London: Macmillan, 1916. (Wade 115)
>   Textual changes occurring in this edition made in copy
>   of RESP POEM 14 that is inscribed to GREG LADY
>   (PR5904 R3).
>   Emory University
>
>   Several copies with corrections, revisions, and
>   instructions for printers, used as copytext for later
>   editions, including LATE POEM 22 (items 2412, 2412a,
>   2412c, 2412d).
>   Yeats, Anne
>
>   Copy inscribed to GREG LADY, dated October 1916.
>   Wertheim, Stanley
>
>   Copy inscribed (to no one) with the lines from PLAY ASK
>   BL: "The proud & careless notes live on But bless our
>   hands that ebb away."
>   University of London Library
>
>   See Miscellany: MISC for autograph memorandum removed
>   from copy of this book.

Responsibilities: Poems and a Play   RESP POEM 14
>   Dundrum: Cuala, 1914. (Wade 110)
>   Page proofs (incomplete) with Pound's rewriting and
>   corrections by WBY.
>   Yale University

Copy inscribed (to no one) with a note: "This book is not liked in America to judge by the reviews. W.B. Yeats 1917."
    Dublin City Libraries

Copy inscribed to HEAL JAME, dated 1938, with a fair copy of COAT, with slight variations from the final version.
    Stanford University

Copy, with corrections, inscribed to MACB MAUD GO "from W.B. Yeats, June 1914."
    Sparrow, John

AMs of note in this edition about POEM WRIT 13 (Ms 30314).
    National Library of Ireland
    Copy at SUNY SB

Proof sheets with a note: "When done with these proofs please send them to John Quinn." Corrections and revisions in the following poems: BEGG BEGG CR, COLD HEAV, HOUR DAWN, MAGI, MEMO YOUT, PAUD, PEA COCK, REAL, RUNN PARA, TO CHIL DA, TO FRIE WH, TO SHAD, WHEN HELE LI, WITC; and a Play: PLAY QUEE (EC9 Y3455.914 ra).
    Harvard University

AMs of the epigraphs for the book; TMs draft of Table of Contents with corrections; drafts and revisions of poems (Ms 30044, 30096, 13586).
    National Library of Ireland
    Copy at SUNY SB   Box 4

Page proofs with corrections and revisions in APPO, WHEN HELE LI, PARD OLD FA (with note referring to Pound), and WHIL I RE.
    New York Public Library

Copy with revisions throughout, including textual changes to HOUR GLAS, preliminary to the publication of RESP OTHE 16; another copy inscribed to GREG LADY, with comments on TO FRIE WH and on HOUR GLAS (see those works for the comments; PR5904 R3).
    Emory University

Copy inscribed to "Olivia Shakespear from W B Yeats. May 29.1914 (SHAK OLIV).
University of Texas at Austin

See also Books: RESP OTHE 16.

Reveries over Childhood and Youth   REVE CHIL 15
Dundrum: Cuala, 1915. (Wade 111)
TMs with a few corrections, sent to John Quinn; typed date of Christmas 1914.
University of Texas at Austin

TMs (carbon) entitled "A Reverie over Childhood and Youth," with a few autograph corrections, dated Christmas, 1914 (114 pp).
University of Tulsa

TMs (carbon; 113 pp) under title of "A Reverie over Childhood and Youth," with a few revisions and corrections, dated 1914, and sent to John Quinn in New York (MS Eng 821.1).
Harvard University

TMs and AMs in Pound's hand, probably from dictation (about 112 pp; Ms 30868).
National Library of Ireland
Copy at SUNY SB Box 21, 22

Draft, entitled "A Reverie Over Childhood and Youth," dated 1914 (168 pp).
Colby College Library

Two copies inscribed to HEAL JAME: one, dated August 15, 1937: to "the friend of my friend John Quinn;" the other, dated July 30, 1938: "I meant to call this book Memory Harbour from a picture...by my brother. But found ...that somebody else had...taken the name."
Stanford University

Inscribed copy with bookplate of GREG LADY, telling where he wrote the book and noting that it was written "to clear up my own mind...It is for my friends and children" (PR5906 A557 1915).
Emory University

Copy inscribed to ROTH WILL, dated 1916.
University of Texas at Austin

Copy inscribed to TUCK MRS. "from W B Yeats, February 1916."
>> Emory University

Reveries over Childhood and Youth   REVE CHIL 16
New York: Macmillan, 1916. (Wade 112)
>> Copy inscribed (to no one), dated Dec. 1925, with the line: "An aimless joy is a pure joy" (from TOM O'RO).
>>> University of London Library

>> Copy inscribed (to no one), dated May 9, 1920.
>>> Wellesley College

>> Copy inscribed (to no one), dated May 6 1920.
>>> University of Texas at Austin

>> Copy inscribed to "W T Horton from his friend W B Yeats May 16 1916" (HORT WILL).
>>> Harper, George

Second Book of the Rhymers' Club   SECO BOOK 94
London: Matthews, 1894. (Wade 294)
>> Copy of book with a fair copy of OIL BLOO, probably inscribed in 1928 and sent to James B. de Vincheles Payen-Payne (PAYE JAME VI).
>>> University of Toronto

>> Copy with bookplate of GREG LADY, with the following inscription: "This book was the last act of the Rhymers Club...I think it was the fear of another book brought the club to an end. The members who wrote worst wanted another book greatly. W B Y 1901."
>>> Smith, Simon Nowell

The Secret Rose   SECR ROSE 97
London: Lawrence, 1897. (Wade 21)
>> Page proofs, corrected (Ms 30204). See also Prose: COST PROU (Ms 30369).
>>> National Library of Ireland
>>> Copy at SUNY SB   Box 31

>> Copy, with corrections, inscribed to POLL GEOR, dated 1897.
>>> Princeton University Library

Copy inscribed (to no one) with the line "In dreams
begin responsibilities."
    State University of New York at Buffalo

Copy inscribed to JOHN LION. Also an imperfect copy of
an unidentified edition, with corrections and
instructions for a printer, used as copy for EARL POEM
25.
    New York Public Library

Copy inscribed to SYMO ARTH; another "To O. Shakespear,
from W B Yeats April 1st 1897" (SHAK OLIV).
    University of Texas at Austin

Selected Poems   SELE POEM 21
  New York: Macmillan, 1921. (Wade 128)
    Copy of SELE POET 13 with deletions and additions
    intended as copytext for this version (item 2419).
        Yeats, Anne

    Copy inscribed (to no one) with the line from PARD OLD
    FA: "'Only the wasteful virtues earn the sun' W B Yeats
    Jan 1925" (item 2417c).
        Yeats, Anne

    Copy with a cancelled inscription: "W S Nichol
    Service[?] from W B Yeats Nov 13 1921," followed by
    note: "Not to be lent or given as it contains
    corrections W B Yeats 4 Broad St. Oxford," with
    revisions in BAIL AILL, OLD AGE QU, TO SHAD,
    WILD SWAN CO, UNDE MOON, UPON DYIN LA (item 2417).
        Yeats, Anne

Selected Poems   SELE POEM 29
  London: Macmillan, 1929. (Wade 165)
    Incomplete page proofs (pp 49-128), dated 9 April 1929
    (Ms 30009). Individual items not noted in Poems
    section, except for a few with no other known manu-
    scripts, including: MASK, THES ARE CL, TO IRE CO, WHEN
    YOU AR.
        National Library of Ireland
        Copy at SUNY SB   Box 5

Copy inscribed to FODE GWYN "from her friend W.B.
Yeats, April 17, 1932."
  Indiana University

Copy inscribed to GREG LADY, dated September 1930, with
draft of FOR ANNE GR (PR 5902 M3 1929).
  Emory University

A Selection from the Love Poetry   SELE LOVE 13
 Dundrum: Cuala, 1913. (Wade 106)
  Copy with numeric additions to the Table of Contents
  and to p. 3 (PR5900 A6 1913 cop. 1). Copy inscribed
  to GREG LADY, dated June 1922: "I notice that only
  those poems that I dislike are popular" (PR5900 A6 1913
  cop.2).
    Emory University

  Page Proofs.
    National Library of Ireland
    Copy at SUNY SB Box 5

  Copy inscribed to DUGG ELIZ, dated December 1915;
  another "To Thomas Beecham from W B Yeats in gratitude
  for a gift to the Irish Players" (BEEC THOM).
    University of Texas at Austin

A Selection from the Poetry   SELE POET 13
 Leipzig: Tauchnitz, 1913. (Wade 103)
  Copy inscribed to COLU PADR: "Mr Colum from his friend
  the writer April 26 1913" in WBY's hand but not signed,
  with a few corrections (in Rare Books and Mss).
    New York Public Library

  Copy with "The Countess Cathleen" and its notes,
  inscribed to "John Drinkwater from W B Yeats April 4
  1913" (DRIN JOHN); note by Drinkwater indicates that
  corrections are WBY's; printer's date of 10 Dec. 1912.
    University of Texas at Austin

  Copy inscribed to REID FORR, with corrections.
    Princeton University Library

  Copy with deletions and additions intended as the
  copytext for SELE POEM 21 (item 2419).
    Yeats, Anne

Seven Poems and a Fragment   SEVE POEM 22
   Dundrum: Cuala, 1922. (Wade 132)
      Copy inscribed to HEAL JAME, dated 1938, referring to
      NINE HUND NI as the "first poem in...my 'later
      manner.'"
         Stanford University

      Inscribed copy (bookplate of GREG LADY) with the note:
      "I wrote 'Soul's Night' some months ago at Oxford. H...
      is Horton a very dear friend who died three years ago,
      & I have accurately described the chief emotion of his
      life. W B Yeats June 1922"; AMs draft of STAR NEST MY,
      dated July 14, 1922 (PR5904 S35 copy 2). See also
      Poems: ALL SOUL NI.
         Emory University

The Shadowy Waters   SHAD WATE 00
   London: Hodder, 1900. (Wade 30)
      Copy inscribed to MASE JOHN: "A piece of poet's bay
      given to me by Lady Gregory--Feb. 10 1903."
         Princeton University Library

      Copy inscribed to Maire Nic Shiublaigh (WALK MARY).
         Northwestern University Library

      Copy inscribed to HORN MISS AN "from her friend W B
      Yeats Dec. 19, 1900" (item 2420).
         Yeats, Anne

      Copy inscribed to SYMO ARTH, dated Dec. 1900, with one
      correction at end, possibly by WBY; another copy
      inscribed to "Maud Gonne Dec. 19 1900" (MACB MACU GO).
         University of Texas at Austin

The Shadowy Waters   SHAD WATE 01
   New York: Dodd, Mead, 1901. (Wade 31)
      Copy inscribed to GREG LADY, with one minor change:
      "Forgael" changed to "Aibric" in stage directions on
      p. 14.
         New York Public Library

The Shadowy Waters   SHAD WATE 07
   London: Bullen, 1907. (Wade 66)
      Copy with extensive revisions used as the copytext for
      PLAY IRIS 11 (item 2421).
         Yeats, Anne

      Copy with autograph notes, possibly by WBY.
         University of Texas at Austin

      Copy inscribed to GREG LADY "from her friend the
      writer." Also page proofs with corrections.
         New York Public Library

      See also Poems: SHAD WATE.

The Singing Head and the Lady   SING HEAD 34
   n.p.: n.p., 1934. (Wade 180)
      Copy inscribed (to no one): "Best wishes W B Yeats."
         Wellesley College

      One of four preliminary trial copies "Inscribed for
      Frederick Prokosch by W.B. Yeats Nov. 25, 1935" (PROK
      FRED).
         Indiana University

      Copy no. III inscribed (to no one), dated Nov 6, 1935
      (Vault PR5904 S5).
         Emory University

      Copy inscribed to PROK FRED, dated Nov 25, 1935.
         Wesleyan University

      Two copies: one inscribed to PROK FRED (may be bogus),
      dated November 1935; another (to no one) dated Nov. 25,
      1935.
         University of Texas at Austin

Some Essays and Passages by John Eglinton   SOME ESSA 05
   Dundrum: Dun Emer, 1905. (Wade 232)
      Copy inscribed with "Words alone are certain good"
      (from SONG HAPP SH), signed by Eglinton, with note by
      WBY: "John Eglinton is our one Irish writer. He is in
      permanent friendly opposition to our national literary
      movement. He has influenced us all I think even though
      we curse him at times," dated Dec 31 1905
      (Ip.M271.905S. copy 1).
         Yale University

Books

A Speech and Two Poems   SPEE TWO   31
   Dublin: Sign of Three Candles, 1937. (Wade 193)
     Copy inscribed to HEAL JAME, "with gratitude & thanks."
        Stanford University

     Copy inscribed to WALS JAME P.
        Kenyon College Library

Stories of Michael Robartes and his Friends   STOR MICH   31
   Dublin: Cuala, 1931. (Wade 167)
     AMs fragments.
        National Library of Ireland
        Copy at SUNY SB   Box 38

     Page proof with corrections; TMs, fragment; also AMs
     fragments (Ms 30019, 30465, 30390).
        National Library of Ireland
        Copy at SUNY SB   Box 38

     Proof sheets with corrections (25 pp).
        Wesleyan University

     Copy of AMs of Introduction, from white vellum notebook.
     See Miscellany: DIAR JOUR (Partial List...#545).
        Location of original unknown
        Copy at SUNY SB   Box 88

     Copy inscribed to HEAL JAME, dated 1938: "Part of my
     philosophical book A Vision. I have improved the
     stories since and added a new one."
        Stanford University

     Copy inscribed to DULA EDMU, dated Feb. 19, 1932;
     another "To George Russell from W B Yeats, Feb. 5 1932"
     (RUSS GEOR).
        University of Texas at Austin

     See also Miscellany: DIAR JOUR (AMs notebook with date
     24 May; Ms 13577).

Stories of Red Hanrahan: The Secret Rose: Rosa
Alchemica   STOR RED   04
   Dundrum: Dun Emer, 1904. (Wade 59)
   Early and later page proofs, signed, with a few
   corrections; two inscribed copies, both dated
   1905, one with a note indicating that the name Hanrahan
   is imaginary, and that Lady Gregory helped WBY with the
   material; also a note by Lady Gregory.
      New York Public Library

   Copy inscribed to HEAL JAME, dated 1938: "The friend
   was Lady Gregory. The not very successful design on the
   next page was by her son not yet [a] master of design."
      Stanford University

   Copy inscribed with part of I SEE PH: "'The abstract
   joy, The half read wisdom of demonic images, Suffice
   the ageing man as once the growing boy.' W.B. Yeats."
      Washington State University

   Copy inscribed (to no one), dated May 1, 1908.
      Sligo County Library

   Copy inscribed to "Mrs Emery [word crossed out] from
   her friend W B Yeats" (EMER FLOR FA), with some
   astrological symbols.
      Yale University

   Copy inscribed to SHAK OLIV, dated May 1905; another
   inscribed (to no one), dated May 10, 1905.
      University of Texas at Austin

Stories of Red Hanrahan: Secret Rose: Rosa
Alchemica   STOR RED   13
   Longon: Bullen, 1913. (Wade 104)
   Copy inscribed to GREG LADY.
      New York Public Library

Stories of Red Hanrahan   STOR RED   14
   New York: Macmillan, 1914. (Wade 105)
   Copy with revisions (item 2426).
      Yeats, Anne

Books

Stories of Red Hanrahan and The Secret Rose   STOR RED   27
   London: Macmillan, 1927.
      Two AMs and one TMs, dated June 25, 1927.
         Sligo County Library

      Copy inscribed to GREG LADY.
         New York Public Library

Synge and the Ireland of his Time   SYNG IREL 11
   Dundrum: Cuala, 1911. (Wade 88)
      Page proofs with corrections.
         Yale University

      Final proof inscribed to GREG LADY, dated April 1911.
         New York Public Library

      Proof sheets with extensive corrections, signed and
      dated May 16 1924 (EC9. Y3455.911 sa).
         Harvard University

      Copy with textual revisions (Pr 5533 S5).
         Emory University

      Copy inscribed (to no one), dated May 9, 1920.
         Wellesley College

      Copy inscribed to HEAL JAME, dated July 1938, with
      comments about the friendship between Synge and WBY's
      brother, noting that "both had long silences."
         Stanford University

The Tables of the Law The Adoration of the Magi   TABL LAW 97
   Privately printed, 1897. (Wade 24)
      Copy inscribed to YEAT LILY "from W B Yeats Dec. 29th
      97" (item 2428).
         Yeats, Anne

      Copy inscribed to SHAK OLIV, dated June 16, 1897
      (Ip.Y34.897T).
         Yale University

      AMs related to "The Adoration of the Magi" (1 p; Ms
      8762).
         National Library of Ireland
         Copy at SUNY SB   Box 30

Vellum copy inscribed to GREG LADY, with three lines
from RED HANR SO (PR 5904 T32 1897).
   Emory University

Copy inscribed to SHAR WILL, dated July 2nd, 1897;
another inscribed (to no one), dated April 20 1917.
   University of Texas at Austin

The Tables of the Law The Adoration of the Magi   TABL LAW   04
London: Matthews, 1904. (Wade 25)
   TMs (carbon) of Preface (1 p).
      University of Texas at Austin

   AMs, beginning "After I had put out," referring to
   "Rosa," "Alchemica," "Tables of the Law," and "The
   Adoration of the Magi" (5 lines; Ms 30442).
      National Library of Ireland
      Copy at SUNY SB   Box 30

   Copy inscribed to MARR RAYM, dated Nov. 6, 1904.
      University of Texas at Austin

The Tables of the Law   TABL LAW   14
   Stratford: Shakespeare Head, 1914. (Wade 26)
   Copy with a fair copy of ROSE PEAC inserted.
      New York Public Library

   Copy inscribed to WELL CARO, dated Jan. 27 1920.
      University of Texas at Austin

The Ten Principal Upanishads   TEN PRIN 37
   London: Faber, 1937. (Wade 252)
   TMs (carbon), AMs (Ms 30130, 30530).
      National Library of Ireland
      Copy at SUNY SB   Box 19

   Inscribed copy: "James Stephens from W B Yeats April
   19 1937" (STEP JAME).
      Finneran, Richard

The Tower   TOWE   28
   London: Macmillan, 1928. (Wade 158)
      Copy with a few revisions, inscribed to SATO JUNZ "from
      his friend W B Yeats" (item 2430c).
         Yeats, Anne

Copy with the note: "George Yeats' copy not to be given away or taken to cut up or for any other purpose by me W B Y" (item 2430e).
    Yeats, Anne

AMs list of poems; also drafts and revisions of poems (Ms 13589, 30760).
    National Library of Ireland
    Copy at SUNY SB Box 5

Copy inscribed to SHAK OLIV. Additional note in another hand, dated 6 December 1946 and signed PR, reads: "Lennox Robinson told me today that Olivia Shakespear was WBY's first mistress. So Mrs. Yeats told him."
    Princeton University Library

Four inscribed copies: one with a line beginning "I would be ignorant" (from DAWN) on an inserted slip; another with a letter to WHEL dated Sept. 26; another to "Iseult Stuart from W B Yeats" (GONN ISEU); another (may be a bogus inscription) "For Frederic Prokosch from W B Yeats 1935" (PROK FRED).
    University of Texas at Austin

The Trembling of the Veil   TREM VEIL 22
  London: Privately printed, 1922. (Wade 133)
    TMs with corrections (Ms 30252).
        National Library of Ireland
        Copy at SUNY SB Box 21, 22

AMs drafts of parts of "Ireland after Parnell" (Ms 30821); two TMs of parts of "The Tragic Generation" and "The Stirring of the Bones" (Ms 30616).
    National Library of Ireland
    Copy at SUNY SB Box 21, 22

Page proofs; AMs drafts of parts of "The Tragic Generation"; AMs of final section; TMs of sections 4 and 5 with corrections (8 pp); TMs of section 17 (2 pp); TMs (fragment) of section 20 with corrections (2 pp); AMs fragments (Ms 30016, 30491, 30504, 30531, 30810, 30811, 30812).
    National Library of Ireland
    Copy at SUNY SB Box 21, 22

Copy inscribed to GREG LADY, dated October 20, 1922.
    New York Public Library

Copy inscribed (to no one) with the line "Only the wasteful virtues earn the sun" (from PARD OLD FA).
    University of London Library

Copy inscribed to TUCK MRS. "From W B Yeats, Oct. 21 1922" (item 2432); copy heavily corrected and revised in pencil with TMs insertions used as copytext for AUTO REVE 26 (item 2432a).
    Yeats, Anne

Two Plays for Dancers   TWO   PLAY 19
  n.p.: Cuala, 1919. (Wade 123)
    Copy inscribed with line from TOM O'RO: "An aimless joy is a pure joy," with revisions and deletions throughout, dated Sept 1927 (PR5904 T9 cop. 2).
        Emory University

    Copy inscribed to HEAL JAME, dated 1938: "I made a different version of this second play more suitable to the ordinary stage. It permits the use of many dancers. That great dancer Ninnette de Valois came to Ireland & danced for us."
        Stanford University

    Copy inscribed to SHAK OLIV, dated March 12, 1918.
        University of Texas at Austin

    AMsS; Preface.
        National Library of Ireland
        Copy at SUNY SB   Box 16

The Unicorn From the Stars   UNIC STAR 08
  New York: Macmillan, 1908. (Wade 73)
    Copy inscribed to DULA EDMU.
        Pierpont Morgan Library

    Lady Gregory's proof copy with revisions and deletions by WBY and Lady Gregory throughout (PR5904 U6).
        Emory University

    Copy inscribed (to no one) with the note: "Proofs sent from America to W B Y & given by him to A G."
        Indiana University

    See also Plays: UNIC STAR.

Unpublished: Macmillan Edition de Luxe   UNPU MACM ED
   Also known as the Coole Edition.
      AMs, TMs, page proofs, and galley proofs, with
      corrections and revisions in many of WBY's works, for
      an edition that was never published. Items include
      Table of Contents (Ms 30120, 30139, 30202),
      Autobiographies (Ms 30140), Mythologies (Ms 30030),
      Plays (MS 30006, 30007, 30185, 30375), Poems (Ms 30241,
      30262, 30263), and Winding Stair Material (MS 30242).
      Items are not listed separately in the individual
      sections of this CENSUS, except for a few poems with
      no other known manuscripts, including Poems: EVER VOIC,
      UNAP HOST.
         National Library of Ireland
         Copy at SUNY SB   Box 28, 29, 30

      Many page proofs and some galley proofs of plays,
      essays, introductions, and poems with corrections by
      WBY, Thomas Mark, and George Yeats (Add. Ms
      55877-55897).
         British Library

      See also Books: LAST POEM 39.

Unpublished: Scribner Edition   UNPU SCRI ED
   Also known as the Dublin Edition.
      Correspondence and materials related to this edition in
      the Archives of Charles Scribner's Sons.
         Princeton University Library

      Various materials, including AMs and TMs of lists, the
      Introductions, and numerous plays and poems, with
      revisions and corrections (Ms 30119, 30181, 30395,
      30628, 30798).
         National Library of Ireland
         Copy at SUNY SB   Box 25

      Extensive collection of materials, including pages torn
      from books, photostats of books, page proofs, and
      typescripts; a few with corrections in the hand of WBY;
      others corrected by George Yeats and one or more
      Scribner editors.
         University of Texas at Austin

Unpublished: The Rosy Cross   UNPU ROSY CR
    AMs; homemade hand-bound collection of autograph poems,
    entitled "The Rosy Cross" including "He who measures
    gain and loss" (early form of SONG ROSY CR), "A
    Salutation" (early form of HE TELL PE), "I dreamed they
    laid thee" (early form of HE WISH BE), "The Pathway"
    (early form of HE WISH CL, dated August 5th 1891), and
    several Unpublished Poems: HE WHO BI, dated October
    1891 and TO SIST CR, dated August 1891 (Ms 30318).
        National Library of Ireland
        Copy at SUNY SB   Box 8

Unpublished: The Speckled Bird   UNPU SPEC BI
    A few pages included in a copy of the Introduction to
    WORD WIND 34 (MS 842).
        University of Reading Library

    Photocopies of drafts (Ms N5854,P6072; N6196,P6930).
        National Library of Ireland

    AMs, two drafts, and TMs (hundreds of pages; Ms 30275,
    30315, 30316, 30317); also an AMs under title of "The
    Lilies of the Lord" (Ms 30503).
        National Library of Ireland
        Copy at SUNY SB   Box 17

Unpublished: Ye Pleiades   UNPU YE   PL
    Homemade, handwritten and bound book edited by E.C.
    Yeats, with autograph copy of the "Priest of Coloony"
    (BALL FATH O'), signed by WBY (Ms 12160).
        National Library of Ireland

A Vision   VISI   25
    London: Privately Printed, 1925. (Wade 149)
        Copy inscribed to DULA EDMU.
        Pierpont Morgan Library

    Copy marked "Copy for Printer, July 26, 1937," with
    revisions; inscribed "To Dobbs [George Yeats] in memory
    of all tribulation when we were making this work   W.B.
    Yeats" (item 2433a).
        Yeats, Anne

Books   61

> Copy revised and annotated (item 2433b); another copy, extensively revised and corrected, used as copytext for VISI 37, inscribed in WBY's hand: "This copy must not be given to any body on any excuse however plausible W B Yeats George Yeats" (item 2433c).
> > Yeats, Anne
>
> Copy inscribed to Iseult Stuart (GONN ISEU).
> > University of Texas at Austin

A Vision   VISI   37
> London: Macmillan, 1937. (Wade 191)
> Copy with a few corrections by WBY, more by George Yeats; inscribed "George Yeats' own copy not to be taken by me W B Yeats, December, 1937" (item 2434).
> > Yeats, Anne
>
> TMs (carbon, 1 p), with revisions of "The Great Year"; Ams (6 pp); early notes in hand of George Yeats, entitled "Experiences of the Desire of Growth"; fragment of a draft (2 pp) mentioning Plotinus; TMs of the end of section V and start of section VI; TMs (carbon) of note one (Ms 30309, 30501, 30048, 30059, 30063, 30276).
> > National Library of Ireland
> > Copy at SUNY SB Box 32-40
>
> Three copies: one inscribed to MARK T; one to SHAK OLIV, dated October 12, 1937; one to MANN ETHE, dated Oct. 1937.
> > University of Texas at Austin
>
> See also Books: PACK EZRA 29, PAGE DIAR 30, VISI 25, and VISI MATE.

Vision Material   VISI MATE
> AMs (11 pp), TMs (22 pp), and TMs, carbon (20 pp), with extensive revisions and corrections in ink and pencil.
> > Southern Illinois University
>
> Extensive collection of uncatalogued materials used as background.
> > Yeats, Senator Michael
> > Copy at SUNY SB Box 32-40

Copy of notebook headed "4 Broad Street," with material
for VISI 25 and section on "Summary of sleeps 1923 July-
Nov. 27."
    Location of original unknown
    Copy at SUNY SB   Box 88

Two TMs (carbon), intended for A Vision but not used (9
pp), under title of "Michael Robartes Foretells."
    Southern Illinois University

TMs with revisions of an Introduction [by] Owen Aherne
(11 pp).
    University of Texas at Austin

Various and extensive Vision manuscripts: AMs (17 pp)
and TMs (1 p) of "The Great Year" (Ms 30322); a maroon
notebook with notes (Ms 30361); TMs (fragment of Book
II, Ms 30428); AMs (1 p, Contents of "The Great Wheel";
Ms 30443); AMs version of "The Gates of Pluto" (Ms
30526); another page (Ms 30529); AMs of a draft, mostly
of section XV (20 pp; Ms 30757); the Introduction to
"The Great Wheel" (20 pp; Ms 30758); AMs fragment of
du Heme's System of the World, probably related to A
Vision (Ms 30840, 30841); AMs fragment referring to
spirits (Ms 30057); See also Miscellany: DIAR JOUR
(Ms 13576, 13578, 13579, 13580, 13582, 30354, 30359,
30361, 30373)
    National Library of Ireland
    Copy at SUNY SB   Box 32-40

Copies of various extensive notes and other items,
including a draft of the Dedication and a 3 x 5 card
file (A-Z) of thoughts and notations from a white
vellum notebook. See Miscellany DIAR JOUR (Partial
list...#545).
    Location of original unknown
    Copy at SUNY SB   Box 88

The Wanderings of Oisin   WAND OISI 89
  London: Kegan Paul, 1889. (Wade 2)
  Page proofs marked "2nd Rev." with some revisions and
  corrections in ANAS VIJA, EPHE, INDI GOD, KANV HIMS,
  MADN KING GO, PHAN SHIP, QUAT APHO, SONG HAPP SH,
  STOL CHIL, TIME WITC VI (156 pp).
      University of Texas at Austin

Books 63

    Many corrections in copy with note by WBY: "Corrections in this book made at my dictation May 7 1889 W B Yeats" (Ellis Collection: 97936).
        University of Reading Library

    Copy inscribed to ELLI MRS. "with the author's kind regards April 9th 1889" (Ellis Collection: 97937).
        University of Reading Library

    Copy with corrections, inscribed to GARN EDWA "from W.B. Yeats Sept 26 1890."
        Princeton University Library

    Copy inscribed to RADF E. "from the writer," dated March 189[?].
        Princeton University Library

    Copy inscribed to HENL W.E.: "with the good wishes of W B Y Jan 19 1889."
        Pierpont Morgan Library

    Copy inscribed to WILL A.M. "with the author's complts."
        Providence Public Library

    Copy inscribed to GRIF MONT "from his friend W.B. Yeats. London Feby 1889."
        University of Kansas

    Copy with a fair copy of HE WISH CL inscribed on front flyleaf, dated October 1904.
        Indiana University

    Four copies: one inscribed to HENL W.E., dated May 1892; another to NETT MRS. J., dated 17 Jan 1889; another with two lines from ROSE UPON RO beginning "To find in all poor foolish things"; another to "Lilly Yeats from her brother the author March 1889."
        University of Texas at Austin

Wheels and Butterflies   WHEE BUTT 34
   London: Macmillan, 1934. (Wade 175)
    Proof sheets with corrections of the Introduction to "Fighting the Waves," from DUBLIN MAGAZINE, April-June 1932.
        Boston University

Corrected and rejected passages from the Introductions
to several plays: one referring to Lunacharski and
Gorki, another to cellars and garrets (Ms 30600,
30628); TMs (Ms 30377).
 National Library of Ireland
 Copy at SUNY SB Box 16

Reference to "cellars and garrets" in Prose: UNPU I PR
(TMs, beginning "I press that thought upon the cellars
and garrets"; Ms 30865).
 National Library of Ireland
 Copy at SUNY SB

Textual revisions of the Introduction to "Fighting the
Waves" (Ms 13567). See Plays: ONLY JEAL EM.
 National Library of Ireland
 Copy at SUNY SB Box 13

Copy inscribed to KROP HILD "with apologies for
dedicating to him 'Fighting the Waves' without
remembering to ask his leave W B Yeats" (item 2347a).
 Yeats, Anne

Copy of AMs, with corrections and additions, from white
vellum notebook. See Miscellany: DIAR JOUR (Partial
List....#545).
 Location of original unknown
 Copy at SUNY SB Box 88

Copy inscribed to SATO JUNZ "with apologies for
dedicating to him 'Resurrection' without remembering to
ask leave W B Yeats" (item 2437).
 Yeats, Anne

Copy inscribed to HAYW JOHN, dated Dec. 20, 1934.
 University of Texas at Austin

Where There Is Nothing (Samhain) WHER THER 02
 Supplement to Samhain, 1902. (Wade 41)
  Copy inscribed to GREG ROBE.
   New York Public Library

Books

Where There Is Nothing (Lane)　　　　　　　　　WHER THER 02
   n.p.: John Lane, 1902. (Wade 42)
      Galley proofs (21 pp) and several copies: one marked
      "corrected copy"; another with WBY's name deleted, then
      signed; and one inscribed to GREG LADY, dated August
      11, 1903.
         New York Public Library

      Copy inscribed to WADE ALLA, dated Jan. 24 1909.
         Indiana University

      Copy inscribed to GREG LADY, offered as "a book which
      is part your own," and noting that there were "only ten
      copies printed of this edition...to secure American
      rights" (PR 5904 W4).
         Emory University

      Copy of privately printed large paper edition (see Wade
      43), inscribed with note beginning "This is the edition
      Quinn had," dated Mar [?], 1902.
         University of Texas at Austin

Where There Is Nothing (London)　　　　　　　　WHER THER 03
   London: Bullen, 1903. (Wade 44)
      Copy inscribed "To Tommy the Song," dated August 1904
      (BERE J.C.).
         New York Public Library

      Copy with corrections, inscribed to SHAW GEOR BE.
         Princeton University Library

      Copy inscribed to Lyall Swete [?], "in memory of
      'Paul'" (SWET LYAL); another inscribed (to no one):
      "W B Yeats May 25 1903."
         University of Texas at Austin

Where There Is Nothing (New York)　　　　　　　WHER THER 03
   New York: Macmillan, 1903. (Wade 45)
      Two copies: one inscribed to POLL GEOR, dated June 20,
      1903; another to RUSS GEOR, dated May 1903.
         University of Texas at Austin

The Wild Swans at Coole, Other Verses and a
Play in Verse   WILD SWAN 17
  Dundrum: Cuala, 1917. (Wade 118)
    Corrected page proofs of title page and facing page;
    final proof; Table of Contents (Ms 30208, 13583).
        National Library of Ireland
        Copy at SUNY SB   Box 5

    Galley proofs with corrections in IN MEMO MA and BROK
    DREA. Also a copy inscribed to BOYD ERNE.
        New York Public Library

    Two sets of page proofs (one 47 pp, one 43 pp) with
    corrections in AT HAWK WE, BROK DREA, DAWN, EGO DOMI
    TU, FISH ERMA N, HER COUR AG, HER COUR TE, HIS PHOE, IN
    MEMO MA, PEOP, THOU PROP.
        University of Texas at Austin

    Copy of EIGH POEM 16 used as copytext for this edition.
        New York Public Library

    Copy inscribed to "Eva Ducat from W B Yeats February
    1918 at Oxford" (DUCA EVA).
        Smith, Simon Nowell

    Copy inscribed to HEAL JAME, dated July 1938, with
    comments on Mabel Beardsley and UPON DYIN LA.
        Stanford University

    Copy inscribed to "Olivia Shakespear from W B Yeats"
    (SHAK OLIV).
        University of Texas at Austin

    See also Books: EIGH POEM 16.

The Wild Swans at Coole (London)   WILD SWAN 19
  London: Macmillan, 1919. (Wade 124)
    Copy inscribed to BATE KATH "from W B Yeats, May 26 1920
    in memory of some pleasant days."
        Wellesley College

    Copy with note to GREG LADY, and page proofs with
    corrections of IRIS AIRM FO and LINE WRIT DE.
        New York Public Library

    Advance copy inscribed with two lines beginning "And
    wisdom is a butterfly" (TOM O'RO).
        Colby College Library

Books

> Copy with some revisions not used for later editions; inscribed "this copy not to leave the house W B Y" (item 2444).
> Yeats, Anne
>
> Copy inscribed (to no one) with the lines from SONG: "O who could have foretold That the heart grows old."
> University of London Library
>
> Copy inscribed to SHAK OLIV, dated April 1919; another copy inscribed to "Maud Gonne from W B Yeats March 15 1919" (MACB MAUD GO).
> University of Texas at Austin
>
> See also Poems: IRIS AIRM FO.

The Wild Swans at Coole (New York)   WILD SWAN 19
  New York: Macmillan, 1919. (Wade 125)
> Copy with annotations and corrections.
> University of California Los Angeles

The Wind Among the Reeds   WIND REED 99
  London: Mathews, 1899. (Wade 27)
> AMs; small white notebook begun 29 August 1893, with drafts of many poems. See Miscellany: DIAR JOUR (Partial List...#548) for list of specific works. SUNY SB does not have a copy, but has a manuscript by George Yeats keyed to it--see next item.
> Yeats, Senator Michael
>
> AMs by George Yeats, "M.S.S. of 1893," keyed to small white notebook begun 29 August 1893 (Partial list... #496).
> Yeats, Senator Michael
> Copy at SUNY SB   Box 5
>
> TMs; five folders labelled "Typescripts of 20 poems," most with autograph corrections; multiple copies of some. Folders include the following poems: BLES, CAP BELL, POET TO HI, TO HEAR BI, HE GIVE HI, HE HEAR CR, HE MOUR CH, HE REME FO, HE TELL PE, HE TELL VA, HE THIN HI, HE THIN TH, HE WISH HI, HOST SIDH, LOVE ASKS FO, LOVE MOUR LO, LOVE PLEA HI, LOVE TELL RO, SONG WAND AE, VALL BLAC PI.
> New York Public Library

Vellum copy inscribed to GREG LADY with drafts of
the unpublished THOU LOUD YE, dated April 14, 1899
and HAPP TOWN UNDER title of "Rider to the North,"
dated March 25, 1903 on endpapers; AMs revison of
HE HEAR CR (PR5904 W6 1899a).
    Emory University

Copy inscribed (to no one) with the line from TOM O'RO:
"An aimless joy is a pure joy," dated Sept. 1907.
    Indiana University

Copy inscribed to QUIN JOHN, dated March 1904, with a
short passage from TO ROSE RO.
    Wake Forest University Library

Copy inscribed to YEAT JOHN: "J B Yeats from W B Yeats"
(item 2445).
    Yeats, Anne

Copy inscribed (to no one) with HAPP TOWN under title
of "Rider to the North," dated March 25, 1903.
    Emory University

Copy inscribed to "Arthur Symons from W B Yeats, April
24, 1899" (SYMO ARTH).
    Smith, Simon Nowell

Copy belonging to QUIN JOHN inscribed with a note about
SONG WAND AE, dated March, 1904.
    New York Public Library

Portrait of WBY intended for this book, inscribed to
GYLE ALTH. See Miscellany: PHOT.
    New York Public Library

AMs of second page of a list of Contents, with 23
titles (Ms 30344).
    National Library of Ireland
    Copy at SUNY SB   Box 6

Copy inscribed to MOOR GEOR, dated 14 April 1889, with
the line from HE HEAR CR, "Your head will not lie on
the breast" changed to "Your breast will not lie by the
breast."
    Pierpont Morgan Library

Copy inscribed to HEAL JAME, dated [1938], with
comments: "The cover for this book was designed by an
Irish artist" whom the neighbors considered "stuck up."
    Stanford University

Copy inscribed "To Maud Gonne from W B Yeats, April 24
1899" (MACB MAUD GO); copy of fourth edition (1903)
inscribed (to no one) with two lines from TO ROSE RO
beginning "To find in all poor foolish things."
    University of Texas at Austin

The Wind Among the Reeds   WIND REED 03
  London: Matthews, 1903.
    Copy inscribed to GREG LADY.
      New York Public Library

The Winding Stair (Gaige)   WIND STAI 29
  New York: C. Gaige, 1929.
    Mock-up for this edition, with instructions to printer
    and revisions in a number of poems, including BLOO
    MOON, DIAL SELF SO, IN MEMO EV, and WOMA YOUN OL; had
    been inscribed to "Crosby Gaige from W B Yeats," but
    inscription was inked out.
      University of Texas at Austin

The Winding Stair (Fountain)   WIND STAI 29
  New York: Fountain, [1929]. (Wade 164)
    Copy inscribed to Shotaro Oshima (OSHI SHOT), "for my
    friend," with lines from TOM O'RO: "Wisdom is a
    butterfly   And not a gloomy bird of prey" (item 2447).
      Yeats, Anne

Copy belonging to PROK FRED with line inscribed from
TOM O'RO: "An aimless joy is a pure joy," dated June
15, 1933" (inscription may be bogus).
    University of Texas at Austin

The Winding Stair   WIND STAI 33
  London: Macmillan, 1933. (Wade 169)
    Proofs (Add. MS 55878).
      British Library

Copy inscribed (to no one) with a line from TOM O'RO:
"An aimless joy is a pure joy."
    Yeats Tower

Copy with note about reasons not to send books to authors for autographs: "Thomas Hardy once showed me a corner cupboard full of such books. He gave them to his friends on their birthdays. W B Yeats" (item 2448b).
    Yeats, Anne

AMs of the Table of Contents; also TMs of first two pages, apparently done on Lady Gregory's typewriter with corrections by WBY; AMs, notes; AMs and TMs with drafts and revisions of poems (Ms 30040, 30312, 13590).
    National Library of Ireland
    Copy at SUNY SB   Box 6, 7

Copy "Inscribed for Lilian Davidson" (DAVI LILI), dated Nov 28 1935; another copy inscribed to SHAK OLIV, dated Sept 1933.
    University of Texas at Austin

Winding Stair Material   WIND STAI MA
   Draft versions of many poems (See Miscellany: DIAR JOUR, Rapallo notebooks, Ms 13578, 13580, 13581).
    National Library of Ireland
    Copy at SUNY SB   Box 90

TMsS, with a few corrections of BLOO MOON, DEAT, DIAL SELF SO, IN MEMO EV, WOMA YOUN OL, dated Rapallo March 1928.
    University of Texas at Austin

AMs and TMs of numerous poems from WIND STAI including AT ALGE ME, BLOO MOON, BYZA, COOL PARK 19, COOL PARK BA, CRAZ MOON, DEAT, DIAL SELF SO, FOR ANNE GR, FROM ANTI, GRAT UNKN IN, IN MEMO EV, MOHI CHAT, MOTH GOD, NINE CENT AF, OIL BLOO, QUAR OLD, REMO INTE SP, RESU THOU, SEVE SAGE, SPIL MILK, STAT, STRE SUN GL, SWIF EPIT, SYMB, THRE MOVE, VERO NAPK, VACI (Ms 13590).
    National Library of Ireland
    Copy at SUNY SB   Box 6, 7

Copies of various versions of WIND STAI poems and related material in white vellum notebook. See Miscellany: DIAR JOUR (Partial List...#545).
    Location of original unknown
    Copy at SUNY SB   Box 88

See also Books: UNPU MACM ED.

Books

Words for Music Perhaps and Other Poems   WORD MUSI 32
   Dublin: Cuala, 1932. (Wade 168)
     AMs note (3 pp); AMs and TMs of drafts and revisions of
     poems (Ms 30802, 13591).
        National Library of Ireland
        Copy at SUNY SB

     Copy inscribed to HEAL JAME, dated 1938, with long note
     about the death of Lady Gregory, including an anecdote
     about her deceiving a parson about her impending death:
     "She would not have let him speak of religion that was
     her souls secret."
        Stanford University

     Copy inscribed to "Iseult Stuart from W B Yeats" (GONN
     ISEU).
        University of Texas at Austin

The Words upon the Window Pane   WORD WIND 34
   Dublin: Cuala, 1934. (Wade 174)
     Fragment of Introduction; a few pages of SPEC BIRD
     included (Ms 842). See Books: UNPU SPEC BI.
        University of Reading Library

     Revised galley proofs for a commentary written for the
     DUBLIN MAGAZINE (1930; Ms 15598).
        National Library of Ireland
        Copy at SUNY SB

     AMs and TMs; corrected pages, page proofs, and drafts
     of the introductory essay (Ms 30211, 30324, 30325).
        National Library of Ireland
        Copy at SUNY SB Box 16

     Copy inscribed to HEAL JAME: "I wrote this play as a
     help to bring back a part of the Irish mind which we
     have been thrusting out as if it were foreign. Now
     that our period of violent protest is over we claim
     the Anglo-Irish eighteenth century as our own."
        Stanford University

The Works of William Blake 3 vols   WORK WILL 93
   London: Quaritch, 1893. (Wade 218)
     Copy inscribed to GREG LADY, with notes about his
     editing of Blake.
        New York Public Library

Notes and fragments of proofs, with corrections (MS 30289); AMs drafts (Ms 30534).
   National Library of Ireland
   Copy at SUNY SB Box 40

Copy inscribed with long note to P.I.A.L. (MACB MAUD GO), with comments on the publisher Quaritch who said he would pay nothing but free copies, and on WBY's co-editor Ellis: "a wild man & I a most ignorant boy," and a claim that they persuaded people "that Blake knew what he was talking about if we did not."
   University of Kansas

Drafts, various papers, and letters relating to the editorial work of Ellis and WBY; also a photocopy of a copy of "The Marriage of Heaven and Hell" with annotations by WBY (MS293/2/2, MS293/2/3/1 and MS1154).
   University of Reading Library

Long note in vol. 1 (quoted in Wade 218) about the making of this edition, dated May 3, 1900 (item 220).
   Yeats, Anne

Annotations and marginalia in numerous works by Blake, Swedenborg, and others, in the holdings of Anne Yeats. See Bibliography: O'Shea, CATALOG.

Inscriptions

This section includes items WBY inscribed, usually to his friends and relatives. It does not include items with only a signature. The descriptions, arranged here by the names of the persons to whom inscribed, duplicate information also found in other sections. Thus, THE LAND OF HEART'S DESIRE (1903) inscribed to Florence Earle Coates with lines from "The Withering of the Boughs" is described here under COAT FLOR EA, but noted also in the Books section under LAND HEAR 03, and in the Poems section under WITH BOUG.

Ahern, Katharine   AHER KATH
    Copy of PLAY CONT 24 inscribed with line from PARD
    OLD FA: "only the wasteful virtues earn the sun."
    Note by Ahern says she asked WBY for an inscription
    after a lecture in Hartford.
        University of Louisville

Allen, Charles Dexter   ALLE CHAR DE
    Copy of HINK MIDD 16 with inscription on bookplate:
    "The earlier & later poems in this book mark a change
    that is coming to Ireland--a change from collective to
    individual intellect--from Thomas Davis to 'A.E.'"
        Harper, George

Baker, Gladys   BAKE GLAD
    Copy of AUTO 27 "inscribed for Gladys Baker."
        University of Delaware Library

Bates, Katherine   BATE KATH
    Copy of WILD SWAN 19 inscribed "To Miss Katherine
    Bates from W B Yeats, May 26 1920 in memory of some
    pleasant days."
        Wellesley College

Beecham, Thomas   BEEC THOM
    Inscribed copy of SELE LOVE 13, given "in gratitude
    for a gift to the Irish Players."
        University of Texas at Austin

Bender, Albert   BEND ALBE
    Inscribed copy of LATE POEM 26, dated March 10, 1911.
        Mills College Library

Beresford, J. Cooke (Tommy the Song)   BERE J.C.
    Copy of WHER THER 03 inscribed to "Tommy the Song."
        New York Public Library

Blunden, Edmund and Helen   BLUN EDMU HE
    Inscribed copy of DRAM PERS 36, dated June 6, 1936.
        University of Texas at Austin

Boggs, Tom   BOGG TOM
    Inscribed copy of AUTO REVE 27, dated Jan. 19, 1933.
        University of Texas at Austin

Boyd, Ernest   BOYD ERNE
    Inscribed copy of WILD SWAN 17.
        New York Public Library

    Inscribed copy of EAST 16, dated June 22, 1917 (Ip Y34
    916g).
        Yale University

Browne, Maurice   BROW MAUR
    Inscribed copy of COUN CATH 12, dated July 1912.
        Princeton University Library

Bullen, A.H.   BULL A.H.
    Inscribed copy of CELT TWIL 12.
        New York Public Library

Carmichael, Miss   CARM MISS
    Copy of GREG IDEA 01 inscribed to "Miss Carmichael
    from W B Yeats March 1902."
        University of California Los Angeles

Coates, Florence Earle   COAT FLOR EA
    Copy of POEM 99 inscribed with five lines from WITH
    BOUG, beginning "The boughs have withered," with
    mistakes and corrections.
        Wake Forest University Library

    Copy of LAND HEAR 03 inscribed with two lines: "No
    boughs have withered because of the wintry
    wind," dated Dec. 1903 (from WITH BOUG).
        Indiana University

Inscriptions   75

Cockerell, Sydney   COCK SYDN
    Inscribed copy of CELT TWIL 02, dated 1902.
    University of Texas at Austin

Collinson, Margaret   COLL MARG
    Inscribed copy of GOLD HELM 08, with a note about GREE
    HELM, signed "W.B. Yeats, Thoor Ballylee 1922."
    Dublin City Libraries

Colum, Padraic   COLU PADR
    Copy of SELE POET 13 inscribed to "Mr Colum from his
    friend the writer April 26 1912," with a few
    corrections (in Rare Books and Ms).
    New York Public Library

Davidson, Lilian   DAVI LILI
    Copy of WIND STAI 33 "Inscribed to Lilian Davidson,"
    dated Nov 28, 1935.
    University of Texas at Austin

Dickinson, Mabel   DICK MABE
    Inscribed copy of LAND HEAR 12, "from her friend W.B.
    Yeats, June 22, 1912."
    Indiana University

Dodd, Loring Holmes   DODD LORI HO
    Inscribed photograph (PHOT) thanking the Dodds for
    their hospitality.
    Clark University

Drinkwater, John   DRIN JOHN
    Inscribed copies of POEM WRIT 13 and SELE POET 13
    (with "Countess Cathleen" and its notes).
    University of Texas at Austin

Ducat, Eva   DUCA EVA
    Inscribed copy of WILD SWAN 17, dated "February 1918
    at Oxford."
    Smith, Simon Nowell

Duggan, Elizabeth   DUGG ELIZ
    Inscribed copy of SELE LOVE 13, dated December 1913.
    University of Texas at Austin

Dulac, Edmund   DULA EDMU
    Inscribed copy of UNIC STAR 08.
        Pierpont Morgan Library

    Inscribed copy of STOR MICH 31, dated Feb. 19, 1932.
        University of Texas at Austin

    Inscribed copy of NEW POEM 38, dated May 24, 1938.
        Wesleyan University

    Inscribed copy of PLAY PROS 22, dated Dec. 22, 1922.
        University of Texas at Austin

    Inscribed copy of VISI 25.
        Pierpont Morgan Library

Dulac, Helen   DULA HELE
    Inscribed copy of ESSA W.B. 37.
        University of Texas at Austin

Eaton, Nolan   EATO NOLA
    Copy of AUTO REVE 26 inscribed "with love from W B
    Yeats Xmas 1932."
        University of Victoria

Ellis, Edwin J.   ELLI EDWI J.
    Inscribed copy of COUN CATH 92, dated August 30, 1892
    (Ellis Collection: 97943).
        University of Reading Library

    Inscribed copy of CELT TWIL 93, dated December 1893
    (Ellis Collection: 97934).
        University of Reading Library

    Inscribed copy of POEM 95, dated August 27, 1895
    (Ellis Collection: 97940).
        University of Reading Library

Ellis, Mrs.   ELLI MRS.
    Inscribed copy of WAND OISI 89, dated April 9, 1889
    (Ellis Collection: 97937).
        University of Reading Library

Emery, Florence Farr   EMER FLOR FA
    Copy of POEM 01, with inserted letter to EMER FLOR FA.
        University of Texas at Austin

Copy of STOR RED 04 inscribed to "Mrs. Emery [word crossed out] from her friend W B Yeats," with some astrological symbols.
   Yale University

Fay, William   FAY WILL
   Inscribed copy of POEM 1899 06.
   New York Public Library

   Inscribed copy of IDEA GOOD 03, dated May 1903.
   University of Texas at Austin

Ffrench, Rhona   FFRE RHON
   Copy of PALG CHIL 98 inscribed to "Rhona Ffrench from W.B. New Year 1914."
   University of Kansas

Foden, Gwyneth   FODE GWYN
   Copy of AUTO REVE 26 inscribed "to my friend Gwyneth Foden. This book about my friends W B Yeats May 1935."
   University of Victoria

   Inscribed copy of SELE POEM 29 "from her friend W.B. Yeats, April 17, 1932."
   Indiana University

Garnett, Edward   GARN EDWA
   Inscribed copies of CELT TWIL 93 and POEM 95.
   Princeton University Library

   Inscribed copy of WAND OISI 89, dated 1890.
   Princeton University Library

Gonne, Iseult   GONN ISEU
   Inscribed copy of NINE POEM 18 to "Maurice from W B Y. Dec. 5, 1918."
   Wake Forest University Library

   Copies of OCTO BLAS 27, TOWE 28, VISI 25, and WORD MUSI 32 inscribed to "Iseult Stuart."
   University of Texas at Austin

   See also Inscriptions: STUA FRAN.

Gonne, Maud   GONN MAUD
   See Inscriptions: MacBride, Maude Gonne (MACB MAUD GO).

Gosse, Edmund   GOSS EDMU
   Inscribed copies of HOUR CATH 04, POEM SECO 09, and
   TAGO GITA (may be bogus inscriptions).
      University of Texas at Austin

Gregory, Lady   GREG LADY
   The New York Public Library (Berg Collection) has an
   extensive collection of Lady Gregory material,
   including the following books inscribed to her: AUTO
   REVE 26, BOOK RHYM 92, CATH HOOL 02, CELT TWIL 93,
   COLL WORK 08, COUN CATH 12, CUTT AGAT 12, DEIR 11,
   EARL POEM 25, EAST 16, ESSA 24, FAIR FOLK 88, GOLD
   HELM 08, GREE HELM 12, HOUR GLAS 03, HOUR GLAS 05,
   HOUR GLAS 14 (2 copies), IDEA GOOD 03, IN SEVE 03,
   KING THRE 04, KING BAIL 04, KING THRE 05, LAND HEAR
   94, LATE POEM 22, ON BAIL 05, PLAY CONT 23, PLAY IRIS
   11, PLAY PROS 22, POEM WRIT 13, SHAD WATE 01, SHAD
   WATE 07, STOR RED 13, STOR RED 27, SYNG IREL 11, TREM
   VEIL 22, WHER THER 02, WIND REED 03, WORK WILL 93.
      New York Public Library

   There are many copies of books inscribed to Lady
   Gregory at Emory University, including BELT 00, CELT
   TWIL 93, COUN CATH 99, DEAT SYNG 28, EGLI LITE 04,
   FOUR YEAR 21, HORT BOOK 98, JOHN SHER 91, POEM 95,
   POEM 99, POEM 01, POEM 04, POEM BALL 88, POET WORK
   06, RESP POEM 14, REVE CHIL 15, SELE LOVE 13, SELE
   POEM 29, SEVE POEM 22, TABL LAW 97, WHER THER 02,
   WIND REED 99.
      Emory University

   WBY's copy of Shelley's SELECT WORKS (See Other
   Authors: SHEL SELE 66) inscribed with note to Lady
   Gregory (in Pforzheimer Collection).
      New York Public Library

   Two inscribed copies of LAND HEAR 03, one of the
   Mosher edition, one of the Bibelot edition.
      University of Reading Library

Inscribed copy of CARL STOR 89, dated 1901, with a
lengthy note about the Introduction.
    Sligo County Library

Inscribed copy of RESP OTHE 16, dated October 1916.
    Wertheim, Stanley

Inscribed copy of O'KE CAIT 05, "from her friend."
    University of Kansas

TMs of notes for CAT MOON 24, dedicated to
Lady Gregory (Ms 30273).
    National Library of Ireland
    Copy at SUNY SB Box 1

See Prose: MICH CLAN GR, for an inscribed copy of an
article from a Christmas Annual.

See also Books: BOOK RHYM 92 and SECO BOOK 94.

Gregory, Robert   GREG ROBE
    Inscribed copy of CATH HOOL 02.
        New York Public Library

Griffin, Montagu   GRIF MONT
    Inscribed copy of WAND OISI 89, dated London February
1889.
        University of Kansas

Grigsby, Miss   GRIG MISS
    Copy of YEAT SLIG 30 inscribed to "Miss Grigsby from
W B Yeats, July 21, 1930" (item 2309).
        Yeats, Anne

Harris, Frank   HARR FRAN
    Inscribed copy of AUTO REVE 26, dated Feb. 27, 1927.
        Crawford, William

Hayward, John   HAYW JOHN
    Inscribed copy of WHEE BUTT 34, dated Dec. 20, 1934.
        University of Texas at Austin

Healy, James   HEAL JAME
   Some fifty books inscribed to Healy, apparently by
   way of thanks for his contribution to a rest for WBY
   and his wife in the south of France in 1938; books
   (details in Books section and Other Authors section)
   include ALLI SIXT 05, BOUN SWED 25, CAT MOON 24, DEAT
   SYNG 28, DISC VOLU 07, DOWD WOMA 13, DRAM PERS 35,
   DUNS SELE 12, EGLI SOME 05, ESSA W.B. 37, ESTR 26,
   FENO CERT 16, FLOW LOVE 25, FOUR YEAR 21, GOGA OFFE
   23, GOGA WILD 30, GREE HELM 10, GREG BOOK 26, GREG
   COOL 31, GREG KILT 18, HIGG ARAB 33, HINK TWEN 07,
   HYDE LOVE 04, IN SEVE 03, JOHN TWEN 04, KING GREA 34,
   MASE JOHN 15, MICH ROBA 20, MOOR LYRI 29, NEW POEM
   38, O'CO LORD 38, O'CO WILD 32, OCTO BLAS 27, PACK
   EZRA 29, PARN POEM 27, POEM WRIT 13, POET IREL 08,
   RESP POEM 14, REVE CHIL 15, ROBI LITT 28, ROSS PILG
   33, RUSS BY 06, RUSS SOME 36, SELE LOVE 13, SEVE POEM
   22, SPEE TWO 31, STOR MICH 31, STOR RED 04, SYNG DEIR
   10, SYNG IREL 11, TAGO POST 14, TWO PLAY 19, WILD
   SWAN 17, WIND REED 99, WORD MUSI 32, WORD WIND 34,
   YEAT EARL 23, YEAT FURT 20, YEAT PASS 17.
       Stanford University

   Inscribed copy of JOHN SHER 91; also a copy of KING
   THRE 04 inscribed to Healy "in memory of our friend
   John Quinn."
       Colby College Library

   Inscribed copy of KING THRE 04.
       University of Texas at Austin

Henley, W.E.   HENL W.E.
   Inscribed copy of WAND OISI 92, dated May 1892.
       University of Texas at Austin

   Copy of WAND OISI 89 inscribed to "W E Henley with the
   good wishes of W B Y Jan 19 1889."
       Pierpont Morgan Library

Higgins, Fred   HIGG FRED
   Inscribed copy of TWO SONG RE.
       New York Public Library

Hinkson, Katherine Tynan   HINK KATH TY
   Copy of CARL STOR 89 inscribed "To the author of
   'Shamrocks.'"
       Sligo County Library

Copy of COUN KATH 92 inscribed to Katherine Tynan.
   Colby College Library

Copy of FAIR FOLK 88 inscribed "To my good friend Katherine Tynan," dated July 21st, 1889; with corrections.
   New York Public Library

Holland, Nora   HOLL NORA
   Copy of MOOR MAXI ND inscribed to "Nora Holland from W.B. Yeats."
      University of Kansas

Horniman, Miss Annie   HORN MISS AN
   Copy of BELT 00 inscribed to "Miss Horniman from her friend the editor" (no signature).
      University of Kansas

   Copy of SHAD WATE 00 inscribed to "Miss Horniman from her friend W B Yeats Dec. 19, 1900" (item 2420).
      Yeats, Anne

Horton, William   HORT WILL
   Inscribed copies of POEM 95, REVE CHIL 16, and EIGH POEM 16, latter with the note, "I have had nothing to do with the publication of this pretentious pamphlet."
      Harper, George

Howe, W.T.   HOWE W.T.
   Inscribed copies of AUGU BOOK 27 and AUTO REVE 26. Copy of POEM 95 inscribed "With pleasant memories," dated Dec. 1, 1932.
      New York Public Library

Johnson, Lionel   JOHN LION
   Copy of CELT TWIL 93 inscribed to "Lionel Johnson from his friend W B Yeats Dec 93" (item 2320).
      Yeats, Anne

   Inscribed copy of SECR ROSE 97.
      New York Public Library

   Inscribed copy of POEM BALL 90.
      Newberry Library

Kinder, Margaret Martin KIND MARG MA
   Inscribed copy of COUN CATH 12, dated July 1912
   (PR5904 C6 1912 cop. 2).
      Emory University

King, Richard Ashe KING RICH AS
   Inscribed copy of EARL POEM 25, dated September 29,
   1925.
      University of Texas at Austin

Laird, Helen LAIR HELE
   Copy of CATH HOUL 02 inscribed to "Miss Helen Laird
   from W B Yeats Nov 1902."
      University College Dublin

Lambert, Mrs. Enid LAMB MRS. EN
   Inscription in Mrs. Enid Lambart's autograph album,
   dated 23 June 1910, with three lines of verse, beginning
   "Come now a tale of some old time not worth remembering"
   (variant of line from DEIR; MS. 1-1958).
      Fitzwilliam Museum

Lane, Hugh LANE HUGH
   Inscribed copy of POEM WRIT 13 with two lines from
   PAUD, dated Oct, 1913.
      Wesleyan University

Linley, Laura LINL LAUR
   A copy of her OUT OF THE VORTEX (LINL OUT 16), with
   inscription, beginning "I knew the writer of this
   book," dated Nov 1921.
      University of Texas at Austin

MacBride, Maud Gonne MACB MAUD GO
   Copies of a number of books inscribed to Maud Gonne,
   including CUTT AGAT 19, dated April 1919; EARL POEM 25,
   from "her friend," dated Sept 27, 1925; LAND HEAR 94,
   dated April 20, 1894; SHAD WATE 00, dated Dec. 19 1900;
   and WIND REED 99, dated April 24, 1899.
      University of Texas at Austin

   Copy of JOHN SHER 91 inscribed with eight-line poem,
   beginning "We poets labour all our days," dated
   September 1, 1891 (from TO MAUD GO, related to HE TELL
   PE).
      University of Texas at Austin

Inscriptions

    Inscribed copy of POEM 1899 06, dated 1906.
       Princeton University Library

    Copy of RESP POEM 14, with corrections, inscribed to
    "Maud Gonne from W. B. Yeats, June 1914."
       Sparrow, John

    Copy of WORK WILL 93, with long note to P.I.A.L. and
    comments on the publisher Quaritch, on the co-editor
    Ellis, and on Blake.
       University of Kansas

    Copy of BOOK IRIS 95 inscribed to "Miss Maud Gonne from
    W.B. Yeats March 16th 1896."
       University of Kansas

    Copy of DISC VOL 07 inscribed to "Maud Gonne from her
    friend W.B. Yeats."
       Sparrow, John

MacGreevy, T.   MACG T.
    Inscribed copy of PLAY PROS 24, dated 24 April 1924.
       University of Kansas

Mannin, Ethel   MANN ETHE
    Inscribed copy of VISI 37, dated Oct. 1937, with note
    saying he is "not so discourteous" that he expects
    her to read this "difficult book."
       University of Texas at Austin

Mark, T.   MARK T.
    Inscribed copy of VISI 37 with note of thanks for
    his "laborious correction" of the text.
       University of Texas at Austin

Markiewicz, Constance   MARK CONS
    Copy of LAND HEAR 94 inscribed to "Miss Constance
    Gore Booth with the authors compliments July 18th
    1894."
       University of British Columbia

Marriott, Raymond   MARR RAYM
    Inscribed copy of TABL LAW 04, dated Nov. 6, 1904.
       University of Texas at Austin

Masefield, John   MASE JOHN
   Inscribed copy of GREE HELM 12 with the comment "This
   cover was a great effort on the part of the publisher.
   He describes it as the kind of cover I prefer!
   W B Y," dated Dec 1912.
      Smith, Simon Nowell

   Inscribed copy of SHAD WATE 00: "A piece of poet's bay
   given to me by Lady Gregory--Feb. 10 1903."
      Princeton University Library

Mathers, Mr. and Mrs.   MATH MRMS
   Inscribed copy of JOHN SHER 91.
      Colby College Library

Mattheson, Hilda   MATT HILD
   Inscribed copy of OXFO BOOK 36, dated November 1935.
      University of Texas at Austin

Meiklejohn, Mrs.   MEIK MRS.
   Inscribed copy of HOUR GLAS 14, dated March 1914.
      Princeton University Library

Meynell, Alice   MEYN ALIC
   Inscribed copy of CELT TWIL 05, dated 15 Jan 1905,
   commenting on the uncertainty of WBY's plans and
   further contact.
      Boston College

Moore, George   MOOR GEOR
   Inscribed copy of WIND REED 99.
      Pierpont Morgan Library

Moore, Sturge   MOOR STUR
   Copy of GREE HELM 12, dated Dec. 1912, with a note
   that the cover is the work of the American publisher
   and "He says it is he believes the kind of cover I
   like."
      University of London Library

   Copy of POEM 22 with a line from TOM O'RO: "'An
   aimless joy is a pure joy' W B Yeats" (item 2402a).
      Yeats, Anne

   Copy of COLL POEM 33 inscribed "To Sturge Moore from
   W.B. Yeats November 1933."
      University of London Library

Copy of COUN CATH 12 inscribed "to Sturge Moore from
W.B. Yeats, 1912 June 5."
University of London Library

Morrell, Lady Ottoline   MORR LADY OT
Inscribed copy of NINE POEM 18, dated July 15, 1933,
with note about WBY's lecture tour in New York just
before the war.
University of Texas at Austin

Inscribed copy of FOUR PLAY 21.
University of Texas at Austin

Copy of FOUR YEAR 21 inscribed to "Lady Ottoline
Morrell from W B Y Xmas 1921."
Pierpont Morgan Library

Inscribed copy of NINE POEM 14, dated March 15, 1922.
Kenyon College Library

Inscribed copy of HOUR GLAS 14, dated October 14, 1914.
Kenyon College Library

Copy of POEM WRIT 13 inscribed to "Lady Ottoline
Morrell from W.B. Yeats, Dec 20 1921."
University of Kansas

Inscribed copy of POEM WRIT 13, dated Oct. 14, 1914.
University of Texas at Austin

Moynan, Thomas King   MOYN THOM KI
Inscribed copy of LAKE ISLE 24, dated May 15, 1924.
University of Texas at Austin

Nettleship, Mrs. J.T.   NETT MRS. J.
Inscribed copy of WAND OISI 89, dated 17 Jan 1889.
University of Texas at Austin

Nic Shiubhlaigh, Maire   NIC SHIU MA
See Inscriptions: Walker, Mary (WALK, MARY).

O'Connor, Frank   O'CO FRAN
Proof sheets for HERN EGG 38, dated 1937, with
corrections and revisions; "for Frank O'Connor" on
cover sheet.
Harvard University

O'Leary, Ellen   O'LE ELLE
    Inscribed copy of FAIR FOLK 88.
    University of Texas at Austin

O'Leary, John   O'LE JOHN
    Inscribed copy of MOSA 86.
    New York Public Library

    Inscribed copy of CELT TWIL 93 "from W B Yeats
    February 1894."
    University of Victoria

Oshima, Shotaro   OSHI SHOT
    Copy of WIND STAI 29 inscribed: "for my friend
    Shotaro Oshima W B Yeats 'Wisdom is a butterfly and
    not a gloomy bird of prey'" (from TOM O'RO; item
    2447).
        Yeats, Anne

Payen-Payne, James B. de Vincheles   PAYE JAME B.
    Inscribed copy of SECO BOOK 94, with fair copy of OIL
    BLOO, probably inscribed in 1928.
    University of Toronto

Peabody, Josephine Preston   PEAB JOSE PR
    Inscribed copy of HOUR GLAS 04.
    Harvard University

Phelan, James   PHEL JAME
    Photograph of WBY inscribed to Phelan, dated March
    1904 (Robinson Jeffers Collection).
    Occidental College Library

Pollexfen, George   POLL GEOR
    Inscribed copy of WHER THER 03 (Wade 45), dated June
    20, 1903; and of CELT TWIL 02, dated July 1902.
    University of Texas at Austin

    Inscribed copy of SECR ROSE 97, with corrections.
    Princeton University Library

Pollexfen, Henrietta   POLL HENR
    Copy of FAIR FOLK 88 inscribed to "Henrietta," dated
    May 16, 1889.
        University of Texas at Austin

    Copy of MOSA 86 inscribed to "H.A. Pollexfen"
    University of California Los Angeles

Price, Franklin   PRIC FRAN
   Copy of EARL POEM 25 inscribed to "Franklin Price
   from W B Yeats Nov 12, 1925" (item 2344).
      Yeats, Anne

Prokosch, Frederic   PROK FRED
   Copy of SING HEAD 34 "Inscribed for Frederic Prokosch
   by W.B. Yeats Nov. 25 1935."
      Indiana University

   Inscribed copy of SING HEAD 34, dated Nov 25, 1935.
      Wesleyan University

   Inscribed copies of two Cuala hand-colored prints, no.
   50 (lines from WILD SWAN CO), and no. 88 (LOVE TELL
   RO).
      Wesleyan University

   Inscribed copies of POEM 95 and WIND STAI 29 (may be
   bogus inscriptions).
      University of Texas at Austin

   Inscribed copy of KING BAIL 04 (Wade 56), and of SING
   HEAD 34, dated Nov. 1935.
      University of Texas at Austin

Quinn, John   QUIN JOHN
   Inscribed copy of KING THRE 04, dated Nov 11, 1904,
   with fair copies of NEVE GIVE AL and chorus from
   DEIR.
      New York Public Library

   Inscribed copy of HOUR GLAS 01, dated March 1914,
   noting that it is the first copy of his plays.
      New York Public Library

   Inscribed copy of HOUR GLAS 04 (Bullen edition) with
   one alteration in text (p. 77).
      New York Public Library

   Inscribed copy of SAMH 05 "from W B Yeats," dated
   Nov. 1905.
      University of Victoria

   Inscribed copy of BOOK IRIS 95: "John Quinn's book
   W B Yeats, 1904."
      University of Victoria

Copy of PER AMIC 18 inscribed "To my friend John
Quinn for much kindness & good conversation," dated
May 26, 1920; copy of POEM 01 inscribed as "Quinn's
book," dated November twelveth 1904; copy of REPR
IRIS 91 with note quoted by Wade; inscribed copy of
HOUR GLAS 14, dated April 1914.
    University of Texas at Austin

Inscribed copy of BROO TREA 00: "I had this book with
me to read out of when lecturing."
    Wake Forest University Library

Inscribed copy of IN SEVE 03, dated March 1904: "This
is the first book of mine that it is a pleasure to
look at--a pleasure whether open or shut."
    Stanford University

Inscribed copy of COUN KATH 92, dated March 1904, with
autograph note referring to Browning, and to the
creation of evil as a "sublime conception."
    New York Public Library

Inscribed copy of WIND REED 99, with a short passage
from TO ROSE RO, dated March 1904.
    Wake Forest University Library

Inscribed copy of IRIS FAIR 95, with note describing
it as a "good...but...pretty recklessly & ill written"
book.
    Wake Forest University Library

Inscribed copy of CELT TWIL 94 with note by W B Y
describing it as his first book with "a style," saying
it was written for W.E. Henley.
    Wake Forest University Library

Radford, E.   RADF E
    Copy of WAND OISI 89 inscribed "from the writer,"
dated March 189[6?].
        Princeton University Library

Rees, J. Rogers   REES J.   RO
    Copy of LAND HEAR 94 belonging to Rees, inscribed with a
note about the book.
        Indiana University

Inscriptions

Reid, Forrest   REID FORR
    Inscribed copy of SELE POET 13, with corrections.
        Princeton University Library

Robinson, Lennox   ROBI LENN
    Copy of CAT MOON 24 with two lines from POET OWN HA
    inscribed on Robinson's bookplate, beginning "Call
    down a blessing on the blossom of the May."
        Stanford University

    Inscribed copies of SWAM INDI 32 and PLAY PROS 22,
    latter dated 6 Dec. 1922.
        Princeton University Library

    Inscribed copies of EARL POEM 25, ESSA 24, and OXFO
    BOOK 36.
        University of Texas at Austin

    Inscribed copy of PLAY CONT 23, "from his friend,"
    dated Feb 27 1924.
        University of Delaware Library

    Inscribed copy of LAND HEAR 25, "from his friend the
    writer. W.B. Yeats."
        Indiana University

    Inscribed copy of LATE POEM 22, dated Dec. 6, 1922.
        University of Texas at Austin

Rose, Edward   ROSE EDWA
    Inscribed copy of POEM 95 "from the author."
        Smith, Simon Nowell

Rothenstein, William   ROTH WILL
    Inscribed copy of REVE CHIL 15, dated 1916.
        University of Texas at Austin

Russell, Father   RUSS FATH
    Copy of JOHN SHER 91 inscribed to "Father Russell from
    his friend the author," with WBY's signature beneath
    the pseudonym "Gonconagh" (Ip.Y34.891b).
        Yale University

Russell, George   RUSS GEOR
    Inscribed copies of CELT TWIL 02, dated July 8, 1902;
    POEM 95, dated August 26, 1895; STOR MICH 31, dated
    Feb 5 1932; and WHER THER 03 (Wade 45), dated May 1903.
        University of Texas at Austin

Inscribed copy of KING BAIL 04 (Wade 56), dated March 1904; originally inscribed to YEAT JOHN.
University of Texas at Austin

Inscribed copy (author's presentation copy 1) of CELT TWIL 93, dated Dec. 1893.
University of Texas at Austin

Sandymount Castle School Library   SAND CAST SC
Copy of BOOK IRIS 00 inscribed "To Sandymount Castle School library from W. B. Yeats, July 1901."
Indiana University

Sato, Junzo   SATO JUNZ
Copy of TOWE 28 inscribed "To Sato from his friend W B Yeats" (item 2430c).
Yeats, Anne

Copy of WHEE BUTT 34 inscribed "To Junzo Sato with apologies for dedicating to him 'Resurrection' without remembering to ask his leave W B Yeats" (item 2437).
Yeats, Anne

Shakespear, Olivia   SHAK OLIV
Inscribed copy of TABL LAW 97, dated June 16, 1897 (Ip.Y34.897T).
Yale University

Inscribed copy of TOWE 28, with note in another hand saying Lennox Robinson was told by Mrs. Yeats that Olivia was WBY's first mistress.
Princeton University Library

Inscribed copies of numerous books, including the following: AUTO REVE 26, BOOK IRIS 95, BOUN SWED 25, CUTT AGAT 12, DRAM PERS 26, EARL POEM 25, ESTR 26, FOUR PLAY 21, FOUR YEAR 21, HERN EGG 38, HOUR CATH 04, IDEA GOOD 03, LATE POEM 22, MICH ROBA 20, PLAY CONT 23, PLAY IRIS 11, PLAY PROS 22, POEM 01, POEM 95, RESP POEM 14, SECR ROSE 97, STOR RED 04, TWO PLAY 19, VISI 37, WILD SWAN 17, WILD SWAN 19, and WIND STAI 33.
University of Texas at Austin

Sharp, William   SHAR WILL
Inscribed copy of Macmillan edition of IN SEVE 03.
New York Public Library

Inscriptions   91

    Inscribed copy of TABL LAW 97, dated July 2nd, 1897.
       University of Texas at Austin

    Inscribed copy of Dun Emer edition of IN SEVE 03.
       New York Public Library

Shaw, George Bernard   SHAW GEOR BE
    Inscribed copy of WHER THER 03, with corrections.
       Princeton University Library

Smith, J.   SMIT J.
    Inscribed copy of POEM 99.
       Boston College

Smith, Pamela   SMIT PAME
    Inscribed copy of BOOK IRIS 95 with the bookplate of
    SMIT PAME and the lines: "Though leagues asunder our
    opinions tend   We are one in heart as Ireland's
    friend," (THOU LEAG AS), dated 26 Oct. 1901.
       Emory University

Spare, A.   SPAR A.
    Inscribed copy of EIGH POEM 16.
       New York Public Library

Squire, J.   SQUI J.
    Copy of COLL POEM 33 with an inscription:
    "To this book only begetter J. Squire from W B Y
    Dec 1933" (may be bogus).
       University of Texas at Austin

Stephens, James   STEP JAME
    Copy of TEN PRIN 37 inscribed to "James Stephens from
    W B Yeats April 19 1937."
       Finneran, Richard

Stoker, Bram   STOK BRAM
    Copy of COUN KATH 92 inscribed "with the compliments
    and best regards of W B Yeats, Sept 1892."
       New York Public Library

Stuart, Francis and Iseult   STUA FRAN IS
    Copy of EARL POEM 25 inscribed to "Francis and Iseult
    Stuart," dated Oct. 7, 1925; copy of ESSA 24 inscribed
    to "Iseult and Francis Stuart," dated 1924.
       University of Texas at Austin

    See also Inscriptions: Gonne, Iseult (GONN ISEU).

Swete, Lyall [?]   SWET LYAL
    Inscribed copy of WHER THER 03, in memory of 'Paul.'
        University of Texas at Austin

Symons, Arthur   SYMO ARTH
    Inscribed copy of SECR ROSE 97.
        University of Texas at Austin

    Inscribed copy of SHAD WATE 00, dated Dec. 1900.
        University of Texas at Austin

    Copy of WIND REED 99 inscribed to "Arthur Symons from
    W B Yeats, April 24, 1899."
        Smith, Simon Nowell

Tage, Philip   TAGE PHIL
    Inscribed copy of GREG CASE 26 "from W.B. Yeats, Oct.
    11, 1926."
        Indiana University

Todhunter, John   TODH JOHN
    Inscribed copy of COUN KATH 92.
        University of Texas at Austin

Trantis, Edith B.   TRAN EDIT B.
    Copy of POEM 95 "Inscribed to Edith B. [Trantis] by W B
    Yeats, Nov 22 1932."
        University of Virginia

Tucker, Mrs.   TUCK MRS.
    Inscribed copy of REVE CHIL 15 "from W B Yeats
    February, 1916" (PR5906 .A557 1915 cop. 2).
        Emory University

    Copy of TREM VEIL 22 inscribed to "Mrs. Tucker From
    W B Yeats, Oct. 21 1922" (item 2432).
        Yeats, Anne

Turner, W.J.   TURN W.J.
    Inscribed copy of COLL POEM 33, "from W.B. Yeats,
    June 6, 1935."
        Indiana University

Inscriptions

Unknown Recipient   UNKN RECI
WBY has inscribed many books with lines of poetry or
brief notes, but has not addressed the inscription to
anyone in particular. These include the following
(details on inscriptions given under the titles in
the Books section and Other Authors section): ALLI
SIXT 05, BLUN SONN 75, BOOK RHYM 92, CELT TWIL 12,
CELT TWIL 93, COLL WORK 08, COUN CATH 29, COUN KATH
92, CUTT AGAT 19, DEIR 07, DISC VOLU 07, DRAM PERS
36, EGLI LITE 04, EIGH POEM 16, ESSA W.B. 37, FOUR
PLAY 21, GOLD HELM 08, GREG CUCH 02, GREG GODS 04,
GREG POET 03, HORT BOOK 02, HOUR GLAS 03, HOUR GLAS
04, HOUR GLAS 14 (private), HOUR GLAS 14 (Cuala),
IDEA GOOD 04, IN SEVE 03, IN SEVE 03, IRIS FAIR 92,
JOHN SHER 91, KING GREA 34, KING THRE 04, LAND HEAR
12, LAND HEAR 94, MOSA 86, NEW POEM 38, NINE POEM 14,
PER AMIC 18, PLAY CONT 24, PLAY IRIS 11, PLAY PROS
22, POEM 01, POEM 12, POEM 13, POEM 22, POEM 95, POEM
99, POEM 1899 06, POEM WILL 93, POEM WRIT 13, POET
IREL 08, POET WORK 06, POET WORK 12, RESP OTHE 16,
RESP POEM 14, REVE CHIL 15, REVE CHIL 16, REVE CHIL
16, SECO BOOK 94, SECR ROSE 97, SELE POEM 21, SING
HEAD 34, SOME ESSA 05, STOR RED 04, SYNG IREL 11,
TABL LAW 97, TOWE 28, TREM VEIL 22, TWO PLAY 19, UNIC
STAR 08, WAND OISI 89, WHEE BUTT 34, WHER THER 02,
WHER THER 03, WILD SWAN 19, WIND REED 99, WIND STAI
33, WORK WILL 93.

Two copies of an article on WBY by Patrick MacDonagh;
WBY has signed and dated (June) his photo (PHOT) that
appears on the cover of the periodical SCHOLASTIC (Vol.
37, 1904).
     University of Notre Dame

Letter inscribed (to no one) in front of HOUR GLAS 04,
dated August 31, 1920.
     University of Reading Library

Photograph (PHOT) inscribed with the line: "We perish
into God and sink away into reality" (from ONLY JEAL
EM; MS Vault File).
     Yale University

Van Krop, Hildo   VANK HILD
    Copy of WHEE BUTT 34 inscribed "To Hildo van Krop
    with apologies for dedicating to him 'Fighting the
    Waves' without remembering to ask his leave W B
    Yeats" (item 2437a).
        Yeats, Anne

Veasey, Miss   VEAS MISS
    Inscribed copy of MOSA 86: "With good wishes for the
    New Year from her friend The Author."
        State University of New York at Buffalo

Viele-Griffin, Francis   VIEL FRAN
    Inscribed copy of COUN CATH 12, dated June 19, 1912.
        University of Texas at Austin

Vynne, Nora   VYNN NORA
    Copy of CELT TWIL 93 inscribed to "Miss Nora Vynne
    from her friend William Butler Yeats Dec. 19, 1893."
        University of Louisville

Wade, Allan   WADE ALLA
    Copy of CUTT AGAT 12 inscribed to "Allan Wade from
    his friend W B Yeats Dec 4 1912."
        Indiana University

    Copy of WHER THER 02 inscribed to "Allan Wade from
    W.B. Yeats Jan 24 1909"; copy of KING THRE 04 to
    "Allan Wade from W.B. Yeats Jan. 24th 1909"; copy of
    GREE HELM 12 "from his friend W.B. Yeats, Dec. 1912.
    The cover of the book is the unaided work of the
    American publisher. He says he believes it the kind
    of work I like."
        Indiana University

Walker, Mary (Maire Nic Shiubhlaigh)   WALK MARY
    Inscribed copy of SHAD WATE 00.
        Northwestern University Library

Walsh, James P.   WALS JAME P.
    Inscribed copy of SPEE TWO 31.
        Kenyon College Library

Wellesley, Dorothy   WELL DORO
    Copy of NEW POEM 38 "Inscribed for my dear friend
    Dorothy Wellesley, W B Yeats July 1938," with some
    pencilled corrections in MODE LAUR.
        Smith, Simon Nowell

Inscriptions

Wells, Caroline   WELL CARO
    Inscribed copy of TABL LAW 14, dated Jan 27, 1920.
        University of Texas at Austin

Williams, A.M.   WILL A.M.
    Copy of WAND OISI 89 inscribed "with the author's
    complts," with a few corrections in text.
        Providence Public Library

Wolley, Miss   WOLL MISS
    Copy of KING BAIL 04 inscribed to "Miss Wolley from
    W. B. Yeats, March 1904."
        Washington State University

Yeats, Anne   YEAT ANNE
    Copy of GREG THRE 23 inscribed to "Anne Yeats from
    her father W B Yeats. My dear Anne, I give you three
    'Wonder Plays' by my greatest friend. You will be
    able to act some scenes out of them. W B Yeats"
    (item 810).
        Yeats, Anne

Yeats, Elizabeth   YEAT ELIZ
    Copy of LATE POEM 22 inscribed "To Loll, from Willie.
    Xmas 1922."
        University of Louisville

    Copy of COLL POEM 33 inscribed to "E.C.Y. from W.B.Y.,
    affectionately. 1933" (Yeats 211).
        Trinity College Dublin

    Copy of REPR IRIS 91 inscribed to "Lolly C. Yeats from
    her brother Willie October 1891" (Yeats 213, 214).
        Trinity College Dublin

    Copy of CUTT AGAT 19 inscribed to "Lolly Yeats from
    W B Yeats April 1919" (Yeats 191).
        Trinity College Dublin

    Copy of WHIT POET 86 inscribed to "Lolly from Willy
    Xmas 1886."
        University of Kansas

    Copy of ARNO POEM 00 inscribed to "Lolly Yeats from
    W.B. Yeats. Xmas 1900."
        University of Kansas

Yeats, George   YEAT GEOR
   Copy of VISI 25 inscribed "To Dobbs in memory of all
   tribulation when we were making this work W.B. Yeats"
   (item 2433a).
        Yeats, Anne

   Copy of COLL POEM 33 inscribed to "George Yeats From
   W.B.Y. November 1933" (item 2323).
        Yeats, Anne

   Copy of LATE POEM 22 inscribed with the note: "Not to
   be given away. Dates written in by George. W B Y"
   (item 2382b).
        Yeats, Anne

   Copy of PLAY IRIS 11 with note on 2nd flyleaf:
   "George's copy. I am not to take it whatever the
   need W B Y" (item 2397).
        Yeats, Anne

   Two copies of PLAY PROS 22 with notes: "George Yeats
   (not to be taken by me. W B Y)" and "George Yeats
   her book not to be taken by me. W B Yeats" (items
   2398, 2398a).
        Yeats, Anne

   Copy of SELE POEM 21 with note: "Not to be lent or
   given as it contains corrections W.B. Yeats 4 Broad
   St. Oxford." (item 2417).
        Yeats, Anne

   Copy of TOWE 28 with the note: "George Yeats' copy
   not to be given away or taken to cut up or for any
   other purpose by me WBY" (item 2430e).
        Yeats, Anne

   Copy of VISI 37 with the note: "George Yeats' own
   copy not to be taken by me W B Yeats, December, 1937"
   (item 2434).
        Yeats, Anne

   Copies of many additional books from WBY's library
   in possession of Anne Yeats have other comments
   to or about George Yeats, and annotations by her.
   See Bibliography: O'Shea, CATALOG.

Inscriptions

Yeats, Jack   YEAT JACK
    Inscribed copy of DEIR 07.
    New York Public Library

Yeats, John Butler   YEAT JOHN BU
    Copy of LITE IDEA 90 inscribed to "J B Yeats from
    W B Yeats July 18, 1899" (Yeats 30. no.1).
        Trinity College Dublin

    Copy of KING BAIL 04 inscribed to "J B Yeats from
    W B Yeats. March 1904" (Yeats 196).
        Trinity College Dublin

    Inscribed copy of KING BAIL 04 (Wade 56); same copy
    later inscribed to RUSS GEOR (dated March 1904).
        University of Texas at Austin

    Copy of IDEA GOOD 03 inscribed "To my father
    W B Yeats May 12, 1903" (Yeats 195).
        Trinity College Dublin

    Copy of WIND REED 99 inscribed to "J B Yeats from
    W B Yeats" (item 2445).
        Yeats, Anne

    Copy of POEM 1899 06 inscribed "To my father.
    W B Yeats" (item 2400).
        Yeats, Anne

Yeats, Lily   YEAT LILY
    Copy of JOHN SHER 91 inscribed to "Lily Yeats Sep
    1891 Bedford Park London   W" (186.q.77 no. 13).
        Trinity College Dublin

    Copy of TABL LAW 97 inscribed to "Lily Yeats from
    W B Yeats Dec 29th 97" (item 2428).
        Yeats, Anne

    Copy of HINK MIRA 95 inscribed to "Lily Yeats from
    W.B. Yeats. Xmas'95. Hyeres."
        University of Kansas

    Copy of WAND OISI 89 inscribed to "Lilly Yeats from
    her brother the author March 1889."
        University of Texas at Austin

Yeats, Michael   YEAT MICH
    Copy of VERN NOVE 29 with a long inscription noting
    that "These stories pleased me very much when I was
    your age" (Press L.7.28).
        Trinity College Dublin

    Copy of COLL POEM 33, with corrections, inscribed to
    "Michael Yeats from W.B. Yeats November 1933."
        Yeats, Senator Michael

Young, Ella   YOUN ELLA
    Copy of POET IREL 08 inscribed to "Ella Young from
    W B Yeats Xmas 1908."
        The Huntington Library

Young, James Carleton   YOUN JAME CA
    Inscribed copy of DISC VOLU 07 with a note about the
    origin of the book, dated Dec. 16, 1907 (Ip. y34 907d).
        Yale University

    Copy of LAND HEAR 04 inscribed with note saying that
    WBY likes this American edition better than the English
    one (Ip.Y34.894b).
        Yale University

    Copy of CELT TWIL 93 with a note about summer visits to
    Sligo and Galway, and saying that WBY considers this
    "among the best" of his books (Ip.Y34.893C).
        Yale University

Letters

This section includes letters, notes, cards, telegrams, invitations, and signed form letters.

A.E.   A.E.
　　See Russell, George (RUSS GEOR).

Abbey Theatre Board   ABBE THEA BO
　　One TMs draft, two AMs drafts (Ms 30229).
　　　　National Library of Ireland
　　　　Copy at SUNY SB

Aberdein, Jeanie Watson   ABER JEAN WA
　　One ALS (1919; Ms 2618).
　　　　University of Aberdeen

Academy Editor   ACAD EDIT
　　One ALS (16 Mar [1892]).
　　　　University of Texas at Austin

　　One ANS (28 Nov, 1902).
　　　　Brown University

Aldington, Brigit (Patmore)   ALDI BRIG
　　One ALS (4 Nov, [1935]), addressed to "Dear Mrs. Aldington."
　　　　University of California Los Angeles

Aldington, Richard   ALDI RICH
　　One ALS.
　　　　University of California Los Angeles

　　One ALS.
　　　　University of Kansas
　　　　Copy at SUNY SB   Box 56

Allgood, Sara (Sally)   ALLG SARA
　　ALS (January 15 [1922]).
　　　　New York University

One ALS, two TLS (1935?).
   New York Public Library

One ALS (7 Jan. 1922).
   McMaster University

Copies of three TLS and ALS (one, 1935; Ms 15395).
   National Library of Ireland

Allingham, Helen   ALLI HELE
   One ALS; one TLS, dated 7 Dec. 1904.
      University of Illinois at Urbana

Alma-Tadema, Miss Laurence   ALMA TADE MI
   One ALS (Osborn Shelves e.2).
      Yale University

Archer, William   ARCH WILL
   One ALS, dated 4 April [1903]; one ALS dictated, dated
   18 June 1902; two TLS, dated 23 Aug. [1904] and 25
   Sept [1904] (Add. MS 45297, ff. 252-257).
      British Library

   One ALS (in Archer papers, box 1).
      Regent's College

Armsby-Wilson, R.   ARMS WILS R.
   One ALS.
      University of Texas at Austin

Arndt, Mrs.   ARND MRS.
   TLS, dated March 27, 1934.
      Pennsylvania State University Library

Arthur, Chester   ARTH CHES
   One ALS (1938).
      Colby College Library

Asquith, Lady   ASQU LADY
   One ALS, with comment about WBY retiring to his tower
   to discover his sins.
      Crawford, William

Bagnold, Enid   BAGN ENID
   Photocopy of a letter (in RP2105).
      British Library

Letters

Bailey, William F.   BAIL WILL F.
    One TL (25 June, 1915).
        New York Public Library

    Two ALS.
        University of Texas at Austin

    TL draft (June 23, 1915; Ms 13068).
        National Library of Ireland
        Copy at SUNY SB   Box 56

Ball, Mrs. [Frances]   BALL MRS. FR
    One LS dictated to A. Horniman, dated July 8, 1903.
        Emory University

Barnes, George   BARN GEOR
    Nine TLS, dated Jan 15, 1937-Dec 13, 1938 (Ms 5918).
        National Library of Ireland

Barry, William   BARR WILL
    ALS (March 24, 1899; 4 pp).
        National Library of Ireland
        Copy at SUNY SB   Box 56

Bates, Katherine Lee   BATE KATH LE
    One ALS to "Miss Bates" (May 26 1920).
        Wellesley College
        Copy at SUNY SB   Box 56

Bax, Clifford   BAX CLIF
    One LS (22 Jan, 1903), in hand of A. Horniman.
        University of Texas at Austin

Beardsley, Mabel   BEAR MABE
    21 ALS ([1913-1915]), edited and dated by Harold Adams.
        University of Texas at Austin

    Two letters (January 15, 1920 and March 25, 1920).
        Princeton University

Beardsley, Mrs.   BEAR MRS.
    Two letters.
        Princeton University

Beauclerk, Miss [Helen]   BEAU MISS HE
    See Letters: Dulac, Helen (DULA HELE).

Beech, Stella Campbell BEEC STEL CA
    One ALS ([1909]).
    New York Public Library

Bell, C.C. BELL C.C.
    ALS (Mar 3 1900; Add. MS 45498C).
    British Library

Bell, Edward Price BELL EDWA PR
    One ALS.
    Newberry Library

Belmont, Eleanor Robson BELM ELEA RO
    One ALS.
    Columbia University

Bender, Albert BEND ALBE
    Four TLS, two ALS (1923-31).
    Mills College Library

Benson, A.C. BENS A.C.
    TLS (in S.721.d.89.9); LS, dictated (Add. 7339/30).
    Cambridge University Library

Bertram, Mr. BERT MR.
    TLS (Sept 21 1921; 1 p).
    Princeton University Library

Best, R.I. BEST R.I.
    Two ALS; TLS, with last paragraph in script (Sept.
    28 [1904]; Ms 11004); LS (Ms 10543).
    National Library of Ireland

Biggar, Francis J. BIGG FRAN J.
    One ALS (Nov 1893).
    University of Texas at Austin

    Four letters.
    New York Public Library

Birrell, Augustine BIRR AUGU
    Copy of dictated letter to "Professor Birrell" (20 Dec.
    1917) about Hugh Lane's will (Ms 30134).
    National Library of Ireland
    Copy at SUNY SB Box 56

    One ALS (9 Aug [1911]).
    University of Liverpool

Letters

Blacker, Dr.   BLAC DR.
   Four letters: two TLS to the Secretary of the Eugenics
   Society (1937-38); one TLS and one ALS to Dr. Blacker
   (the Secretary).
      Wellcome Institute for History of Medicine

Blackwood & Sons, William   BLAC SONS WI
   Letters (Ms. 4684).
      National Library of Scotland

Blair, Mr.   BLAI MR.
   One ALS.
      Mills College Library

Blake, Warren Barton   BLAK WARR BA
   One TLS (10 July 1911).
      Harvard University

Bland, Henry Mead   BLAN HENR ME
   Three letters (1907-1909).
      University of California Berkeley

   One ALS (1926; I:72).
      Emory University

Blunden, Edmund C.   BLUN EDMU C.
   One TLS (12 Dec, 1936).
      University of Texas at Austin

Blunt, Wilfrid   BLUN WILF
   One TLS (4 July [1902]); ALS (12 June 1903); one
   dictated letter (24 November 1902).
      University of Delaware Library

   One ALS (26 July [1903]); one TLS (7 May [1905]).
      University of Texas at Austin

   One letter, in hand of Pound, with copies of
   poems, including WBY's (1914; in Blunt Ms Box 61,
   49).
      West Sussex Record Office

Blythe, Ernest   BLYT ERNE
   Two ALS; three ALS and TLS; letter from WBY and Lady
   Gregory, signed by both (Ms 20704, 20714-15, 20705).
      National Library of Ireland

AMs draft (3 pp; Ms 30887); TLS copy (22 June 1925; 4 pp; Ms 31017).
   National Library of Ireland
   Copy at SUNY SB

Two letters (Ms 20715).
   National Library of Ireland

One letter (1928; in Archives Dept. P24/470).
   University College Dublin

Bodkin, Thomas   BODK THOM
   Letters and notes, mostly ALS (MS 7001/1728-29,
   1732-47, 1749-50, 1752-57).
      Trinity College Dublin

Booth, Miss Gore   BOOT MISS GO
   See Letters: Markievicz, Constance (MARK CONS).

Bottomley, Gordon   BOTT GORD
   One ALS (5 July [1932]).
      New York Public Library

Boughton, Rutland   BOUG RUTL
   One TLS (1938; Add. MS. 52366).
      British Library

Bourgeois, M.   BOUR M.
   One ALS.
      Stanford University

Boyd, Ernest   BOYD ERNE
   Transcriptions of nine letters (1915-18, and unknown
   dates).
      Stanford University

Boylan, Josephine   BOYL JOSE
   See Letters: Jacobson, Josephine Boylan (JACO JOSE BO).

Bradley, Katherine   BRAD KATH
   See Letters: Field, Michael (FIEL MICH).

Brett [George]   BRET GEOR
   TL copy (Nov. 18, 1935; 1 p).
      National Library of Ireland
      Copy at SUNY SB Box 56

Bridges, Mrs. Robert   BRID MRS. RO
    One letter (1930; Dep. Bridges 118, fol. 72).
        Bodleian Library

Bridges, Robert   BRID ROBE
    One letter (Ms 5918).
        National Library of Ireland

    Letters (1896-1930; Dep. Bridges 105; 120, fols. 159-60,
    and MS.Don.d. 135).
        Bodleian Library

Bright, Mary Chavelita   BRIG MARY CH
    Two letters.
        Princeton University Library

Brisbane, Arthur   BRIS ARTH
    TLS (Feb. 4, 1912).
        Syracuse University

Brittain, Vera Mary   BRIT VERA MA
    Two ALS.
        University of California Los Angeles

Brooke, Rupert   BROO RUPE
    One ALS (1913; in Brooke papers).
        King's College Library

Brophy, John   BROP JOHN
    One TLS.
        University of Texas at Austin

    One letter.
        Princeton University Library

Brown, Tom   BROW TOM
    One ALS ([Feb 28 1910]).
        Wellesley College
        Copy at SUNY SB Box 56

Browne   BROW
    One ALS to a Mr. Browne, in care of Harriet Monroe.
        New York Public Library

    One TLS (1912 September 29).
        University of Texas at Austin

One ALS, addressed to Mr. Browne (1933; Ms 31060).
National Library of Ireland
Copy at SUNY SB Box 56

Bryers, Mr.   BRYE MR.
See Letters: Sealy, Bryan, and Walker (SEAL BRYE WA).

Bullen, A.H.   BULL A.H.
One ALS (Ms 434).
Birmingham Reference Library

Seven ALS, four TLS (1902-1906). Four letters in hand
of A. Horniman, two in hand of Lady Gregory; TLS
signed for WBY by John Quinn (2 Jan 1904).
University of Texas at Austin

Four ALS (1907-1909).
University of California Los Angeles

Seven TLS, six ALS, one TL.
Harvard University

Eight ALS and TLS ([1903]-1913).
State University of New York at Buffalo

Over 90 letters, about half ALS, half TLS (some
dictated). Other related letters to Bullen's
Secretary, Miss Lister (LIST MISS E.).
University of Kansas
Copy at SUNY SB Box 56

One ALS.
University of Reading Library

One ALS.
Southern Illinois University

Bynner, Witter   BYNN WITT
Three ALS, one TLS (1905-[1916]).
Harvard University

Campbell, Mrs. B.   CAMP MRS. B.
LS (1924; Add. MS 48974, f. 81).
British Library

Campbell, Mrs. Joseph   CAMP MRS. JO
Copy of a letter (March 24, 1906).
New York Public Library

Letters

Campbell, Mrs. Patrick   CAMP MRS. PA
    One ALS.
        University of Texas at Austin

    One ALS.
        New York University

Carter, Mr.   CART MR.
    One TLS (March 31 1910).
        Kenyon College Library

Carton   CART
    One ALS.
        University of Texas at Austin

Chakravarty, Amiya   CHAK AMIY
    Copy (in Chakravarty's handwriting) of letter from WBY.
        Boston University

Chambers, Maria C.   CHAM MARI C.
    One ALS.
        University of Texas at Austin

Chatto & Windus Ltd.   CHAT WIND LT
    Letters (1921-1936).
        University of Reading Library

Chesson, Nora   CHES NORA
    One ALS (27 Jan [1895]).
        University of Texas at Austin

Chesson, Wilfrid H.   CHES WILF H.
    One ALS (12 Aug [1910]).
        University of Texas at Austin

Chew, Prof. Samuel C.   CHEW PROF SA
    LS, dictated (9 April 1918).
        Pierpont Morgan Library

Childers, Mary Alden   CHIL MARY AL
    One letter (1921; 7847-51/1328).
        Trinity College Dublin

Church, Richard   CHUR RICH
    Two ALS, one TLS (1937).
        University of Texas at Austin

Clarke, Austin   CLAR AUST
    One TLS (29 Sep 1912).
        Harvard University

Clemens, Cyril   CLEM CYRI
    Six ALS and TLS photocopies (MS 3987/2-7).
        Trinity College Dublin

    Two TL copies (5 March-25 March, 1938).
        University of Texas at Austin

Clifton, [Harry]   CLIF HARR
    TLS; copy with corrections (1 p; Ms 13068).
        National Library of Ireland

Clinton-Baddeley, V.C.   CLIN BADD V.
    Two letters (Ms 5918).
        National Library of Ireland

Clodd, Edward   CLOD EDWA
    6 ALS (25 Dec [1898], others undated; in Clodd
    Correspondence).
        University of Leeds

Cockerell, Sydney   COCK SYDN
    One ALS ([21 June, 1904]).
        University of Texas at Austin

Coffey, [George]   COFF GEOR
    Three ALS.
        University of Texas at Austin

Colton, Mr.   COLT MR.
    One ALS (Ms 5918).
        National Library of Ireland

Colum, Padraic   COLU PADR
    Ten ALS, three TLS (1905-1922).
        New York Public Library

Colville, Warner   COLV WARN
    One handwritten post card (24 May, 1916).
        Southern Illinois University

Conant, [James]   CONA JAME
    ALS, ca 1935; dictated draft (2 pp; Ms 31003).
        National Library of Ireland
        Copy at SUNY SB   Box 56

Connell, Norreys CONN NORR
   (pseudonym of Conal O'Riordan)
   12 ALS (one dated 9 March 1908), seven TLS (one
   dictated to Conal Holmes O'Connell), and three ANS
   (1907-1919).
      Southern Illinois University

   One ALS (24 Dec, 1919).
      Southern Illinois University

   One ALS (Ms 24543).
      National Library of Ireland

   One ALS.
      University of Texas at Austin

Coomaraswamy, Amanda Kentish COOM AMAN KE
   One ANS.
      Boston Public Library

Cooper, Mrs. [Edith] COOP MRS. ED
   See Letters: Field, Michael (FIEL MICH).

Corri, Madame Ghita CORR MADA GH
   One letter (11 Sept, 1927).
      Princeton University Library

Cosgrave, William T. COSG WILL T.
   One TLS by "W B Y" and Lady Gregory offering the Abbey
   Theatre to the nation (1923; Ms 20670).
      National Library of Ireland

Cotton, James COTT JAME
   One ANS (1902).
      Brown University

Coulter, John COUL JOHN
   One ALS (Oct. 30 [1918]).
      McMaster University

Cousins, James H. COUS JAME H.
   One ALS.
      Theosophical Society Archives

   One ALS (17 Sept, 1914).
      University of Texas at Austin

Craig, Edward Gordon CRAI EDWA GO
    Letters.
        Bibliotheque de l'Arsenal

Crangle, Mrs. Roland CRAN MRS. RO
    Three ALS and two TLS (1914-1924).
        Cornell University

Crangle, Roland CRAN ROLA
    One telegram, dated Feb. 18, 1914.
        Cornell University

Cronan, Mary CRON MARY
    AMs; pencil draft of letter, with poem FLOW HAS BL on
    verso (Ms 30439).
        National Library of Ireland
        Copy at SUNY SB   Box 56

Crone, Dr. J.S. CRON DR. J.
    Two TLS and five ALS.
        Belfast City Libraries

Crook, William Montgomery CROO WILL MO
    Letters (1887-1889; Ms. Eng. hist. d. 369, fols. 3-6;
    d. 372, fol 20).
        Bodleian Library

Cummings, Hubertis M. CUMM HUBE M.
    One letter (June 23 1933).
        Princeton University Library

Curran, Constantine P. CURR CONS P.
    Two letters (one dated 1936; in CUR.1.5-6).
        University College Dublin

Curtis, Mr. CURT MR.
    ALS, regarding the amount to be paid for an article
    (1910).
        Trent University

Darragh, Florence Leticia DARR FLOR LE
    TL (copy), dated 28 March 1913 (2 pp; Ms 31037).
        National Library of Ireland
        Copy at SUNY SB   Box 56

Das, Mr. DAS MR.
    One letter (Ms 5918).
        National Library of Ireland

Letters

Davitt, Michael   DAVI MICH
    One ALS ([1899]; MS 9418/1994).
      Trinity College Dublin

Davray, Henry   DAVR HENR
    One ALS (November 21, [1899]).
      Northwestern University Library

    One ALS (13 Nov, 1904).
      Scripps College

    Two ALS.
      Harvard University

Day, F. H.   DAY F.H.
    One ALS (27 Oct, 1894).
      Southern Illinois University

    One ALS.
      Boston College

    One ALS.
      University of Texas at Austin

De Blaghd, Earndn   DE   BLAG EA
    See Letters: Blythe, Ernest (BLYT ERNE).

De Valera, Eamon   DE   VALE EA
    TLS ([Feb 1933; 2 pp; Ms 30161); TLS draft (March 1933;
    3 pp; Ms 31039); TL copy with carbons (Jan 1937; 2 pp;
    Ms 30229).
      National Library of Ireland
      Copy at SUNY SB   Box 56

DeLury, Alfred   DELU ALFR
    ALS (November 30 [1923]).
      Trent University

    One telegram (Feb. 13, 19--).
      University of Toronto

Dial   DIAL
    Seven ALS, TLS, dictated letters; one postcard, signed
    (ca 1923-28; Za Dial).
      Yale University

Dickinson, Mabel   DICK MABE
    15 letters (1908-1911).
    University of California Berkeley

Digges, Dudley   DIGG DUDL
    One TLS.
    Colby College Library

Dillon, John and Miles   DILL JOHN MI
    Three ALS and one signed card (Ms 29043).
    National Library of Ireland

Dircks, W.H.   DIRC W.H.
    One ALS (Osborn files; Yeats).
    Yale University

Dixon, W. Macneile   DIXO W.   MA
    Two letters (MS. Gen. 512 [19-20]).
    University of Glasgow Library

Dobell, Bertram   DOBE BERT
    One letter (MS Dobell c. 53, fols. 201-3).
    Bodleian Library

Dolan, M.J.   DOLA M.J.
    One TLS (July 31, 1925; Ms 22555).
    National Library of Ireland

Doone, Rupert   DOON RUPE
    Two ALS, one ANS (1937?).
    New York Public Library

Dowden, Edward   DOWD EDWA
    One TL (19 May, 1895).
    University of California Los Angeles

    Three ALS.
    Southern Illinois University

Doyle, Miss C.M.   DOYL MISS C.
    One ALS (Ms 5918).
    National Library of Ireland

Drinkwater, John   DRIN JOHN
    One TLS (MS Vault Shelves Drinkwater).
    Yale University

Dryhurst, Norah   DRYH NORA
    One letter (1901; Add. MS 46362, f. 60).
        British Library

    One ALS.
        University of Texas at Austin

Dublin Magazine Editor   DUBL MAGA ED
    One letter.
        Indiana University

Duckworth, Gerald   DUCK GERA
    One letter (in Duckworth papers).
        University of London Library

Duff, Arthur   DUFF ARTH
    Letters (1934-1939) about music for WBY's plays (in
    Add.Ms.55003).
        British Library

Duffy, Charles Gavan   DUFF CHAR GA
    Three ALS (one of them fragmentary; ca 1890; Ms 8005).
        National Library of Ireland

Dulac, Edmund   DULA EDMU
    93 ALS, nine TLS, two initialled L, one TL fragment,
    one telegram (1916-1937). 18 letters in hand of George
    Yeats, signed by WBY.
        University of Texas at Austin

    TL and AMs describing a performance of AT HAWK WE at
    the Abbey (Ms 13583).
        National Library of Ireland
        Copy at SUNY SB

Dulac, Helen   DULA HELE
    Two TLS (16 Nov-4 Dec, 1937); two ALS addressed to
    "Miss Beauclerk."
        University of Texas at Austin

Dulanty   DULA
    Typed copies and carbons of letters about Lane pictures
    (15 January 1937; Ms 30161).
        National Library of Ireland
        Copy at SUNY SB   Box 56

Duncan, Ellen Douglas   DUNC ELLE DO
    Seven ALS, five LS (10 Jan-16 May 1918).
        Columbia University

    One TLS.
        University of Texas at Austin

    One ALS.
        National Library of Ireland
        Copy at SUNY SB Box 56

    One ALS.
        Harvard University

Duncan, James   DUNC JAME
    ALS draft (Ms 31027).
        National Library of Ireland

    One TL (13 Nov, [1908]).
        New York Public Library

Dunn, Mr.   DUNN MR.
    One ALS, asking that he be sent what is due for "Peter
    Gilligan."
        Kain, Richard M.

    One ALS.
        Bucknell University

    Two ALS.
        University of Texas at Austin

    Letter asking if Dunn owes him any money for his
    poem CRAD SONG, which is tipped in to WAND OISI 89.
        Tulane University

Dunsany, Lady   DUNS LADY
    Six ALS (1909-1919).
        New York Public Library

Dunsany, Lord   DUNS LORD
    14 ALS, seven LS, one AL, one ANS (1909-1935).
        New York Public Library

Letters   115

Editor   EDIT
    For manuscripts of WBY's letters to Editors, see titles
    of specific publications: Academy, Dublin Magazine,
    Freeman's Journal, Nationales, Times. See also
    SCOT JAME (Editor, London Mercury).

Ellis, Edwin J.   ELLI EDWI J.
    Five letters (MS 293/1/1).
       University of Reading Library

    Two ALS, two TLS, six TL copies (1890-1912; Ms 30550).
       National Library of Ireland
       Copy at SUNY SB   Box 56

Ellis, Mrs.   ELLI MRS.
    Eight letters (Ms 30550).
       National Library of Ireland
       Copy at SUNY SB   Box 56

    Four letters (MS 293/1/1).
       University of Reading Library

Ellis, P.D.   ELLI P.D.
    Photocopy of a letter-card about WBY's definition of
    imagination (in RP 2885).
       British Library

Emery, Florence Farr   EMER FLOR FA
    Letter asking when she will return, inserted in copy of
    POEM 01. Four ALS, one TLS (1906-1907).
       University of Texas at Austin

    One ALS.
       Pennsylvania State University Library

    AMs; draft of a letter to S.S.D.D. (her code name in
    the Golden Dawn).
       National Library of Ireland

    TMs copies of letters (38 pp; Ms 30585).
       National Library of Ireland
       Copy at SUNY SB   Box 56

    One ALS (1906; A.L. 203/25).
       University of London Library

    One ALS, dated 21 Jan 1911.
       Boston Public Library

One telegram, one letter (in Berg); two ALS (one a
fragment; in Rare Books and Ms).
   New York Public Library

Ervine, St. John   ERVI ST. JO
   One ALS ([1916]; Ms 13068).
      National Library of Ireland
      Copy at SUNY SB   Box 56

   One letter (MS. Autogr. c. 25, fol. 263).
      Bodleian Library

   11 ALS, 10 ANS, four TLS, one form letter signed
   (1912-1937).
      University of Texas at Austin

Eugenics Society   EUGE SOCI
   See Letters: Dr. Blacker (BLAC DR.).

Evans, Edward   EVAN EDWA
   One ALS ([1907]).
      Southern Illinois University

Fagan, Mr.   FAGA MR.
   Five copies of letters, dated 1921-1922 (Ms 5918).
      National Library of Ireland

   Four ALS.
      Wake Forest University Library

   One ALS.
      Southern Illinois University

Fallon, Gabriel   FALL GABR
   TLS (31 July 1925).
      Sligo County Library

Farr, Florence   FARR FLOR
   See Letters: Emery, Florence Farr (EMER FLOR FA).

Farrell, Mr.   FARR MR.
   One TLS [1937].
      McMaster University

Letters 117

Fay, Frank FAY FRAN
TMs copy (August 13 1908; Ms 31058); TLS (Jan 13 1908; Ms 10952).
National Library of Ireland
Copy at SUNY SB   Box 56

One telegram (30 Dec, 1905).
New York Public Library

Copies of 20 letters, some ca 1901-1905, some undated (in Appendix to a dissertation by John Stokes; originals in possession of Fay family).
University of Reading Library

Fay, Mrs. FAY MRS.
ALS (1933; Ms 2652).
National Library of Ireland

Fay, William FAY WILL
One TLS ([1903]; in CUR.L.4).
University College Dublin

One TLS, with TMs of "new passages" for SHAD WATE, and comments on how they will affect the play.
University of Kansas
Copy at SUNY SB   Box 56

ALS ([1923]) and two TLS (Ms 2652, 10952, 27619); two ALS (Ms 2652).
National Library of Ireland

One TLS (31 Aug [1903]); two ALS.
Harvard University

LS (Ms 13068).
National Library of Ireland
Copy at SUNY SB

Fergusson, Lady FERG LADY
One ALS.
University of Tulsa

Field, Michael FIEL MICH
(pseudonym of Katharine Bradley and Edith Cooper)
ALS (11 June [1903]) and TLS (27 July [1903]).
University of Delaware Library

    One ALS (2 pp), to a Mrs. Cooper [Edith?].
        National Library of Ireland
        Copy at SUNY SB   Box 56

Fisher, H.A.L.   FISH H.A.
    One letter (Ms fisher 72, fol. 124).
        Bodleian Library

Fitts, [William B.]   FITT WILL B.
    One ALS (19 Aug [1900?]).
        Harvard University

Fitzgerald, Miss   FITZ MISS
    Photocopy of a letter (1899; in RP1889).
        British Library

Foden, Gwyneth   FODE GWYN
    One ALS (21 May 1935).
        University of Delaware Library

    Seven ALS, two TLS, one AL, initialed.
        University of Texas at Austin

Ford, Ford Madox   FORD FORD MA
    One TLS, one ALS.
        New York Public Library

Ford, Julia   FORD JULI
    Two letters, one of them dictated to Ezra Pound
        (Za Ford, Julia).
        Yale University

Forster, E.M.   FORS E.M.
    One ALS ([1935]; in Forster papers).
        King's College Library

Foster, Jeanne   FOST JEAN
    Four TLS, four ALS, and two LS (dictated) (1908-23;
    Rare Books and Ms).
        New York Public Library

Francis, Rene   FRAN RENE
    One TLS (5 Sept, 1911).
        Bucknell University

Fraser, Dr.   FRAS DR.
    One letter with photograph (4630-4649/4325).
        Trinity College Dublin

Letters

   One ALS.
      University of California Los Angeles

Fredman, Miss   FRED MISS
   One letter (5 Feb, 1921).
      Indiana University

   Two ALS ([1919]).
      State University of New York at Buffalo

Freemans Journal Editor   FREE JOUR ED
   One TLS (23 May, 1902).
      New York Public Library

Freund, Frank   FREU FRAN
   One ALS (20 Feb, 1906).
      New York Public Library

Frohman, Charles   FROH CHAR
   TL copy (March 4 1908; 1 p; Ms 18694).
      National Library of Ireland
      Copy at SUNY SB   Box 56

Frost, William H.   FROS WILL H.
   One ALS.
      Brown University

Gardner, Fredrick   GARD FRED
   Post card noting that WBY will lecture on "The Nature
   of Beauty" ([10 July 1893]).
      State University of New York at Albany

Garnett, Edward   GARN EDWA
   Nine ALS.
      University of Texas at Austin

Garnett, Porter   GARN PORT
   One ALS.
      Mills College Library

Garvey, Maire   GARV MAIR
   One TLS (Dec. 18, 1905; Ms 8320).
      National Library of Ireland

Garvin, James L.   GARV JAME L.
   One ALS (24 Oct, 1919).
      University of Texas at Austin

Gaunt, William GAUN WILL
    Microfiche copy of ALS (TAM59/13).
        Tate Gallery Archive

Gawsworth, John GAWS JOHN
    TLS, accompanied by two identical ALS to the Trustees
    of the Civil List Pension Fund on behalf of Edward
    Jepson's daughter (January, 1939).
        Wellesley College

Gibbon, Monk GIBB MONK
    Three ALS.
        Queen's University (Canada)

    TLS (17 October 1932; Ms 31045).
        National Library of Ireland
        Copy at SUNY SB Box 56

Gibson, Mr. GIBS MR.
    One ALS (in Ms.Eur.E.276/70).
        India Office Library and Records

Gibson, Wilfrid GIBS WILF
    One ALS (probably to Gibson, but librarian not
    certain).
        Wake Forest University Library

Gill, Thomas Patrick GILL THOM PA
    Letters (photocopies; 1898-1908; 4733/74-5, 80, 76,
    77-9, 81-7).
        Trinity College Dublin

Gogarty, Oliver St. John GOGA OLIV ST
    TLS (Ms 9933).
        National Library of Ireland

    One ALS, two TLS (1924-[1937]).
        Harvard University

    ANS, addressed to "Senator Gogarty."
        University of California Berkeley

    One TLS (1929).
        Colby College Library

    One ALS (11 July, [191-]).
        State University of New York at Buffalo

Letters

>Three ALS.
>Sligo County Library

>One TLS.
>Stanford University

>One letter (7 Sept, 1918).
>Princeton University Library

>One TLS.
>Boston University

>Four TLS, nine ALS, two dictated letters (1919-1935).
>Bucknell University

Gonne, Iseult (Stuart)   GONN ISEU
>Four ALS (three of these addressed to "Maurice").
>University of Kansas
>Copy at SUNY SB Box 56

>One ALS.
>Northwestern University Library

>One ALS.
>University of Texas at Austin

Goodman, Edward   GOOD EDWA
>Two ALS (in Billy Rose Theatre Collection).
>New York Public Library

Gorell, Elizabeth   GORE ELIZ
>32 ALS (in Gorell 5).
>Bodleian Library

Gorman, Eric   GORM ERIC
>One ALS (1937 or 1938; I:76).
>Emory University

Gosse, Edmund   GOSS EDMU
>One ALS.
>New York Public Library

>24 ALS ([20 Nov. 1905]-23 Nov. [1923]; in Gosse Correspondence).
>University of Leeds

>Letters (1895-1914; Ashley Ms 5739 and B. 4679*).
>British Library

Gosse, Lady   GOSS LADY
    Three letters (Add. 7023/8).
        Cambridge University Library

Gosse, Phillip   GOSS PHIL
    One letter (4 Mar, 1929).
        The Huntington Library

Gough, Mrs.   GOUG MRS.
    One ALS (29 May, 1932).
        University of Louisville

    One TLS (1933 June 27; I:74).
        Emory University

Graham, R.B. Cunningham   GRAH R.B. CU
    One TLS (Dep. 205, Box 1a).
        National Library of Scotland

Graves, Alfred Perceval   GRAV ALFR PE
    One ALS.
        Harvard University

    One ALS (Feb 1901; 3 pp; Ms 31029).
        National Library of Ireland
        Copy at SUNY SB   Box 56

Gregg, Fredrick J.   GREG FRED J.
    One ALS ([191-]).
        State University of New York at Buffalo

Gregory, Lady   GREG LADY
    76 ALS, 20 TLS, four LS, 11 TL, five TL (copies), nine
    telegrams, one ANS (1898-1931).
        New York Public Library
        Copy at SUNY SB   Box 65-76

    ALS (Nov. 25 [1917?]; 2 pp; Ms 13068); TMs copies
    and carbons (19 June 1925; Ms 30161); TLS ([Jan. ?
    1914]; 3 pp; Ms 30227).
        National Library of Ireland
        Copy at SUNY SB   Box 65-76

    Other letters and excerpts in notebooks with other
    items. See Miscellany: DIAR JOUR (Ms 30361, 30593).
        National Library of Ireland
        Copy at SUNY SB   Box 88

Letters

    Telegram (1903; Ms 19844).
       National Library of Ireland

    Two ALS, one TLS (1928-1932).
       University of Delaware Library

    One AL (1912?) possibly to Lady Gregory, with reference to Bourgeois.
       Stanford University

    Two ALS, two TLS (1926-1932).
       University of Louisville

    21 ALS, one TLS (1913-14, 1919-1920).
       Northwestern University Library

    Two TL (copies), dated April 20 and 25, 1928.
       University of Texas at Austin

    Eight ALS, three TLS (1904-1910).
       Emory University

    One ALS (March 14 [1914]).
       Wellesley College

Gregory, Mr.   GREG MR.
    TLS about anthologies and publishers, with corrections (June 25 1913; Ms 26752).
       National Library of Ireland

Gregory, Mrs. Margaret   GREG MRS. MA
    ALS (Ms 30901).
       National Library of Ireland
       Copy at SUNY SB

Gregory, Robert   GREG ROBE
    One letter; one ALS (May 1912; 1 p).
       National Library of Ireland
       Copy at SUNY SB   Box 56

Grierson, H.J.C.   GRIE H.J.
    One letter.
       Bodleian Library

    15 letters (MS. 9331).
       National Library of Scotland

Grigsby, Miss [Emilie]   GRIG MISS EM
    One letter ([1930]; MS. Eng. lett. c. 650, fols. 1-2).
        Bodleian Library

    Two LS, one dated May 17 [1925].
        Washington State University

Grigson, Geoffrey   GRIG GEOF
    One ALS.
        State University of New York at Buffalo

Guinan, John   GUIN JOHN
    Three TLS, three ALS (1908-1934).
        University of Texas at Austin

Guiney, Louise Imogen   GUIN LOUI IM
    Three ALS.
        College of the Holy Cross

    One ALS to "Miss Guiney."
        Pierpont Morgan Library

Guthrie, Mr.   GUTH MR.
    Two letters.
        Indiana University

Gwynn, Denis   GWYN DENI
    ALS (Ms 10737).
        National Library of Ireland

Gwynn, Stephen   GWYN STEP
    Three TLS (1906).
        State University of New York at Buffalo

    One ALS.
        University of California Los Angeles

    One ALS ([1887]; WBY I:57).
        Emory University

    One ALS.
        New York Public Library

    One ALS.
        Harvard University

Letters   125

  Four ALS and one signed form letter from the Irish
  Academy of Letters (1900-1925; Ms 8600); another letter
  about restoration work at Thoor Ballylee ([1917]; Ms
  18475).
     National Library of Ireland

  One TL, initialled (3 Nov [1912]).
     University of Texas at Austin

Hackett   HACK
  One ALS.
     University of Texas at Austin

Haggard, Rider   HAGG RIDE
  Two ALS (1910-[1915]).
     State University of New York at Buffalo

Haldane, Richard Burdon   HALD RICH BU
  One letter (MS. 5914).
     National Library of Scotland

Hall, Agnes   HALL AGNE
  LS (dictated), dated Dec. 18, 1908 (Ms 5918).
     National Library of Ireland

Halle, Mrs. Louis   HALL MRS. LO
  AL.
     Wellesley College

Hamilton, Miss   HAMI MISS
  One LS (5 Mar, 1908).
     New York Public Library

Hamsa, Shri   HAMS SHRI
  One ALS (12 March 1937).
     University of Delaware Library

Harding, W.G.   HARD W.G.
  One ALS.
     Wake Forest University Library

Hardy, Thomas   HARD THOM
  One letter.
     Dorset County Museum

Harmsworth, Edward   HARM EDWA
  AL draft (Ms 31026).
     National Library of Ireland
     Copy at SUNY SB   Box 56

Harris, Frank   HARR FRAN
    One ALS.
    University of Texas at Austin

Harris, Fred   HARR FRED
    ALS (Dec 14 [1918]; 1 p).
    National Library of Ireland
    Copy at SUNY SB Box 56

Harrison   HARR
    TLS (copy), dated Monday 13 December 1926 (Ms 30896).
    National Library of Ireland
    Copy at SUNY SB Box 56

Harrison, Clifford   HARR CLIF
    ALS (April 1 1914; 2 pp).
    University of Virginia

Hayes, Dr. Carlton   HAYE DR. CA
    One TLS (1 Feb, 1935).
    Southern Illinois University

Hays, Mr.   HAYS MR.
    Letter on theatre business, in a green notebook; see
    Miscellany: DIAR JOUR (Ms 30385).
        National Library of Ireland
        Copy at SUNY SB Box 88

Hayward, John   HAYW JOHN
    One ALS (26 Nov, 1934).
    University of Texas at Austin

Heald, Edith Shackleton   HEAL EDIT SH
    Fragment of TL (1938 Feb. 21).
    National Library of Ireland
    Copy at SUNY SB Box 56

    One TLS (26 Feb, 1938).
    University of Texas at Austin

    AL; note on his good days and bad days, with copy of
    his "latest poem" (not included, but note, not by WBY,
    says it may have been THOS IMAG) possibly the ending of
    a letter to Heald.
        Harvard University

    61 ALS (1937-1938).
        Harvard University

Healy, James A.   HEAL JAME
    One ALS, one TN, one ANS ([1937-1938]).
        Stanford University

    One letter (Ms 5918).
        National Library of Ireland

Henderson, W.A.   HEND W.A.
    Three ALS, two TLS (ca 1913).
        University of Kansas
        Copy at SUNY SB   Box 56

    One TLS, one ALS (1910-1911).
        New York Public Library

    One ALS.
        University of Texas at Austin

Henley, W.E.   HENL W.E.
    One ALS ([1890]).
        Wellesley College
        Copy at SUNY SB   Box 56

Higgins, Frederick   HIGG FRED
    Printed invitation from Senator W.B. Yeats to F.R.
    Higgins (1924; Ms 10864).
        National Library of Ireland

    23 ALS, 12 TLS, one signed form letter, three signed
    cards; copy of poem JOHN KINS LA enclosed in one letter
    (ca 1937-39).
        University of Texas at Austin

    Two ALS and four TLS (1936-1938; Ms 27884).
        National Library of Ireland

    Form letter about the Irish Academy of Letters, signed
    by G. Bernard Shaw and WBY ([1932]; Ms 27886).
        National Library of Ireland

Higginson, T.W.   HIGG T.W.
    One letter from Rosses Point concerning a possible
    meeting in London, and asking for Miss Guiney's
    address.
        Higginson Family Museum

Hill, Edwin Bliss HILL EDWI
    Four letters (1918-1920).
        The Huntington Library

Hinkson, Henry Albert HINK HENR
    One ALS (17 Apr 1901).
        Harvard University

Hinkson, Katherine Tynan HINK KATH TY
    Two letters: one TL, incomplete; one dated March 21 [1889] (Ms 31035).
        National Library of Ireland
        Copy at SUNY SB Box 56

    Letters (in Hanson/Tynan collection).
        John Rylands University Library

    Nine TLS (in Shorter Collection).
        University of Leeds

    20 ALS; one TLS, dictated (1893-1918).
        Harvard University

    72 ALS, some with AMs drafts of "The Fairy Doctor" and "In Church" (see Poems: FAIR DOCT and IN CHUR; 1887-1895), and of an unpublished poem beginning "Wherever in the wastes of wrinkling sand" (WHER WAST WR).
        The Huntington Library

    One ALS; one AL, initialled.
        University of Texas at Austin

    One letter (2 July [1888]).
        Princeton University Library

Hodgson, Ralph HODG RALP
    One mimeographed letter, asking for permissions (Uncat MS Vault 263).
        Yale University

Holland, Miss HOLL MISS
    One ALS ([1903]).
        Southern Illinois University

Letters

Holloway, Joseph   HOLL JOSE
    Two TLS (Dec 18 1907, Nov 28 1923; Ms 13267).
    National Library of Ireland
    Copy at SUNY SB   Box 56

    TNS; one letter (Ms 13267-69, 4455).
    National Library of Ireland

Holroyd, Charles   HOLR CHAR
    One TLS (9 Oct, 1915).
    New York Public Library

Hone, Joseph M.   HONE JOSE M.
    Five telegrams (1913-1932).
    Northwestern University Library

    One ALS; one signed form letter about an Irish Academy
    of Letters, signed by G.B. Shaw and WBY.
    Wellesley College

    Six ALS ([1912-1932]).
    State University of New York at Buffalo

    Four ALS.
    Kenyon College Library

    One TL, with paragraph in script, signed; two ALS (Ms 5918).
    National Library of Ireland

    Six ALS, five TLS ([1907-1936]).
    University of Texas at Austin

Horn   HORN
    ALS to "My Dear Horn [?]" (probably Herbert Horne),
    dated 19 January 1891.
    Pennsylvania State University Library

Horniman, Miss Annie   HORN MISS AN
    One TL (15 Aug. 1909); three drafts; TLS from WBY and
    Lady Gregory; TLS (some carbons, copies) (Ms 30230,
    30908, 10952).
        National Library of Ireland
        Copy at SUNY SB   Box 56

    One TLS (May 19, 1910; 1 p; Ms 13068); ALS (1 p; Ms
    13068); one AL (2 pp; Ms 13068).
        National Library of Ireland
        Copy at SUNY SB   Box 56

One ALS (Sept, 1906).
   New York Public Library

Two ALS (1906-1910; in Horniman Collection).
   John Rylands University Library

Carbon copy of a telegram (5 Nov, 1907).
   Southern Illinois University

Horton, William   HORT WILL
   86 letters transcribed by John Gawsworth (1896-1918; Ms 289).
      University of Reading Library

   67 ALS, seven TLS, four telegrams, one post card (1896-1918).
      University of Texas at Austin
      Copy at SUNY SB   Box 56, 57

   One TLS (17 Jul [1903]); one ALS (3 Feb 1915).
      Harvard University

Howe, W.T.H.   HOWE W.T.
   One LS (3 Dec, 1932).
      New York Public Library

Hughes, Richard   HUGH RICH
   ALS (18 May [1922]).
      Pierpont Morgan Library

   ALS (April [1921]; 2 pp).
      Princeton University Library

Hunt, Violet   HUNT VIOL
   One ALS, declining an invitation to tea ([July 9, 1903]).
      Kain, Richard M.

   Six ALS, five TLS (1902-1923).
      New York Public Library

Hutchinson, Thomas   HUTC THOM
   Autograph postcard, signed, dated 24 June 1898.
      Pierpont Morgan Library

   One ALS.
      University of Kansas
      Copy at SUNY SB   Box 57

Letters   131

          ALS (1894; Special coll. 821.91.Y34.68).
          John Rylands University Library

Hyde, Douglas   HYDE DOUG
     One telegram.
     New York Public Library

Jackson, Arthur   JACK ARTH
     One TL (May 1910).
     New York Public Library

Jackson, Holbrook   JACK HOLB
     One ALS ([1917?]; WBY I:65).
     Emory University

     Two ALS, two ANS.
     University of California Los Angeles

     One letter.
     Princeton University Library

Jackson, Schuyler B.   JACK SCHU B.
     Six letters (1922-1924).
     Indiana University

Jacob, Miss   JACO MISS
     One ALS.
     New York Public Library

     ALS (July 30 [1919]; Ms 31022); ALS (July 30 [1922];
     5 pp).
     National Library of Ireland
     Copy at SUNY SB   Box 57

Jacobson, Josephine Boylan   JACO JOSE BO
     One ALS (1931).
     Boston University

James, Henry   JAME HENR
     One ALS (20 Aug [1915]).
     Harvard University

Johnson, Fred   JOHN FRED
     TLS (Ms 31040).
     National Library of Ireland
     Copy at SUNY SB   Box 57

Jones, Jennie Ina   JONE JENN IN
   One LS (27 April, 1902).
   Southern Illinois University

Joyce, James   JOYC JAME
   Four ALS, one AL, one TLS (1902-04, and undated; MS
   Vault; Joyce; Box 3).
   Yale University

   Five ALS, two TLS, one TL, one TLS copy (1902-1924).
   Cornell University

   One TL (18 Dec, 1902).
   Southern Illinois University

Karlfeldt, Eric   KARL ERIC
   One ALS (Nov. 21st [1923]).
   Svenska Akademiens Nobelbibliotek

Keeble, Lillah McCarthy   KEEB LILL MC
   One ALS regretting inability to attend her recital; one
   TN, apologizing for not being able to write a preface.
   Kain, Richard M.

   One ALS.
   University of Texas at Austin

Keller, Mr.   KELL MR.
   TLS, with enclosure (1935 August 13).
   Emory University

Kennedy, W.S.   KENN W.S.
   Five ALS ([1919]).
   State University of New York at Buffalo

Keynes, Geoffrey   KEYN GEOF
   Two letters (MS 1372).
   University of Reading Library

Kiernan, Thomas J.   KIER THOM J.
   Seven TLS, four ALS (1928-1939).
   New York Public Library

King, Frederick A.   KING FRED A.
   One ALS.
   University of Texas at Austin

Letters

King, Richard Ashe   KING RICH AS
    ALS.
        Trent University

    One TLS (26 Oct, 1924).
        University of Texas at Austin

Kingston, Gertrude   KING GERT
    Two ALS and one postcard, signed (in Kingston papers).
        King's College Library

Kinkead, Eugene   KINK EUGE
    One letter (Ms 5918).
        National Library of Ireland

    One transcribed letter (7 April, [1938]).
        Stanford University

Kleeman, Rita Sulzbacher Halle   KLEE RITA SU
    One ALS (1927).
        Wellesley College

Knight, W.A.   KNIG W.A.
    LS, dictated (June 19th 1902).
        Pierpont Morgan Library

Knole, Lady   KNOL LADY
    Two TN.
        Kain, Richard M.

Koehler, Thomas   KOEH THOM
    One letter (18 Nov, 1908).
        Indiana University

Laird, Helen   LAIR HELE
    LS, signed also by Maud Gonne, the Fays and others (in
    Curran Collections).
        University College Dublin

Lambert, Maurice   LAMB MAUR
    Three ALS (Ms 15544).
        National Library of Ireland

Lane, Hugh   LANE HUGH
    One TLS (24 March 1906), two LS, dictated (one dated 28
    March 1906).
        Southern Illinois University

Letter with copy of Poem: TO WEAL MAN enclosed
(MS 7001/1728).
    Trinity College Dublin

Nine ALS, one dated 14 April 1905; one TLS; two TLS,
(dictated, dated 12 Mar. 1905 and 5 April 1905); page
with notes about theatre (Ms 22743). See Miscellany:
THEA MATE.
    National Library of Ireland

ALS ([1913]; Ms 13072).
    National Library of Ireland

Langbridge, Fred   LANG FRED
    Two ALS, one TLS (1910).
        University of Texas at Austin

    One ALS.
        Southern Illinois University

Langbridge, Rosamund   LANG ROSA
    Four ALS (1889-1907; WBY I:60).
        Emory University

Laurie, Thomas Werner   LAUR THOM WE
    Two ALS (1900).
        University of Texas at Austin

    One ALS (1924).
        Colby College Library

Law, Mr.   LAW MR.
    TL copy about the blacklisting of George Moore by the
    Irish Literary Society, (March 16 1901; Ms 31038).
        National Library of Ireland
        Copy at SUNY SB   Box 57

Le Fanu, Mrs.   LEFA MRS.
    One ALS.
        University of Texas at Austin

LeGallienne, Richard   LEGA RICH
    One ALS (1916 May 28; Za Pound Film 7).
        Yale University

    One ALS.
        New York University

Letters   135

   One ALS.
       Brandeis University Library

   Three ALS.
       University of Texas at Austin

Lecky, W.E.H.   LECK W.E.
   One letter (Ms 1827-1836/2624).
       Trinity College Dublin

Lerine, Isaac Esq.   LERI ISAA ES
   Dictated letter, dated March 26, 1918.
       Kenyon College Library

Leventhal, A.J.   LEVE A.J.
   ALS with envelope (17 Dec 1921; 2 pp).
       University of Victoria

Leveson, George Granville   LEVE GEOR GR
   One ALS (8 Jan 1900).
       Harvard University

Lewis, P. Wyndham   LEWI P.   WY
   Four ALS, two TL, one TLS (1914-1930).
       Cornell University

   TL (copy; Ms 30570).
       National Library of Ireland
       Copy at SUNY SB   Box 57

Linati, Carlo   LINA CARL
   TLS; LS ([1913]).
       Pierpont Morgan Library

Linc(?)   LINC
   ANS, sending wishes and love "To dearest [Linc?]."
       University of Tulsa

Linnell, Mr.   LINN MR.
   One ALS (Oct 28, 1894; MS. 78-1950).
       Fitzwilliam Museum

Lister, Miss E.M.   LIST MISS E.
   Nine ALS, three TLS (ca 1908-09).
       Harvard University

   Three ALS ([1908-1911]).
       State University of New York at Buffalo

One letter (Ms 24563).
    National Library of Ireland

Eight letters to Miss Lister as Secretary to A.H. Bullen (BULL A.H.).
    University of Kansas

Little, Mr.   LITT MR.
   Typed copies and carbons of letters about Lane pictures (15 January 1937; Ms 30161).
    National Library of Ireland
    Copy at SUNY SB   Box 57

Londonderry, Lady   LOND LADY
   ALS (4 pp; Ms 30886).
    National Library of Ireland
    Copy at SUNY SB   Box 57

Longford Printing Press   LONG PRIN PR
   TLS (10 January 1939; Ms 30513).
    National Library of Ireland
    Copy at SUNY SB   Box 57

Lowell, Amy   LOWE AMY
   One ALS, one TLS (1914).
    Harvard University

Lynd, [Robert]   LYND ROBE
   Six ALS, one TLS, including one dated May 28 1928.
    Northwestern University Library

Lyster, Jane R.   LYST JANE R.
   One letter, copied by T.W. Lyster (Ms 5919).
    National Library of Ireland

Lyster, T.W.   LYST T.W.
   One letter, dictated (1918), and one ALS; letter copied out by Lyster (Ms 21749, 5915).
    National Library of Ireland

Lyttelton, Edith   LYTT EDIT
   TMs copies of two letters (18 July [1914] and 25 July [?]; Ms 30025).
    National Library of Ireland
    Copy at SUNY SB

   Four letters (in CHAN I 5/21).
    Churchill College

Lyttelton, Lady Katherine   LYTT LADY KA
    ALS (Sept 6 [1909]; in Lyttelton papers).
        Westfield College

MacBride, Maud Gonne   MACB MAUD GO
    AL to Maud Gonne (2 pp; [1893]) with suggested rules
    for a lending library (3 pp; Ms 30686).
        National Library of Ireland
        Copy at SUNY SB

    Three TL copies (14 Jan, 1907-16 June 1938).
        University of Texas at Austin

    One AL (fragment; [1893]).
        Yeats, Michael

MacColl, D.S.   MACC D.S.
    Seven ALS (MacColl Y22-32).
        University of Glasgow Library

MacDermott, Norman   MACD NORM
    One ALS.
        Bucknell University

MacDonagh, Thomas   MACD THOM
    TLS (1909; Ms 18474).
        National Library of Ireland

    Three ALS, two TLS (1907-1915).
        University of Texas at Austin

    Three photocopied ALS and TS (Ms 15395).
        National Library of Ireland

    ALS (January 26 [1909]).
        New York University

MacDonald, Sir Anthony   MACD SIR AN
    ALS (Ms 30894).
        National Library of Ireland
        Copy at SUNY SB

MacGreevy, Thomas   MACG THOM
    Two TLS and copy (Ms 8104/53a, 71a; 8104/20).
        Trinity College Dublin

MacHugh, Ignatius   MACH IGNA
    Two ALS (1921-1925).
        The Huntington Library

MacManus, Mr.   MACM MR.
    One TNS (1937; Ms 10716).
        National Library of Ireland

Mackenna, Stephen   MACK STEP
    One ALS. (Ms 10751).
        National Library of Ireland

    One LS, dictated (3 May 1902).
        Southern Illinois University

Mackintosh, Graham   MACK GRAH
    One ALS (27 May, [1917]).
        University of Texas at Austin

Maclagan, [E.R.D.]   MACL E.R.
    One ALS.
        University of Kansas

Macmillan Company   MACM COMP
    Letters (Ms 31057).
        National Library of Ireland
        Copy at SUNY SB Box 57

    Letters (1932-1935; Ms 1089).
        University of Reading Library

    100 ALS, 19 TLS, two ANS, six signed cards, all
    addressed to "Dear Sir"; five ALS and 11 TLS, addressed
    to Sir Frederick Macmillan; 23 ALS and 26 TLS,
    addressed to Harold Macmillan; one ALS addressed to Mr.
    [Harold] Watt; one ALS addressed to Mr. [Thomas] Mark
    (Add MS 55003).
        British Library

Macmillan, Frederick   MACM FRED
    See Letters: Macmillan Company (MACM COMP).

Macmillan, Harold   MACM HARO
    See Letters: Macmillan Company (MACM COMP).

Magee, William Kirkpatrick   MAGE WILL KI
    See also entries in Inscriptions and Other Authors
    under his pseudonym of John Eglinton (EGLI JOHN).

Letters

>One ALS.
>>Kain, Richard M.

>One ALS, one TLS.
>>Southern Illinois University

>One ALS.
>>New York Public Library

>One ALS.
>>Pierpont Morgan Library

Mahaffy, J.P.   MAHA J.P.
>Letters (2075/337-338).
>>Trinity College Dublin

Mair, George   MAIR GEOR
>Two TLS (typed by Pound; ca 1914-16).
>>New York Public Library

Mallarme, Stephane   MALL STEP
>One ALS.
>>Bibliotheque Literaire Jacques Doucet

Mannin, Ethel   MANN ETHE
>Some 50 ALS (March 1935-Dec. 1938).
>>Sligo County Library

Mark, Mr.   MARK MR.
>See Letters: Macmillan Company (MACM COMP).

Markiewicz, Constance   MARK CONS
>Copy of letter (dictated; Ms 31030); AL (4 pp).
>>National Library of Ireland
>>Copy at SUNY SB   Box 57

>One ALS to Miss Gore Booth.
>>Northwestern University Library

>One letter. (Harvard lists as "unidentified correspondent"; note by F.S.L. Lyons says it is to Markewicz; call no. bMS Am 1787 561).
>>Harvard University

>Seven ALS and TLS ([1895-1911]).
>>Harvard University

Marriott, Mr.   MARR MR.
    One ALS.
    Southern Illinois University

Marsh, Edward   MARS EDWA
    Two TLS (1910 and 1912; 8400/235, 236).
    Trinity College Dublin

    Three ALS, one LS ([1917-1923]).
    New York Public Library

Martin, Harvey   MART HARV
    One ALS (27 October 1909).
    University of Delaware Library

Martyn, Edward   MART EDWA
    ALS ([1899]; 4 pp; Ms 13068).
    National Library of Ireland
    Copy at SUNY SB   Box 57

    Autographed, signed postcard (Ms 16703).
    National Library of Ireland

Masefield, Constance   MASE CONS
    Two ALS.
    University of Texas at Austin

Masefield, John   MASE JOHN
    One ALS.
    Colby College Library

    Two letters (MS. Eng. lett. c. 255, fols. 159, 161).
    Bodleian Library

    Two ALS, one dated 7 May [1930].
    Columbia University

    Four TLS (1912-1934).
    University of Vermont

    Eight ALS, one TLS, one telegram (1905-1935).
    University of Texas at Austin

Mathews, Elkin   MATH ELKI
    Six letters (MS 392/1/1).
    University of Reading Library

One ALS (30 Oct, [190?]).
    Connecticut College

One letter ([May 29, 1916]).
    University of California Berkeley

28 ALS (one a copy; 30 Dec [1894]-23 Jan [1914]).
    University of Leeds

One ALS (1916 May 28).
    Yale University

One ALS (Jan 25 [1893]; 7 pp).
    Princeton University Library

One ALS ([1899]).
    State University of New York at Buffalo

29 TL (carbon copies), three ALS, one ACS, one TLS (1894-1914).
    University of Texas at Austin

One ALS (17 Feb, 1898).
    Southern Illinois University

Matthews, Mr.   MATT MR.
    ALS to "My dear Mr. Matthews."
    Wellesley College

Matthews, Seymour Freeman   MATT SEYM FR
    ALS, dated May 1, 1908.
    Kenyon College Library

Maude, Mary   MAUD MARY
    Two ALS, one postmarked Nov 20, 1907.
    Southern Illinois University

Mavor, James   MAVO JAME
    One ALS; one TLS.
    University of Toronto

McCartan, Patrick   MCCA PATR
    One ALS (22 Jan, [1937]).
    Southern Illinois University

    One TLS (28 July 1935); one ALS.
    Case Western Reserve University Library

One ALS.
University of Texas at Austin

Three TLS, four ALS (1933-1937).
Boston University

One ALS.
Northwestern University Library

McCarthy, Lillah MCCA LILL
See Letters: Keeble, Lillah McCarthy (KEEB LILL MC).

McColl, Dugald S. MCCO DUGA S.
One letter (5 Jan, [1917]).
New York Public Library

McDermott, Mary Scudder MCDE MARY SC
One ALS and one ANS.
Wellesley College

McDonagh, Thomas MCDO THOM
Two letters (Ms 10854); photocopies of three letters (Ms 13663).
National Library of Ireland

TLS (May 5 1909; Ms 18474).
National Library of Ireland

McDonald, Mr. MCDO MR.
TLS (10 June 1924).
Pierpont Morgan Library

McElligott, J.J. MCEL J.J.
Copy of letter concerning government control of the Abbey Theatre (1933; Ms 26198).
National Library of Ireland

McGuinness, Norah MCGU NORA
Three ALS.
Sligo County Library

McMahon, Mr. MCMA MR.
One ALS (in Ms Eur. E. 267/70).
India Office Library and Records

Letters

McManus, Mr.   MCMA MR.
   TLS about a letter WBY wanted published (May 13, 1937;
   Ms 10716).
      National Library of Ireland

   TLS, with a reply to Noyes in the IRISH PRESS (Feb 12,
   1937; Ms 5460).
      National Library of Ireland

Meiklejohn, Alexander   MEIK ALEX
   Two letters [1914?].
      Amherst College Library

Meo, Mrs. Craig (Elena)   MEO MRS. CR
   One ALS.
      University of Texas at Austin

Methuen and Co.   METH CO.
   Three ALS, relating to second edition of BOOK IRIS OO.
      New York Public Library

Meynell, Alice   MEYN ALIC
   ANS, pasted in copy of CELT TWIL 05, given by
   W. Meynell to Shane Leslie; note dated 15 Jan. 1905.
      Boston College

Meynell, Wilfred   MEYN WILF
   ALS (July 13 [1916]).
      New York University

   Two ALS.
      University of Texas at Austin

Milligan, Alice   MILL ALIC
   Two ALS.
      University of California Los Angeles

   One AL (23 Sept, [1897]).
      University of Texas at Austin

   One ALS.
      University of Kansas
      Copy at SUNY SB   Box 57

Minchin, Mr.   MINC MR.
   ALS (January 10 1912).
      Northwestern University Library

Monck, Nugent   MONC NUGE
    LS (1 p; Ms 13068).
        National Library of Ireland
        Copy at SUNY SB Box 57

    One ALS (23 June [1912]).
        University of Louisville

Monro, Alida   MONR ALID
    Letters (Add. MS 57752).
        British Library

Monro, Harold   MONR HARO
    Nine ALS, two TLS, one signed card; body of one ALS in hand of George Yeats, two TLS typed by Ezra Pound.
        University of Texas at Austin

Monroe, Harriet   MONR HARR
    Eight TLS, seven ALS, two L, one TL (1913-1932).
        University of Chicago

    One ALS, introducing Lennox Robinson.
        Southern Illinois University

    See also Letters: BROW, for letter to Mr. Browne in care of Harriet Monroe.

Moon, Mrs.   MOON MRS.
    One ALS (Za Gilman).
        Yale University

Mooney, Ria   MOON RIA
    One TLS, dated Aug. 23, 1936.
        New York Public Library

Moore, David F. (Solicitor)   MOOR DAVI F.
    Copy of letter to Dr. Moore, of Whitney and Moore law firm, regarding Horniman dispute (Ms 31010).
        National Library of Ireland
        Copy at SUNY SB Box 59

    One TLS (2 Oct, 1910).
        New York Public Library

Moore, George   MOOR GEOR
    Letters about the Play: DIAR GRAI (Ms 8777).
        National Library of Ireland
        Copy at SUNY SB Box 57

Letters 145

    One ALS.
       New York Public Library

Moore, Isabel   MOOR ISAB
    One TLS (15 Dec 1903).
       Harvard University

Moore, Sturge   MOOR STUR
    Two ALS (10 July [1932-33?] and 25 April [1932?]; in
    Sturge Moore papers, box 2:76-77).
       University of London Library

    85 ALS, 21 TLS, five AL, one post card (1901-1936).
       University of Texas at Austin

    Five ALS (February-April [1932]; Add. MS 45732).
       British Library

    19 letters (Jan 16 [1926]-July 1 [1936]; Ms 31004).
       National Library of Ireland
       Copy at SUNY SB   Box 57

Morel, Auguste   MORE AUGU
    One ALS (Ms 31023).
       National Library of Ireland
       Copy at SUNY SB   Box 57

Morgan, Louise   MORG LOUI
    One ALS, one TLS (14 Dec, 1930-1 May [1931]).
       University of Texas at Austin

Morrell, Lady Ottoline   MORR LADY OT
    One ALS.
       Kenyon College Library

    One ALS (Jan 6 [1922]).
       Pierpont Morgan Library

    One ALS (15 Nov, [1922]).
       Southern Illinois University

    34 ALS, five TLS ([1911]-1937).
       University of Texas at Austin

Morrell, Philip   MORR PHIL
    Two ALS.
       University of Texas at Austin

Morris, May   MORR MAY
    One letter (MS. Top. Oxon. c. 369, fol 54).
        Bodleian Library

    TLS (Oct 30 1930; Add. MS 45348, f. 31); one letter
    (Add. MS 45348, f. 93).
        British Library

    One TLS (1934).
        Colby College Library

Morrison, George E.   MORR GEOR E.
    One TLS.
        University of Texas at Austin

Morton, David   MORT DAVI
    TLS (July 12, 1929).
        Amherst College Library

Mosher, Thomas Bird   MOSH THOM BI
    One TLS (1 Aug 1912).
        Harvard University

Munroe, Miss   MUNR MISS
    One ALS.
        Southern Illinois University

Murphy, Diana   MURP DIAN
    Three letters (Ms 5918).
        National Library of Ireland

    Two ALS.
        Southern Illinois University

Murray, Gilbert   MURR GILB
    Letter dictated to A. Horniman, signed (22 Jan 1903);
    three letters dictated to Lady Gregory, signed (17 March
    1903, 7 April 1903, 21 July 1903); TLS (14 Aug 1903);
    ALS (24 Jan. 1905). (Ms Gilbert Murray 9, 13, 33, 116).
        Bodleian Library

Murray, John   MURR JOHN
    One ALS.
        University of Texas at Austin

Murray, Thomas   MURR THOM
    Two ALS, two TLS (1910).
        New York Public Library

Letters

Myers, Mrs. E.   MYER MRS. E.
    Six letters (Myers 22, 25).
       Trinity College Library (Cambridge)

National Bank   NATI BANK
    Drafts and copies of letters about Cuala Press affairs,
    dated 1937-38 (14 pp; Ms 30904).
       National Library of Ireland
       Copy at SUNY SB

Nationales Editor   NATI EDIT
    One ALS (draft).
       New York Public Library

Needham, Mr.   NEED MR.
    One ALS (6 Nov, 1921).
       Southern Illinois University

Nevinson, [Henry Woodd]   NEVI HENR WO
    One ALS (19 April, 1904).
       Southern Illinois University

    One ALS.
       University of Tulsa

Neylan, John Francis   NEYL JOHN FR
    One letter (Mar 1938).
       University of California Berkeley

Nicoll, William R.   NICO WILL R.
    One ALS (1 Aug [1899]).
       New York Public Library

Noyes, Alfred   NOYE ALFR
    One TLS (Oct 25; Ms 5918).
       National Library of Ireland

O'Brien, Edward Joseph   O'BR EDWA JO
    One TLS (3 Feb 1910).
       Harvard University

    Two ALS (Ms 5918).
       National Library of Ireland

O'Brien, R. Barry   O'BR R.   BA
    One letter (in Archives Dept. LA15/1665).
       University College Dublin

O'Brien, Reverend Henry   O'BR REVE HE
    Seven ALS, LS and TLS (1902-1907).
        Pierpont Morgan Library

O'Brien, [George]   O'BR GEOR
    One TL (Sept 10 1925; 2 pp).
        National Library of Ireland
        Copy at SUNY SB   Box 57

O'Casey, Sean   O'CA SEAN
    One TL copy (20 April, 1928).
        University of Texas at Austin

    One TL, one TLS, one ALS, and two LS (dictated to
    George Yeats).
        New York Public Library

    TMs (draft of copy; 20 April 1928); TL (May 4 1928;
    1 p; Ms 30889).
        National Library of Ireland
        Copy at SUNY SB   Box 57

O'Connell, John   O'CO JOHN
    One TL (1923 Nov 25; Ip.Y34 C895Pch).
        Yale University

    One AL fragment (1908; Ms 1742).
        National Library of Ireland
        Copy at SUNY SB   Box 57

O'Connor, Frank   O'CO FRAN
    Four ALS (1930, 1931, 1937, n.d.).
        Boston University

    Two TL copies (26 April 1932 and 4 November [1936?]; Ms
    31021).
        National Library of Ireland
        Copy at SUNY SB

O'Connor, Miss Moya Llewelyn-Davies   O'CO MISS MO
    15 TL copies (1936-1937).
        University of Texas at Austin

O'Donaghue, Paidh   O'DO PAID
    One ALS (19 May [1888]).
        State University of New York at Buffalo

Letters

O'Donahue   O'DO
    ALS.
       Amherst College Library

O'Donnell, Charles   O'DO CHAR
    One TLS (January 19th, 1933).
       University of Notre Dame

O'Donnell, Frank   O'DO FRAN
    Six ALS, one TLS, one dictated LS, one telegram (1918-1922).
       University of Delaware Library

O'Donoghue, D.J.   O'DO D.J.
    One ALS to an O'Donoghue (note in Berg says it is probably D.J.).
       New York Public Library

    One TLS.
       Kenyon College Library

    Two ALS.
       University of Texas at Austin

    One TLS.
       Southern Illinois University

    One ALS.
       University of California Los Angeles

O'Donovan, Michael   O'DO MICH
    See Letters: O'Connor, Frank (O'CO FRAN).

O'Donovan, [Fred]   O'DO FRED
    Three letters (1919-1932).
       National Library of Ireland
       Copy at SUNY SB   Box 57

O'Faolain, Sean   O'FA SEAN
    Two ALS.
       University of Tulsa

    One letter.
       University of California Berkeley

    Copies of two ALS.
       National Library of Ireland
       COPY at SUNY SB   Box 57

O'Grady, Standish   O'GR STAN
    One ALS.
       University of Kansas
       Copy at SUNY SB   Box 57

O'Hegarty, Patrick   O'HE PATR
    Three ALS, one TLS, one LS (dictated).
       University of Kansas
       Copy at SUNY SB   Box 57

O'Higgins, Mrs. Kevin   O'HI MRS. KE
    AMs; draft (12 July [1927]; Ms 31041).
       National Library of Ireland
       Copy at SUNY SB   Box 57

O'Leary, Ellen   O'LE ELLE
    One ALS.
       Harvard University

    One ALS (3 Feb, [1889]).
       New York Public Library

O'Leary, John   O'LE JOHN
    Ten ALS (1888-1896).
       New York Public Library

    Two ALS (1889).
       University of Texas at Austin

    Two TL ([1889]).
       Harvard University

    ALS (January 21 [1891]).
       University of Delaware Library

    45 letters, mostly ALS (Ms 5918, 5925); TMs copies of two letters (July 12 1887, Oct 25 [1903]; Ms 30577).
       National Library of Ireland
       Copy at SUNY SB   Box 57

    57 ALS (1884-1889); TLS, with corrections (Oct. 25, 1903; Ms 5925).
       National Library of Ireland

    Two TL copies (1889; Ms 5918).
       National Library of Ireland

Letters

O'Neill, Maire   O'NE MAIR
    Two ALS, two TLS (1909-1911).
        University of Texas at Austin

O'Riordan, Conal   O'RI CONA
    See Letters: Connell, Norreys (CONN NORR).

O'Sullivan, Seumas   O'SU SEUM
    Form letter about the Irish Academy of Letters, signed
    by G.B. Shaw and WBY (Ms 15566).
        National Library of Ireland

    Three letters, two dated 1903 and 1904 (4630-49/42, 55,
    4325).
        Trinity College Dublin

Ormerod, Mr.   ORME MR.
    Two TLS (1910-1911).
        The Huntington Library

Orpen, R.C.   ORPE R.C.
    Three letters (Ms 31031).
        National Library of Ireland
        Copy at SUNY SB   Box 57

Owen, Mary   OWEN MARY
    One ALS (1903 May 9; Osborn files).
        Yale University

Owlett, F.C.   OWLE F.C.
    One telegram (1931; MS. Eng. misc. d. 895, fol. 51).
        Bodleian Library

Oxford University   OXFO UNIV
    Copy of TL (Feb 21 1931; 1 p; Ms 31007).
        National Library of Ireland
        Copy at SUNY SB   Box 57

Oxford University Press   OXFO UNIV PR
    One letter.
        Princeton University Library

PEN   PEN
    Four TLS, three ALS, one telegram (1922-1933).
        University of Texas at Austin

Palmer, Herbert E.   PALM HERB E.
    One ALS (9 Aug [1922]).
        University of Delaware Library

    TL (Ms 5918).
        National Library of Ireland

    One ALS (10 Sept, [1922]).
        Southern Illinois University

    One ALS.
        New York University

Palmstierna, Baron   PALM BARO
    One ALS (3 June, [1933]).
        State University of New York at Buffalo

Parkhill, D.   PARK D.
    One TLS (18 May 1904).
        Harvard University

Payen-Payne, James B. de Vincheles   PAYE JAME B.
    ALS, in which WBY had enclosed a copy of OIL BLOO,
    noting that it illustrated the spirit of the nineties,
    dated June 23 [1928?].
        University of Toronto

Payne, Leonidas W.   PAYN LEON W.
    Two ALS, one TLS.
        University of Texas at Austin

Payne, [Iden]   PAYN IDEN
    One TLS (13 Apr 1910).
        Harvard University

Peters, Mr.   PETE MR.
    One TLS (8 Jan, 1913).
        Wesleyan University

Phelps, William Lyon   PHEL WILL LY
    One ALS (Feb 12 1920; Za Phelps).
        Yale University

Plomer, William C.F.   PLOM WILL C.
    One letter.
        Indiana University

Letters

Plunkett, Count PLUN COUN
    ALS (2 pp; Ms 5918).
        National Library of Ireland

Plunkett, Horace Curzon PLUN HORA CU
    Letters (1899-1931).
        Plunkett Foundation for Co-operative Studies

    ALS (3 pp).
        National Library of Ireland
        Copy at SUNY SB   Box 57

    Two ALS, one TL draft with corrections (Ms 31005).
        National Library of Ireland
        Copy at SUNY SB   Box 57

Poel, William POEL WILL
    One LS (1 p; Ms 13068).
        National Library of Ireland
        Copy at SUNY SB   Box 57

    One TLS with autograph note (May 7, 1909).
        University of Kansas

    One TL copy.
        University of Texas at Austin

Pollexfen, George POLL GEOR
    One ALS ([1905]; 4 pp).
        Yeats, Senator Michael
        Copy at SUNY SB   Box 57

Pollock, Dr. POLL DR.
    Two ALS; one TLS (July 25, 1934).
        Southern Illinois University

Pond, James POND JAME
    Five ALS, five LS, one TLS (1912-1923).
        Southern Illinois University

Porter, Mr. PORT MR.
    One ALS.
        Pennsylvania State University Library

Pound, Dorothy POUN DORO
    One letter (12 July, 1918).
        Indiana University

Pound, Ezra   POUN EZRA
    11 letters (10 dated, 1914-1926).
        Indiana University

    One ALS (25 Mar, 1913).
        Hamilton College Library

    One ALS.
        University of Chicago

    One ALS (11 Feb, [1917]).
        Cornell University

    One ALS (1919 Jul 15); two other letters, one dated
    May [1909], another 22 August [1920] (MS Vault;
    Joyce; Box 4; Folder 21).
        Yale University

Power   POWE
    TL (June 20, 1935; Ms 5918).
        National Library of Ireland

Prokosch, Frederick   PROK FRED
    One ALS (15 July 1935), one TLS (25 Nov, 1935).
        University of Texas at Austin

Purohit, Shri Swami   PURO SHRI SW
    53 ALS, seven TLS, three TL, one ANS, one AL, one
    telegram (1931-1938).
        University of Delaware Library

    ALS and TMs copy of two letters (one dated 23 August
    1937; Ms 31019).
        National Library of Ireland
        Copy at SUNY SB Box 57

Purser, Sarah   PURS SARA
    10 ALS, TLS, one ALS note (1899-1935; Ms 10201).
        National Library of Ireland

Purves, John   PURV JOHN
    Two ALS (in Acc. 7175 no. 2).
        National Library of Scotland

Pyper, J.S.   PYPE J.S.
    Photocopies of three letters and a telegram (in
    RP1018).
        British Library

Letters

Quinn, John   QUIN JOHN
    Five ALS (7 pp; Ms 5918).
        National Library of Ireland

    61 ALS, 46 TLS, 16 LS (dictated), 11 telegrams
    (1901-24; in Rare Books and Ms).
        New York Public Library

Quinn, Joseph   QUIN JOSE
    One ALS (9 February [1894?]; Ms 31028).
        National Library of Ireland
        Copy at SUNY SB   Box 57

Radin, Herman   RADI HERM
    One ALS (12 Feb [1924]).
        University of Delaware Library

Rae, J.A.   RAE J.A.
    One TLS (1923; Ms 18476).
        National Library of Ireland

Raferty, Mr.   RAFE MR.
    Three letters, one an ALS (July 9 1921).
        National Library of Ireland
        Copy at SUNY SB

Raffalovich, Marc-Andre   RAFF MARC AN
    One letter (Acc. 8035).
        National Library of Scotland

Ratcliffe, Dorothy Una   RATC DORO UN
    Two ALS (20 Aug. 1927 and 22 April 1928).
        University of Leeds

Rattray, R.F.   RATT R.F.
    Two ALS.
        University of Texas at Austin

Rawley, Mr.   RAWL MR.
    One ALS.
        Southern Illinois University

Ray, Mr.   RAY MR.
    Two TLS (1 Aug 1912 and 21 Nov 1912).
        University of Texas at Austin

    Three letters.
        Princeton University Library

Read, Herbert   READ HERB
    TLS (1936).
        University of Victoria

Reardon   REAR
    One ALS (8 April, 1904), body in hand of A. Horniman.
        University of Texas at Austin

Redman, Miss   REDM MISS
    One ALS
        University of Texas at Austin

Redmond, John   REDM JOHN
    One letter ([1898]; Ms 15234).
        National Library of Ireland

Rees, J. Rogers   REES J.   RO
    One ALS, about a lecture, possibly to Rees (Feb 5 [1903]).
        Wellesley College

Rees, Mrs.   REES MRS.
    ALS (April 16 [1903]).
        Wellesley College

Reith, Lord   REIT LORD
    One letter (1936; in BBC Written Archives, Special Collections S/60/6).
        Reading University

Reynolds, Horace Mason   REYN HORA MA
    One TLS, two ALS, one ANS (24 Dec, 1932-9 June [1933]).
        Harvard University

Rhys, Ernest   RHYS ERNE
    Ten ALS, one TLS, one LS (dictated).
        University of Kansas
        Copy at SUNY SB   Box 57

    Seven ALS, one dated Dec. 1981; two TLS, dated 11 Nov. 1905 and 21 Dec. 1906 (Eg 3248, ff 92-108).
        British Library

    One ALS (19 November 1890).
        University of Delaware Library

Letters

Rhys, Grace RHYS GRAC
    Copy of letter (Ms 30578).
        National Library of Ireland
        Copy at SUNY SB Box 57

Richards, Grant RICH GRAN
    One ALS.
        University of Texas at Austin

Ricketts, Charles RICK CHAR
    Three letters ([1904-1922]; Add. Ms 58090, ff. 41, 125; 58091, ff. 189-192).
        British Library

    Letters (MS. Walpole d. 19, fol 129).
        Bodleian Library

Riding, Laura RIDI LAUR
    One ALS (23 May [1936]).
        University of Delaware Library

    Three ALS.
        University of Texas at Austin

Roberts, Arthur Llewelyn ROBE ARTH LL
    Two ALS (29 July 1915 and 4 August 1915).
        The Royal Literary Fund

Roberts, George ROBE GEOR
    17 TLS and ALS (1903-1911).
        Harvard University

    One letter, dictated (Ms 21946 [xiii]).
        National Library of Ireland

    LS (dictated; 7 pp; Ms 21946).
        National Library of Ireland

Roberts, Michael ROBE MICH
    One TLS (Nov 12 '35).
        New York Public Library

Robertson, Walford ROBE WALF
    Three letters (1904-1913).
        The Huntington Library

Robins, Elizabeth   ROBI ELIZ
    ALS (January 5, 1920).
        New York University

Robinson, Corinne (Roosevelt)   ROBI CORI
    Two TLS, one ALS (16 Dec, 30 Dec 1932; [11 Dec 1932]).
        Harvard University

Robinson, Lennox   ROBI LENN
    One ALS (11 Nov, [1921]).
        University of Texas at Austin

    One letter.
        Indiana University

    83 ALS, 16 TLS (1913-1930).
        Southern Illinois University

    Two TL, one L (1929-1931).
        New York Public Library

    Four ALS, one LS (dictated to George Yeats), three TLS,
    with corrections (1914-1931).
        Meisei University

Rolleston, [Thomas William]   ROLL THOM WI
    One ALS.
        Harvard University

Rossi, Mario   ROSS MARI
    One AL.
        University of Texas at Austin

    One ALS.
        Kenyon College Library

Rothenstein, William   ROTH WILL
    61 TL (1902-1939; Ms 5918).
        National Library of Ireland

    64 ALS and TLS.
        Harvard University

Royal Irish Academy   ROYA IRIS AC
    TL draft; copies of two letters (27 July 1926 and
    27 November 1927; Ms 31006).
        National Library of Ireland
        Copy at SUNY SB Box 57

TL copy about the setting up of a Literary Institute
(3 pp; Ms 31070).
   National Library of Ireland
   Copy at SUNY SB   Box 57

Ruffort, Walter   RUFF WALT
   One ALS (29 July, [1917]).
   University of Texas at Austin

Rummel, Walter Morse   RUMM WALT MO
   One ALS.
   University of Texas at Austin

Russell, Father Matthew   RUSS FATH MA
   Nine ALS ([1888-189-]).
   Archivae Provincia Hibernia

Russell, George   RUSS GEOR
   One ALS.
   Northwestern University Library

   51 letters (1899-1932).
   Indiana University

   Two ANS.
   Stanford University

   One ALS.
   University of Tulsa

   One ALS ([1904]).
   Harvard University

   45 TL (copies; 1891-1932).
   University of Texas at Austin

   Two ALS, one dated 1932.
   Colby College Library

   One ALS.
   Wake Forest University Library

   Two TL (April 1919 and April 26 1932); four ALS; three
   TLS (17 Oct. 1932, 21 Dec. 1932, and 5 Nov. 1933; Ms
   27887).
      National Library of Ireland

TL; purple type, probably copies, of 46 letters, with
typed signatures (1889-1932; Ms 15600).
    National Library of Ireland
    Copy at SUNY SB   Box 57

Ryan, Mr.   RYAN MR.
   Short T note.
      Belfast City Libraries

Salt, Dr.   SALT DR.
   One ALS.
      University of Kansas
      Copy at SUNY SB   Box 58

Sassoon, Siegfried   SASS SIEG
   One ALS (1925).
      Colby College Library

Schepeler, Alexandria   SCHE ALEX
   22 ALS (1914-1917).
      The Huntington Library

Schroeder, [William Lawrence]   SCHR WILL LA
   TLS (7 May 1909).
      Harvard University

Scott, C.P.   SCOT C.P.
   Four letters (in C.P. Scott correspondence).
      John Rylands University Library

Scott-James, Rolfe (Editor, London Mercury)   SCOT ROLF
   Nine TLS, eight ALS, two telegrams (1934-1939).
      University of Texas at Austin

Scribner   SCRI
   One ALS.
      University of Texas at Austin

      Letters. See Books: UNPU SCRI ED.
      Princeton University

Scroope, Mr.   SCRO MR.
   Five letters (Ms 30573).
      National Library of Ireland
      Copy at SUNY SB

   AL (Jan 2, 1918; Ms 30904).
      National Library of Ireland
      Copy at SUNY SB

Letters

Sealy, Bryers, and Walker   SEAL BRYE WA
   Two ALS ([1904]), to Mr. Bryers of the firm Sealy,
   Bryers, and Walker.
      New York Public Library

Secretary of Royal Society   SECR ROYA SO
   Five ALS, three TLS (1911, 1913 and 1931).
      Royal Society of Literature

Settle, Miss   SETT MISS
   One LS (dictated).
      University of Kansas
      Copy at SUNY SB   Box 58

Shahan, Thomas   SHAH THOM
   TLS (March 8, 1904).
      The Catholic University of America

Shakespear, Olivia   SHAK OLIV
   One ALS (12 Oct, [1937]).
      University of Texas at Austin

   122 letters (Aug 6 [1894]-Sept 17 [1936]). AMs drafts
   of poems enclosed in some letters. See Poems: AMON
   SCHO CH, EMPT CUP, FIRS LOVE, and FROM OEDI CO
   (Partial List...#673).
      Yeats, Senator Michael
      Copy at SUNY SB   Box 58, 59

   Three letters (1900-1938).
      Indiana University

Shakespeare Memorial   SHAK MEMO
   Copy of TL (Feb 4 1910; 2 pp; Ms 31008).
      National Library of Ireland
      Copy at SUNY SB   Box 59

Shannon, Charles   SHAN CHAR
   Two letters ([1908]-1924; Add. MS 58090, ff. 86-87;
   58091, ff. 202-203).
      British Library

   One ALS.
      University of California Los Angeles

   AL about DIAR GRAN (29 August 1913).
      University of Texas at Austin

Sharp, William   SHAR WILL
    One letter (MS. 15941, fols. 149-152).
    National Library of Scotland

Shaw-Taylor, John   SHAW TAYL JO
    TL (Aug 18 1908; 3 pp).
    National Library of Ireland
    Copy at SUNY SB Box 59

Shaw, Charlotte   SHAW CHAR
    Two ALS.
    University of Texas at Austin

Shaw, George B.   SHAW GEOR B.
    One ALS (2 May 1905).
    University of Texas at Austin

    Seven ALS; three TLS, two dated 26 April 1932 and 15
    Sept 1932 (Add. MS 50554, ff. 142-167).
    British Library

    Letters and copies (Ms 31052, 31020).
    National Library of Ireland
    Copy at SUNY SB Box 59

Shaw, T.E.   SHAW T.E.
    AMs; draft with corrections of invitation for
    membership in Irish Auxiliary of Letters, addressed to
    Air Craftsman T.E. Shaw (T.E. Lawrence; Ms 31015).
    National Library of Ireland
    Copy at SUNY SB

Sheil, Frank J.   SHEI FRAN J.
    One TLS (1923 Dec 3; Za Clark Clark).
    Yale University

Sherman, Philip   SHER PHIL
    Four ALS, two ANS (1884-1915).
    Brown University

Sherrard, Mr.   SHER MR.
    One ALS (Sept 29, 1905).
    New York University

Letters

Shine, Mrs.   SHIN MRS.
    Two ALS ([13 Jan. 1913] and Oct. 8 [1913]; Ms
    27743[3]); five ALS and one TLS, postmarked 4 Feb.
    1915-4 May 1916 (Ms 27743[4]).
        National Library of Ireland

Shiubhaligh, Maire   SHIU MAIR
    See Letters: Walker, Mary (WALK MARY).

Shorter, Clement   SHOR CLEM
    Letters (1899-1918 and undated; Add. MS 63596; Ashely
    Ms 2283, 2284, 2285, 2287, 2288, A. 4677, B. 5658,
    5750).
        British Library

    Two ALS (29 June and 29 Jan [1918]).
        University of Texas at Austin

    Three ALS (in Shorter Correspondence).
        University of Leeds

    24 ALS, one LS ([1897-1919]).
        New York Public Library

    Letters (MS. 9864, fols. 161-162).
        National Library of Scotland

Shorter, Mrs. Dora   SHOR MRS. DO
    Letters (1896 and undated; Ashley Ms 2284, 2288, A.
    4678).
        British Library

    Two ALS.
        New York Public Library

Siberry, Charles E.   SIBE CHAR E.
    LS (dictated; June 19, 1925).
        Sligo County Library

Sidgewick, Frank   SIDG FRAN
    One ALS, one TLS.
        University of Texas at Austin

Sigerson, George   SIGE GEOR
    Two ALS (Ms 31025).
        National Library of Ireland
        Copy at SUNY SB   Box 59

LS (1 p; Ms 13068).
    National Library of Ireland
    Copy at SUNY SB

Simpson, Dr. Robert   SIMP DR. RO
    TL copy (April 3, 1924; 3 pp; Ms 30582).
    National Library of Ireland
    Copy at SUNY SB   Box 59

Simson, Theodore   SIMS THEO
    See Letters: Spicer-Simson, Theodore (SPIC SIMS TH).

Sinclair, Mr.   SINC MR.
    One ALS.
        University of California Los Angeles

Sir John   SIR JOHN
    One TLS (Oct 5 1918).
    National Library of Ireland
    Copy at SUNY SB   Box 59

Sitwell, Dame Edith   SITW DAME ED
    One TLS (13 Dec, 1936).
        University of Texas at Austin

Smith   SMIT
    One ALS.
        University of Texas at Austin

Smith, Mrs. Travers   SMIT MRS. TR
    One ALS.
        Harvard University

    One ALS.
        Southern Illinois University

Smith, T.R.   SMIT T.R.
    One ALS (1915).
        Colby College Library

Solomons, Dr. B.   SOLO DR. B.
    Four ALS (ca 1920; WBY I:67).
        Emory University

Sparling, Henry H.   SPAR HENR H.
    One ALS.
        Brown University

Letters   165

Speyer, Edward   SPEY EDWA
    One letter (1917; Add. MS 46716, f. 23).
        British Library

Spicer-Simson, Theodore   SPIC SIMS TH
    Two letters (August 8, 1922 and November 15, 1922).
        Princeton University Library

    Two ALS (10 May 1922 and 11 October 1923).
        Southern Illinois University

Squire, John   SQUI JOHN
    13 ALS (1920-1922).
        University of Texas at Austin

    One ANS, seven ALS, and one TLS (ca 1914-28; Uncat MS
    Vault File).
        Yale University

St. Lawrence, Mrs.   ST. LAWR MR
    Photostat of a TLS.
        University of Kansas

Starkey, James   STAR JAME
    Three ALS, one TLS.
        University of Texas at Austin

    Two letters (1926-1930).
        Indiana University

Stead, W.F.   STEA W.F.
    One ALS, dated Sept 26, to "Dear Father Stead," about
    the symbol in WBY's ring.
        Martin, Walter

    21 letters, 18 of them ALS (1921-1939; Osborn Shelves:
    Stead Boxes).
        Yale University

Stephens, A.G.   STEP A.G.
    One ALS (3 Sept. 1899).
        State Library of New South Wales

Stephens, James   STEP JAME
    One ALS.
        New York Public Library

Two ALS.
Harvard University

One ALS.
University of California Los Angeles

Steven, [Hilda A.] STEV HILD A.
    One ALS (February 17, 1926).
        State Library of Victoria

Stokes, Margaret STOK MARG
    AL fragment.
        National Library of Ireland
        Copy at SUNY SB   Box 59

Stone, Melville STON MELV
    Invitation to Chicago Journalist Melville Stone to
    visit Ireland in Aug. 1924, signed by WBY as Chairman
    of a Distinguished Visitors Committee.
        Newberry Library

Stone, Miss STON MISS
    One TLS (19 Jan, 1907).
        University of Texas at Austin

Strong, L.A.G. STRO L.A.
    14 ALS, five TLS, one invitation (1919-1937).
        University of Texas at Austin

Stuart, Frances STUA FRAN
    Two ALS, one TLS.
        University of Texas at Austin

    Two ALS, one LS (dictated).
        University of Kansas
        Copy at SUNY SB   Box 59

Stuart, Iseult STUA ISEU
    See Letters: Gonne, Iseult (Stuart) (GONN ISEU).

Stuart, Mr. STUA MR.
    One ALS (October [1897]).
        Southern Illinois University

Sturm, Frank Pearce STUR FRAN PE
    One TLS.
        University of Illinois at Urbana

Letters

    22 letters (Mar 26 1916-Jan 21 1938).
    National Library of Ireland
    Copy at SUNY SB   Box 59

Sutherland, Duchess   SUTH DUCH
   One ALS.
      Princeton University Library

      Four ALS (1903-1904).
      University of California Los Angeles

Swanton, F.C.J.   SWAN F.C.
   One letter (2 Apr. 1934; Ms 23312).
     National Library of Ireland

Symons, Arthur   SYMO ARTH
   Two letters.
     Princeton University Library

   Two TLS, one ALS (1905-1915).
     University of Texas at Austin

   One ALS ([7 Nov, 1901]).
     New York Public Library

Synge, John   SYNG JOHN
   More than 50 ALS and TLS (Ms 4424-4426).
     Trinity College Dublin

   TLS ([1906]; 4 pp; Ms 1036).
     National Library of Ireland
     Copy at SUNY SB   Box 59

Tagore, Rabindranath   TAGO RABI
   One ALS ([1912]).
     Harvard University

   Letters (Ms 5918).
     National Library of Ireland

Thayer, Scofield   THAY SCOF
   One ALS, one TLS (ca 1924; Za Dial Thayer).
     Yale University

Thompson, Mr.   THOM MR.
   One ALS (27 March 1922).
     University of Delaware Library

Thorpe, Mr.   THOR MR.
    One ALS, regretting WBY's inability to attend a
    birthday celebration for Sir Samuel Ferguson.
        Kain, Richard M.

Thring, Herbert   THRI HERB
    One TLS (March 19, 1912).
        New York University

    Two TL (copies, with corrections; June 1928; Ms 30897).
        National Library of Ireland
        Copy at SUNY SB   Box 59

    Nine ALS, one dated 30 Feb. 1910; two cards, signed
    (Add. MS 56851).
        British Library

Times Editor   TIME EDIT
    One TL (11 Dec, 1916).
        New York Public Library

    AMs draft and typed copy of letter about the burning of
    dwellings in Andrahan (2 pp; Ms 31080).
        National Library of Ireland
        Copy at SUNY SB

Torrence, Ridgeley   TORR RIDG
    One letter (October 7 [1920]).
        Princeton University Library

Travers-Smith, Dorothy   TRAV SMIT DO
    One ALS.
        Meisei University

Trevelyan, R.C.   TREV R.C.
    One ALS (RCT 17).
        Trinity College Library (Cambridge)

Turner, W.J.   TURN W.J.
    14 letters (1935?-1937?).
        National Library of Ireland
        Copy at SUNY SB   BOX 54

University of Cairo   UNIV CAIR
    TLS to English Department recommending W.F. Stead for a
    Professorship (Osborn Shelves; Stead Boxes).
        Yale University

Unknown Correspondent   UNKN CORR
    Two ALS ([191?]).
        State University of New York at Buffalo

    One LS (1903; In CUR.L.3).
        University College Dublin

    ALS (dictated), dated February 28 1903.
        University College Dublin

    One ALS.
        Stanford University

    One ALS about sending copy for the Spenser selections
    (1 p; Ms 13068).
        National Library of Ireland
        Copy at SUNY SB   Box 56

    Two letters, one about being away for two weeks,
    another about a quarrel with Count Markievicz (Ms
    31009, 31011).
        National Library of Ireland
        Copy at SUNY SB   Box 56

    MS copy of letter about Warrior's Day and veterans from
    France and Italy (2 pp; Ms 30890).
        National Library of Ireland
        Copy at SUNY SB   Box 56

    AL; draft beginning "Sir" with reference to the Lane
    controversy (Ms 30068).
        National Library of Ireland
        Copy at SUNY SB   Box 56

    AL about papers for Ballylee Castle, dated March 9
    [1917?] (1 p, incomplete; Ms 13068).
        National Library of Ireland
        Copy at SUNY SB   Box 56

    ALS about a work, 'Soul Shadows,' evidently sent to WBY
    (1 p; Ms 30374).
        National Library of Ireland
        Copy at SUNY SB   Box 56

    AMs about a copy of a corrected speech, dated August
    15, 1926 (Ms 5918).
        National Library of Ireland

TLS to a "Dear Madam" expressing his regret that he
cannot attend a Centenary Celebration (Ms 26752).
    National Library of Ireland

TLS, about a poem on Roger Casement, dated January 29,
1937 (1 p; Ms 5460).
    National Library of Ireland

ALS to "Dear Madam," with references to symbolism,
illustrations, and the Ellis and Yeats edition of Blake.
    University of Tulsa

Letter inscribed in front of HOUR GLAS 04, dated August
31, 1920.
    University of Reading Library

Dictated letter inscribed in front of HOUR GLAS 04,
dated August 31, 1920.
    University of Reading Library

Letter (1923; Ms 1142); TLS (1936; Jonathan Cape
General files).
    University of Reading Library

Letter in WAND OISI 89 (Walpole e. 831).
    Bodleian Library

Letter from W B Yeats as sponsor (in case file 2990).
    The Royal Literary Fund

Three ALS, one LS (1902-1921).
    Southern Illinois University

One letter (December 1, 1922).
    Princeton University Library

One TLS (7 Jan, 1908).
    Cornell University

One TLS, one ALS, and one AL (draft) to an (unknown)
editor.
    New York Public Library

One ALS.
    University of California Los Angeles

Letter beginning "Dear Sir" on Abbey Theatre
Stationery, sending an autograph as requested.
    Harvard University

ALS to a bookseller, ordering two books: CHALDEAN
ASTROLOGY and ESSAYS ON PSYCHIC RESEARCH.
    Harvard University

A form letter, dated February 1937, regarding changes
in the constitution of the Irish Academy of letters,
signed by WBY as President.
    Harvard University

ALS from Gort, Galway, dated 12 Sep [1913?], regarding
earlier editions of PLAYS FOR AN IRISH THEATRE.
    Harvard University

One letter to "Dear Madam."
    University of Leeds

One ANS.
    Brown University

Letter, signed by WBY but not in his hand, with a
list of Schuyler Jackson's library (MS Vault File).
    Yale University

One ALS to a Mrs. Mc[?] (dated Aug. 29 [1928]); two ALS
to an (unknown) printer; one TLS fragment (1905?).
    New York Public Library

ALS; TLS, dated June 8 1910.
    Kenyon College Library

Four letters: three to "Dear Sir," one TLS, dated 10,
1921, others ALS; one TLS to "Dear Madam," dated
December 20, 1902.
    Southern Illinois University

Two ALS; one discussing an essay WBY is returning
and mentioning poor eyesight; the other about his
bookplate.
    McGill University

One ALS to unknown bookstore.
    University of Victoria

One ALS fragment (MS Vault Uncat File).
    Yale University

One TLS and four ALS.
    New York University

One ANS.
    University of California Los Angeles

One ALS.
    Mills College Library

One ALS.
    Northwestern University Library

One ALS; one TLS.
    Pennsylvania State University Library

One letter (20 Dec, 1902). May or may not be WBY's signature.
    Southern Illinois University

Nine ALS: one requesting a copy of two books on the occult; another, a copy of "Simpliccimus"; one about some letters; one mentioning Kathleen; one mentioning Goodman, A.P. Watt, and "The Hour Glass"; one about a publisher; one about a returning a play; one about proof sheets for IN SEVE WOOD; one TNS (July 30 1904); two TLS about a lecture tour and THRE SONG SA; and one ANS listing materials and instructions for two plays.
    University of Texas at Austin

Unwin, Jane Cobden   UNWI JANE CO
    One letter (in Cobden papers 972).
    West Sussex Record Office

Unwin, T. Fisher   UNWI T.   FI
    ALS and ALS draft ([1892-93]; Ms 31024).
    National Library of Ireland
    Copy at SUNY SB   Box 59

    Two unsigned drafts of a letter inserted in copy of COLL WORK 08 (item 2325).
        Yeats, Anne

    63 ALS, one signed post card (1892-1901).
        University of Texas at Austin

Letters

Ussher, Arland USSH ARLA
 One ALS, one TLS.
  University of Kansas
  Copy at SUNY SB Box 59

Vaughan VAUG
 LS objecting to the inclusion of the play HOUR GLAS in a program; another LS (Ms 13068).
  National Library of Ireland
  Copy at SUNY SB Box 59

Vernandulaynstett VERN
 ALS and TLS (1910; Ms 31032).
  National Library of Ireland
  Copy at SUNY SB Box 59

Wade, Allan WADE ALLA
 24 copies of letters (June 12 1902-Feb 13 1922; Ms 30560).
  National Library of Ireland
  Copy at SUNY SB Box 59

 30 letters (1902-1922).
  Indiana University

Waggett, Mr. [E.S.] WAGG MR. E.
 TL (April 3, 1924; Ms 30582).
  National Library of Ireland
  Copy at SUNY SB Box 59

Wagstaff, W.H. WAGS W.H.
 TL (Feb 21 1931).
  National Library of Ireland
  Copy at SUNY SB Box 59

Waithman, Miss WAIT MISS
 One ALS.
  Kenyon College Library

Walker, Emery WALK EMER
 Five ALS, one TLS (1907).
  Bucknell University

 Four ANS, three ALS, one signed post card (1913-1916).
  University of California Los Angeles

 One ALS (1919; Add. Ms 54316-54317).
  British Library

One ALS (29 Sept, 1923).
   Brown University

Walker, Mary   WALK MARY
   One AL fragment, ca 1906, to Maire Nic Shiubhlaigh.
      Yeats, Senator Michael
      Copy at SUNY SB   Box 59

   One ALS, to Marie Shiebhlaigh.
      Northwestern University Library

   One TL (23 Dec, [1905]).
      New York Public Library

Walkley, A.B.   WALK A.B.
   One TLS.
      University of Kansas

Ward, James   WARD JAME
   One ALS.
      Bucknell University

Watkins, Vernon   WATK VERN
   Three letters, dated March 19, June 2 and Oct 23, 1938.
      Southern Illinois University

   Letters (Ms 5918).
      National Library of Ireland

Watson, Lady   WATS LADY
   Two TLS (dictated to George Yeats; 1935).
      Wake Forest University Library

Watt, A.P.   WATT A.P.
   Typed draft, with corrections (Ms 31018).
      National Library of Ireland
      Copy at SUNY SB   Box 59

   Six ALS, two TLS, 2 LS (1918-24?).
      New York Public Library

Watt, Mr.   WATT MR.
   See Letters: Macmillan Company (MACM COMP).

Weber, William   WEBE WILL
   One ALS (12 May [1914]).
      University of California San Diego

Wellesley, Dorothy   WELL DORO
    AL fragment ([July 2 1936]), with corrections in WBY's
    hand of her poem, "The Lady, The Squire, and the
    Serving Man."
         National Library of Ireland
         Copy at SUNY SB   Box 59

    Seven ALS, one TLS (1936-1938).
         University of Texas at Austin

    122 letters, mostly ALS, including the originals of
    those published in LETTERS ON POETRY...TO DOROTHY
    WELLESLEY, with unpublished parts; some with drafts of
    poems enclosed, including LONG LEGG FL, POLI, SPUR,
    STAT UES, and UNDE BEN BU (1935-1938).
         Meisei University

Wells, James R.   WELL JAME R.
    One TLS (1927 Sep 16), and one ALS (MS Vault File).
         Yale University

Wetherell, J.E.   WETH J.E.
    ALS, dated Feb 18, 1921, suggesting poems to be
    selected.
         University of Toronto

Wharton, Mrs.   WHAR MRS.
    One ANS (August 20 [1915]; Za).
         Yale University

Whelan   WHEL
    One ALS, dated Sept 26, inserted in copy of TOWE 26.
         University of Texas at Austin

    Three ALS.
         University of Kansas

White, Elizabeth   WHIT ELIZ
    One letter (30 Jan. 1899; 3777/132).
         Trinity College Dublin

White, H.O.   WHIT H.O.
    Six letters (MS 3777/132-137).
         Trinity College Dublin

Wilkinson, Marguerit   WILK MARG
    Two ALS.
        Northwestern University Library

Williamson, George   WILL GEOR
    TL copy (Dec 22 [1920]; Ms 30566).
        National Library of Ireland
        Copy at SUNY SB   Box 59

    Two letters (Nov 10, 1920 and Dec 22, 1920).
        Princeton University Library

Wilson, David   WILS DAVI
    Seven ALS (ca 1917).
        Wake Forest University Library

Wilson, John Gideon   WILS JOHN GI
    Two ANS [193?].
        Boston Public Library

Wilson, Mr.   WILS MR.
    LS mentioning Lady Gregory and payments (Ms 13068).
        National Library of Ireland
        Copy at SUNY SB   Box 59

    One TLS (June 26, 1935).
        New York University

    One TLS (Jan 2 1934).
        University of Tulsa

Wilson, Mrs.   WILS MRS.
    Two ALS.
        Southern Illinois University

Wilson, Rathmell   WILS RATH
    One ALS [17 June 1911].
        University of Texas at Austin

Wingfield, Sheila   WING SHEI
    One TS (10 Sept. 1938); three AMs (Oct. 2 [1938], Nov.
    21, [1938], and Nov. 24 [1938]).
        National Library of Ireland
        Copy at SUNY SB   Box 59

Withers, Percy   WITH PERC
    Letters (PW Misc).
        Somerville College Library

Letters

Wolfe, Humbert   WOLF HUMB
    One TLS (March 31, 1927).
        New York Public Library

Wollman, Maurice   WOLL MAUR
    One TLS (23 Sept, 1935).
        State University of New York at Buffalo

Wood, Mrs.   WOOD MRS.
    Two ALS ([1930 and 1934]).
        Wellesley College

Wright, Mr.   WRIG MR.
    Two TLS (July 12, 1912 and September 29, 1912).
        New York University

Wright, Mrs.   WRIG MRS.
    Four ALS.
        University of Texas at Austin

Yeats, Anne   YEAT ANNE
    One ALS (Partial List...#892).
        Yeats, Senator Michael
        Copy at SUNY SB   Box 59

    Three ALS, one dated April 6 [1938].
        National Library of Ireland
        Copy at SUNY SB   Box 59

    Signed postcard, referring to recent return from N.Y.
    (Dec. 27; Ms 10751).
        National Library of Ireland

Yeats, Elizabeth   YEAT ELIZ
    One letter (1 May, 1916).
        Princeton University Library

    62 TLS and ALS (1913-1938; Partial List...#1089).
        Yeats, Senator Michael
        Copy at SUNY SB   Box 59, 60

    One TLS.
        Bucknell University

    One ALS.
        Brown University

One ALS.
New York Public Library

Yeats, George   YEAT GEOR
440 letters (Oct 3 [1917]-Nov 1 [1938]), including one
with a change in the text of VACI (Partial List...
#1012).
    Yeats, Senator Michael
    Copy at SUNY SB   Box 58, 59, 60

Yeats, John Butler   YEAT JOHN BU
Two ALS, one TMs (copy) (Rare Books and Ms).
New York Public Library

63 ALS and TLS (Partial List...#1084).
    Yeats, Senator Michael
    Copy at SUNY SB   Box 60, 61

One AL excerpt (18 Jan 1915).
University of Texas at Austin

Two letters (Za Ford, Julia).
Yale University

Two ALS ([4 April 1909 and 29 April 1909]).
Pierpont Morgan Library

Yeats, Lily   YEAT LILY
73 letters and one postcard ([Oct 11 1891-Dec 15 1915];
Partial List...#1099, 1103, 1104).
    Yeats, Senator Michael
    Copy at SUNY SB   Box 60, 61

Two letters (1939).
The Huntington Library

One ALS (1917; Ms 21819).
National Library of Ireland

Yeats, Michael   YEAT MICH
Two autographed signed cards and one ALS (Oct 6 1931-
Dec 23 [1931]; Partial List...#907, 1047).
    Yeats, Senator Michael
    Copy at SUNY SB   Box 60

Young, Ella   YOUN ELLA
One ALS; one LS, dictated.
Library of Congress

Young, Miss   YOUN MISS
    Three ALS, one TLS.
        New York Public Library
Young, Stark   YOUN STAR
    One ALS ([24 Aug 1912]).
        University of Texas at Austin

Zabel, Morton   ZABE MORT
    Four TLS (1931-1937).
        University of Chicago

Miscellany

This section includes material that does not fit in other sections, arranged in subcategories: Diaries and Journals; Documents; Folklore, Myth, and Legend; Irish Academy Material; Lane Material; Lists; Miscellaneous; Occult Material; Photographs; Quoted and Paraphrased Material; Reviews (of plays); and Theatre Material.

Diaries and Journals   DIAR JOUR
Because of the numerous cross references to the Diaries and Journals, entries here include as a heading the Partial List number (#) or the manuscript number (Ms) for items in the possession of Senator Michael Yeats or at the National Library of Ireland (copies at SUNY SB also noted), arranged in numerical order.

#351
AMs; leather-bound diary, first entry dated "Rapallo June 1934," with drafts of SUPE SONG, PRAY OLD AG, TWO SONG RE, and KING GREA CL (Partial List...#351).
    Yeats, Senator Michael
    Copy at SUNY SB   Box 90

#353
AMs; notebook (10 Ashfield Terrace) with some prose, and draft of "The Cromwellian Speaks" (Unpublished Poem: PROT LEAP), and WAND OISI material (45 pp; Partial List...#353).
    Yeats, Senator Michael
    Copy at SUNY SB   Box 88

#496
AMs by George Yeats, keyed to small white notebook (item #548 below). Has copies, not in WBY's hand, of numerous unpublished poems (I WILL NO, ON CHIL DE, TO SIST RO) and variants (including omitted stanzas) of published poems.
    Yeats, Senator Michael
    Copy at SUNY SB

#537
AMsS; notebook labelled "Private" (XYZ journal), ca
[1908]-1917, with entries in hand of WBY, Maud Gonne,
and Lady Gregory (71 pp); later published by Macmillan
in 1972 as MEMOIRS (Partial List...#537).
    Yeats, Senator Michael
    Copy at SUNY SB   Box 24

#544
AMs; white vellum journal, published as latter part of
MEMOIRS by Macmillan in 1972 (Partial List...#544).
    Yeats, Senator Michael
    Copy at SUNY SB   Box 24

#545
White vellum notebook, sold at Sotheby's in 1985 and now
in unknown hands, but copy available at SUNY SB (and on
microfilm at Harvard and NLI). Has extensive manuscript
material, with more details under individual entries.
See Books: STOR MICH 21, WHEE BUTT 34, VISI MATE; WIND STAI
MA; Plays: CAT MOON, DEIR, DREA BONE, FIGH WAVE (ONLY JEAL
EM), RESU, WORD WIND PA; Poems: COOL PARK BA, CRAZ JANE
BI, CRAZ JANE GO, CRAZ JANE JA, DANC CRUA CR, DELP ORAC
PL, DIAL SELF SO, GRAT UNKN IN, HUDD DUDD DA, MOTH GOD,
OLD AGE QU, OLD TOM AG, PARN FUNE, QUAR OLD AG, REMO
INTE SP, RESU THOU, RIBH ECST, SEVE SAGE, STAT ISTI CS,
STRE SUN GL, THRE MOVE, TOM CRUA, TOM LUNA, VACI;
Prose: BISH BERK, IRIS CENS, LOUI LAMB, UNPU DEAT LA,
UNPU MODE IR; Poems, Unpublished: GARD EDEN, ONLY DEAD
HA (Partial List...#545).
    Location of original unknown
    Copy at SUNY SB   Box 88

#548
AMs; small white notebook begun 29 August 1893, with
drafts of many works from WIND REED 99, including
Poems: CAP BELL, EVER VOIC, GLOV CLOA, HE BID HI, HE
GIVE HI, HE TELL PE, HEAR WOMA, HOST AIR, HOST SIDH,
LOVE ASKS FO, LOVE SPEA HE, LOVE TELL RO, MAID QUIE,
MOOD, POET HIS BE, POET PLEA, RED HANR SO, SHAD WATE,
SONG OLD MO, SONG ROSY CR, TO SOME I, TRAV PASS, VALL
BLAC PI, WISD DREA; and Poems, Unpublished: GOD LOVE
RO, I WILL NO, ON CHIL DE, THOU LOUD YE, WHIT DAUG IR,
YOU ARE ET (Partial List...#548; SUNY SB does not have
copy, but has copy of notebook by George Yeats keyed
to it; see item #496 above). See also Books:
WIND REED 99.
    Yeats, Senator Michael

Miscellany: Diaries and Journals   183

Ms 13570
   AMsS; an occult diary and notebook, ca 1889-90, in an
   "Acton Post Office Book" (photocopy at NLI; Ms 13570).
      Yeats, Senator Michael
      Copy at SUNY SB   Box 87

Ms 13576
   AMs; notebook dated 1921 April 7-1927 July, with VISI
   MATE and diary entry for AMON SCHOOL CH (Ms 13576).
      National Library of Ireland
      Copy at SUNY SB   Box 88

Ms 13577
   AMs; notebook, dated "24 May," with material for
   STOR MICH 31, and an unpublished poem: CONC LANE (41 pp;
   Ms 13577).
      National Library of Ireland
      Copy at SUNY SB   Box 88

Ms 13578
   AMs; Rapallo notebook A with comments on CAT MOON,
   rewritten parts of A VISION (VISI MATE), parts of PLAY
   QUEE, CENS ST.T AQ, IRIS CENS, WIND STAI, and a letter
   (UNKN CORR) about Miss Horniman and Wagner (Ms 13578).
      National Library of Ireland
      Copy at SUNY SB   Box 90

Ms 13579
   AMs; Rapallo notebook B, with extensive VISI MATE (Ms
   13579).
      National Library of Ireland
      Copy at SUNY SB   Box 90

Ms 13580
   AMs; Rapallo notebook [C], finished June or July 1929,
   with VISI MATE, two unpublished poems (IMAG BRID and
   CRAZ JANE KI), and poems from WIND STAI 33 and WORD
   MUSI 32, including AT ALGE, some CRAZ JANE poems, GIRL
   SONG, HER ANXI, HER DREA, HIS BARG, HIS CONF, LULL,
   MAD MIST SN, MOHI CHAT, NINE CENT AF, RESU THOU, SYMB,
   THOS DANC DA, THRE THIN, YOUN MAN SO (Ms 13580).
      National Library of Ireland
      Copy at SUNY SB   Box 90

Ms 13581
Rapallo notebook [D], headed "Dublin August 1929," with
drafts and notes about many poems in WIND STAI and WORD
MUSI PE, including AFTE LONG SI, BYZA, COOL PARK 19,
CRAZ JANE DA, CRAZ JANE TA, I AM IR, SWIF EPIT, VERO
NAPK, and some OCCU material (Ms 13581).
    National Library of Ireland
    Copy at SUNY SB   Box 90

Ms 13582
AMs; Rapallo notebook E, with VISI MATE and
manuscripts of RESU and WORD WIND PA (105 pp; Ms
13582).
    National Library of Ireland
    Copy at SUNY SB   Box 90

Ms 13589
AMsS; notebook with Table of Contents from TOWE 28,
and drafts and revisions of poems: AMON SCHO CH, ALL
SOUL NI, DEAT HARE, I SEE PH, LEDA SWAN, MEDI TIME WA,
NINE HUND NI, SAIL BYZA, TOWE, TWO SONG PL, and Prose:
Adoration of the Magi (TABL LAW) (Ms 13589).
    National Library of Ireland
    Copy at SUNY SB   Box 88

Ms 18748
AMs; copy of brown exercise book, entitled "Thoughts
and Second Thoughts," with reminiscences of Parnell,
Gladstone, Salome, etc. (24 pp; Ms 18748).
    National Library of Ireland
    Copy at SUNY SB   Box 90

Ms 30336
AMsS; red (maroon) looseleaf notebook, ca 1934, with
notes on Higgins's ARABLE HOLDINGS (HIGG ARAB 33), the
beginning of a review of Rossi's PILGRIMAGE IN THE WEST
(ROSS PILG 33) entitled "A Poetry of the West," lines
from FULL MOON MA, commentary on SUPE SONG for KING
GREA CL, a note on BROA 35, and Prefaces to WHEE BUTT
34 and COLL PLAY 34 (47 pp; Ms 30336).
    National Library of Ireland
    Copy at SUNY SB   Box 88

Ms 30354
AMs notebook labelled "Private," ca 1930-[1931], "begun
at Rapallo," with VISI MATE and subjects for Byzantium
(BYZA) poems; also TMs with corrections. Published by
Cuala in 1944 as PAGE DIAR 30 (Ms 30354).
    National Library of Ireland
    Copy at SUNY SB   Box 87

Miscellany: Diaries and Journals 185

Ms 30358
AMs; red notebook, inscribed from Maud Gonne, dated Christmas 1912, with writing in automatic script of Elizabeth Radcliff and drafts of or lines from ADAM CURS, BROK DREA, DAWN, DEEP SWOR VO, DOLL, EGO DOMI TU, FISH ER MA, LINE WRIT DE, MAGI, MEDI TIME WA, ON THOS HA, ON WOMA, OWEN AHER DA, PRES, RIDD IS HA, ROSE TREE, RUNN PARA, TO FRIE, TO SHAD, TO YOUN GI, TWO YEAR LA, WHEN HELE LI, and WITC. Also random notes on political and mystical subjects; an account in Maud Gonne's hand (so noted by WBY), dated 14th May 1914, of their visit to a shrine, beginning "After Mass Abbie Vachur said pointing to Mr. Yeats" (Ms 30358).
 National Library of Ireland
 Copy at SUNY SB Box 88

Ms 30359
AMs; leather notebook, ca 1927, with VISI MATE, drafts of poems, including BEFO WORL WA, DEAT, DIAL SELF SO, EGO DOMI TU, FROM ANTI, IN MEMO EV, OIL BLOO, PRES, ROSE TREE (Ms 30359).
 National Library of Ireland
 Copy at SUNY SB Box 88

Ms 30361
AMs; maroon notebook containing CALV, PLAY QUEE, notes toward A Vision (VISI MATE), and a letter to GREG LADY (95 pp; Ms 30361).
 National Library of Ireland
 Copy at SUNY SB Box 88

Ms 30362
Looseleaf notebook with contents for NEW POEM 38, one page of PURG, and other material (Ms 30362).
 National Library of Ireland
 Copy at SUNY SB

Ms 30373
AMs; red looseleaf notebook with VISI MATE, Introduction to the MIDNIGHT COURT (see Other: MERR MIDN), drafts of TOWE, a note about Count Stenbock and Blake, and other material (50 pp; Ms 30373).
 National Library of Ireland
 Copy at SUNY SB Box 88

Ms 30385
AMs; green looseleaf notebook with passages from Plays: COUN CATH, HOUR GLAS, and PLAY QUEE; and Poem: COLD HEAV. Also a letter to HAYS MR. (Ms 30385).
    National Library of Ireland
    Copy at SUNY SB   Box 88

Ms 30535
AMs; small exercise book with random notes, begun May 24, 1908, mentioning "The Doctor in Spite Himself," Hugh Lane, and the theatre (over 30 pp; Ms 30535).
    National Library of Ireland
    Copy at SUNY SB   Box 88

Ms 30546
AMs; brown vellum notebook with gilt trim, with "W.B. Yeats Prose" on spine, ca 1933-34, with notes on the Genealogical Tree of Knowledge (See OCCU), THRE SONG SA, KING GREA CL, and other miscellany (17 pp; Ms 30546).
    National Library of Ireland
    Copy at SUNY SB   Box 87

Ms 30547
AMs; brown vellum notebook with gilt trim, with "W.B. Yeats Poetry" on spine; drafts of a number of poems, including COME GATH RO, PARN FUNE, THRE MARC SO, THRE SONG SA, and parts of plays, including FULL MOON MA and a song from POT BROT (Ms 30547).
    National Library of Ireland
    Copy at SUNY SB   Box 4

Ms 30593
AMs; blue exercise book, with notes about the work on Thoor Ballylee and excerpts from letters to GREG LADY (Ms 30593).
    National Library of Ireland
    Copy at SUNY SB

Ms 30759
AMs; small red diary from 1930, with a few brief notes, mostly about illness (Ms 30759).
    National Library of Ireland
    Copy at SUNY SB   Box 87

Ms 31061, 31062
AMs; two small diaries, with engagements and random notes, one for 1932, another for 1934 (Ms 31061, 31062).
National Library of Ireland

AMsS; small notebook ("The Museum Notebook") with selection, entitled "The Conversation of Cuchulain and Emer," with a four-line poem about the "apple tree of Ailinn" and the "yew of Baile." See also Other Authors: GREG CUCH 02.
New York Public Library

Red-covered loose-leaf notebook given to Lady Gregory, blank, but signed.
New York Public Library

See also Books: AUTO MATE (green notebook; Partial List...#405); WIND REED 99 (small white notebook; Partial List...#548); VISI MATE and Miscellany: FOLK MYTH LE (small red notebook; Ms 30367); OCCU (various journals and diaries; Ms 13568, 13569, 13570); and QUOT PARA MA (small bound notebook and "Literary Notes"; Ms 13575, 30363).

Documents   DOCU
TMsS; deed of the National Theatre Society Limited, beginning "This instrument made the twelfth day of April 1911 between W B Yeats for 1 pound to Philip Hanson for 9 shares" (Ms 21952).
National Library of Ireland

Agreement between Maire Nic Shiubhlaigh and The National Theatre Society, signed by Lennox Robinson and WBY, dated 1 Nov. 1910 (Ms 22562).
National Library of Ireland
Copy at SUNY SB

Agreement between Padraic Colum and the Directors of the Abbey Theatre for permission to perform his play "Thomas Muskerry," signed by WBY and Colum (1 p).
New York Public Library

Agreement between Maire O'Neill and the National Theatre Society, dated July 1, 1911, relating to an American tour; signed by WBY and Robinson.
New York Public Library

TMs; contract with Little Theatre of Chicago for
production of ON BAIL ST and SHAD WATE, dated 30
November 1913, with autograph corrections and signature
of Maurice Brown and WBY. Other contracts with
publishers include Macmillan and Methuen, but not in
WBY's hand. (Ms 30643).
    National Library of Ireland
    Copy at SUNY SB

Copy of marriage certificate for WBY and George
Hyde-Lees, dated 19 July 1921, giving 20 Oct. 1917 for
date of marriage (Partial List...#78).
    Yeats, Senator Michael
    Copy at SUNY SB Box 93

WBY's passports, dated 17 June 1916 and 29 Nov. 1923
(Partial List...#219).
    Yeats, Senator Michael

WBY's will and letters about burial and estate
(Partial List...#642).
    Yeats, Senator Michael
    Copy at SUNY SB Box 93

WBY's will, dated Dec. 21, 1929 on Rapallo stationery
bequeathing "whatever I die possessed of" to his wife
"Bertha George Yeats for the benefit of my children,"
witnessed by Ezra Pound and Basil Bunting (Ms 30201).
    National Library of Ireland
    Copy at SUNY SB Box 93

AMsS; last will and testament, signed by WBY.
    Indiana University

Folklore, Myth, and Legend   FOLK MYTH LE
  AMs; fragment (1 p), perhaps of a folktale, including
  the line "his love changed to pity and (I?) became
  snowy white" (Ms 30490).
      National Library of Ireland
      Copy at SUNY SB

  Two pages on Celtic Mysteries in notebook of SPEC BIRD
  (Ms 30275).
      National Library of Ireland
      Copy at SUNY SB

Miscellany: Irish Academy Material 189

Various AMs on Irish myths, gods, and legends (Ms 13574, 13575).
    National Library of Ireland
    Copy at SUNY SB   Box 31

AMs and TMs (over 100 pp), entitled "Fairy Belief" and "Notes on the Faery People," possibly related to Lady Gregory's VISIONS AND BELIEFS (GREG VISI 20) (Ms 13575, 30114, 30269).
    National Library of Ireland
    Copy at SUNY SB   Box 30

AMs; notes (over 40 pp) on Mary Battle (Ms 30481).
    National Library of Ireland
    Copy at SUNY SB   Box 31

Small red notebook containing folklore collected in Sligo, Frenchpark, Lissadell and Lough Gill [1890's] (Ms 30367).
    National Library of Ireland
    Copy at SUNY SB   Box 31

Photocopy of notes: "Visions of an old Irish mythology ...begun Dec. 13 1898," beginning "Less my own visions than the visions of others" (17 pp; Ms 18749).
    National Library of Ireland
    Copy at SUNY SB   Box 31

Scrap of paper, beginning "The fairies, the gentry, the Royal Gentry, the other as they are called by Irish countrymen" (119 pp); another scrap, just before the typed version of the same, marked "corrected proofs and typescripts"; notes to Lady Gregory's VISIONS & BELIEFS and Oscar Wilde's FAIRY TALES; note on first page beginning, "Swedenborg, Mediums, and the Desolate Places" (Prose: SWED MEDI DE) (40 pp; Ms 13575).
    National Library of Ireland
    Copy at SUNY SB   Box 31

See also Miscellany: QUOT PARA MA and LIST.

Irish Academy Material   IRIS ACAD MA
TMsS; discussing funding and list of proposed members for the Irish Academy of Letters (2 pp).
    Boston University

AMs; fragment of a draft proposing that the Irish
Academy award prizes and medals.
  New York Public Library

TMsS; carbon copy of a proposal about financial matters,
captioned "Irish Academy of Letters."
  Pennsylvania State University Library

AMs; a reply to a questionnaire from the Irish Academy
about whether Academicians should be eligible for money
prizes; WBY thought younger members should.
  New York Public Library

Form letter, dated February 1937, regarding changes in
constitution of the Irish Academy (also listed under
Letters: UNKN CORR).
  Harvard University

Lane Material   LANE MATE
  AMs; fragments on the Lane gallery (3 pp).
  New York Public Library

TMs entitled "Clairvoyant Search for the Will (of Hugh
Lane)" Also listed in Miscellany: OCCU (Ms 30081).
  National Library of Ireland
  Copy at SUNY SB

AMs of statement on Hugh Lane, beginning "May I ask
your readers support for an act of generosity and
justice" (14 pp; Ms 30283).
  National Library of Ireland
  Copy at SUNY SB

AMs fragment, beginning "It is now about the pictures,
etc. had spoken of this to Lady Gregory and her
sister," probably about the Lane controversy (1 p; Ms
31054).
  National Library of Ireland
  Copy at SUNY SB

Miscellaneous copies of letters, with corrections;
comments on Hugh Lane's pictures (Ms 30250).
  National Library of Ireland
  Copy at SUNY SB

Miscellany: Lists							191

A few comments on Lane in Miscellany: DIAR JOUR
(small exercise book; Ms 30535).
    National Library of Ireland
    Copy at SUNY SB

TMs; copy of an extract from a two-page leaflet
announcing a private performance of "The Shewing up of
Blanco Posnet" at the Court Theatre, 14 July [1913?],
as a benefit for the Lane Gallery, with typed signature
of WBY (Ms 30131).
    National Library of Ireland
    Copy at SUNY SB

Lists   LIST
TMs; list entitled "Swans at Coole" with autograph
annotations, mostly indicating that certain poems are
"complete" (4 pp; Ms 30752).
    National Library of Ireland
    Copy at SUNY SB

Printed booklet of "Early Cuala Press Lists" with the
note: "This is an old list we made ourselves" in WBY's
hand; two copies, one with writing (4 pp each; Ms
30743).
    National Library of Ireland
    Copy at SUNY SB

AMs; two lists of articles by WBY that appeared in
various periodicals: one includes titles such as
"Nationality and Literature," "The Message of the
Folklorist," and "The Ainu"; the other, subtitled
"Folklore and Legend," includes "Irish Faeries,"
"Village Ghosts," and others; most appeared in the
1890's (Ms 12147).
    National Library of Ireland
    Copy at SUNY SB

AMs; list of members of the "Committee of Coinage
Design," including WBY as Chairman (1 p; Ms 30893).
    National Library of Ireland
    Copy at SUNY SB

AMs; list of names on a scrap of paper, including
Parnell, Gogarty, Stephens, Belloc, Higgins and others
(Ms 30724).
    National Library of Ireland
    Copy at SUNY SB

AMs list of names of poets, with page numbers, originally enclosed in Stephen Brown's FROM THE REALMS OF POETRY, in the library of Lennox Robinson.
    Southern Illinois University

AMs; list of Synge's works, apparently for a posthumous collection, with notes (4 pp; Ms 30805).
    National Library of Ireland
    Copy at SUNY SB

AMs; list of rules for the theatre (1 p; Ms 13068).
    National Library of Ireland
    Copy at SUNY SB

AMs; list of 17 plays, divided into "Vol 1," beginning with "Land of Heart's Desire," and "Vol 2," beginning with "The Hour Glass" and "The Player Queen" (1 p; Ms 30045).
    National Library of Ireland
    Copy at SUNY SB

TMs; "List of Contents for Selected Poems (Golden Treasury)," (3 pp and carbon 3 pp; nothing in WBY's hand; Ms 30110).
    National Library of Ireland
    Copy at SUNY SB

TMs with revisions of manuscripts and Contents for "The Wild Swans at Coole" (4 pp; Ms 30762).
    National Library of Ireland
    Copy at SUNY SB

AMs; list of Contents for CELT TWIL 93 (1 p; Ms 12147).
    National Library of Ireland
    Copy at SUNY SB

AMs; list of Contents for TOWE (Ms 13589).
    National Library of Ireland
    Copy at SUNY SB

List of Contents, beginning with "Dedication," "The Countess Kathleen," "Song and Ballads," "Father Gilligan," etc. (1 p; Ms 30345).
    National Library of Ireland
    Copy at SUNY SB

Looseleaf notebook containing list of poems related to
NEW POEM 38, but not in order of contents; including
GYRE, LAPI LAZU, and others (6 pp; Ms 30362).
    National Library of Ireland
    Copy at SUNY SB

TMs of "List of Poems Suppressed by Yeats": Version A
(1 p and carbon); Version B (1 p and carbon) (Ms
30199).
    National Library of Ireland
    Copy at SUNY SB   Box 1

Empty envelopes that had contained TMs and AMs of poems
and essays, with autograph lists (Ms 30265); contents
(1 p, numbered "2") for an early volume, with
twenty-three titles, beginning with "O Everlasting
Voices," "The Folk of the Air," "Out of the Twilight,"
and "Into the Twilight" (Ms 30344).
    National Library of Ireland
    Copy at SUNY SB

AMs; notes listing "Books by W B Yeats" including POEMS
(Unwin), THE WIND AMONG THE REEDS (Matthews), POEMS
1899-1906 (Bullen), THE SECRET ROSE, THE CELTIC
TWILIGHT, THE STORIES OF RED HANRAHAN, IDEAS OF GOOD &
EVIL, and DEIRDRE (Ms 30046).
    National Library of Ireland
    Copy at SUNY SB

See also Miscellany: THEA MATE and Speeches:
AMER TOUR LE.

Miscellaneous   MISC
Accounts of various kinds, including expenditures for
American tour (1932-1933; Ms 30659); signed checks
(1932-1933; Ms 30658); small green notebook with
expenses (21 pp; Ms 30720); statement on earnings
(1913-1917; Ms 30398); royalty accounts (1933-1939; Ms
30659); other accounts from late 1920's (Ms 30912).
    National Library of Ireland
    Copy at SUNY SB

Typed carbon of a petition to Sir Edward Grey, signed
by WBY and Lady Gregory (2 pp; 1907?; WBY I:61).
    Emory University

Clipping from MANCHESTER GUARDIAN, dated in WBY's hand, "February 24" [1932 or 1933], entitled "Irish Ban on 'the Puritan,'" with corrections by WBY (Ms 30224).
   National Library of Ireland
   Copy at SUNY SB

TMs of notes about poetry (1 p; Ms 30332).
   National Library of Ireland
   Copy at SUNY SB

Minutes related to a T.W. Lyster Memorial, dated May 4, 1923 (1 p; Ms 10543).
   National Library of Ireland

Clipping about the works of WBY, signed and dated, May 1, 1908.
   Kenyon College Library

TMs and AMs with revisions, beginning "in the rafters, and played them till the women came back again," with reference to a child "screeching for the breast," and to bagpipes (20 lines).
   New York Public Library

Photographic copy of WBY's response to a survey from Cambridge University on the creative process, with some specific questions and written responses (Ms 30098).
   National Library of Ireland
   Copy at SUNY SB

AMsS; a report, dated June 21 1893, beginning "The Library Committee of this National Literary Society has held a large number of meetings" (Ms 5918).
   National Library of Ireland

TMs; memo, beginning "After Synge's death I was given a letter," quoting a letter from Synge regarding the posthumous publication of Synge's works, with
the response of WBY and Lady Gregory to that request; a few handwritten notes by WBY (2 pp).
   New York Public Library

Handwritten prospectus to help establish Dun Emer Press, with mention of IN SEVE WO.
   Bucknell University

White vellum address book, begun 1923 (Ms 30549).
   National Library of Ireland

Miscellany: Miscellaneous

AMs with a few notes, probably in WBY's hand; an index removed from Synge's THE ARAN ISLES (1 p).
    New York Public Library

Printed petition, entitled "An Appeal: Weldon Subscription Fund," with printed signature of WBY.
    University of Texas at Austin

Copy of Lett's POCKET DIARY AND ALMANAC for 1903, with entries in the hand of WBY.
    Sligo County Library

Signed memo, undated, removed from RESP OTHE 16: "By the by, my permanent address is that upon this paper" (4.Broad Street, Oxford; MS Vault File).
    Yale University

AMs and TMs; comments on four essays submitted for "the Society's Gold and Silver Medals" (Ms 30435).
    National Library of Ireland
    Copy at SUNY SB

Materials on coinage, including WBY's TMs with corrections of "The Report of the Coinage Committee" (Ms 30866). See also Miscellany: LIST.
    National Library of Ireland
    Copy at SUNY SB Box 88

Two hand-colored Cuala prints: no. 50, with lines from WILD SWAN CO; and no. 88, with lines from LOVE TELL RO, inscribed to PROK FRED.
    Wesleyan University

WBY's desk blotter, with drafts of CIRC ANIM DE and other fragments of poems (Ms 30253).
    National Library of Ireland
    Copy at SUNY SB

Notes on backs of envelopes reading "The Land of Heart's Desire, Avenue Theatre," dated March 29-April 21, 1894 (Ms 13068).
    National Library of Ireland
    Copy at SUNY SB

See also Prose: UNPU UNID MA.

Occult Material   OCCU
   Occult writings, dated July-August, 1919, with early
   draft of IF I 40 (Ms 18750).
       National Library of Ireland

   Ms; fragmentary record of seance, beginning "Grammercy.
   What do you want? Your mind is an open book to me"
   (1 p; Ms 31049).
       National Library of Ireland
       Copy at SUNY SB

   AMs of Leo Africanus material (Ms 30499).
       National Library of Ireland
       Copy at SUNY SB   Box 87

   Automatic writing, dated 10 May 1933 (1 p; Ms 30011).
   AMs; fragment of notes for a seance (Ms 30910).
       National Library of Ireland
       Copy at SUNY SB   Box 80-85

   AMs, entitled "Script giving name of my guide" (2 pp),
   with reference to Horatio the Roman and Isabella of the
   Castillo (Ms 30047).
       National Library of Ireland
       Copy at SUNY SB

   TMs (carbon) with corrections, entitled "Clairvoyant
   Search for the Will" (of Hugh Lane), describing a seance
   (13 pp). Also listed in Miscellany: LANE MATE.
       National Library of Ireland
       Copy at SUNY SB

   A Genealogical chart of the Star family (ancestors of
   Swedenborg?), with note saying chart belonged to WBY;
   nothing in WBY's hand (Ms 30737).
       National Library of Ireland
       Copy at SUNY SB

   AMs; notes on the "Genealogical Tree of Revolution"
   (Childers correspondence, 7847-51/132930).
       University College Dublin

   TMs; "Genealogical Tree of Revolution," with
   corrections; note in another hand indicates that WBY
   "drew this up ca 1925."
       University of Texas at Austin

Miscellany: Photographs

Two diagrams related to the phases of the moon, with notes and jottings, and a note by Dulac that these are WBY's suggestions for the "Phase" design.
    Pierpont Morgan Library

AMs; thousands of pages of occult material, mostly uncatalogued: automatic writing, horoscopes, astrological notes, items related to Golden Dawn and Rosicrucians, etc. (Partial List...#1094).
    Yeats, Senator Michael
    Copy at SUNY SB Box 80-85

Various journals, with notes on a Celtic order (Ms 13568); notes on mystical topics (Ms 13569); and a photocopy of an occult diary, dated 1889 (Ms 13570).
    National Library of Ireland
    Copy at SUNY SB Box 87

TMsS; many items: a "Genealogical Tree of Revolution"; "A Race Philosophy" (1 p); "Seven Propositions"; a statement, beginning "Reality is a timeless and spaceless community of Spirits" (2 pp); sayings, dated December 23, 1938, beginning "Discoveries in Eugenics" and including the well-known "We can express truth but cannot know it" (1 p); a note dictated to George Yeats (Ms 30280). See also Miscellany: DIAR JOUR (Ms 30546).
    National Library of Ireland
    Copy at SUNY SB Box 87

Astrological material, including a few items in WBY's hand: a geneology of Irish gods, a horoscope for Dorothy Shakespear, and miscellaneous notes (Ms 31094).
    National Library of Ireland
    Copy at SUNY SB Box 31

AMs; horoscope with diagram (Ms 30064); other horoscope material, one entitled "Admission, July 24, 1914" that may have to do with admission of Mrs. Yeats to Golden Dawn (Ms 30069, 30764); another with diagram (Ms 30913).
    National Library of Ireland
    Copy at SUNY SB Box 89, 90

Photographs   PHOT
    Photograph of Maud Gonne inserted in copy of POEM 01, with caption, "was married Sat. last."
        University of Texas at Austin

Photograph of WBY, inscribed to DODD LORI HO.
   Clark University

Childhood photograph, inscribed "Taken at Sligo when I lived with my grandmother at Merville," in copy of COLL WORK 08, vol. 2.
   New York Public Library

Inscribed portrait: "by Althea Gyles. Meant to go in 'Wind among the Reeds' but Plate was I think lost. This is I believe the only copy." See also Books: WIND REED 99.
   New York Public Library

Two copies of an article on WBY by Patrick MacDonagh; WBY has signed and dated (June) his photo that appears on the cover of the periodical SCHOLASTIC (Vol. 37, 1904).
   University of Notre Dame

Photograph, signed in lower left corner.
   Southern Illinois University

Photograph inscribed (to no one) with a line from ONLY JEAL EM: "We perish into God and sink away into reality" (MS Vault file).
   Yale University

Inscribed photograph: "To Hon. James D. Phelan with kind regards from W.B. Yeats, March, 1904" (Robinson Jeffers Collection).
   Occidental College Library

A photograph of WBY's tower at Ballylee with a note on the back: "The cottage at back is my kitchen. In front you will see on[e] parapet of the old bridge, the other was blown up during our civil war W B Y."
   University of London Library

Quoted and Paraphrased Material   QUOT PARA MA
   AMs, seven lines "From Hafiz," beginning "From unbeginning eternity my heart made a bargain with your ringlet" (Ms 30049).
      National Library of Ireland
      Copy at SUNY SB   Box 88

Miscellany: Quoted and Paraphrased Material   199

AMs; two quotations, one beginning "Ah lord my God give
me quiet and seclusion," the other beginning "In the
eyes of the world" (8 lines; Ms 30464).
    National Library of Ireland
    Copy at SUNY SB Box 20

AMs, entitled "Literary Notes" in a small notebook,
beginning "A society in stable equilibrium is by
definition" with quotations from Henry Adams (5 pp; Ms
30363).
    National Library of Ireland
    Copy at SUNY SB Box 88

AMs; notes on the army crisis of 1924.
    National Library of Ireland

AMs; notes on clothing worn by ancient Irish,
arranged by rank (Ms 30072).
    National Library of Ireland
    Copy at SUNY SB

AMs; notes on tyranny quoted from unknown source,
beginning "I [can?] compare with Brutus...was told
that her ancestor princes, Socrates" (1 p; Ms
30408).
    National Library of Ireland
    Copy at SUNY SB

AMs; fragments of notes on Valery, Rilke, Stefan
George, Wellesley, and Auden (1 p).
    National Library of Ireland
    Copy at SUNY SB Box 20

AMs; small bound notebook with extensive notes WBY
took on GREG VISI 20, and other random jottings (34
pp; Ms 13575).
    National Library of Ireland
    Copy at SUNY SB

Quotations, beginning "Here he follows his own reason
and his own way," on Kildare Street Club stationery
(16 lines; Ms 30806).
    National Library of Ireland
    Copy at SUNY SB

AMs fragment of prose, numbered 52, beginning "got to the kitchen he and the two menservants, the cook and the girl from the village," possibly on folklore (1 p; Ms 30851).
    National Library of Ireland
    Copy at SUNY SB

TMs, entitled "Notes. The Fairy People," beginning "The first detailed account of the Faery People of the Gaelic race was made by the Reverend Robert Kirk in 1691." Nothing in WBY's hand (Ms 30114).
    National Library of Ireland
    Copy at SUNY SB   Box 30

AMs; botanical or medical note (a few lines), beginning "Polygonum Cuspidatum" (Ms 30480).
    National Library of Ireland
    Copy at SUNY SB   Box 88

AMs fragment of prose numbered 90-91, beginning "most of these moments brought," possibly on folklore (3 pp; Ms 30853).
    National Library of Ireland
    Copy at SUNY SB

Article, entitled "The Bishop of Toronto on Emigration," copied by WBY out of a journal called THE IRISH PEOPLE (1864 or 1865).
    The Huntington Library

AMs; notes and quotations from THE YELLOW BOOK OF LUCAN, mostly on the Deirdre legends.
    New York Public Library

AMs; notes on Nutt's OSSIAN AND OSSIANIC LITERATURE (4 pp).
    New York Public Library

AMs; 15 lines (listed as Holograph fragment) about ancient peoples, dreamers, and things, with reference to the Roman, the Englishman, and "grey stone and grey clouds."
    New York Public Library

Miscellany: Reviews

AMs; short poem, entitled "Little Old Mud Cabin," beginning "These were the words my father spoke," probably a copy of a folk song (1 p).
    New York Public Library

TMsS, with corrections, of some Irish historical notes (8 pp).
    Southern Illinois University

See also Miscellany: DAIR JOUR, for various notebooks.

Review of "A China Shop"   REVI CHIN SH
    AMs and TMs, beginning "I have spent hours over this play" (1 p each; Ms 13068).
        National Library of Ireland
        Copy at SUNY SB Box 41

Review of "The Crimson and the Tricolour"   REVI CRIM TR
    AMsS; review of O'Casey's play "The Crimson and the Tricolour," dated June 19, 1922.
        Southern Illinois University

Review of "Gombeenism"   REVI GOMB
    TMs (2 pp), with a few notations in WBY's hand, of the play "Gombeenism," submitted to the Abbey.
        University of Texas at Austin

Review of "The Red Petticoat"   REVI RED PE
    AMs, beginning "An infuriating play!" (Ms 13068).
        National Library of Ireland
        Copy at SUNY SB Box 41

Review of MacNamara's play   REVI MACN PL
    AMs; comments on (an untitled) McNamara play, beginning "When I read the first act of this play" (10 pp; Ms 31053).
        National Library of Ireland
        Copy at SUNY SB Box 41

TMs with comments; reader's opinion on Mr. MacNamara's play, beginning "When I read the first act of this play" (3 pp).
    New York Public Library

Review of MacNutty's Play   REVI MAC NU
   AMs and TMs, beginning "An impossible play, and what a
   pity" (1 p each; Ms 13068).
        National Library of Ireland
        Copy at SUNY SB   Box 41

Review of Shiels's Play   REVI SHIE PL
   Ms; notes about a play by George Shiels, beginning "A
   Work of art can have only one subject and I have tried
   to find the subject of this play"; also suggests that
   character roles must be credulous (6 pp; Ms 30895).
        National Library of Ireland
        Copy at SUNY SB   Box 41

Reviews, Miscellaneous   REVI MISC
   Random notes on plays by other authors probably sent to
   the Abbey for review (4 pp; Ms 13068).
        National Library of Ireland
        Copy at SUNY SB   Box 41

Theatre Material   THEA MATE
   TMsS, with corrections, on the reasons for and against
   the establishment of a Gaelic Company (7 pp).
        New York Public Library

   Short prose passage headed "April 30 1906," beginning
   "A possible cause of vulgarity," about the theatre
   (1 p; Ms 30330).
        National Library of Ireland
        Copy at SUNY SB

   Page with note in WBY's hand about asking more of
   theatre people, enclosed in a letter to LANE HUGH (Ms
   22743).
        National Library of Ireland

   AMs; list of rules for the theatre (1 p; Ms 13068).
   Also noted under Miscellany: LISTS.
        National Library of Ireland
        Copy at SUNY SB

   TMs of a section on "The binding in Our Irish theatre"
   by Lady Gregory, with AMs corrections and comments by
   WBY (Ms 21856).
        National Library of Ireland

Corrected TMs draft and final version (carbon) of a statement about the refusal to allow the Abbey to be rented for Saor Eire meeting (Ms 30159).
    National Library of Ireland
    Copy at SUNY SB Box 93

TMs, with corrections, of proposal related to Annie Horniman, beginning "The players have submitted their statement of facts."
    New York Public Library

TMs (carbon), entitled "Why the Abbey Theatre Remained Open on May 7th [1910]," signed and dated, Feb 3 1911 (23 pp).
    New York Public Library

TMsS, entitled "Reasons for Dismissal of Manager" with autograph addition, dated July 17th, 1915 (2 pp; Ms 30559).
    National Library of Ireland
    Copy at SUNY SB Box 93

AMs, not in WBY's hand but signed by him, beginning "PRIVATE I have made number 1 proposal" (regarding Annie Horniman).
    New York Public Library

AMs; list of plays, including "New Country," "Spreading the News," "On Baile's Strand," "Well of the Saints," and "Land of Heart's Desire" (1 p).
    New York Public Library

AMs; draft of proposal, entitled "The Celtic Theatre," beginning "We propose to have performed in Dublin every spring" (2 pp).
    New York Public Library

TMs, entitled "Private and Confidential, Samhain 1910," beginning "We have carried on the dramatic movement in Ireland for ten years" (3 pp; Ms 13068).
    National Library of Ireland
    Copy at SUNY SB

Minutes of committee meetings from 1908-10, usually in the hand of someone else; some signed by WBY, others by Lennox Robinson (20 pp; Ms 21569).
    National Library of Ireland

Sketches of sets for various plays, including COUN CATH, DEIR, HOUR GLAS, ON BAIL ST, and PURG.
    National Library of Ireland
    Copy at SUNY SB Box 88

See also Miscellany: DIAR JOUR (small exercise book; Ms 30535), DOCU, and LISTS; and Speeches: ABBE SUBS, BURL HOUS LE, DEFE ABBE TH, THEA BEAU, and others.

Other Authors

This section includes items, mostly books, by other authors to which WBY contributed (introductions and prefaces, for example), or in which he wrote inscriptions or marginalia.

Allingham, William
SIXTEEN POEMS   ALLI SIXT 05
   Dundrum: Dun Emer, 1905. (Wade 234)
      Copy inscribed to HEAL JAME, dated July 1938, with note
      stating that Allingham was the poet of Ballyshannon,
      near Sligo.
         Stanford University

      Copy inscribed (to no one) with a long note about
      Allingham and Ballyshannon, "one beautiful Irish town,"
      and a comment on the absence of a tombstone on
      Allingham's grave: "as though the carver said 'the name
      is enough. He is in all our hearts,'" dated Dec 31
      1900 (Ip.A155.C905).
         Yale University

Arnold, Matthew
   POEMS   ARNO POEM 00
      London: Dent, 1900.
      Copy inscribed to "Lolly Yeats from W.B. Yeats. Xmas
      1900" (YEAT ELIZ).
         University of Kansas

Blake, William
   See Books: WORK WILL 93.

Blunden, Edmund
   SONNETS AND SONGS   BLUN SONN 75
      London: Murray, 1875.
      Note inscribed on flyleaf: "Wilfrid Blunt left me this
      book in his will. it was sent me after his death by
      Dorothy Carleton   W B Y. March 9, 1922" (item 229).
         Yeats, Anne

Carleton, William
STORIES FROM CARLETON   CARL STOR 89
  London: Walter Scott, 1889.
  Copy inscribed to GREG LADY, with a lengthy note on
  WBY's Introduction, dated 1901.
        New York Public Library

  Copy inscribed "To the author of Shamrocks" (HINK
  KATH).
        Sligo County Library

Dowden, Edward
A WOMAN'S RELIQUARY   DOWD WOMA 13
  Dundrum: Cuala, 1913.
  Copy inscribed to HEAL JAME, dated July 1938, with the
  note: "Had nothing to do with this book, a temporary
  rebellion...of my sisters."
        Stanford University

Dunsany, Lord Edward
SELECTIONS FROM THE WRITINGS OF LORD DUNSANY   DUNS SELE 12
  Dundrum: Cuala, 1912. (Wade 247)
  Copy inscribed to HEAL JAME: "This book of a fine
  writer but a nuisance of a man. July 1938."
        Stanford University

  TMs of Introduction (10 pp; Ms 30272).
        National Library of Ireland
        Copy at SUNY SB   Box 25

Eglinton, John
LITERARY IDEALS IN IRELAND   EGLI LITE 99
  London: Unwin, 1899. (Wade 297)
  Copy inscribed to "J B Yeats from W B Yeats July 18,
  1899," with one correction on p. 72 (Yeats 30. no.1).
        Trinity College Dublin

  Copy inscribed to GREG LADY with TMsS of "John Eglinton
  and Spiritual Art" (3 pp) tipped in (PR8714 .L5 1899).
  Also listed in Prose: JOHN EGLI SP.
        Emory University

  Copy inscribed (to no one) with the note: "This was a
  stirring row while it lasted & we were all very angry
  W B Yeats."
        University of Victoria

Other Authors

———.
SOME ESSAYS AND PASSAGES   EGLI SOME 05
   Dundrum: Dun Emer, 1905. (Wade 232)
      Inscribed copy: "W B Yeats May 1 1908."
         Sligo County Library

      Copy signed by Eglinton (1926), by WBY (1933), and
      later inscribed to HEAL JAME: "Eglinton was the skeptic
      of our movement, always for the individual against the
      race. We lived in our better moments W B Y July,
      1938."
         Stanford University

Erdman, Johann Eduard
A HISTORY OF PHILOSOPHY   ERDM HIST 24
   London: Allen & Unwin, 1924.
   Three AMs drafts of SPIL MILK on inside of back cover
   (item 638).
      Yeats, Anne

Fenollosa, Ernest
CERTAIN NOBLE PLAYS OF JAPAN   FENO CERT 16
   Dundrum: Cuala, 1916. (Wade 269)
      Copy inscribed to HEAL JAME, dated July 1938, with note
      explaining that books published by Cuala had some
      connections with Irish themes.
         Stanford University

      AMs, AMsS, TMs; drafts of the Introduction (Ms 30527).
         National Library of Ireland
         Copy at SUNY SB Box 25

      AMs of the Introduction, with corrections (8 pp).
         Yale University

Flower, Robin
LOVE'S BITTERSWEET: TRANSLATIONS FROM THE IRISH
POETS OF THE SIXTEENTH AND SEVENTEENTH
CENTURIES   FLOW LOVE 25
   Dublin: Cuala, 1925.
      Copy, dated 1938, inscribed to HEAL JAME, on the
      difference between Frank O'Connor and Flower:
      O'Connor's "Translations are better poetry....Flower is
      however a great scholar."
         Stanford University

Goethe, Johann W.
GOETHE'S BOYHOOD   GOET GOET 88
   London, 1888.
      Copy with date (1888, Sept. 6) and WBY's signature on
      cover (PT2027 .A2 092).
         Emory University

Gogarty, Oliver St. John
AN OFFERING OF SWANS   GOGA OFFE 23
   Dublin: Cuala, 1923.
      Copy inscribed to HEAL JAME, dated 1938: "That dip in
      the Liffey made Gogarty a poet."
         Stanford University

      AMs and TMs with autograph corrections, some possibly
      by WBY (12 pp; Ms 30781); TMs of Preface; carbon, with
      corrections; incomplete (1 p; Ms 30299).
         National Library of Ireland
         Copy at SUNY SB   Box 25

_____.
WILD APPLES   GOGA WILD 30
   Dublin: Cuala, 1930. (Wade 279)
      Copy inscribed to HEAL JAME, dated 1938: "Some of
      Gogarty's best poetry."
         Stanford University

Gregory, Lady Augusta
CASE FOR THE RETURN OF SIR HUGH LANE'S
PICTURES TO DUBLIN   GREG CASE 26
   Dublin: Talbot Press, 1926
      Copy inscribed to "Philip Tage from W B Yeats Oct 11
      1926" (TAGE PHIL).
         Indiana University

_____.
COOLE   GREG COOL 31
   Dublin: Cuala, 1931. (Wade 319)
      Copy inscribed to HEAL JAME, with tribute to GREG LADY
      as "the noblest person I have ever known."
         Stanford University

_____.
COUNTRY OF THE YOUNG   GREG COUN YO
   For WBY's version of this play, See Plays: UNPU COUN YO.

Other Authors   209

---------.
CUCHULAIN OF MUIRTHEMNE   GREG CUCH 02
London: Murray, 1902. (Wade 256)
    Copy with revisions in pencil, used as copytext for
    CUTT AGAT 12 (item 792).
        Yeats, Anne

    Copy inscribed (to no one): "This book is our bible of
    romance there is enough in it? for generations of
    poets" (March, 1904; Iq.G862.902).
        Yale University

    Copy with revisions in pencil, used as copytext for
    GREG GODS 04 (item 792).
        Yeats, Anne

    TMs, with corrections by WBY and Lady Gregory, dated
    Feb. 1902 (12 pp).
        New York Public Library

    AMsS of four-line poem entitled "The Conversation of
    Cuchulain and Emer," beginning "The apple tree of high
    Ailinn The yew of Baile of little land"; appeared as
    endnote to section of Lady Gregory's book.
        New York Public Library

---------.
GODS AND FIGHTING MEN   GREG GODS 04
London: Murray, 1904. (Wade 258)
    Copy inscribed (to no one): "I have already spoken
    about this book...I am empty of words--it and the
    Cuchulain are the best we have. W.B. Yeats. March
    1904."
        Wake Forest University Library

    Second page proof, dated 1903, with corrections, and a
    note, dated March 1904, saying WBY gave this copy to
    John Quinn "the morning of sailing"; also, an AMs of
    the Preface.
        New York Public Library

    Proof sheets, with revisions in WBY's Preface, and his
    comments in the main body of the text (PB1421 .G7).
        Emory University

IDEALS IN IRELAND   GREG IDEA 01
   London: Unicorn, 1901. (Wade 300)
      TMsS of the postscript, possibly corrected by WBY (Ms
      30112).
         National Library of Ireland
         Copy at SUNY SB

      Copy inscribed to CARM MISS, dated March 1902.
         University of California Los Angeles

      TMs with corrections by WBY, Lady Gregory, Douglas
      Hyde, and others (incomplete; 57 pp).
         New York Public Library
         Copy at SUNY SB

THE KILTARTAN POETRY BOOK   GREG KILT 18
   Dublin: Cuala, 1918.
      Copy inscribed to HEAL JAME, dated July 1938: "Augusta
      Gregory has surpassed all our translations from the
      Gaelic, because she alone took for her motto
      Aristotle's saying: 'To think like a wise man but
      express yourself like the common people.' She
      constantly quoted it."
         Stanford University

POETS AND DREAMERS   GREG POET 03
   Dublin: Hodges, Figgis, 1903.
      Inscribed copy with note about "The Lost Saint,"
      finding it "more full of the spirit of old Irish
      Christians" than modern writing and describing Dr. Hyde
      as the only writer able to write not in the "style of
      his own age but altogether in the mood of an age long
      past" (Iq G862 903P).
         Yale University

SEVEN SHORT PLAYS   GREG SEVE 09
   Dublin: Maunsel, 1909 (Wade 304)
      Page proofs with revisions and deletions by WBY and
      Lady Gregory, including revisions to "The Travelling
      Man" (PR4728 .B5 S4).
         Emory University

Other Authors   211

THE TRAVELLING MAN   GREG TRAV 09
  Dublin: Maunsel & Co., Ltd, 1909
    TMsS, corrected (11 pp; Ms 30287).
      National Library of Ireland
      Copy at SUNY SB   Box 8

THREE LAST PLAYS   GREG THRE 23
  London: G.P. Putnam's, [1923].
    Copy inscribed to YEAT ANNE (item 810).
      Yeats, Anne

VISIONS & BELIEFS IN THE WEST OF IRELAND   GREG VISI 20
  London: Putnam, 1920. (Wade 312)
    AMs notes and fragments (MS 30172); TMs and Ms (notebook
    and three folders; Ms 13575); corrected galley proofs (Ms
    30276). See also Prose: WIZA WITC IR and SWED MEDI DE.
      National Library of Ireland
      Copy at SUNY SB   Box 31

    Reference to the book in Miscellany: FOLK MYTH LE
    ("Scrap of paper"; Ms 13575).
      National Library of Ireland
      Copy at SUNY SB

    See also Miscellany: OCCU and QUOT PARA MA.

Hamsa, Shri Bhagwan
THE HOLY MOUNTAIN   HAMS HOLY 34
  London: Faber, 1934. (Wade 282)
    Corrections in the article "Initiation upon a Mountain"
    (Criterion, 1934; Wade 282 and 1934; Ms 30106).
      National Library of Ireland
      Copy at SUNY SB

    AMs (incomplete); AMs of Introduction (Ms 30507,
    13556).
      National Library of Ireland
      Copy at SUNY SB   Box 25

    TMs, with corrections, of Introduction (15 pp).
      Southern Illinois University

Higgins, Frederick R.
ARABLE HOLDINGS   HIGG ARAB 33
  Dublin: Cuala, 1933.
    Inscription to HEAL JAME, dated 1938: "Higgins, immature
    in this book, though 'Father and Son' [and 'Padraic
    O'Conaire'] are fine poems & perhaps his best, will
    soon be a beautiful poet and song writer."
      Stanford University

    See also Miscellany: DIAR JOUR (red looseleaf
    notebook; Ms 30373).

Hinkson, Katherine Tynan
THE MIDDLE YEARS   HINK MIDD 16
  London: Constable, 1916.
    Copy with inscription on bookplate of Charles Dexter
    Allen (ALLE CHAR DE): "The earlier & later poems in
    this book mark a change that is coming upon Ireland--a
    change from collective to individual intellect--from
    Thomas Davis to 'A.E.'"
      Harper, George

MIRACLE PLAYS   HINK MIRA 95
  London: Lane, 1895.
    Copy inscribed to "Lily Yeats from W.B. Yeats. Xmas'95.
    Hyeres" (YEAT LILY).
      University of Kansas

TWENTY ONE POEMS   HINK TWEN 07
  Dundrum: Dun Emer, 1907. (Wade 238)
    Copy inscribed to HEAL JAME, dated July 1938, with an
    earlier inscription by Hinkson: "Dear Sir,-- Certainly!
    Very sincerely yours."
      Stanford University

Horton, W.T.
A BOOK OF IMAGES   HORT BOOK 98
  London: Unicorn, 1898. (Wade 255)
    Copy inscribed to GREG LADY, dated 28 July 1899, with
    revisions in the Introduction that appeared in SYMB PAIN
    in IDEA GOOD 03 (NC1115 H7).
      Emory University

Other Authors 213

    WBY's copy with a note about Horton's interest in things
mystical, and about his work: "crude though it is [it]
has some personality, a queer energy of a sort," dated
June 1902 (Ip Y34 898).
        Yale University

Hyde, Douglas
THE LOVE SONGS OF CONNAUGHT   HYDE LOVE 04
  Dundrum: Dun Emer, 1904. (Wade 260)
  AMs of Preface (2 pp).
      New York Public Library

    Copy inscribed to HEAL JAME, dated July 1938, with a
long note explaining that Hyde had given up writing
dialect after negative comments from a priest, and
concluding, "Like Augusta Gregory Hyde writes Norman
English badly. She learned her beautiful poetic style
from [this book]."
      Stanford University

Johnson, Lionel
TWENTY ONE POEMS   JOHN TWEN 04
  Dundrum: Dun Emer, 1904.
  Two copies: one dated May 1905, stating "Lionel Johnson
was once my greatest friend"; the other, dated July
1938, and inscribed to HEAL JAME, praises Johnson as a
reader of his own poetry, concluding "I shall not again
meet courtesy like his."
      Stanford University

Johnston, Denis
SHADOWDANCE   JOHN SHAD
  First TMs draft of "Shadowdance," later called "The old
lady says No!" (1926) with holograph corrections by WBY
and others.
      University of Victoria

Linley, Laura
OUT OF THE VORTEX   LINL OUT 16
  London, 1916.
  Copy with signed inscription, beginning "I knew the
writer of this book," dated Nov 1921.
      University of Texas at Austin

Magee, William
SOME ESSAYS AND PASSAGES   MAGE SOME ES
  See Other Authors: EGLI SOME 05.

Masefield, John
JOHN M. SYNGE: A FEW PERSONAL RECOLLECTIONS   MASE JOHN 15
   Dundrum: Cuala, 1915.
      Copy inscribed to HEAL JAME, dated July 30 1938, noting
      that Masefield probably met Synge in WBY's room in
      Bloomsbury, and that Synge "had much influence on Mase-
      fields dramatic work," especially on "Nan."
         Stanford University

Merriman, Brian
MIDNIGHT COURT   MERR MIDN ND
   London: Cape, n.d. Trans. Ussher (Wade 276)
      AMs of the Introduction, in a red looseleaf notebook.
      See also Miscellany: DIAR JOUR (Ms 30373).
         National Library of Ireland
         Copy at SUNY SB   Box 88

Milton, John
THE POETICAL WORKS   MILT POET 35
   London: Oxford, 1935.
      WBY's copy, with no marginalia but a draft of first
      stanza of NEWS DELP OR on back end page, entitled
      "A Letter to the Delphic Oracle."
         University of Tulsa

Moore, George
MAXIMS OF GEORGE MOORE   MOOR MAXI ND
   London: Harrap, n.d.
      Copy inscribed to HOLL NORA.
         University of Kansas

Moore, Thomas
LYRICS AND SATIRES   MOOR LYRI 29
   Dublin: Cuala, 1929.
      Copy inscribed to HEAL JAME, stating: "I dislike this
      book. There was much persuasion used upon me by the
      girls at the press & my sister to get me to
      consent...O'Faolain is a vigorous personality but no
      kind of justice is done to Moore. I am ashamed of
      myself."
         Stanford University

NIETZSCHE AS CRITIC, PHILOSOPHER AND PROPHET   NIET AS   01
   London: Richard, 1901.
      WBY's personal copy, heavily annotated.
         Northwestern University Library

Other Authors   215

O'Connor, Frank
  LORDS AND COMMONS   O'CO LORD 38
    Dublin: Cuala, 1938.
    Copy inscribed to HEAL JAME, dated Oct 14 1938, with a
    short comment: "A fine book."
      Stanford University

  THE WILD BIRD'S NEST   O'CO WILD 32
    Dublin: Cuala, 1932.
    Copy inscribed to HEAL JAME, dated July 1938,
    describing O'Connor as "a good poet & novelist. He had
    a command from the I.R.A."
      Stanford University

O'Kelly, Seumas
  CAITLIN NI UALLACHAIN   O'KE CAIT 05
    Dublin: Gill, 1905.
    Copy inscribed to GREG LADY "from her friend."
      University of Kansas

Palgrave, Francis Turner
  CHILDREN'S TREASURY OF LYRICAL POETRY   PALG CHIL 98
    London: Macmillan, 1898.
    Copy inscribed to "Rhona Ffrench with love fr. W.B. New
    Year 1914" (FFRE RHON).
      University of Kansas

Parnell, Thomas
  POEMS   PARN POEM 27
    Dublin: Cuala, 1927.
    Copy inscribed to HEAL JAME, dated 1938, with brief
    comment: "Parnell the poet was a dull dog but Lennox
    Robinson liked him."
      Stanford University

Patanjali, Shri Baghwan
  APHORISMS OF YOGA   PATA APHO 38
    London: Faber, [1938]. (Wade 286)
    Several TMs of the Introduction, some with corrections
    (Ms 30043, 30148); AMs drafts (Ms 30462).
      National Library of Ireland
      Copy at SUNY SB Box 25

AMs; a green looseleaf notebook with WBY's
condensations and interpretations of "Karma-Yoga
Aphorisms of Shri Purohit Swami" (Ms 30389); AMs of
Introduction (Ms 30400).
  National Library of Ireland
  Copy at SUNY SB   Box 25

Phillimore, Cecily
  PAUL: THE CHRISTIAN   PHIL PAUL 30
  London: Hodder & Stoughton, 1930.
    Copy with draft of song from the Play: RESU (item 1564).
      Yeats, Anne

RAPHAEL'S ASTRONOMICAL EPHEMERIS OF THE PLANETS   RAPH ASTR ND
  London: [privately printed].
    A few marginal scribblings, probably by WBY.
      University of Texas at Austin

Robinson, Lennox
  A LITTLE ANTHOLOGY OF MODERN IRISH VERSE   ROBI LITT 28
  Dublin, Cuala, 1928.
    Copy inscribed to HEAL JAME (1938) with anecdote about
    a priest who disapproved of Robinson's selection of
    poetry.
      Stanford University

Rossi, Mario
  PILGRIMAGE IN THE WEST   ROSS PILG 33
  Dublin: Cuala, 1933.
    Copy inscribed to HEAL JAME, dated 1938, with anecdote
    about a visit of Rossi to Lady Gregory who, though
    aged, "needed neither ear trumpet nor spectacles."
      Stanford University

Ruddock, Margot
  THE LEMON TREE   RUDD LEMO 36
  London: Dent, 1936. (Wade 284)
    AMs of opening section (3 pp; Ms 30388).
      National Library of Ireland
      Copy at SUNY SB

    TMs; two drafts of an article "Prefatory Notes..."
    (Wade 1936), dated December 1936, used as Introduction
    to this book (Ms 30321).
      National Library of Ireland
      Copy at SUNY SB   Box 25

Other Authors 217

Russell, George
BY STILL WATERS   RUSS BY   06
  Dundrum: Dun Emer, 1906.
    Copy inscribed to HEAL JAME, dated July 30, 1938, with
    comments on George Russell: "AE & I were always great
    friends & sometimes great enemies...."
        Stanford University

Sage, Michael
MRS. PIPER AND THE SOCIETY FOR PSYCHICAL
RESEARCH   SAGE PIPE 03
  London: R. Brimley Johnson, 1903.
    Copy of book with pencilled notes by WBY (198.s.128).
        Trinity College Dublin

Shelly, Percy Bysshe
SELECT WORKS   SHEL SELE 66
  London: Milner and Sowerby, 1866.
    WBY's copy, with marked passages and marginalia,
    inscribed to GREG LADY: "This was the first book I ever
    read Shelley in. I lost it & years after a friend
    bought it in Dublin. & now I give it to Lady Gregory,
    Oct 14 1902." (in Pforzheimer Collection).
        New York Public Library

Stuart, Francis
PIGEON IRISH   STUA PIGE 32
  London: Gollancz, 1932.
    AMs with corrections, entitled "Pigeon Irish," probably
    notes toward a review, commenting on two of Stuart's
    poems and his book: "the same cold, exciting
    strangeness."
        University of Texas at Austin

Swami, Shri Purohit
AN INDIAN MONK   SWAM INDI 32
  London: Macmillan, 1932. (Wade 281)
    AMs, TMs, and two carbons of the Introduction (Ms
    30042, 30506).
        National Library of Ireland
        Copy at SUNY SB   Box 20, 25

    Copy inscribed to ROBI LENN.
        Princeton University Library

_____.
THE TEN PRINCIPAL UPANISHADS   SWAM TEN 37
  See Books: TEN PRIN 37.

Synge, John M.
POEMS AND TRANSLATIONS   SYNG POEM 09
  Dundrum: Cuala, 1909.
    Copy inscribed to HEAL JAME: "Synge was the most
    characteristic genius of our movement & will grow
    greater with the passage of time."
      Stanford University

    Copy with a few revisions in WBY's hand (PR5532 .P6).
      Emory University

    AMs of Introduction, dated April 4, 1909.
      New York Public Library

COLLECTED PLAYS (SHINGU GIKYOKU ZENSHU)   SYNG COLL 23
  Tokyo: Shincho-Sha, 1923.
    AMs; draft of an essay, freely edited (presumably by a
    Japanese editor) for this Japanese edition of the plays
    of Synge (2 pp; Ms 30101).
      National Library of Ireland
      Copy at SUNY SB

Tagore, Rabindranath
  GITANJALI   TAGO GITA 12
  London: India Society, 1912. (Wade 263)
    Two AMs; one TMsS with corrections, dated Sept.
    1912, of the Introduction.
      New York Public Library

    Several TMs of Tagore's poems slightly revised in WBY's
    hand. Revisions in "In desparate hope I go and search
    for her," and "Thou deity of the ruined temple" (from
    GITANJALI), and in one other poem: "O woman thou camst
    for a moment to my side."
      Harvard University

    Copy inscribed to "Edmund Gosse from W.B. Yeats. Dec.
    8.1912" (may be in hand of Gosse).
      University of Texas at Austin

THE POST OFFICE   TAGO POST 14
  Dundrum: Cuala, 1914. (Wade 267)
    Copy inscribed to HEAL JAME, dated July 1938: "When we
    published this book 'The Post Office' had just been
    played by the Abbey Theatre."
      Stanford University

Other Authors   219

   AMs of Preface (Ms 30292).
      National Library of Ireland
      Copy at SUNY SB   Box 25

A TREASURY OF IRISH POETRY IN THE ENGLISH
TONGUE   TREA IRIS 00
   New York: Macmillan, 1900.
      Inscribed copy: "I had this book with me to read out
      of when lecturing."
         Wake Forest University Library

Verne, Jules
NOVELS   VERN NOVE 29
   London: Victor Gollancz, 1929
      Copy inscribed to Michael Yeats (YEAT MICH) with the
      comment: "These stories pleased me very much when I was
      your age" (Press L.7.28).
         Trinity College Dublin

Villiers de L'Isle-Adam
AXEL   VILL AXEL 25
   London: Jarrolds, 1925. (Wade 275)
      AMs of Preface (Ms 30285).
         National Library of Ireland
         Copy at SUNY SB   Box 25

      Copy of prospectus of book with WBY's Preface and
      quotations from WBY (not recorded in Wade).
         University of London Library

Virgil
AENEID   VIRG AENE
   WBY's personal copy with his name and address in his own
   hand.
      Northwestern University Library

Wardrop, Marjory Scott
GEORGIAN FOLK TALES   WARD GEOR 94
   London: Nutt, 1894.
      Copy with scattered notes in margins and on back
      pastedown.
         University of Kansas

Wellesley, Dorothy
  POEMS OF TEN YEARS, 1924-1934   WELL POEM 34
    London: Macmillan, 1934.
      Two copies; some of her poems revised by WBY (items
      2235 and 2235A).
        Yeats, Anne

  SELECTIONS FROM THE POEMS   WELL SELE 36
    London: Macmillan, 1936. (Wade 283)
      TMs (carbon) of Introduction (Ms 30151).
        National Library of Ireland
        Copy at SUNY SB   Box 25

      AMs; fragment of the Introduction (2 pp).
        New York Public Library

Whittier, John Greenleaf
  THE POETICAL WORKS   WHIT POET 86
    London: Scott, 1886.
      Copy inscribed to "Lolly from Willy Xmas 1886" (YEAT
      ELIZ).
        University of Kansas

Wilde, Oscar
  THE COMPLETE WORKS OF OSCAR WILDE   WILD COMP 23
    Garden City: Doubleday, 1923. (Wade 271)
      TMs of Introduction to Vol 3: THE HAPPY PRINCE AND
      OTHER FAIRY TALES (Ms 30158); AMs (Ms 30489).
        National Library of Ireland
        Copy at SUNY SB   BOX 25

      Reference to the book in Miscellany: FOLK MYTH LE
      ("Scrap of paper..."; Ms 13575).
        National Library of Ireland
        Copy at SUNY SB

Yeats, Jack
  SLIGO   YEAT SLIG 30
    London: Wishart, 1930.
      Copy inscribed to "Miss Grigsby from W B Yeats, July
      21, 1920" (GRIG MISS; item 2309).
        Yeats, Anne

Yeats, John Butler
PASSAGES FROM THE LETTERS OF JOHN BUTLER YEATS   YEAT PASS 17
  Dundrum: Cuala, 1917.
    Copy inscribed to HEAL JAME, dated 1938: "My father wrote whenever an idea came into his head. I seldom commented. I found that if I commented it checked the flow of his thought."
        Stanford University

_____. FURTHER LETTERS OF JOHN BUTLER YEATS   YEAT FURT 20
  Dundrum: Cuala, 1920.
    Copy inscribed to HEAL JAME, dated 1938.
        Stanford University

_____.
EARLY MEMORIES   YEAT EARL 23
  Dundrum: [Cuala], 1923. (Wade 272)
    Copy inscribed to HEAL JAME, dated 1938, with comments on "my uncle George Pollexfen," who "was a great judge of horses and raced them as advised by their horoscopes."
        Stanford University

Plays

This section includes material related to the published plays under the title from Alspach's VARIORUM EDITION, and other dramatic material under an "Unpublished: ..." heading.

At the Hawk's Well   AT   HAWK WE
   Page proofs with corrections in WILD SWAN 17.
      University of Texas at Austin

   AMs; preface with revisions and deletions (24 October 1916; I:33).
      Emory University

   Corrections, note, and autograph additions in Lady Gregory's copy of play in the periodical TO-DAY (June 1917); also a TMs (carbon) inscribed to GREG LADY, dated May 1917.
      New York Public Library

   Fragment, including draft of Preface and of the song beginning "He has lost what may not be found" (Poems: HE HAS LO; Ms 13583).
      National Library of Ireland
      Copy at SUNY SB   Box 10

   Various versions of the play (Ms 8773).
      National Library of Ireland
      Copy at SUNY SB

   AMs fragment (3 pp); Ms diary extract, probably dictated by WBY, referring to a rehearsal (Ms 30187, 30065). See also Poems, Unpublished: KEEP FAR OF (Ms 30182).
      National Library of Ireland
      Copy at SUNY SB   Box 10

   See also Letters: DULA EDMU for a description of a performance at the Abbey (Ms 13583).
      National Library of Ireland
      Copy at SUNY SB

Calvary   CALV
   AMs fragment (16 pp) entitled "On the Road to
   Calvary," related to "Calvary," but with
   variants that do not appear in the published
   version (MS Eng 338.8).
         Harvard University

   Two versions and a note about the play (Ms 8776).
         National Library of Ireland
         Copy at SUNY SB   Box 10

   TMs (5 pp) of "Note on the Symbolism" (Ms 30789).
         National Library of Ireland
         Copy at SUNY SB   Box 10

   Page proof of the Note on the play, date-stamped 7
   Oct. 1920 (Ms 30125); also an AMs in a maroon notebook.
   See also Miscellany: DIAR JOUR (Ms 30336).
         National Library of Ireland
         Copy at SUNY SB   Box 10

The Cat and the Moon   CAT   MOON
   TMs, with revisions (Ms 21500).
   See also Poems: GIFT HAR AL and OWEN AHER DA.
         National Library of Ireland

   AMs fragment, apparently of Preface; corrected page
   proofs; AMs, draft of part of Introduction; AMs of
   the notes (Ms 30070, 30108, 30302, 30376, 8774).
         National Library of Ireland
         Copy at SUNY SB   Box 10

   Copy of AMs of Introduction, in white vellum notebook.
   See Miscellany: DIAR JOUR (Partial List...#545).
         Location of original unknown
         Copy at SUNY SB   Box 88

   TMs (carbon and original) and galley proofs (Za Dial).
         Yale University

   See also Miscellany: DIAR JOUR (Ms 13570).

Cathleen Ni Houlihan   CATH HOUL
   Revisions in copy of HOUR GLAS 04 (item 2360, 2362).
   See also Books: PLAY IRIS 11.
         Yeats, Anne

Plays   225

Revisions in copy of HOUR GLAS 04 (item 2360).
    Yeats, Anne

AMs entitled "Chant," with music.
    Northwestern University Library

One draft and one fragment of WBY's play in Lady
Gregory's hand, signed by her. See also Books: CATH
HOOL 02.
    New York Public Library

TMs, with corrections not made by WBY (Ms 10950).
    National Library of Ireland

AMs; drafts of first and second "Old Woman's Song,"
with revisions and deletions (3 pp; I:34).
    Emory University

The Countess Cathleen   COUN CATH
Printed copy labelled by WBY as "prompt copy," with
typed inserts and autograph revisions, some by
Florence Farr, some possibly by WBY (96 pp).
    University of Texas at Austin

Quotation from play, beginning "The years like great
black oxen," inscribed in copy of LAND HEAR 94.
    University of Texas at Austin

Printed copy labelled by WBY as "prompt copy," with
some inked revisions in WBY's hand.
    University of Kansas

Copy of COUN CATH 12 inscribed to GREG LADY with
lines from scene 1: "This 'unknown thing' that may
be nothing--but that's the buyer's risk."
    New York Public Library

TMs (carbon) with corrections in unidentified hand,
with inscription to GREG LADY: "this old prompt copy
which she has preserved so many years," dated June,
1926.
    New York Public Library

Three TMs, with revisions (Ms 21147, 21501, 21502).
    National Library of Ireland

AMs; fragments (6 pp; Ms 30447). Cast list; various
versions and partial versions (9 notebooks and 146 pp
in 9 folders; Ms 30419, 8758).
    National Library of Ireland
    Copy at SUNY SB   Box 10

AMs in Miscellany: DIAR JOUR (green looseleaf
notebook; Ms 30385).
    National Library of Ireland
    Copy at SUNY SB   Box 88

Revisions and variant lines in COLL WORK 08.
    Yeats, Anne

Corrected proof sheets, signed.
    Yale University

AMs; fragment of speech near end of second scene
(I:35).
    Emory University

AMs and TMs with revisions and corrections (27 pp);
typed and autograph revisions and corrections of
play in a copy of POEM 99 (MS Eng 338.2).
    Harvard University

See also Books: SELE POET 13 and Poems, Unpublished:
IMPE HEAR BE.

The Death of Cuchulain   DEAT CUCH
    TMs, with corrections by WBY and another hand,
    possibly F.R. Higgins (18 pp; Ms 30087).
        National Library of Ireland
        Copy at SUNY SB   Box 10

    AMs draft of closing lines; TMs, revised (Ms 30192,
    8772). Also AMs fragment (4 pp; Ms 30433) and other
    fragments (Ms 13583).
        National Library of Ireland
        Copy at SUNY SB   Box 10

Deirdre   DEIR
    AMs (11 pp); TMs with corrections in carbon; TMs
    with corrections by WBY and Lady Gregory; TMs
    with typed corrections.
        New York Public Library

TMs (47 pp) with a few corrections, entitled "The Entrance of Deirdre."
　　　New York Public Library

Fair copy of chorus written in copy of KING THRE 04 inscribed to QUIN JOHN.
　　　New York Public Library

Three lines (variant) from play, beginning "Come now a tale of some old time not worth remembering" inscribed in album of LAMB MRS. EN.
　　　Fitzwilliam Museum

AMs in copy of POEM 01 belonging to GREG LADY, beginning "Why is it,' queen Edain said," entitled "Entrance of Deirdre" (from QUEE EDAI; I:32).
　　　Emory University

Revisions and variant lines in COLL WORK 08.
　　　Yeats, Anne

TMs of note, with comments and corrections, used as a basis for a later edition (Ms 13571).
　　　National Library of Ireland
　　　Copy at SUNY SB　Box 15

TMs, with revisions (Ms 21493).
　　　National Library of Ireland

Printed copy with corrections (Ms 21148).
　　　National Library of Ireland

TMs carbon with corrections (24 pp); AMs version of extract; TMs (260 pp) and AMs (185 pp); fragments (Ms 30150, 30343, 8760, 13583).
　　　National Library of Ireland
　　　Copy at SUNY SB　Box 11

Copy of AMs, with corrections, in white vellum notebook. See Miscellany: DIAR JOUR (Partial List...#545).
　　　Location of original unknown
　　　Copy at SUNY SB　Box 88

See also Books: COLL WORK 08, DEIR 07, PLAY IRIS 11 and Poems: QUEE EDAI.

Diarmuid and Grania   DIAR GRAN
   Twelve items, some holograph, some typewritten, some
   carbons, with corrections in WBY's and other hands.
   Fragments, separate acts, and songs.
      New York Public Library

   TMs (two carbon copies) with revisions (88 pp and 116
   pp).
      University of Texas at Austin

   Versions of text and correspondence between the two
   authors, WBY and George Moore (several hundred pages;
   Ms 8777); TMs of Act II (Ms 30437).
      National Library of Ireland
      Copy at SUNY SB Box 9

   Proof sheets (14 pp), though nothing in WBY's hand
   (951d).
      Harvard University

   TMs (106 pp).
      Washington University Libraries

   See also Poems: SPIN SONG.

The Dreaming of the Bones   DREA BONE
   Two TMs fragments; AMs fragment and note; various
   versions; fragments (Ms 30051, 30071, 8775, 13583).
      National Library of Ireland
      Copy at SUNY SB Box 12

   AMs and TMs, with revisions (25 pp), dated Aug 1917 (MS
   Eng 338.6). Also TMs, with a few revisions and
   corrections (21 pp; MS Eng 821).
      Harvard University

   Copy of Program Note for an Abbey revival, in white
   vellum notebook. See Miscellany: DIAR JOUR (Partial
   List...#545).
      Location of original unknown
      Copy at SUNY SB Box 88

   TMs (carbon) with revisions, dated 1917 August; also
   page proofs with corrections (16 pp).
      University of Texas at Austin

Proof sheets of the play with a note, not in WBY's hand, saying they are "corrected by Yeats"; another TMs with revisions possibly by WBY, with typed date: August 1917.
    University of Texas at Austin

A Full Moon in March   FULL MOON MA
TMs, corrected but not in WBY's hand (10 pp); AMs of the last page; AMs copy of Preface; AMs of Table of Contents (Ms 30186, 30800, 8769).
    National Library of Ireland
    Copy at SUNY SB   Box 12

Copy with heavy revisions of THRE SONG SA (item 2351).
    Yeats, Anne

TMs (10 pp) with revisions.
    University of Texas at Austin

TMs.
    University of Chicago

Portion of text, entitled "The Swineherd" (Ms 8906).
    National Library of Ireland
    Copy at SUNY SB

See also Miscellany: DIAR JOUR (red looseleaf notebook; Ms 30336) and Books: LAST POEM 38 (Ms 30547).

The Golden Helmet   GOLD HELM
    See Books: GOLD HELM 08.

The Green Helmet   GREE HELM
TMs of note, with comments and corrections, used as a basis for a later edition (Ms 13571).
    National Library of Ireland
    Copy at SUNY SB   Box 12

TMs, with revisions (Ms 8761).
    National Library of Ireland
    Copy at SUNY SB   Box 12

TMs (Ms 21503).
    National Library of Ireland

See also Books: PLAY IRIS 11 and GOLD HELM 08.

The Herne's Egg   HERN EGG
    AMs; text with revisions (Ms 8770).
        National Library of Ireland
        Copy at SUNY SB   Box 12

    See also Books: HERN EGG 38 and HERN OTHE 38.

The Hour-Glass   HOUR GLAS
    Copy of play from NORTH AMERICAN REVIEW (1903) with
    deletions and revised ending; also a note in GREG
    LADY's copy of RESP POEM 14 about "this seemingly
    final version" (I:36).
        Emory University

    Proofs with corrections.
        Yale University

    AMs corrections to be inserted after the play was
    published (5 pp) in PLAY IRIS 11; changes appeared in
    PLAY PROS 24.
        Southern Illinois University

    AMs (37 pp) with revisions.
        University of Texas at Austin

    A comment in a copy of RESP POEM 14 inscribed to GREG
    LADY: "This seemingly final version of The Hour Glass
    had to be revised again..." (1922; I:37).
        Emory University

    Three page AMs; TMs (15 pp) with corrections; TMs
    (carbon; 18 pp) with notes. Other TMs and page proofs
    with corrections (in Rare Books and Ms).
        New York Public Library

    Revisions in copy of Book: HOUR GLAS 04 (item 2362).
    See also Books: PLAY IRIS 11.
        Yeats, Anne

    Revisions and variant lines in COLL WORK 08.
        Yeats, Anne

    AMs of song beginning "As I was going the road one day"
    (See Poems: AS I WA; Ms 30381).
        National Library of Ireland
        Copy at SUNY SB

Plays

    TMs, with revisions, marked Prompt Copy (Ms 21504); TMs
of Preface, with corrections (Ms 10950).
        National Library of Ireland

    TMs of note, with comments and corrections in Preface,
used as a basis for a later edition (Ms 13571).
        National Library of Ireland
        Copy at SUNY SB Box 15

    AMs entitled "A Preface to the New Version" (Ms 30761);
TMs with AMs revisions (Ms 8763); printed text with
revisions used as copy for PLAY PROS 22 (Ms 30251).
Some passages in a green notebook; see Miscellany: DIAR
JOUR (Ms 30385).
        National Library of Ireland
        Copy at SUNY SB Box 15

The Island of Statues   ISLA STAT
    See Poems: ISLA STAT.

The King of the Great Clock Tower   KING GREA CL
    AMs notes for the Preface; final page proof (1934);
text and revisions (25 pp; Ms 8769, 30306, 30020).
        National Library of Ireland
        Copy at SUNY SB Box 26

    TMs (carbon), with corrections, with the comment
"Corrected April 1934" (17 pp). TMs, with corrections
and sketch of scenery by WBY (9 pp).
        Southern Illinois University

    See also Miscellany: DIAR JOUR (leather-bound diary, Ms
30351; red looseleaf notebook, Ms 30373; and brown
vellum notebook, Ms 30546).

The King's Threshold   KING THRE
    One TMs, two AMs drafts; on back of one page are eight
lines of poetry, beginning "If I had given way." See
also galley proofs of POEM 1899 06.
        New York Public Library

    Two Ms notebooks of play in Lady Gregory's hand (note
by her reads "dictated by W B Y to A. Gregory"); TMs
fragment (15 pp) with corrections by WBY and Lady
Gregory.
        New York Public Library

Revisions and variant lines in COLL WORK 08.
  Yeats, Anne

TMs of early version, with revisions (Ms 21381).
  National Library of Ireland

TMs (36 pp) with a few corrections, probably by WBY (in Rare Books and Ms).
  New York Public Library

TMs (carbon), with revisions and corrections. TMs of acting version; one page TMs in with TMs of ON BAIL ST (MS Eng 338.3).
  Harvard University

TMs of note, with comments and corrections, used as a basis for a later edition; TMs and Ms, with revisions (Ms 13571, 8760).
  National Library of Ireland
  Copy at SUNY SB   Box 13

AMs fragment; two AMs and TMs, revised (Ms 8759, 21867, 30156). Also printed text used as copy for PLAY PROS 22 (Ms 30251).
  National Library of Ireland
  Copy at SUNY SB   Box 13

The Land of Heart's Desire   LAND HEAR DE
Two AMs fragments (2 pp); one TMs and some unbound printed sheets (in Berg); one TMs (33 pp) with underlinings, revisions, and stage directions (in Rare Books and Ms).
  New York Public Library

TMs (5 pp) of Bridget Bruin's part (b MS Thr 24 [211]).
  Harvard University

TMs of Child's part, with AMs revisions (1894; 8 pp); AMs (25 pp).
  Princeton University Library

AMs of appendix (never used); AMs; draft of preface as it appeared in PLAY CONT 23 (Ms 30074, 30326, 30296).
  National Library of Ireland
  Copy at SUNY SB   Box 13

Plays

Inscribed copy of LAND HEAR 94 with lines from COUN CATH beginning "the years like great black oxen" and a note about his hating the play.
University of Texas at Austin

Mosada   MOSA
  See Poems: MOSA.

On Baile's Strand   ON   BAIL ST
TMs of note, with comments and corrections, used as a basis for a later edition; TMs, carbon (Ms 13571).
  National Library of Ireland
  Copy at SUNY SB Box 13, 15

TMs, with revisions (Ms 21498).
  National Library of Ireland

Ms draft of "May this fire have driven out"; TMs (3 pp) prose scenario; AMs draft of a dialogue between Cuchulain and Conchubar; AMs fragment of a draft; page proofs of POEM 1899 06 with parts of SHAD WATE (Ms 30475, 30331, 30032, 30017, 30329).
  National Library of Ireland
  Copy at SUNY SB Box 14

AMs; note on play, notebooks (63 pp), and list of characters; also a statement of central idea of play in Lady Gregory's hand, and revisions of play in galley proofs for POEM 1899 06.
  New York Public Library

Revisions and variant lines in COLL WORK 08, vol. 2 (item 2326). Revisions in copy of POEM 1899 06 (item 2400).
  Yeats, Anne

TMs, with corrections (8 pp of scene I); also has one page TMs of KING THRE (bMS Thr 32).
  Harvard University

See also Poems: AGAI WITC.

Only Jealousy of Emer and Fighting the Waves   ONLY JEAL EM
Proof sheet.
  University of Chicago

Revisions in the play in a copy of TWO PLAY 19, used as
basis for FOUR PLAY 21 (PR5904 T9 cop. 2).
    Emory University

TMs, with revisions (Ms 21494).
    National Library of Ireland

AMs draft (Ms 8774).
    National Library of Ireland
    Copy at SUNY SB   Box 12

TMs of Introduction to Fighting the Waves, with
corrections (8 pp).
    Southern Illinois University

Copy of AMs of Introduction to Fighting the Waves, and
of poem "Move upon Newton's town," used in
Introduction, in white vellum notebook. See
Miscellany: DIAR JOUR (Partial List...#545).
    Location of original unknown
    Copy at SUNY SB   Box 88

A line from the play, "We perish into God and sink away
into reality," inscribed (to no one) in Miscellany:
PHOT.
    Yale University

AMs; notebook with entry of "The Conversation of
Cuchulain and Emer," possibly related to this play.
    New York Public Library

AMs (25 pp; MS Eng 338.7).
    Harvard University

Introduction to Fighting the Waves from DUBLIN MAGAZINE
(Apr-June 1932), corrected for next printing; AMs; AMs
notes and fragments (3 pp); TMs fragment (4 pp); TMs
(10 pp); five TMs, with corrections; revisions for the
Introductions (Ms 30003, 30492, 30079, 30165, 30602,
30872, 13567, 8774).
    National Library of Ireland
    Copy at SUNY SB   Box 13

The Player Queen   PLAY QUEE
    AMs in Miscellany: DIAR JOUR (green looseleaf notebook,
    Ms 30385; and Rapallo notebook A, Ms 13578).
        National Library of Ireland
        Copy at SUNY SB   Box 88, 90

Plays   235

TMs of note, with comments and corrections, used as
a basis for a later edition (Ms 13571).
    National Library of Ireland
    Copy at SUNY SB   Box 15

AMs headed "Corrections in Player Queen to make it
suitable for use by Abbey Ballet" (6 pp); AMs and
pages; AMs of Preface and portions of play and TMs
draft of final page; partial and complete versions with
revisions (Ms 30138, 30484, 30286, 8764, 8758); other
passages noted in Miscellany: DIAR JOUR (green
looseleaf notebook, Ms 30385; and in a maroon notebook,
Ms 30361).
    National Library of Ireland
    Copy at SUNY SB   Box 13, 14

TMs (Za Dial).
    Yale University

The Pot of Broth   POT   BROT
    TMs, with corrections (14 pp; Ms 10950).
    National Library of Ireland

Photocopy of TMs with revisions (Ms 21492; N6385,
P7465).
    National Library of Ireland

Revisions in copy of HOUR GLAS 04 (item 2360).
    Yeats, Anne

TMs of note, with comments and corrections, used as a
basis for a later edition (Ms 13571).
    National Library of Ireland
    Copy at SUNY SB   Box 15

AMs; fragment with revisions and deletions (April 1922;
3 pp; I:38).
    Emory University

See also Books: LAST POEM 39 and HOUR CATH 05.

Purgatory   PURG
    AMs; one page with other material in a looseleaf
    notebook. See Miscellany: DIAR JOUR (Ms 30362).
    National Library of Ireland
    Copy at SUNY SB   Box 15

Some AMs with stage directions, possibly in WBY's hand (Ms 21499).
   National Library of Ireland

TMs fragment; pages removed from ON BOIL, dated April 1938; AMs and TMs scenario and various versions (Ms 30169, 30207, 8771).
   National Library of Ireland
   Copy at SUNY SB   Box 15, 27

Carbon TMs with corrections by WBY or his wife George (8 pp).
   Boston University

The Resurrection   RESU
   Draft of song beginning "Astrea's holy child" (item 1564). See Other: PHIL PAUL 30.
      Yeats, Anne

   AMs fragment (19 pp).
      New York Public Library

   AMs in Miscellany: DIAR JOUR (Rapallo notebook finished June 1929; Ms 13580).
      National Library of Ireland
      Copy at SUNY SB   Box 90

   Copy of AMs of Introduction, and of lyrics, with revisions, in white vellum notebook. See Miscellany: DIAR JOUR (Partial List...#545).
      Location of original unknown
      Copy at SUNY SB   Box 88

   AMs, dated June 1927 (16 pp); TMs with corrections; two AMs (4 pp); TMs (carbon, 2 pp) and AMs (9 pp); TMs; TMs of stage directions, dated 21-22 January 1929; AMs and TMs versions and revisions (Ms 30028, 30197, 30305, 30371, 30769, 8766, 13582).
      National Library of Ireland
      Copy at SUNY SB   Box 15

The Seeker   SEEK
   See Poems: SEEK.

The Shadowy Waters   SHAD WATE
   See Poems: SHAD WATE.

Plays

Sophocles' King Oedipus   SOPH KING OE
    TMs, with revisions (Ms 21497).
        National Library of Ireland

    One TMs, with revisions, headed "Nugent Monck Prompt
    Copy"; AMs (3 pp) of preface; two TMs, revised
    (Ms 30426, 30334, 8765, 24932).
        National Library of Ireland
        Copy at SUNY SB   Box 19

    AMs; fragment of a draft beginning, "This version of
    Sophocles play was written for Dublin players" (1 p; Ms
    30753).
        National Library of Ireland
        Copy at SUNY SB   Box 19

    AMs; alteration of "Oedipus" under title of "Make Way
    for Oedipus" (1 p).
        Southern Illinois University

    Copy of "The Oedipus Tyrannus," extensively edited by
    WBY (item 1962).
        Yeats, Anne

Sophocles' Oedipus at Colonus   SOPH OEDI CO
    TMs, with revisions (Ms 21495-97).
        National Library of Ireland

    TMs; TMs with notes and corrections by Lennox Robinson
    (Ms 30605, 8767).
        National Library of Ireland
        Copy at SUNY SB   Box 19

    TMs, with revisions and insert (78 pp).
        University of Texas at Austin

Time and the Witch Vivien   TIME WITC VI
    See Poems: TIME WITC VI.

The Unicorn from the Stars   UNIC STAR
    TMs of note, with comments and corrections, used as a
    basis for a later edition (Ms 13571).
        National Library of Ireland
        Copy at SUNY SB   Box 15

TMs of essay, with corrections by Lady Gregory and WBY,
discussing the relationship between this play and WHER
THER IS (1 p). Several other TMs; Ms in Lady Gregory's
hand, with her corrections.
New York Public Library

See also Books: UNIC STAR 08.

Unpublished: Bishop and the Monk   UNPU BISH MO
AMs; draft of early unidentified play, with characters
named The Bishop Monk, and the Accused, a shepherdess
(10 pp; Ms 30060).
 National Library of Ireland
 Copy at SUNY SB

Unpublished: The Blindness   UNPU BLIN
See Plays: UNPU EPIC FO.

Unpublished: Chairman and Parliamentary Party UNPU CHAI PA
AMs fragment, beginning "Chairman wants to form
parliamentary party," with character of Madman and
directions: "First man enters" (1 p; Ms 30815).
 National Library of Ireland
 Copy at SUNY SB

Unpublished: Country of the Young   UNPU COUN YO
TMs with revisions (11 pp) of WBY's version of Lady
Gregory's play (GREG COUN YO; Ms 30287).
 National Library of Ireland
 Copy at SUNY SB Box 8

Unpublished: Cyprian   UNPU CYPR
Ms; fragment of play, headed Scene I, beginning
"Cyprian--I live in this Lake" (3 pp; Ms 30839).
 National Library of Ireland
 Copy at SUNY SB

Unpublished: The Dagger still in his Hand UNPU DAGG ST
Ms; fragment of play, beginning "the dagger still in
his hand" (12 lines; Ms 30838).
 National Library of Ireland
 Copy at SUNY SB

Unpublished: Door of a Large House   UNPU DOOR LA
   TMs; scenario for a play evidently not written
   beginning "Door of a large house. Enter a young man
   and a young woman" about a king, queen, and lovers
   (3 pp; Ms 30337).
      National Library of Ireland
      Copy at SUNY SB

Unpublished: Epic of the Forest   UNPU EPIC FO
   AMs; a series of related scenes and fragments under
   various titles: "The Village of the Elms" (3 pp); "The
   Starving of Rothsay" (35 pp); "Sans Eyes" (hundreds of
   pp); "Pedro's Song"; "A Dialogue: Peasant Girl and Boy"
   (1 p); and "The Blindness" (Ms 30352, 30402, 30414,
   30440, 30459).
      National Library of Ireland
      Copy at SUNY SB Box 8, 9

Unpublished: Giddy day goes barefoot   UNPU GIDD DA
   AMs (8 pp).
      National Library of Ireland
      Copy at SUNY SB

Unpublished: Girl and Goatherd   UNPU GIRL GO
   AMs; fragment of play about a Girl and Goatherd (Ms
   30182).
      National Library of Ireland
      Copy at SUNY SB Box 8

Unpublished: He is out [of?] his wits   UNPU HE IS
   AMs; fragment beginning "He is out [of?] his wits, with
   reference to "hollow cheeks and yellow [hair?]"
      New York Public Library

Unpublished: Island Faeries at Evening   UNPU ISLA FA
   AMs; small black notebook containing draft of a verse
   play entitled "Island Fairies at Evening" with
   characters named "He" and "She" (Ms 30066).
      National Library of Ireland
      Copy at SUNY SB

Unpublished: Laying of the Foundations   UNPU LAYI FO
   TMs, beginning with Act II, with corrections not by WBY
   (Ms 10950).
      National Library of Ireland

Unpublished: Love and Death: A Tragedy   UNPU LOVE DE
    AMs; several notebooks with some 300 pages, ca 1884
    (Partial List...#356).
        Yeats, Senator Michael
        Copy at SUNY SB   Box 9

Unpublished: Love's Decay   UNPU LOVE 'S
    AMs; early play about a river, a boat, and the rushes
    (8 pp).
        National Library of Ireland
        Copy at SUNY SB   Box 9

Unpublished: Old Man and Girl   UNPU OLD   MA
    AMs; fragment with characters of Old Man and Young Girl
    (20 pp; Ms 30488).
        National Library of Ireland
        Copy at SUNY SB   Box 9

    AMs; draft entitled "A Play Begun and Never Finished,"
    with characters "Old Man" and "Girl" (over 20 pp; Ms
    30427).
        National Library of Ireland
        Copy at SUNY SB

Unpublished: Opening Ceremony for the Masquers   UNPU OPEN CE
    TMs; a few lines describing an "opening ceremony,"
    with instructions for a man to enter and blow a horn,
    with autograph cancellations (2 pp).
        New York Public Library

Unpublished: Peter and the Shepherd   UNPU PETE SH
    Scrap of play about Peter and Shepherd (1 p; Ms 30469).
        National Library of Ireland
        Copy at SUNY SB

Unpublished: The Poet and the Actress   UNPU POET AC
    AMs (20 pp) and TMs (14 pp) of dialogue entitled "The
    Poet and the Actress." Unclear whether it is intended
    as a play, poem, or story (Ms 30410).
        National Library of Ireland
        Copy at SUNY SB   Box 17

Unpublished: Sans Eyes   UNPU SANS EY
    See Plays: UNPU EPIC FO.

Unpublished: Sea Spirit   UNPU SEA   SP
    AMs; fragment of early play about a Sea Spirit (3 pp;
    Ms 30407).
        National Library of Ireland
        Copy at SUNY SB   Box 9

Plays

Unpublished: The Rover and Lord of the Tower   UNPU ROVE LO
   AMs.
      National Library of Ireland
      Copy at SUNY SB

Unpublished: The Starving of Rothsay   UNPU STAR RO
   See Plays: UNPU EPIC FO.

Unpublished: You Have Gray Hair   UNPU YOU HA
   AMs; fragment beginning "You have grey hair and hollow
   cheeks" (2 pp).
      New York Public Library

Unpublished: The Village of the Elms   UNPU VILL EL
   See Plays: UNPU EPIC FO.

Where There Is Nothing   WHER THER IS
   Five TMs, with corrections and revisions (by Lady
   Gregory as well as WBY), and some suggestions for a
   printers proof (Rare Books and Ms).
      New York Public Library

   Part of a letter about the play (Ms 30343).
      National Library of Ireland
      Copy at SUNY SB

   See also Plays: UNIC STAR.

The Words Upon the Window-Pane   WORD WIND PA
   AMs (22 pp; fMS Eng 338.9); TMs (23 pp; bMS Am 1787
   [604]).
      Harvard University

   Copy of part of the Introduction, along with part of
   another manuscript. See Books: UNPU SPEC BI (MS842).
      University of Reading Library

   TMs of commentary (8 pp); TMs, revised, with
   Introduction; revised galley proofs (Ms 30874, 8768,
   15598, 13582).
      National Library of Ireland
      Copy at SUNY SB   Box 16, 90

   Draft of Introductions, and some notes, in Miscellany:
   DIAR JOUR (Rapallo notebook E; Ms 13582).
      National Library of Ireland
      Copy at SUNY SB   Box 90

AMs in Miscellany: DIAR JOUR (Rapallo notebook finished
June 1929; Ms 13580).
    National Library of Ireland
    Copy at SUNY SB

See also Books: WHEE BUTT 34.

Poems

This section includes the poems published in Allt's VARIORUM EDITION and in Finneran's POEMS OF W.B. YEATS: A NEW EDITION. Poems from the VARIORUM EDITION for which no manuscripts have been found are listed with the note "No Ms Located."

Accursed who brings to light of day   ACCU WHO BR
   No Ms located.

An Acre of Grass   ACRE GRAS
   AMs; TMs, with corrections (Ms 13593).
      National Library of Ireland
      Copy at SUNY SB Box 3

Adam's Curse   ADAM CURS
   Two AMs of various stanzas, with additional notes by
   Lady Gregory; one TMs, with corrections by Lady Gregory.
      New York Public Library

   Revisions in copy of POEM SECO 09.
      Yeats, Anne

   AMs draft in "red notebook...from Maud Gonne."
   See Miscellany: DIAR JOUR (Ms 30358).
      National Library of Ireland
      Copy at SUNY SB Box 88

   Galley proofs with revisions in POEM 1899 06.
      New York Public Library

   Proof sheets with corrections (Ms 13584).
      National Library of Ireland
      Copy at SUNY SB Box 1

After Long Silence   AFTE LONG SI
   AMs (Ms 13591).
      National Library of Ireland
      Copy at SUNY SB Box 6

AMs draft. See Miscellany: DIAR JOUR (Rapallo notebook
D headed "Dublin August 1929"; Ms 13581).
    National Library of Ireland
    Copy at SUNY SB   Box 90

Against Unworthy Praise   AGAI UNWO PR
  No Ms located.

Against Witchcraft   AGAI WITC
  (From the Play: ON BAIL ST)
  Two AMsS; AMs fragment (Ms 30384, 30403).
    National Library of Ireland
    Copy at SUNY SB   Box 7

All Souls' Night   ALL SOUL NI
  Note on the poem in copy of SEVE POEM 22 inscribed to
  GREG LADY, dated June 1922, claiming: "I have
  accurately described the chief emotion" of the life
  of Horton (I:1).
    Emory University

  AMs. See Miscellany: DIAR JOUR (Ms 13589).
    National Library of Ireland
    Copy at SUNY SB   Box 5

All Things can Tempt me   ALL THIN CA
  Copy, dated 1908 September, with revisions and
  deletions on upper flyleaf of copy of POET WORK 06
  that belonged to GREG LADY (I:2).
    Emory University

  Fair copy in COLL WORK 08, vol. 7.
    New York Public Library

  Fragment (prose, 9 lines) with line that echoes ALL
  THIN CA: "nothing ready to his hand."
    University of Delaware Library

Alternative Song for the Severed Head in 'The
King of the Great Clock Tower'   ALTE SONG SE
  AMs in Miscellany: DIAR JOUR (Partial List...#351).
    National Library of Ireland
    Copy at SUNY SB   Box 4

Among School Children   AMON SCHO CH
  TMs (carbon; Za Dial).
    Yale University

Poems   245

>   AMs; TMs. See Miscellany: DIAR JOUR (Ms 13589).
>   National Library of Ireland
>   Copy at SUNY SB   Box 5
>
>   Theme for this poem written in journal with material
>   for VISI 37. See Miscellany: DIAR JOUR (notebook begun
>   April 1921; Ms 13576).
>   National Library of Ireland
>   Copy at SUNY SB   Box 88
>
>   AMs draft enclosed in letter to SHAK OLIV.
>   Yeats, Senator Michael
>   Copy at SUNY SB   Box 58, 59
>
>   Copy of IN SEVE 03 inscribed (to no one) with the line
>   "How shall we know the dancer from the dance."
>   University of Texas at Austin

Anashuya and Vijaya   ANAS VIJA
>   Page proofs with corrections in POET WORK 06.
>   New York Public Library
>
>   Page proof with revisions in WAND OISI 89.
>   University of Texas at Austin
>
>   Inscribed copy of WAND OISI 89 with a few corrections
>   in this poem entitled "Jealousy."
>   Providence Public Library
>
>   AMs (Ms 30453).
>   National Library of Ireland
>   Copy at SUNY SB   Box 1

Ancestral Houses   ANCE HOUS
>   AMs (Ms 13589).
>   National Library of Ireland
>   Copy at SUNY SB   Box 5
>
>   See also Poems: MEDI TIME CI.

Another Song of a Fool   ANOT SONG FO
>   No Ms located.

The Apparitions   APPA
>   AMs (2 pp); TMs, with corrections (Ms 13593).
>   National Library of Ireland
>   Copy at SUNY SB   Box 2

An Appointment   APPO
    TMs, revised (Ms 21855).
        National Library of Ireland

    Page proofs with revisions in RESP POEM 14.
        New York Public Library

    12 lines with revisions and deletions and an
    explanatory note by Lady Gregory on blank page
    of her copy of POEM 01, dated Aug 25 1907 (I:3).
        Emory University

Are You Content?   ARE   YOU   CO
    AMs (3 pp); TMs copy (Ms 13593).
        National Library of Ireland
        Copy at SUNY SB   Box 4

The Arrow   ARRO
    Revisions in copy of COLL WORK 08, vol. 1 (item 2325).
        Yeats, Anne

    Revisions in copy of POEM SECO 09 (item 2401).
        Yeats, Anne

    AMs, on Coole Park stationery.
        New York Public Library

    Proof, with corrections (1 p; Ms 30188).
        National Library of Ireland
        Copy at SUNY SB   Box 1

At Algeciras--A Meditation upon Death   AT   ALGE ME
    AMs. See Miscellany: DIAR JOUR (Rapallo notebook
    finished June 1929; Ms 13580).
        National Library of Ireland
        Copy at SUNY SB   Box 90

    TMs, with corrections (Ms 13590). See Books: WIND STAI
    MA.
        National Library of Ireland
        Copy at SUNY SB   Box 6

At Galway Races   AT   GALW RA
    Revisions in copy of GREE HELM 12 (item 2355).
        Yeats, Anne

    Fair copy in COLL WORK 08, vol. 7.
        New York Public Library

Poems   247

   16 lines with deletions, on blank page of copy of POET
   WORK 06, vol. 1, belonging to GREG LADY, dated Sept
   1908 (I:4).
      Emory University

At the Abbey Theatre   AT   ABBE TH
   No Ms located.

At the Grey Round of the Hill   AT   GREY RO
   AMs, with revisions and a note, dated 1917 July 9.
      University of Texas at Austin

Baile and Aillinn   BAIL AILL
   Page proofs with corrections in POET WORK 06; galley
   proofs with revisions in POEM 1899 06.
      New York Public Library

   Page proofs (Ms 13584).
      National Library of Ireland
      Copy at SUNY SB   Box 1, 5

   Revisions in copies of LATE POEM 22, POEM SECO 09, and
   SELE POEM 21 (items 2382, 2401, 2417).
      Yeats, Anne

The Ballad of Earl Paul   BALL EARL PA
   Three copies: one in purple, two in black type; third
   has typed signature, dated Sligo, April 4, 1893.
      University of Texas at Austin

The Ballad of Father Gilligan   BALL FATH GI
   Corrections in page proofs of POET WORK 06.
      New York Public Library

The Ballad of Father O'Hart   BALL FATH O'
   Autograph copy, probably in WBY's hand (but unusually
   legible), entitled "The Priest of Coloony," in
   homemade, handbound book. See Books: UNPU YE PL.
      National Library of Ireland

   Corrections and notes in WBY's copy of Sparling's IRISH
   MINSTRELSY; poem entitled "The Priest of Coloony"
   (item 1967).
      Yeats, Anne

The Ballad of Moll Magee   BALL MOLL MA
   No Ms located.

The Ballad of the Foxhunter   BALL FOXH
    AMs; another AMs, entitled "The Ballad of the Old
    Foxhunter," with five quatrains, beginning "Now lay me
    in a cushioned chair" (Ms 30423, 30418).
        National Library of Ireland
        Copy at SUNY SB   Box 1

The Balloon of the Mind   BALL MIND
    AMs (Ms 13587).
        National Library of Ireland
        Copy at SUNY SB   Box 6

    AMs.
        New York Public Library

    TMs, typed by Ezra Pound, with comments by him and sent
    to Harriet Monroe (Aug 1, 1917).
        University of Chicago

Beautiful Lofty Things   BEAU LOFT TH
    AMs; TMs, with corrections in punctuation (Ms 13593).
        National Library of Ireland
        Copy at SUNY SB   Box 3

    Rough pencil draft in WBY's copy of Sacheverell
    Sitwell's CANONS OF GIANT ART (item 1936).
        Yeats, Anne

Before the World Was Made   BEFO WORL WA
    TMs and two carbon copies (Ms 13592).
        National Library of Ireland
        Copy at SUNY SB   Box 7

    AMs draft. See Miscellany: DIAR JOUR (leather notebook
    ca 1927; Ms 30359).
        National Library of Ireland
        Copy at SUNY SB   Box 88

Beggar to Beggar Cried   BEGG BEGG CR
    AMs (Ms 13586).
        National Library of Ireland
        Copy at SUNY SB   Box 4

The Black Tower   BLAC TOWE
    AMs (11 pp); TMs, with corrections (Ms 13593).
        National Library of Ireland
        Copy at SUNY SB   Box 2

Poems   249

> TMs (carbon), dated January 21 1939 (Ms 30200).
> National Library of Ireland
> Copy at SUNY SB   Box 2

The Blessed   BLES
> Page proofs with corrections in POET WORK 06.
> New York Public Library
>
> Two TMs with revisions.
> New York Public Library
>
> See also Books: WIND REED 99.

Blood and the Moon   BLOO MOON
> AMs draft (Ms 13583).
> National Library of Ireland
> Copy at SUNY SB
>
> AMs. See Books: WIND STAI MA.
> National Library of Ireland
> Copy at SUNY SB   Box 6

The Blood Bond   BLOO BOND
> AMsS, with revisions and deletions (I:5).
> Emory University

The bravest from the gods but ask   BRAV FROM GO
> No Ms located.

Broken Dreams   BROK DREA
> Galley proofs with corrections in WILD SWAN 17.
> New York Public Library
>
> Page proofs with corrections in WILD SWAN 17.
> University of Texas at Austin
>
> AMs (Ms 13587).
> National Library of Ireland
> Copy at SUNY SB   Box 5
>
> AMs draft in "red notebook...from Maud Gonne."
> See Miscellany: DIAR JOUR (Ms 30358).
> National Library of Ireland
> Copy at SUNY SB   Box 88

A Bronze Head   BRON HEAD
    AMs (4 pp); two TMs copies, with corrections (Ms
    13593).
        National Library of Ireland
        Copy at SUNY SB   Box 2

Brown Penny   BROW PENN
    AMs; fragments (Ms 30409).
        National Library of Ireland
        Copy at SUNY SB   Box 1

    AMsS; fair copy (I:6).
        Emory University

Byzantium   BYZA
    AMs. See Books: WIND STAI MA.
        National Library of Ireland
        Copy at SUNY SB   Box 6

    Photocopies of drafts (Ms 30155).
        National Library of Ireland
        Copy at SUNY SB

    TMs, AMs, and proof draft, all with corrections (Ms
    13589).
        National Library of Ireland
        Copy at SUNY SB   Box 88

    AMs draft. See Miscellany: DIAR JOUR (Rapallo
    notebook headed "Dublin August 1929"; Ms 13580).
        National Library of Ireland
        Copy at SUNY SB   Box 90

    See also Poems, Unpublished: WHEN CONS DE (Ms 13590).

The Cap and Bells   CAP BELL
    TMs, with revisions.
        New York Public Library

    AMs in small white notebook. See Miscellany: DIAR JOUR
    (Partial List...#548).
        Yeats, Senator Michael

    See also Books: WIND REED 99.

Poems

The Cat and the Moon   CAT MOON
    AMs (Ms 13587).
        National Library of Ireland
        Copy at SUNY SB   Box 6

Certain Artists Bring Her Dolls and Drawings   CERT ARTI BR
    TMs, with variant readings.
        University of Reading Library

    See also Poems: UPON DYIN LA.

The Chambermaid's First Song   CHAM FIRS SO
    AMs, TMs, with corrections, page proofs (Ms 13593).
        National Library of Ireland
        Copy at SUNY SB   Box 3

The Chambermaid's Second Song   CHAM SECO SO
    AMs; TMs, with corrections (Ms 13593).
        National Library of Ireland
        Copy at SUNY SB   Box 3

The Choice   CHOI
    No Ms located.

Chosen   CHOS
    AMs and TMs (Ms 13592).
        National Library of Ireland
        Copy at SUNY SB   Box 7

    See also Poems: WOMA YOUN OL.

Church and State   CHUR STAT
    AMs draft (Ms 30795). See also Poems: THRE SONG SA
    (Ms 30521).
        National Library of Ireland
        Copy at SUNY SB

The Circus Animal's Desertion   CIRC ANIM DE
    AMs, dated Nov 1937 (5 pp); TMs and carbon, with
    corrections (Ms 13593).
        National Library of Ireland
        Copy at SUNY SB   Box 2

The Cloak, the Boat, and the Shoes   CLOA BOAT SH
    No Ms located.

A Coat   COAT
    Fair copy with slight variations, inscribed in RESP
    POEM 14. See Inscriptions: HEAL JAME.
        Stanford University

    AMs (2 pp; Ms 30514); AMs (Ms 13586).
        National Library of Ireland
        Copy at SUNY SB   Box 4

    Opening lines inscribed in copy of CATH HOOL 02.
        New York Public Library

The Cold Heaven   COLD HEAV
    Revisions in copy of LATE POEM 22 (item 2382).
        Yeats, Anne

    TMs, revised (Ms 21871).
        National Library of Ireland

    AMs (Ms 13586). AMs in a green notebook. See
    Miscellany: DIAR JOUR (Ms 30385).
        National Library of Ireland
        Copy at SUNY SB   Box 4, 88

The Collar-Bone of a Hare   COLL BONE HA
    AMs (Ms 13587).
        National Library of Ireland
        Copy at SUNY SB   Box 5

Colonel Martin   COLO MART
    AMs (9 pp); TMs, with corrections (2 pp; Ms 13593).
        National Library of Ireland
        Copy at SUNY SB   Box 4

Colonus' Praise   COLO PRAI
    AMs (3 pp; Ms 13589).
        National Library of Ireland
        Copy at SUNY SB   Box 5

Come Gather Round me, Parnellites   COME GATH RO
    AMs and TMs copies with corrections (2 pp; Ms 13593).
        National Library of Ireland
        Copy at SUNY SB   Box 4, 20

Poems   253

>   AMs of note on poem (6 pp; Ms 30394); AMs (Ms 30394);
>   AMs draft in Miscellany: DIAR JOUR (Ms 30547).
>   National Library of Ireland
>   Copy at SUNY SB   Box 4, 87
>
>   Page with poem, entitled "Come stand about me
>   Parnellites," enclosed in letter to WELL DORO.
>   Meisei University

Come ride and ride to the garden   COME RIDE RI
>   AMs, entitled "The Travelling Man sings" (Ms 21866).
>   National Library of Ireland

The Coming of Wisdom with Time   COMI WISD TI
>   No Ms located.

Conjunctions   CONJ
>   TMs, with commentary.
>   University of Chicago

Consolation   CONS
>   AMs and TMs (Ms 13592).
>   National Library of Ireland
>   Copy at SUNY SB   Box 7
>
>   See also Poems: WOMA YOUN OL.

Coole Park, 1929   COOL PARK 19
>   TMs. See Books: WIND STAI MA.
>   National Library of Ireland
>   Copy at SUNY SB   Box 6
>
>   AMs draft. See Miscellany: DIAR JOUR (Rapallo notebook
>   headed "Dublin August 1929"; Ms 13581).
>   National Library of Ireland
>   Copy at SUNY SB   Box 90
>
>   AMs; drafts, one dated 7 Sept. 1929 (Ms 13590, 21862,
>   21871).
>   National Library of Ireland
>
>   TMs (carbon) with corrections, entitled "Coole," and
>   dated Sept. 7, 1929.
>   New York Public Library

Coole Park and Ballylee, 1931   COOL PARK BA
    Corrected copy (Ms 30026); TMs. See Books: WIND STAI MA.
    National Library of Ireland
    Copy at SUNY SB   Box 6, 136

    Copy of drafts from white vellum notebook.
    See Miscellany: DIAR JOUR (Partial List...#545).
        Location of original unknown
        Copy at SUNY SB   Box 88

    TMsS with corrections, entitled "Coole. 1932."
    New York Public Library

The Countess Cathleen in Paradise   COUN CATH PA
    Photostat of AMsS, entitled "A Dream of a Blessed
    Spirit."
    University of Texas at Austin

    AMs draft enclosed in letter to SHAK OLIV.
    Yeats, Senator Michael
    Copy at SUNY SB   Box 58, 59

A Cradle Song   CRAD SONG
    Page proofs with corrections in POET WORK 06; TMs.
    New York Public Library

    AMs draft in letter to HINK KATH TY.
    The Huntington Library

    AMs copy of poem tipped in copy of WAND OISI 89.
    Tulane University

A Crazed Girl   CRAZ GIRL
    AMsS, AMs and TMs, entitled "At Barcelona" (Ms 13593).
    National Library of Ireland
    Copy at SUNY SB   Box 3

The Crazed Moon   CRAZ MOON
    AMs and TMs. See Books: WIND STAI MA.
    National Library of Ireland
    Copy at SUNY SB   Box 6

Crazy Jane and Jack the Journeyman   CRAZ JANE JA
    Copy of drafts and fair copy from white vellum notebook.
    See Miscellany: DIAR JOUR (Partial List...#545).
        Location of original unknown
        Copy at SUNY SB   Box 88

Poems

>Two TMs; AMs (Ms 13591).
> National Library of Ireland
> Copy at SUNY SB   Box 6

Crazy Jane and the Bishop   CRAZ JANE BI
>Copy of drafts and fair copy from white vellum notebook.
>See Miscellany: DIAR JOUR (Partial List...#545).
> Location of original unknown
> Copy at SUNY SB   Box 88

>TMs, with corrections (Ms 13591).
> National Library of Ireland
> Copy at SUNY SB   Box 6

>AMs. See Miscellany: DIAR JOUR (Rapallo notebook
>finished June 1929; Ms 13580).
> National Library of Ireland
> Copy at SUNY SB   Box 90

Crazy Jane Grown Old Looks at the Dancers   CRAZ JANE GR
>TMs (Ms 13591); AMs in Miscellany: DIAR JOUR (Rapallo
>notebook finished June 1929; Ms 13580).
> National Library of Ireland
> Copy at SUNY SB   Box 6, 90

Crazy Jane on God   CRAZ JANE GO
>Copy of drafts and fair copy from white vellum
>notebook. See Miscellany: DIAR JOUR (Partial
>List...#545).
> Location of original unknown
> Copy at SUNY SB   Box 88

>TMs and AMs (Ms 13591).
> National Library of Ireland
> Copy at SUNY SB   Box 88

Crazy Jane on the Day of Judgment   CRAZ JANE DA
>AMs draft in Miscellany: DIAR JOUR (Rapallo notebook D,
>headed "Dublin August 1929"; Ms 13581).
> National Library of Ireland
> Copy at SUNY SB   Box 90

>AMsS; TMs, with corrections (Ms 13591).
> National Library of Ireland
> Copy at SUNY SB   Box 6

Crazy Jane on the Mountain   CRAZ JANE MO
    AMs; rough draft (bMS Eng 338.12 95-15).
        Harvard University

    AMs (2 pp); TMs, with corrections (Ms 13593).
        National Library of Ireland
        Copy at SUNY SB   Box 4, 27

    Copy in corrected page proofs (Add. MS 55881).
    See Books: ON BOIL 39.
        British Library

Crazy Jane Reproved   CRAZ JANE RE
    TMs, with corrections (Ms 13591).
        National Library of Ireland
        Copy at SUNY SB   Box 6

Crazy Jane Talks With the Bishop   CRAZ JANE TA
    TMs, with corrections in punctuation (Ms 13591).
        National Library of Ireland
        Copy at SUNY SB   Box 6

    AMs draft in Miscellany: DIAR JOUR (Rapallo notebook D,
    "Dublin August 1929"; Ms 13581).
        National Library of Ireland
        Copy at SUNY SB   Box 90

Crossways   CROS
    AMs notes on WAND OISI and CROS (Ms 13583).
        National Library of Ireland
        Copy at SUNY SB

Cuchulain Comforted   CUCH COMF
    AMs fragment; TMs (carbon, 1 p); TMs (2 pp) of prose
    subject (Ms 30067, 30132, 30196).
        National Library of Ireland
        Copy at SUNY SB   Box 2

    AMs (2 pp); TMs, with corrections; TMs copy; two
    carbons (Ms 13593).
        National Library of Ireland
        Copy at SUNY SB   Box 2

Cuchulain's Fight with the Sea   CUCH FIGH SE
    Page proofs with corrections in POET WORK 06.
        New York Public Library

Poems   257

The Curse of Cromwell   CURS CROM
    AMs; TMs, with corrections (Ms 13593).
    National Library of Ireland
    Copy at SUNY SB   Box 3

The Danaan Quicken Tree   DANA QUIC TR
    No Ms located.

The Dancer at Cruachan and Cro-Patrick   DANC CRUA CR
    Copy of draft, entitled "The One and the Dancer,"
    from white vellum notebook. See Miscellany: DIAR JOUR
    (Partial List...#545).
        Location of original unknown
        Copy at SUNY SB   Box 88

    TMs; TMs, with corrections; AMsS, dated Aug. 1931 (Ms
    13591).
        National Library of Ireland
        Copy at SUNY SB   Box 6

The Dawn   DAWN
    Copy of TOWE 28 inscribed (to no one), beginning "I
    would be ignorant."
        University of Texas at Austin

    TMs; typed by Ezra Pound with comments by him, sent
    to Harriet Monroe (Aug 1, 1917).
        University of Chicago

    Corrections in copy of EIGH POEM 16.
        New York Public Library

    Page proofs with corrections in WILD SWAN 17.
        University of Texas at Austin

    AMs; fair copy of last five lines.
        Boston College

    AMs (Ms 13587).
        National Library of Ireland
        Copy at SUNY SB   Box 5

    AMs draft in "red notebook...from Maud Gonne."
    See Miscellany: DIAR JOUR (Ms 30358).
        National Library of Ireland
        Copy at SUNY SB   Box 88

A Dawn-Song   DAWN SONG
    No Ms located.

Death   DEAT
    AMs draft. See Miscellany: DIAR JOUR (leather note-
    book ca 1927; Ms 30359).
        National Library of Ireland
        Copy at SUNY SB   Box 88

    AMs and TMs. See Books: WIND STAI MA.
        National Library of Ireland
        Copy at SUNY SB   Box 6

The Death of the Hare   DEAT HARE
    AMs. See Miscellany: DIAR JOUR (Ms 13589).
        National Library of Ireland
        Copy at SUNY SB   Box 5

Dedication   DEDI
    AMs and TMs drafts (Ms 13590).
        National Library of Ireland
        Copy at SUNY SB   Box 6, 7

The Dedication to a Book of Stories selected
from the Irish Novelists   DEDI BOOK ST
    Page proofs with corrections in POET WORK 06.
        New York Public Library

A Deep-Sworn Vow   DEEP SWOR VO
    AMs draft in "red notebook...from Maud Gonne."
    See Miscellany: DIAR JOUR (Ms 30358).
        National Library of Ireland
        Copy at SUNY SB   Box 88

The Delphic Oracle upon Plotinus   DELP ORAC PL
    Copy of drafts and fair copy from white vellum
    notebook. See Miscellany: DIAR JOUR (Partial
    List...#545).
        Location of original unknown
        Copy at SUNY SB   Box 88

    AMsS; TMs copy (Ms 13591).
        National Library of Ireland
        Copy at SUNY SB   Box 6

Demon and Beast   DEMO BEAS
    TMs (original and carbon) with additions and
    corrections (Za Dial).
        Yale University

    AMs (Ms 13588).
        National Library of Ireland
        Copy at SUNY SB   Box 3

A Dialogue of Self and Soul   DIAL SELF SO
    AMs and TMs. See Books: WIND STAI MA.
        National Library of Ireland
        Copy at SUNY SB   Box 6

    AMs draft. See Miscellany: DIAR JOUR (leather notebook
    ca 1927; Ms 30359).
        National Library of Ireland
        Copy at SUNY SB   Box 88

    See also Miscellany: DIAR JOUR (Ms 13590) and Poems:
    WOMA YOUN OL.

The Dolls   DOLL
    AMs draft in "red notebook...from Maud Gonne."
    See Miscellany: DIAR JOUR (Ms 30358).
        National Library of Ireland
        Copy at SUNY SB   Box 88

    AMs (Ms 13586).
        National Library of Ireland
        Copy at SUNY SB   Box 4

The Double Vision of Michael Robartes   DOUB VISI MI
    TMs and two carbons, with corrections on first copy.
        Yale University

    Revisions in copy of LATE POEM 22.
        Yeats, Anne

    Copy of POEM 01 inscribed (to no one), with the lines
    "For what but eye and ear silence the mind With the
    minute particulars of mankind."
        University of London Library

    TMs, revised (3 pp; Ms 21864).
        National Library of Ireland

Down by the Salley Gardens   DOWN SALL GA
    AMsS, entitled "An Old Song Resung," dated 1888.
        University of Tulsa

    AMs; copy entitled "An Old Song Resung."
        University of Texas at Austin

A Dream of Death   DREA DEAT
    Page proofs with corrections in POET WORK 06.
        New York Public Library

    Two AMs, one of a later version (Ms 30318); AMs draft,
    beginning "I dreamed they laid." (Ms 30341).
        National Library of Ireland
        Copy at SUNY SB Box 5, 8

A Drinking Song   DRIN SONG
    Two AMs, with revisions.
        New York Public Library

A Drunken Man's Praise of Sobriety   DRUN MAN' PR
    AMs; TMs, with corrections (Ms 13593).
        National Library of Ireland
        Copy at SUNY SB Box 4

Easter 1916   EAST 1916
    AMs; fair copy entitled "Easter," signed and dated
    April 1917, with two minor corrections (Ashley MS
    2291).
        British Library

    TMs and AMs (Ms 13588).
        National Library of Ireland
        Copy at SUNY SB Box 3

    TMs, with corrections.
        The Huntington Library

    Fair copy of stanza III, dated Sept. 1916, in COLL
    WORK 08, vol. 3.
        New York Public Library

    TMs, with corrections.
        Sligo County Library

    TMs (original and carbon), with additions and
    corrections (Za Dial).
        Yale University

Poems   261

    Fair copy, dated Sept. 25, 1916, inserted in EAST 16.
    New York Public Library

Ego Dominus Tuus   EGO DOMI TU
    AMs (Ms 13587).
    National Library of Ireland
    Copy at SUNY SB   Box 6

    Proof sheet.
    University of Chicago

    AMs, dated Dec 1915 (4 pp; MS Eng 821.4).
    Harvard University

    Copy of PER AMIC 18 inscribed (to no one) with the
    line "By the help of images I call to my own
    opposite."
    University of London Library

    Page proofs with corrections in WILD SWAN 17.
    University of Texas at Austin

    AMs draft. See Miscellany: DIAR JOUR (leather notebook,
    Ms 30359; red notebook, Ms 30358).
    National Library of Ireland
    Copy at SUNY SB   Box 88

    TMs, entitled "The anti-self," with corrections, dated
    Dec. 1915.
    New York Public Library

The Empty Cup   EMPT CUP
    AMs (1 p; Ms 13589).
    National Library of Ireland
    Copy at SUNY SB   Box 5

    AMsS, enclosed in letter to SHAK OLIV.
    Yeats, Senator Michael
    Copy at SUNY SB   Box 58, 59

The End of Day   END DAY
    AMs (1 p; Ms 13587).
    National Library of Ireland
    Copy at SUNY SB   Box 6

    See also Poems: UPON DYIN LA.

The Entrance of Deirdre   ENTR DEIR
    See Poems: QUEE EDAI and Plays: DEIR.

Ephemera   EPHE
    Page proofs with revisions in copy of WAND OISI 89.
        University of Texas at Austin

    AMs (Ms 30348).
        National Library of Ireland
        Copy at SUNY SB   Box 1

    See also Books: POET WORK 06.

The Everlasting Voices   EVER VOIC
    Copy of poem in page proofs for Books: UNPU MACM ED.
        National Library of Ireland
        Copy at SUNY SB   Box 28, 29, 30

    AMs in small white notebook. See Miscellany: DIAR JOUR
    (Partial List...#548).
        Yeats, Senator Michael

A Faery Song   FAER SONG
    AMs draft, entitled "The good People of the Mountain
    Sing" (Ms 30456). See also Poems, Unpublished: OUTL
    BRID.
        National Library of Ireland
        Copy at SUNY SB

    AMsS.
        University of Texas at Austin

The Fairy Doctor   FAIR DOCT
    AMs draft in letter to HINK KATH.
        The Huntington Library

The Fairy Pedant   FAIR PEDA
    No Ms located.

Fallen Majesty   FALL MAJE
    TMsS, with corrections.
        University of Chicago

    AMs (Ms 13586).
        National Library of Ireland
        Copy at SUNY SB   Box 4

Poems

The Falling of the Leaves   FALL LEAV
    AMs (Ms 30422).
        National Library of Ireland
        Copy at SUNY SB   Box 1

The Fascination of What's Difficult   FASC WHAT DI
    No Ms located.

Father and Child   FATH CHIL
    TMs (Ms 13592).
        National Library of Ireland
        Copy at SUNY SB   Box 7

Fergus and the Druid   FERG DRUI
    Page proofs with corrections in POET WORK 06.
        New York Public Library

    Two lines beginning "Take if you will this little
    bag of dreams," inscribed in copy of POEM 95
    (Ip.Y34.C895pb).
        Yale University

    Two lines beginning "Take if you must this little
    bag of dreams," inscribed in copy of POEM 22,
    dated Dec 15 1923.
        University of Massachusetts Amherst

The Fiddler of Dooney   FIDD DOON
    AMsS (2 pp).
        New York Public Library

A First Confession   FIRS CONF
    TMs and AMs (Ms 13589, 13592).
        National Library of Ireland
        Copy at SUNY SB   Box 7, 88

    See also Poems: WOMA YOUN OL.

First Love   FIRS LOVE
    AMs (Ms 13589).
        National Library of Ireland
        Copy at SUNY SB   Box 5

    AMs draft, enclosed in letter to SHAK OLIV.
        Yeats, Senator Michael
        Copy at SUNY SB   Box 58, 59

The Fish   FISH
    One AMs, entitled "Breasal the Fisherman," with
    revisions; another AMs, entitled "The Fisher Aodh."
        New York Public Library

The Fisherman   FISH ERMA N
    Page proofs with corrections in WILD SWAN 17.
        University of Texas at Austin

    Corrections in EIGH POEM 16.
        New York Public Library

    TMs.
        University of Chicago

    AMs draft in "red notebook...from Maud Gonne."
    See Miscellany: DIAR JOUR (Ms 30358).
        National Library of Ireland
        Copy at SUNY SB   Box 88

The Folly of Being Comforted   FOLL BEIN CO
    AMsS, with revisions.
        Fiskin, Jeffrey

    Revisions in POEM SECO 09.
        Yeats, Anne

    Proof sheets (Ms 13584).
        National Library of Ireland
        Copy at SUNY SB   Box 1

For Anne Gregory   FOR ANNE GR
    AMs and TMs. See Books: WIND STAI MA (Ms 13590).
        National Library of Ireland
        Copy at SUNY SB   Box 6

    AMsS; copy with revisions and deletions, dated
    September 1930, in copy of SELE POEM 29 inscribed to
    GREG LADY (I:29).
        Emory University

The Four Ages of Man   FOUR AGES MA
    TMs, with commentary.
        University of Chicago

Fragments   FRAG
    No Ms located.

A Friend's Illness   FRIE ILLN
    Fair copy, dated Feb. 6, 1909, in COLL WORK 08, vol. 1;
    another fair copy in vol. 7.
        New York Public Library

    AMs, along with sections of ESTR 26 (Ms 30350).
        National Library of Ireland
        Copy at SUNY SB   Box 24

Friends   FRIE
    AMs; AMs draft (30515, 13586).
        National Library of Ireland
        Copy at SUNY SB   Box 4

    AMsS; 28 lines with revisions and deletions (Jan 21
    1911; I:7).
        Emory University

The Friends of His Youth   FRIE YOUT
    TMs (Ms 13589).
        National Library of Ireland
        Copy at SUNY SB   Box 5

The friends that have it I do wrong   FRIE THAT HA
    Quatrain inscribed in copy of KING THRE 04; signature
    is followed by five astrological symbols
    (Ip.y34.904kb).
        Yale University

From 'Oedipus at Colonus'   FROM OEDI CO
    AMs (Ms 13589).
        National Library of Ireland
        Copy at SUNY SB   Box 5

    AMs (two stanzas) enclosed in letter to SHAK OLIV.
        Yeats, Senator Michael
        Copy at SUNY SB   Box 58, 59

    See also Poems: MAN YOUN OL.

From the 'Antigone'   FROM ANTI
    TMs, with corrections by Ezra Pound (Ms 13592); AMs.
    See Books: WIND STAI MA (Ms 13590).
        National Library of Ireland
        Copy at SUNY SB   Box 7

AMs draft. See Miscellany: DIAR JOUR (leather notebook
ca 1927; Ms 30359).
    National Library of Ireland
    Copy at SUNY SB Box 88

See also Poems: WOMA YOUN OL.

Full moody is my love and sad   FULL MOOD IS
  See Poems: GIRL SONG JS.

The Ghost of Roger Casement   GHOS ROGE CA
  AMs; four TMs, with corrections (Ms 13593).
    National Library of Ireland
    Copy at SUNY SB Box 3, 4

The Gift of Harun Al-Rashid   GIFT HARU AL
  TMs and galley proofs with corrections (Za Dial).
    Yale University

  AMsS, AMs and TMs (Ms 30540). Revised proofs from Cuala
  edition of CAT MOON 24 (Ms 21858).
    National Library of Ireland
    Copy at SUNY SB Box 7

Girl's Song (from JOHN SHER 91)   GIRL SONG JS
  AMs beginning "Full moody is my love and sad"
  (Ms 30342).
    National Library of Ireland
    Copy at SUNY SB Box 7

  AMs in Miscellany: DIAR JOUR (Rapallo notebook
  finished June 1929; Ms 13580).
    National Library of Ireland
    Copy at SUNY SB Box 90

Girl's Song (from WIND STAI 33)   GIRL SONG WS
  TMs (Ms 13591).
    National Library of Ireland
    Copy at SUNY SB Box 6

The Glove and the Cloak   GLOV CLOA
  AMs entitled "The Glove in the Cloak" in small white
  notebook. See Miscellany: DIAR JOUR (Partial List...
  #548).
    Yeats, Senator Michael

Poems

    AMsS.
        Kenyon College Library

Gratitude to the Unknown Instructors   GRAT UNKN IN
    Copy of draft entitled "System," in white vellum
    notebook. See Miscellany: DIAR JOUR (Partial
    List...#545).
        Location of original unknown
        Copy at SUNY SB   Box 88

    TMs. See Books: WIND STAI MA.
        National Library of Ireland
        Copy at SUNY SB   Box 6

The Great Day   GREA DAY
    AMs and AMsS; TMs (1 p), with corrections (Ms 13593).
        National Library of Ireland
        Copy at SUNY SB   Box 4

The Grey Rock   GREY ROCK
    AMs (15 pp), dated Oct. 21, 1912, with revisions,
    removed from COLL WORK 08; TMs (carbon) with
    corrections.
        New York Public Library

    TMsS (6 pp) with corrections, dated Oct. 1912, entitled
    "Aoife's Lover," and stamped "THE BRITISH REVIEW. Jan
    28 1913."
        Princeton University Library

    AMs (Ms 13586).
        National Library of Ireland
        Copy at SUNY SB   Box 4

    TMsS, dated Oct 1912, entitled "Aoife's Lover," likely
    used as basis for first appearance in POETRY magazine.
        University of Chicago

    Revisions in copy of LATE POEM 22 (item 2382).
        Yeats, Anne

The Gyres   GYRE
    AMs (9 pp; Ms 13593).
        National Library of Ireland
        Copy at SUNY SB   Box 3

The Happy Townland   HAPP TOWN
    Page proofs with corrections in POET WORK 06; galley
    proofs with revisions in POEM 1899 06.
        New York Public Library

    Revisions in poem, entitled "Rider of the North," and
    fair copy of eight lines beginning "The little fox,"
    both in Dun Emer edition of IN SEVE 03.
        New York Public Library

    AMsS; copy with revisions entitled "A Rider from the
    North," dated 1903 March 28, in copy of WIND REED 99,
    inscribed to GREG LADY (I:18).
        Emory University

    Page proofs, entitled "A Rider from the North" (Ms
    13584).
        National Library of Ireland
        Copy at SUNY SB   Box 1

The harlot sang to the beggarman   HARL SANG BE
    TMs (Ms 8772).
        National Library of Ireland

The Harp of Aengus   HARP AENG
    No Ms located.

The Hawk   HAWK
    Corrections in Books: EIGH POEM 16.
        New York Public Library

    AMs (Ms 13587).
        National Library of Ireland
        Copy at SUNY SB   Box 5

    See also Books: WILD SWAN 17.

He and She   HE   SHE
    TMs, with commentary.
        University of Chicago

He bids his Beloved be at Peace   HE   BIDS HI
    AMs entitled "The Dark Horses," in small white
    notebook. See Miscellany: DIAR JOUR (Partial
    List...#548).
        Yeats, Senator Michael

He gives his Beloved certain Rhymes   HE   GIVE HI
    TMs with revisions, entitled "Aodh to Dectora with
    certain rhymes." See also Books: WIND REED 99.
        New York Public Library

    AMs with various related prose notes and an unpublished
    stanza, in small white notebook. See Miscellany: DIAR
    JOUR (Partial List...#548).
        Yeats, Senator Michael

He has lost what may not be found   HE   HAS LO
    (Song from the Play: AT HAWK WE)
    AMs (13583).
        National Library of Ireland
        Copy at SUNY SB Box 10

He hears the Cry of the Sedge   HE   HEAR CR
    Minor revisions in text of WIND REED 99, inscribed to
    GREG LADY. (PR 5904 W6 1902).
        Emory University

    Copy of WIND REED 99, inscribed to MOOR GEOR with
    changed line: "Your head will not lie on the breast"
    changed to "Your breast will not lie by the breast."
        Pierpont Morgan Library

    AMs, entitled "Aodh to Dectora I."
        Pierpont Morgan Library

    TMs, with revisions; also a fair copy, entitled
    "Aodh & Dectora." See also Books: WIND REED 99.
        New York Public Library

    Page proofs with corrections in POET WORK 06.
        New York Public Library

He mourns for the Change that has come upon him
and his Beloved, and longs for the End of the
World   HE   MOUR CH
    Page proofs with corrections in POET WORK 06.
        New York Public Library

    Page proof, entitled "The Desire of Man and of Woman"
    (from THE DOME, June 1897), with corrections.
        New York Public Library

Two TMs, with revisions, entitled "The Desire of Man and of Woman." See also Books: WIND REED 99.
    New York Public Library

He remembers Forgotten Beauty   HE   REME FO
Page proofs with corrections in POET WORK 06.
    New York Public Library

Two TMs, with revisions, entitled "Michael Robartes to his Beloved. II." See also Books: WIND REED 99.
    New York Public Library

He Reproves the Curlew   HE   REPR CU
AMsS, entitled "O'Sullivan Rua to the curlew."
    Kenyon College Library

He tells of a Valley full of Lovers   HE   TELL VA
Page proofs with corrections in POET WORK 06.
    New York Public Library

TMs, with revisions, entitled "A dream of the valley of lovers." See also Books: WIND REED 99.
    New York Public Library

He tells of the Perfect Beauty   HE   TELL PE
Two AMs drafts with revisions and deletions tipped in copy of POEM 95 belonging to GREG LADY (I:9).
    Emory University

AMs, entitled "A Salutation," dated Sept 1 1891 (Ms 30318).
    National Library of Ireland
    Copy at SUNY SB   Box 8

AMs in small white notebook. See Miscellany: DIAR JOUR (Partial List...#548).
    Yeats, Senator Michael

TMs, with revisions, entitled "The Perfect Beauty." See also Books: WIND REED 99.
    New York Public Library

See Poems, Unpublished: TO MAUD GO for a poem related to this one.

He thinks of his Past Greatness when a Part of
the Constellations of Heaven   HE   THIN HI
    TMs, with revisions, and AMs, entitled "A Song of
    Mongan." See also Books: WIND REED 99.
       New York Public Library

    Page proofs with corrections in POET WORK 06.
       New York Public Library

He thinks of those who have Spoken Evil of his
Beloved   HE   THIN TH
    AMsS, entitled "Aodh to Dectora III."
       Pierpont Morgan Library

    TMs, with revisions; AMs entitled "Aodh & Dectora."
    See also Books: WIND REED 99.
       New York Public Library

    Page proofs with corrections in POET WORK 06.
       New York Public Library

He wishes for the Cloths of Heaven   HE   WISH CL
    TMs, entitled "Aedh wishes for the Cloths of Heaven."
       Yale University

    TMs by Pound made ca 1905, entitled "Aedh wishes for
    the Cloths of Heaven."
       Yale University

    Two AMs, entitled "The Cloths of Heaven."
       New York Public Library

    AMsS, entitled "Aedh wishes for the Cloths of Heaven"
    (Ms 22335).
       National Library of Ireland

    AMs (fair copy) written in Sir Edward Marsh's autograph
    book, dated Jan 1920.
       Eton School Library

    Fair copy on front flyleaf of WAND OISI 89, dated
    October 1904.
       Indiana University

    See also Poems, Unpublished: YOUR PATH.

He wishes his Beloved were Dead   HE   WISH HI
   Clipping from SKETCH, 9 February 1898, with AMs
   corrections (1 p); TMs, with corrections, entitled
   "Aodh to Dectora." See also Books: WIND REED 99.
      New York Public Library

The Heart of the Woman   HEAR WOMA
   AMs in small white notebook. See Miscellany: DIAR JOUR
   (Partial List...#548).
      Yeats, Senator Michael

The heart well worn upon the sleeve may be
the best of sights   HEAR WELL WO
   No Ms located.

Her Anxiety   HER ANXI
   TMs (Ms 13591); AMs in Miscellany: DIAR JOUR (Ms 13580).
      National Library of Ireland
      Copy at SUNY SB   Box 6, 90

Her Courage   HER   COUR AG
   TMs with variant readings, significantly different
   from published version.
      University of Reading Library

   Page proofs with corrections in WILD SWAN 17.
      University of Texas at Austin

   See also Poems: UPON DYIN LA.

Her Courtesy   HER   COUR TE
   Page proofs with corrections in WILD SWAN 17.
      University of Texas at Austin

   TMs with variant readings.
      University of Reading Library

   See also Poems: UPON DYIN LA.

Her Dream   HER   DREA
   TMs (Ms 13591); AMs in Miscellany: DIAR JOUR (Ms 13580).
      National Library of Ireland
      Copy at SUNY SB   Box 6, 90

Her Friends Bring Her a Christmas Tree   HER   FRIE BR
   See Poems: UPON DYIN LA.

Her Praise   HER   PRAI
    AMs (Ms 13587).
        National Library of Ireland
        Copy at SUNY SB   Box 5

    One TMs with corrections, entitled "The Thorn Tree" (Ms
    30035); two other TMsS (Ms 30425).
        National Library of Ireland
        Copy at SUNY SB   Box 5

    One proof sheet; one TMs entitled "The Thorn
    Tree."
        University of Chicago

    Corrections in the poem entitled "The Thorn Tree," in
    EIGH POEM 16.
        New York Public Library

Her Race   HER   RACE
    See Books: WILD SWAN 17 and Poems: UPON DYIN LA.

Her Triumph   HER   TRIU
    TMs, with corrections (2 copies); AMs draft (Ms 13568,
    13589, 13592).
        National Library of Ireland
        Copy at SUNY SB   Box 7

Her Vision in the Wood   HER   VISI WO
    TMs; AMs (Ms 13589, 13592).
        National Library of Ireland
        Copy at SUNY SB   Box 7

    See also Poems: WOMA YOUN OL.

The Hero, the Girl, and the Fool   HERO GIRL FO
    AMs (2 pp; Ms 13589).
        National Library of Ireland
        Copy at SUNY SB   Box 7

High Talk   HIGH TALK
    AMs (2 pp); two TMs and one carbon, with corrections
    (Ms 13593).
        National Library of Ireland
        Copy at SUNY SB   Box 2

His Bargain   HIS   BARG
>TMs (Ms 13591).
>>National Library of Ireland
>>Copy at SUNY SB   Box 6

>AMs. See Miscellany: DIAR JOUR (Rapallo notebook finished June 1929; Ms 13580).
>>National Library of Ireland
>>Copy at SUNY SB   Box 90

His Confidence   HIS   CONF
>TMs (Ms 13591); AMs in Miscellany: DIAR JOUR (Ms 13580).
>>National Library of Ireland
>>Copy at SUNY SB   Box 6, 91

His Dream   HIS   DREA
>Photocopy of AMs draft (RP 2429).
>>British Library

His Memories   HIS   MEMO
>Draft (Ms 13589).
>>National Library of Ireland
>>Copy at SUNY SB   Box 5

His Phoenix   HIS   PHOE
>TMsS; carbon, with revisions, entitled "There is a Queen in China."
>>University of Texas at Austin

>AMs (1 p) and TMs (3 pp; Ms 30300).
>>National Library of Ireland
>>Copy at SUNY SB   Box 5

>Page proofs with corrections in WILD SWAN 17.
>>University of Texas at Austin

>Fair copy, dated Sept. 1915, entitled "There is a Queen in China," in COLL WORK 08, vol. 1.
>>New York Public Library

>Corrections in copy of EIGH POEM 16.
>>New York Public Library

>One proof sheet, and one TMs entitled "There is a Queen in China."
>>University of Chicago

Poems   275

His Wildness   HIS   WILD
    AMs and corrected page proofs (Ms 13589).
    National Library of Ireland
    Copy at SUNY SB   Box 5

The Host of the Air   HOST AIR
    AMs in small white notebook. See Miscellany: DIAR JOUR
    (Partial List...#548).
        Yeats, Senator Michael

The Hosting of the Sidhe   HOST SIDH
    One AMs, two TMs, TMs of first line, all with
    revisions. See also Books: WIND REED 99.
        New York Public Library

    AMs in small white notebook. See Miscellany: DIAR JOUR
    (Partial List...#548).
        Yeats, Senator Michael

Hound Voice   HOUN VOIC
    AMs (5 pp); two TMs and two carbon copies, with
    corrections (Ms 13593).
        National Library of Ireland
        Copy at SUNY SB   Box 2

    TMs with revisions (bMSS Eng 338.12 [5-15]).
        Harvard University

The Hour before Dawn   HOUR DAWN
    Copy of FOUR PLAY 21 inscribed (to no one) with three
    lines, beginning "There is no man but cocks his ear."
        University of London Library

    AMs (Ms 13586).
        National Library of Ireland
        Copy at SUNY SB   Box 4

    Correction in a copy of LATE POEM 22 inscribed to
    GREG LADY.
        New York Public Library

How Ferencz Renyi Kept Silent   HOW   FERE RE
    No Ms located.

Huddon, Duddon and Daniel O'Leary HUDD DUDD DA
    Copy of drafts from white vellum notebook. See
    Miscellany: DIAR JOUR (Partial List...#545).
        Location of original unknown
        Copy at SUNY SB   Box 88

Human Dignity HUMA DIGN
    Draft (Ms 13589).
        National Library of Ireland
        Copy at SUNY SB   Box 5

I Am of Ireland I   AM   IR
    AMs (Ms 13591). TMs note on the poem (Ms 13592).
        National Library of Ireland
        Copy at SUNY SB   Box 6

    AMs draft. See Miscellany: DIAR JOUR (Rapallo notebook
    D headed "Dublin August 1929"; Ms 13581).
        National Library of Ireland
        Copy at SUNY SB   Box 90

I See phantoms of Hatred and of the Heart's
Fullness and of the Coming Emptiness I   SEE PH
    AMs. See Miscellany: DIAR JOUR (Ms 13589). See also
    Books: STOR RED 04 and Poems: MEDI TIME CI.
        National Library of Ireland
        Copy of SUNY SB   Box 5

I walked among the Seven Woods of Coole I   WALK SE
    No Ms located.

I was going the road one day I   WAS GO
    (Song from Play: HOUR GLAS).
    AMs (Ms 30381).
        National Library of Ireland
        Copy at SUNY SB   Box 12

An Image from a Past Life IMAG PAST LI
    TMs and AMs; poem and notes (Ms 13588).
        National Library of Ireland
        Copy at SUNY SB   Box 3

Imitated from the Japanese IMIT JAPA
    AMs and TMs (Ms 13593).
        National Library of Ireland
        Copy at SUNY SB   Box 3

Impetuous Heart Be Still   IMPE HEAR BE
    AMsS; fair copy.
        University of Texas at Austin

    AMs beginning "Impetuous heart give heed to my rime."
    See Miscellany: DIAR JOUR (Partial List...#496).
        Yeats, Senator Michael
        Copy at SUNY SB

    AMs under title of "The Lover to his heart," beginning
    "Impetuous heart be still" (Partial List...#548).
        Yeats, Senator Michael

In a Drawing-Room   IN DRAW RO
    AMs (Ms 30826).
        National Library of Ireland
        Copy at SUNY SB   Box 7

In Church   IN CHUR
    AMs draft in letter to HINK KATH TY.
        The Huntington Library

In Memory of Alfred Pollexfen   IN MEMO AL
    AMsS, dated Aug 1918 (Ms 13587).
        National Library of Ireland
        Copy at SUNY SB   Box 6

    Fair copy (Ms 3255).
        National Library of Ireland

In Memory of Eva Gore-Booth and Con Markiewicz IN MEMO EV
    Two TMs (Ms 30149); AMs draft. See Miscellany:
    DIAR JOUR (leather notebook ca 1927; Ms 30359).
        National Library of Ireland
        Copy at SUNY SB   Box 88

    AMs and TMs. See Books: WIND STAI MA.
        National Library of Ireland
        Copy at SUNY SB   Box 6

    Two TMsS (Ms 30149). See also Miscellany:
    DIAR JOUR (Ms 30359, 13590).
        National Library of Ireland
        Copy at SUNY SB   Box 88

In Memory of Major Robert Gregory   IN   MEMO MA
    AMs (3 pp); revised TMs (Ms 30498, 21868, 21869).
        National Library of Ireland

    TMs, with corrected proof for the ENGLISH REVIEW (Wade 1918).
        Yale University

    TMs and AMs; 12 eight-line stanzas typed with corrections; separate sheet, handwritten, with revisions.
        Emory University

    Four-page TMs with corrections; one page (eight lines) AMs with revisions (I:10).
        Emory University

    TMsS (4 pp) with a few corrections, dated July 1918.
        University of Texas at Austin

    TMs; three copies with corrections, one signed and dated May 24, 1918; galley proofs with corrections for WILD SWAN 17.
        New York Public Library

    TMs (carbon) with corrections, entitled "To Major Robert Gregory"; note by Lady Gregory dated Nov. 23, 1920, says she asked that this poem not be published. Different from any published version.
        New York Public Library

    Page proofs with corrections in WILD SWAN 17.
        University of Texas at Austin

    See also Poems: REPR.

In Tara's Halls   IN   TARA HA
    AMs (4 pp); two TMs copies (Ms 13593).
        National Library of Ireland
        Copy at SUNY SB   Box 2

In the Firelight   IN   FIRE
    Copy of poem (differs slightly from version in VARIORUM) in ALS to O'LE ELLE.
        New York Public Library

In the Seven Woods   IN   SEVE WO
   TMs with corrections; also a draft and a note, dated
   April 5, 1902, with instructions relating to IN SEVE
   03. See also Books: POEM 1899 06.
   New York Public Library

   Revised proofs (Ms 13584).
   National Library of Ireland
   Copy at SUNY SB

The Indian to His Love   INDI LOVE
   No Ms located.

The Indian Upon God   INDI GOD
   Page proofs with revisions in WAND OISI 89.
   University of Texas at Austin

   Page proofs with corrections in POET WORK 06.
   New York Public Library

Into the Twilight   INTO TWIL
   AMs (Ms 30349).
   National Library of Ireland
   Copy at SUNY SB   Box 6

   AMsS; fair copy of first stanza in copy of
   CELT TWIL 93 belonging to GREG LADY (I:11).
   Emory University

An Irish Airman Foresees His Death   IRIS AIRM FO
   AMs (Ms 13587).
   National Library of Ireland
   Copy at SUNY SB   Box 5

   Page proof for WILD SWAN 19 with corrections, and note
   to Lady Gregory.
   New York Public Library

   See also Speeches: AMER TOUR LE (Ms 13587) and
   Poems: REPR.

The Island of Statues   ISLA STAT
   Manuscripts and proofs in copy of MOSA 86
   ([1885]; MS3502/4).
   Trinity College Dublin

AMs (49 pp).
   The King's School Library

Four AMs notebooks; AMs, one with draft of the poem
SEEK (Ms 30328, 30457).
   National Library of Ireland
   Copy at SUNY SB   Box 12

John Kinsella's Lament for Mrs. Mary Moore   JOHN KINS LA
AMs, dated July 29; TMs copy (Ms 13593); TMs (1 p; Ms
30143).
   National Library of Ireland
   Copy at SUNY SB   Box 2

   Copy enclosed in letter to HIGG FRED.
   University of Texas at Austin

Kanva on Himself   KANV HIMS
   AMs (Ms 30448).
   National Library of Ireland
   Copy at SUNY SB   Box 7

   Page proofs with revision in WAND OISI 89.
   University of Texas at Austin

King and No King   KING NO   KI
   No Ms located.

The Lady's First Song   LADY FIRS SO
   AMs; TMs, with corrections (Ms 13593).
   National Library of Ireland
   Copy at SUNY SB   Box 3

The Lady's Second Song   LADY SECO SO
   TMs, with corrections, entitled "The lady to her
   chambermaid" (Ms 13593).
   National Library of Ireland
   Copy at SUNY SB   Box 3

   TMs (carbon), entitled "The lady to her chambermaid,"
   enclosed in letter to WELL DORO.
   Meisei University

The Lady's Third Song   LADY THIR SO
   AMs and TMs (Ms 13593).
   National Library of Ireland
   Copy at SUNY SB   Box 3

Poems 281

The Lake Isle of Innisfree LAKE ISLE IN
    Fair copy on Merrion Square stationery.
    Mills College Library

    TMsS; dated Notre Dame Jan 10 1933.
    University of Notre Dame

    AMsS, dated Dec. 11, 1901.
    Rosenbach Museum and Library

    AMs, fair copy (Ms 13585).
    National Library of Ireland
    Copy at SUNY SB Box 5

    AMsS; fair copy, with "on the shore" changed to "by the shore."
    University of Texas at Austin

    AMsS; fair copy of first stanza, inscribed in POEM 95.
    University of Toronto

The Lamentation of the Old Pensioner LAME OLD PE
    No Ms located.

Lapis Lazuli LAPI LAZU
    AMs fragments (Ms 30409).
    National Library of Ireland
    Copy at SUNY SB Box 3

    AMs (3 pp) and TMsS (3 pp; 2 copies; Ms 13593).
    National Library of Ireland
    Copy at SUNY SB Box 3

A Last Confession LAST CONF
    AMs, AMsS, and TMs (Ms 13592).
    National Library of Ireland
    Copy at SUNY SB Box 7

    See also Poems: WOMA YOUN OL.

The Leaders of the Crowd LEAD CROW
    AMs and TMs, with corrections (Ms 13588).
    National Library of Ireland
    Copy at SUNY SB Box 3

Leda and the Swan   LEDA SWAN
   Fair copy (Ms 30413); AMs. See Miscellany:
   DIAR JOUR (Ms 13589).
      National Library of Ireland
      Copy at SUNY SB   Box 5

   TMs and galley proofs with corrections (Za Dial).
      Yale University

A Legend   LEGE
   No Ms located.

Life   LIFE
   AMs of the middle three stanzas, entitled "A Song of
   Sunset," on verso of a page from a draft of "Mosada"
   (Ms 30430).
      National Library of Ireland
      Copy at SUNY SB   Box 8

Lift Up the White Knee   LIFT WHIT KN
   AMs (1 p), dated 1912.
      Stanford University

   AMs; draft (12 lines), beginning "Lift up the white
   knee That's what they sing Those young dancers"
   (Ms 30466).
      National Library of Ireland
      Copy at SUNY SB

   AMs (1 p), dated 1912.
      Colby College Library

Lines Written in Dejection   LINE WRIT DE
   Page proof in copy of WILD SWAN 19.
      New York Public Library

   AMs draft in "red notebook...from Maud Gonne."
   See Miscellany: DIAR JOUR (Ms 30358).
      National Library of Ireland
      Copy at SUNY SB   Box 88

   AMs (photocopy; Ms 13587).
      National Library of Ireland
      Copy at SUNY SB   Box 5

   AMsS, dated Sept 29, 1918.
      University of Texas at Austin

TMs, typed by Ezra Pound with comments by him and sent to Harriet Monroe (Aug 1, 1917).
    University of Chicago

The Living Beauty   LIVI BEAT
    AMs; fragments of lines used in SOLO SHEB and LIVI BEAU (16 lines; Ms 13587).
        National Library of Ireland
        Copy at SUNY SB   Box 5

    Revisions in copy of LATE POEM 22.
        Yeats, Anne

Long-legged Fly   LONG LEGG FL
    TMs with revisions (bMS Eng 338.12 [5-15]).
        Harvard University

    AMs (2 pp); TMs (Ms 13593).
        National Library of Ireland
        Copy at SUNY SB   Box 2

Love and Death   LOVE DEAT
    AMs; draft (3 pp; Ms 31042).
        National Library of Ireland
        Copy at SUNY SB   Box 9

Love Song   LOVE SONG
    No Ms located.

Love's Loneliness   LOVE LONE
    TMs (Ms 13591).
        National Library of Ireland
        Copy at SUNY SB   Box 6

The Lover asks Forgiveness because of his Many Moods   LOVE ASKS FO
    AMsS, entitled "The Twilight of Forgiveness."
        University of California Los Angeles

    TMs, with revisions, entitled "Michael Robartes to his Beloved. II." See also Books: WIND REED 99.
        New York Public Library

    AMs entitled "The Twilight of Forgiveness" in small white notebook. See Miscellany: DIAR JOUR (Partial List...#548).
        Yeats, Senator Michael

The Lover mourns for the Loss of Love   LOVE MOUR LO
   TMs, titled "Aodh to Dectora II," with corrections; one
   AMs, entitled "A Friend"; a clipping of the poem
   with corrections. See also Books: WIND REED 99.
      New York Public Library

   AMs, entitled "Aodh to Dectora II."
      Pierpont Morgan Library

The Lover pleads with his Friend for Old
Friends   LOVE PLEA HI
   TMs with revisions, entitled "Old Friends."
   See also WIND REED 99.
      New York Public Library

The Lover speaks to the Hearers of his Songs in
Coming Days   LOVE SPEA HE
   Revised proofs (Ms 21856).
      National Library of Ireland

   AMs in small white notebook. See Miscellany: DIAR JOUR
   (Partial List...#548).
      Yeats, Senator Michael

   Page proofs with corrections in POET WORK 06.
      New York Public Library

The Lover Tells of the Rose in his Heart   LOVE TELL RO
   Draft in copy of POEM 95 belonging to GREG LADY.
      Emory University

   AMs; copy with corrections and printer's marks. (I:19).
      Emory University

   AMs in small white notebook. See Miscellany: DIAR JOUR
   (Partial List...#548).
      Yeats, Senator Michael

   Cuala hand colored print (no. 88) inscribed to PROK
   FRED.
      Wesleyan University

   TMs, with revisions, entitled "The Rose in my Heart."
   See also Books: WIND REED 99.
      New York Public Library

Poems   285

A Lover's Quarrel among the Fairies   LOVE QUAR FA
   No Ms located.

The Lover's Song   LOVE RS   SO
   AMs draft, entitled "Yang & Yin" (item 21).
      Yeats, Anne

   AMs; TMs, with corrections (Ms 13593).
      National Library of Ireland
      Copy at SUNY SB   Box 3

Lullaby   LULL
   AMs (Ms 13591).
      National Library of Ireland
      Copy at SUNY SB   Box 6

   AMs. See Miscellany: DIAR JOUR (Rapallo notebook
   finished June 1929; Ms 13580).
      National Library of Ireland
      Copy at SUNY SB   Box 90

Mad as the Mist and Snow   MAD MIST SN
   AMs (Ms 13591); another AMs. See Miscellany: DIAR JOUR
   (Rapallo notebook finished June 1929; Ms 13580).
      National Library of Ireland
      Copy at SUNY SB   Box 6, 90

The Madness of King Goll   MADN KING GO
   Page proofs with revision in WAND OISI 89.
      University of Texas at Austin

   AMsS (4 pp), with revisions, and a note by K. Tynan
   Hinkson [1887].
      University of Texas at Austin

The Magi   MAGI
   AMs draft in "red notebook...from Maud Gonne." See
   Miscellany: DIAR JOUR (Ms 30358).
      National Library of Ireland
      Copy at SUNY SB   Box 88

Maid Quiet   MAID QUIE
   AMsS; fair copy entitled "Hanrahan the Red Upon His
   Wanderings," in copy of POEM 95 belonging to GREG LADY
   (I:8).
      Emory University

AMs in small white notebook. See Miscellany: DIAR JOUR
(Partial List...#548).
    Yeats, Senator Michael

AMs, entitled "Sullivan the Red Upon His Wanderings."
New York Public Library

The Man and the Echo   MAN   ECHO
    AMs (4 pp); two copies and two carbons, with
    corrections (Ms 13593).
        National Library of Ireland
        Copy at SUNY SB   Box 2

The Man Who Dreamed of Faeryland   MAN   WHO   DR
    Page proofs with corrections in POET WORK 06.
    New York Public Library

    AMs (3 pp).
    New York Public Library

A Man Young and Old   MAN   YOUN   OL
    AMs, with revisions of the individual poems (9 pp; Ms
    13589).
        National Library of Ireland
        Copy at SUNY SB   Box 5

The Mask   MASK
    Copy of poem in page proofs of Books: SELE POEM 29.
        National Library of Ireland
        Copy at SUNY SB   Box 5

A Meditation in Time of War   MEDI TIME WA
    Copy of CUTT AGAT 19 inscribed (to no one) with the
    lines "I knew that one is animate, Mankind inanimate
    phantasy."
        University of London Library

    TMs (original and carbon) with additions and
    corrections (Za Dial).
        Yale University

    Page proof (Ms 13588); AMs draft in "red notebook...
    from Maud Gonne." See Miscellany: DIAR JOUR (Ms 30358).
        National Library of Ireland
        Copy at SUNY SB   Box 2, 88

Poems

The Meditation of the Old Fisherman   MEDI OLD FI
    AMs (Ms 30421).
       National Library of Ireland
       Copy at SUNY SB Box 1

Meditations in Time of Civil War   MEDI TIME CI
    TMs (carbon) with corrections for poem from the
    DIAL, January 1923 (Za Dial).
       Yale University

    AMs, with revisions of the individual poems (Ms 13589).
       National Library of Ireland
       Copy at SUNY SB Box 5

Meeting   MEET
    AMs and TMs (13592).
       National Library of Ireland
       Copy at SUNY SB Box 7

Memory   MEMO
    AMS; fair copy.
       Boston College

    AMs with title "Upon a Dying Lady" crossed out
    (Ms 13587).
       National Library of Ireland
       Copy at SUNY SB Box 5

    Proof sheet.
       University of Chicago

    Corrections in Book: EIGH POEM 16.
       New York Public Library

A Memory of Youth   MEMO YOUT
    TMs, with corrections, entitled "Love and the Bird."
    Note by WBY says he made corrections in a hurry,
    and "would be much obliged if you would revise
    punctuation."
       University of Chicago

    AMs (Ms 13586).
       National Library of Ireland
       Copy at SUNY SB Box 4

Men Improve With The Years   MEN   IMPR YE
    AMs, dated July 19, 1918 (Ms 13587).
        National Library of Ireland
        Copy at SUNY SB   Box 5

The Mermaid   MERM
    Draft (2 pp; Ms 13589).
        National Library of Ireland
        Copy at SUNY SB   Box 5

Meru   MERU
    AMs draft, under title of "The Summing Up"
    (Ms 30111).
        National Library of Ireland
        Copy at SUNY SB   Box 4

    AMs draft in Miscellany: DIAR JOUR (Partial
    List...#351).
        National Library of Ireland
        Copy at SUNY SB   Box 4

    TMs with commentary.
        University of Chicago

Michael Robartes and the Dancer   MICH ROBA DA
    TMs (original and carbon) with additions and
    corrections (Za Dial).
        Yale University

    AMs (Ms 13588).
        National Library of Ireland
        Copy at SUNY SB   Box 3

A Model for the Laureate   MODE LAUR
    TMs (1 p; 3 stanzas), under title of "A Marriage Ode"
    (bMS Eng 338.12 [5-15]).
        Harvard University

    TMs, under title of "A Marriage Ode," enclosed in
    letter to WELL DORO.
        Meisei University

    AMs (4 pp); TMs, with corrections (Ms 13593).
        National Library of Ireland
        Copy at SUNY SB   Box 4

Poems

    Some pencilled corrections of poem in NEW POEM 38, inscribed to WELL DORO.
        Smith, Simon Nowell

Mohini Chatterjee   MOHI CHAT
    TMs. See Books: WIND STAI MA.
        National Library of Ireland
        Copy at SUNY SB Box 6, 7

    AMs. See Miscellany: DIAR JOUR (Rapallo notebook finished June 1929; Ms 13580).
        National Library of Ireland
        Copy at SUNY SB Box 90

The Moods   MOOD
    AMsS; fair copy with slight variations in punctuation, dated May 2 [1905 or 1908].
        The Historical Society of Pennsylvania

    Two AMs (Ms 30420, 30477).
        National Library of Ireland
        Copy at SUNY SB Box 6

    AMs in small white notebook. See Miscellany: DIAR JOUR (Partial List...#548).
        Yeats, Senator Michael

Mosada   MOSA
    TMs, with comments on differences from the 1889 version (17 pp; Ms 30193); AMs draft (Ms 30430).
        National Library of Ireland
        Copy at SUNY SB Box 7

    See also Books: MOSA 86.

The Mother of God   MOTH GOD
    AMs and TMs. See Books: WIND STAI MA.
        National Library of Ireland
        Copy at SUNY SB Box 6

    Copy of draft entitled "Mary Virgin," from white vellum notebook. See Miscellany: DIAR JOUR (Partial List...#545).
        Location of original unknown
        Copy at SUNY SB Box 88

The Mountain Tomb   MOUN TOMB
    AMs (Ms 13586).
    National Library of Ireland
    Copy at SUNY SB   Box 4

    TMsS, corrected.
    University of Chicago

Mourn--and Then Onward!   MOUR THEN ON
    No Ms located.

The Municipal Gallery Revisited   MUNI GALL RE
    AMs (13 pp); TMs copy (2 pp; Ms 13593).
    National Library of Ireland
    Copy at SUNY SB   Box 4

My Descendants   MY   DESC
    AMs (Ms 13589).
    National Library of Ireland
    Copy at SUNY SB   Box 5

    See also Poems: MEDI TIME CI.

My House   MY   HOUS
    AMs (Ms 13589).
    National Library of Ireland
    Copy at SUNY SB   Box 5

    See also Poems: MEDI TIME CI.

My Table   MY   TABL
    AMs (Ms 13589).
    National Library of Ireland
    Copy at SUNY SB   Box 5

    See also Poems: MEDI TIME CI.

A Nativity   NATI
    AMs; TMs and carbon, with corrections (Ms 13593).
    National Library of Ireland
    Copy at SUNY SB   Box 2

A Needle's Eye   NEED EYE
    TMs with commentary.
    University of Chicago

Poems   291

   Draft under title of "A Crowded Cross" in copy of
   Swedenborg's THE PRINCIPIA (item 2039A).
      Yeats, Anne

Never Give all the Heart   NEVE GIVE AL
   AMsS; fair copy with corrections, framed, presented to
   Witter Bynner, dated Dec 1905 (bMS Am 1891.22).
      Harvard University

   AMs draft, dated 1904.
      Rosenbach Museum and Library

   AMsS, dated 1904 March 6.
      University of Texas at Austin

   Page proofs with corrections in POET WORK 06.
      New York Public Library

   Fair copy in KING THRE 04, inscribed to QUIN JOHN.
      New York Public Library

The New Faces   NEW   FACE
   AMs, enclosed in a letter to GREG LADY, dated Dec. 7,
   1912.
      New York Public Library

   AMs and TMs (1 p; Ms 13589).
      National Library of Ireland
      Copy at SUNY SB   Box 5

   Revisions in copy of COLL WORK 08 (item 2325).
      Yeats, Anne

News for the Delphic Oracle   NEWS DELP OR
   AMs (5 pp); photocopy; TMs and 2 carbon copies,
   with corrections (Ms 13593).
      National Library of Ireland
      Copy at SUNY SB   Box 2

   TMs carbon (1 p); photocopies of Ms drafts (Ms 30084,
   30155).
      National Library of Ireland
      Copy at SUNY SB   Box 2

Draft of first stanza on back end page of WBY's copy
of Milton's POETICAL WORKS. See Other Authors: MILT
POET 35.
    University of Tulsa

Nineteen Hundred and Nineteen   NINE HUND NI
  Two AMsS; one TMs; one AMs (Ms 13589).
    National Library of Ireland
    Copy at SUNY SB   Box 5

  AMs and revised galley proofs (Ms 30533, 21857),
  latter under title of "Thoughts upon the Present State
  of the World."
    National Library of Ireland
    Copy at SUNY SB   Box 5

  TMs under title of "Thoughts upon the Present State of
  the World" (Za Dial).
    Yale University

  Copy of SEVE POEM 22 inscribed to HEAL JAME, dated
  1938, with this description: "the first poem in what
  critics call my 'later manner.' It was written when
  the Black & and Tans were busy..." and the fighting
  depressed him. "Before this I had written of old Myths
  & personal passion."
    Stanford University

The Nineteenth Century and After   NINE CENT AF
  AMs and TMs. See Books: WIND STAI MA.
    National Library of Ireland
    Copy at SUNY SB   Box 6

  AMs. See Miscellany: DIAR JOUR (Rapallo notebook
  finished June 1929; Ms 13580).
    National Library of Ireland
    Copy at SUNY SB   Box 90

No Second Troy   NO   SECO TR
  No Ms located.

Nothing That He Has Done   NOTH THAT HE
  (Song from Play: GREE HELM)
  AMs draft.
    National Library of Ireland
    Copy at SUNY SB   Box 8

Poems   293

O Do Not Love Too Long   O   DO   NO
   TMs, with corrections.
      New York Public Library

   Two AMs, both with revisions and deletions; one
   unsigned; the other in a copy of POEM 95 belonging to
   GREG LADY, signed and dated 1903 July 12 (I:12, 13).
      Emory University

Oil and Blood   OIL BLOO
   Copy inscribed in SECO BOOK 94 sent to James B. de
   Vincheles Payen-Payne (PAYE JAME B.); also AMs
   beginning "No tombs of gold and lapis lazuli."
      University of Toronto

   TMs. See Books: WIND STAI MA. AMs draft. See
   Miscellany: DIAR JOUR (leather notebook ca 1927; Ms
   30359).
      National Library of Ireland
      Copy at SUNY SB   Box 6, 88

The Old Age of Queen Maeve   OLD AGE   QU
   Copy with revisions in SELE POEM 21 (item 2417).
      Yeats, Anne

   Copy of drafts from white vellum notebook. See
   Miscellany: DIAR JOUR (Partial List...#545).
      Location of original unknown
      Copy at SUNY SB   Box 88

   AMs; draft (4 pp; Ms 30799); page proof and AMs of
   "Prelude" (Ms 13584).
      National Library of Ireland
      Copy at SUNY SB   Box 1

   Galley proofs with revisions in POEM 1899 06. Page
   proofs with corrections in POET WORK 06. TMs, with
   corrections.
      New York Public Library

Old Memory   OLD MEMO
   Revisions in copy of COLL WORK 08.
      Yeats, Anne

   AMs (1 p; 1903).
      Princeton University Library

AMs with corrections (Ms 21865).
    National Library of Ireland

AMsS; twelve lines with revisions (I:14).
    Emory University

Proof sheets with corrections (Ms 13584).
    National Library of Ireland
    Copy at SUNY SB   Box 1

Galley proofs with revisions in POEM 1899 06.
    New York Public Library

The Old Men Admiring Themselves in the Water   OLD   MEN AD
   AMS; early draft (14 lines; Ms 21874).
    National Library of Ireland

Four AMs drafts of poem, one entitled "Song of the Old Man."
    New York Public Library

The Old Stone Cross   OLD   STON CR
   AMs (Ms 13593).
    National Library of Ireland
    Copy at SUNY SB   Box 4

Old Tom Again   OLD   TOM AG
   Copy of drafts in white vellum notebook. See
   Miscellany: DIAR JOUR (Partial List...#545).
    Location of original unknown
    Copy at SUNY SB   Box 88

One TMs (Ms 13591).
    National Library of Ireland
    Copy at SUNY SB   Box 6

On a Picture of a Black Centaur by Edmund Dulac ON   PICT BL
   AMs notes (1 p; Ms 13589).
    National Library of Ireland
    Copy at SUNY SB   Box 5

On a Political Prisoner   ON   POLI PR
   TMs (original and carbon) with additions and
   corrections (Za Dial).
    Yale University

Poems 295

  AMs (Ms 13588).
      National Library of Ireland
      Copy at SUNY SB   Box 3

On Being Asked for a War Poem   ON   BEIN AS
  AMsS, under title "A Reason for Keeping Silent,"
  contributed to THE BOOK OF THE HOMELESS, compiled by
  Edith Wharton (MS Vault Shelves Conrad).
      Yale University

  TMs, typed by Ezra Pound with comments by him and sent
  to Harriet Monroe (Aug 1, 1917).
      University of Chicago

  AMs (Ms 30415).
      National Library of Ireland
      Copy at SUNY SB   Box 6

  AMs; fair copy with slight variations, entitled "On
  being asked to write a war poem," sent for inclusion in
  a pamphlet on "The Fatherless Children of France."
      College of the Holy Cross

  AMs; fair copy with slight variations, entitled "On
  being asked to write a poem on the War."
      Boston College

  TMs, typed by Pound with comments by him and sent to
  Harriet Monroe (Aug 1, 1917).
      University of Chicago

  See also Books: LATE POEM 22.

On George Moore   ON   GEOR MO
  No Ms located.

On hearing that the Students of our New
University have joined the Agitation against
Immoral Literature   ON   HEAR TH
  No Ms located.

On Mr. Nettleship's Picture at the Royal
Hibernian Academy   ON   MR. NE
  No Ms located.

On those that hated 'The Playboy of the Western
World,' 1907   ON   THOS TH
    Fair copy and AN about the poem in COLL WORK 08, vol 7.
        New York Public Library

    AMs draft in "red notebook...from Maud Gonne."
    See Miscellany: DIAR JOUR (Ms 30358).
        National Library of Ireland
        Copy at SUNY SB   Box 88

    AMsS; draft with corrections.
        University of Texas at Austin

On Woman   ON   WOMA
    AMs draft in "red notebook...from Maud Gonne."
    See Miscellany: DIAR JOUR (Ms 30358).
        National Library of Ireland
        Copy at SUNY SB   Box 88

    Corrections in copy of EIGH POEM 16.
        New York Public Library

    TMs (3 lines), typed by Pound with comments by him
    and sent to Harriet Monroe (Aug 1, 1917).
        University of Chicago

    See also Books: LATE POEM 22.

The O'Rahilly   O'RA
    AMs and three copies, with corrections (5 pp each; Ms
    13593).
        National Library of Ireland
        Copy at SUNY SB   Box 4

Out of sight is out of mind   OUT   SIGH IS
    Copy in page proofs for Books: UNPU MACM ED.
        National Library of Ireland
        Copy at SUNY SB   Box 28, 29, 30

Owen Aherne and His Dancers   OWEN AHER DA
    Revised proofs from Cuala edition of CAT MOON 24; poems
    entitled "The Lover Speaks" and "The Heart Replies"
    (Ms 21858).
        National Library of Ireland

    TMs and galley proofs with corrections; poems entitled
    "The Lover Speaks" and "The Heart Replies" (Za Dial).
        Yale University

AMs (30 Oct. [n.y.]; 2 pp; Ms 21870); AMs draft in
"red notebook...from Maud Gonne." See Miscellany: DIAR
JOUR (Ms 30358).
    National Library of Ireland
    Copy at SUNY SB   Box 5

Pardon, Old Fathers   PARD OLD FA
AMs (2 pp; Ms 30364); AMs (Ms 13586).
    National Library of Ireland
    Copy at SUNY SB   Box 4

Revisions in copy of LATE POEM 24.
    Yeats, Anne

Page proofs with revisions in RESP POEM 14.
    New York Public Library

Copy of SELE POEM 21 inscribed (to no one) with the
line, "Only the wasteful virtues earn the sun."
    Yeats, Anne

Copy of KING GREA 34 inscribed (to no one) with the
line, "Only the wasteful virtues earn the sun."
    Smith, Simon Nowell

Two copies of HOUR GLAS 14 (one printed privately, one
by Cuala) inscribed (to no one) with the line "Only the
wasteful virtues earn the sun."
    Harvard University

Copy of PLAY CONT 24 belonging to AHER KATH inscribed
with the line, "Only the wasteful virtues earn the sun."
    University of Louisville

Copy of TREM VEIL 22 inscribed (to no one) with the
line, "Only the wasteful virtues earn the sun."
    University of London Library

Copy of IRIS FAIR 92 inscribed (to no one) with the
line, "'Only the wasteful virtues earn the sun' W B
Yeats, Feb 27, 1931" (item 2452).
    Yeats, Anne

Copy of HOUR GLAS 14 inscribed (to no one) with the
line, "Only the wasteful virtues earn the sun."
    Harvard University

Parnell   PARN
   AMs; TMs, with corrections (Ms 13593).
      National Library of Ireland
      Copy at SUNY SB   Box 4

Parnell's Funeral   PARN FUNE
   TMs of "Commentary on Parnell's Funeral" (10 pp;
   Ms 30795).
      National Library of Ireland

   TMs and AMs, with revisions, entitled "To the Tune of
   O'Donnell Abu." AMs draft in Miscellany: DIAR JOUR (Ms
   30547).
      National Library of Ireland
      Copy at SUNY SB   Box 4

   Copy of AMs drafts and notes in white vellum journal.
   See Miscellany: DIAR JOUR (Partial List...#545).
      Location of original unknown
      Copy at SUNY SB   Box 88

   TMsS (2 pp) with corrections, entitled "Somebody at
   Parnell's Funeral," dated April 9, 1933.
      Southern Illinois University

   TMsS of poem and commentary, with revisions and
   corrections, and an AN "corrected April 1934."
      Harper, George

Parting   PART
   AMs, AMsS, and TMs (13592).
      National Library of Ireland
      Copy at SUNY SB   Box 7

   See also Poems: WOMA YOUN OL.

Paudeen   PAUD
   AMs (Ms 13586).
      National Library of Ireland
      Copy at SUNY SB   Box 4

   Two lines, beginning "There cannot be," inscribed
   in POEM WRIT 13 that is, in turn, inscribed to
   LANE HUGH.
      Wesleyan University

Poems   299

Peace   PEAC
    No Ms located.

The Peacock   PEA COCK
    AMs.
        New York Public Library

The People   PEOP
    Page proofs with corrections in WILD SWAN 17.
        University of Texas at Austin

    AMs; draft, dated Jan. 10, 1915 (3 pp; Ms 30424).
        National Library of Ireland
        Copy at SUNY SB   Box 5

    TMs and proof sheet under title of "The Phoenix."
        University of Chicago

    Corrections in EIGH POEM 16, under title of "The
    Phoenix."
        New York Public Library

The Phantom Ship   PHAN SHIP
    Page proofs with revision in WAND OISI 89.
        University of Texas at Austin

    AMs (Ms 30451).
        National Library of Ireland
        Copy at SUNY SB   Box 7

The Phases of the Moon   PHAS MOON
    AMs (Ms 13587).
        National Library of Ireland
        Copy at SUNY SB   Box 6

    TMs with corrections.
        Yale University

The Pilgrim   PILG
    AMs (2 pp); TMs, with corrections (Ms 13593).
        National Library of Ireland
        Copy at SUNY SB   Box 4

The Pity of Love   PITY LOVE
    AMs; fair copy (Ms located by Barbara Rosenbaum).
        Dalhousie University

The Players ask for a Blessing on the Psalteries
and on Themselves   PLAY ASK   BL
    Copy of IN SEVE 03 inscribed (to no one) with two
    lines: "The proud and careless notes live on But bless
    our hands that ebb away."
        Fiskin, Jeffrey

    Copy of RESP OTHE 16 inscribed (to no one) with two
    lines: "The proud and careless notes live on But bless
    our hands that ebb away."
        University of London Library

    Proof sheets with corrections (Ms 13584).
        National Library of Ireland
        Copy at SUNY SB   Box 1

The Poet Owen Hanrahan under a bush of May   POET OWEN HA
    Copy in page proofs for Books: UNPU MACM ED.
        National Library of Ireland
        Copy at SUNY SB   Box 28, 29, 30

    Two lines: "Call down a blessing on the blossom of the
    May Because it blows in beauty and in beauty blows
    away," inscribed in copy of CAT MOON 24, with bookplate
    of ROBI LENN.
        Stanford University

The Poet pleads with the Elemental Powers   POET PLEA EL
    AMs, entitled "Aodh pleads with the Elemental Powers."
        New York Public Library

    AMs entitled "A Mystical Prayer to the Masters of the
    Elements...," in small white notebook. See Miscellany:
    DIAR JOUR (Partial List...#548).
        Yeats, Senator Michael

A Poet to his Beloved   POET HIS   BE
    TMs, with revisions, entitled "Under the moon."
    See also Books: WIND REED 99.
        New York Public Library

    AMs in small white notebook. See Miscellany: DIAR JOUR
    (Partial List...#548).
        Yeats, Senator Michael

Politics   POLI
   AMs; TMs, with corrections (Ms 13593).
      National Library of Ireland
      Copy at SUNY SB   Box 2

   Copy with variant lines inscribed in NEW POEM 38.
   See Inscriptions: HEAL JAME.
      Stanford University

A Prayer for my Daughter   PRAY MY   DA
   TMs.
      University of Chicago

   AMs and TMs; typed copy, dated June 1919 (Ms 13588).
      National Library of Ireland
      Copy at SUNY SB   Box 3

   TMsS (carbon) with corrections, dated June 1919.
      New York Public Library

   Two lines, beginning "Ceremony is a name," inscribed
   (to no one) in PLAY PROS 22, dated May 16 1923.
      University of Louisville

A Prayer for my Son   PRAY MY   SO
   AMs (2 pp); TMs, with corrections (2 pp; Ms 13589).
      National Library of Ireland
      Copy at SUNY SB   Box 5

   Revisions in copy of COLL WORK 08.
      Yeats, Anne

A Prayer for Old Age   PRAY OLD AG
   AMs in Miscellany: DIAR JOUR (Partial List...#351).
      National Library of Ireland
      Copy at SUNY SB   Box 90

A Prayer on Going into my House   PRAY GOIN MY
   AMs (Ms 13587).
      National Library of Ireland
      Copy at SUNY SB   Box 6

Presences   PRES
   AMs draft. See Miscellany: DIAR JOUR (leather notebook
   ca 1927; Ms 30359).
      National Library of Ireland
      Copy at SUNY SB   Box 88

AMs (Ms 13587).
    National Library of Ireland
    Copy at SUNY SB   Box 6

TMs with corrections, dated Nov. 1915.
    New York Public Library

The Priest and the Fairy   PRIE FAIR
    AMs (5 pp).
        State University of New York
        Copy at SUNY SB   Box 7

Quarrel in Old Age   QUAR OLD AG
    TMs. See Books: WIND STAI MA.
        National Library of Ireland
        Copy at SUNY SB   Box 6

    Copy of drafts from white vellum notebook.
    See Miscellany: DIAR JOUR (Partial List...#545).
        Location of original unknown
        Copy at SUNY SB   Box 88

Quatrains and Aphorisms   QUAT APHO
    Page proofs with revisions in WAND OISI 89.
        University of Texas at Austin

    AMs; one stanza under title of "In a Drawing Room"
    (1 p; Ms 30826).
        National Library of Ireland
        Copy at SUNY SB   Box 7

Queen Edaine   QUEE EDAI
    24 lines of verse in copy of POEM 01, inscribed to GREG
    LADY, beginning "'Why is it' queen Edain said."
    (PR5900 A3 1901 cop. 2).
        Emory University

    AMs in COLL WORK 08; page proofs with corrections in
    POET WORK 06; galley proofs with revisions in POEM 1899
    06.
        New York Public Library

    AMs, beginning "'Why is it' Queen Edain said."
        State University of New York
        Copy at SUNY SB   Box 8

    See also Plays: DEIR.

Poems   303

The Ragged Wood   RAGG WOOD
    Revisions in POEM SECO 09. Revisions in copy of COLL
    WORK 08.
        Yeats, Anne

    TMs.
        New York Public Library

    AMs; 16 lines with revisions and deletions; autograph
    note (verso) concerning symbols (I:16).
        Emory University

The Realists   REAL
    TMsS, corrected.
        University of Chicago

    AMs (Ms 13586).
        National Library of Ireland
        Copy at SUNY SB   Box 4

Reconciliation   RECO
    No Ms located.

Red Hanrahan's Song about Ireland   RED HANR SO
    AMsS; three-line excerpt, beginning "Like tufted
    reeds" in copy of TABL LAW 97 belonging to GREG
    LADY (I:17).
        Emory University

    AMs of the poem; another AMs of the first stanza, dated
    Oct., 1904; page proofs with corrections in POET WORK
    06.
        New York Public Library

    AMs in small white notebook. See Miscellany: DIAR JOUR
    (Partial List...#548).
        Yeats, Senator Michael

    Proof sheets with corrections (Ms 13584).
        National Library of Ireland
        Copy at SUNY SB   Box 1

Remembrance   REME
    AMsS, under title "To--," on a card embossed with the
    name of Arthur J. Elder. May not be in the hand of
    WBY (MS Vault File).
        Yale University

Remorse for Intemperate Speech   REMO INTE SP
   AMs and TMs. See Books: WIND STAI MA.
   National Library of Ireland
   Copy at SUNY SB   Box 6

   Copy of drafts and fair copy from white vellum
   notebook. See Miscellany: DAIR JOUR (Partial
   List...#545).
      Location of original unknown
      Copy at SUNY SB   Box 88

Reprisals   REPR
   AMs and TMs, beginning "Some nineteen German planes,
   they say," dated November 23rd 1920 (Ms 13583);
   TMs (Ms 30509). Related to Poems: IRIS AIRM FO.
   National Library of Ireland
   Copy at SUNY SB   Box 8

   TMs (carbon).
   New York Public Library

The Results of Thought   RESU THOU
   AMsS and TMs (Ms 13590). See Books: WIND STAI MA.
   National Library of Ireland
   Copy at SUNY SB   Box 6

   Copy of drafts and fair copy from white vellum
   notebook. See Miscellany: DAIR JOUR (Partial
   List...#545).
      Location of original unknown
      Copy at SUNY SB   Box 88

Ribh at the Tomb of Baile and Aillinn   RIBH TOMB BA
   TMs, with commentary.
   University of Chicago

Ribh Considers Christian Love Insufficient   RIBH CONS CH
   TMs, with commentary.
   University of Chicago

Ribh Denounces Patrick   RIBH DENO PA
   TMs with commentary, under title of "Ribh Prefers
   an Older Theology."
   University of Chicago

Poems

> TMs, under title of "Ribh Prefers an Older Theology,"
> beginning "Abstractions of the Greek Philosophy"
> (bMS Eng 338.12 [5-15]).
> > Harvard University

Ribh in Ecstasy RIBH ECST
> Copy of AMs, prose version, from white vellum notebook.
> See Miscellany: DIAR JOUR (Partial List...#545).
> > Location of original unknown
> > Copy at SUNY SB   Box 88
>
> AMs (Ms 30519).
> > National Library of Ireland
> > Copy at SUNY SB   Box 4
>
> AMs in Miscellany: DIAR JOUR (Partial List...#351).
> > Yeats, Senator Michael
> > Copy at SUNY SB   Box 90

The Road at My Door ROAD DOOR
> AMs (Ms 13589).
> > National Library of Ireland
> > Copy at SUNY SB   Box 5
>
> See also Poems: MEDI TIME CI.

Roger Casement ROGE CASE
> AMs enclosed in letter to MANN ETHE.
> > Sligo County Library
>
> AMs (2 pp); two TMs, with corrections, one initialed
> (Ms 13593).
> > National Library of Ireland
> > Copy at SUNY SB   Box 3, 4
>
> TMsS; carbon copy, with corrections.
> > University of Texas at Austin
>
> Two TMs, revised (Ms 5460).
> > National Library of Ireland

The Rose of Battle ROSE BATT
> No Ms located.

The Rose of Peace   ROSE PEAC
    AMs; version entitled "The Peace of the Rose"
    inserted in TABL LAW 14.
        New York Public Library

The Rose of the World   ROSE WORL
    The line "Like the pale waters in their wintry race"
    pencilled in to replace "More fleeting than the sea's
    foam-fickle face," in copy of COUN CATH 92.
        Ohio State University

The Rose Tree   ROSE TREE
    Two AMs (Ms 13588, 30474). AMs drafts. See Miscellany:
    DIAR JOUR (Ms 30358, 30359).
        National Library of Ireland
        Copy at SUNY SB   Box 3

    AMsS, dated April 6, 1917.
        New York Public Library

    TMs (original and carbon) with additions and
    corrections (Za Dial).
        Yale University

Running to Paradise   RUNN PARA
    AMs draft in "red notebook...from Maud Gonne."
    See Miscellany: DIAR JOUR (Ms 30358).
        National Library of Ireland
        Copy at SUNY SB   Box 88

The Sad Shepherd   SAD SHEP
    AMs and AMs fragments (Ms 30450, 30469).
        National Library of Ireland
        Copy at SUNY SB   Box 1

Sailing to Byzantium   SAIL BYZA
    AMs and TMs (Ms 13589).
        National Library of Ireland
        Copy at SUNY SB   Box 5

The Saint and the Hunchback   SAIN HUNC
    AMs (Ms 13587).
        National Library of Ireland
        Copy at SUNY SB   Box 6

Poems

The Scholars   SCHO
    Revisions in copies of LATE POEM 22 (item 2382) and
    LATE POEM 24 (item 2383).
        Yeats, Anne

    Two AMs (April 1915; Ms 30476, 13587).
        National Library of Ireland
        Copy at SUNY SB   Box 5

    AMsS; one proof sheet.
        University of Chicago

The Second Coming   SECO COMI
    TMs (original and carbon) with additions and
    corrections (Za Dial).
        Yale University

    TMs and AMs; poem and notes (4 pp; Ms 13588).
        National Library of Ireland
        Copy at SUNY SB   Box 3

The Secret Rose   SECR ROSE
    Copy from issue of THE SAVOY (Sept-Dec 1896), with
    corrections (item 1846).
        Yeats, Anne

The Secrets of the Old   SECR OLD
    AMs and TMs (Ms 13589).
        National Library of Ireland
        Copy at SUNY SB   Box 5

The Seeker   SEEK
    AMs draft in notebook with the poem ISLA STAT
    (Ms 30328).
        National Library of Ireland
        Copy at SUNY SB   Box 15

September 1913   SEPT 1913
    TMs, revised (Ms 21873).
        National Library of Ireland

    Fair copy, dated Aug. 1913, in COLL WORK 08, vol. 4.
    Also one TMsS and two carbons, with corrections, under
    title of "New Ireland."
        New York Public Library

Seven paters seven times   SEVE PATE SE
   Copy in page proofs for Books: UNPU MACM ED.
   National Library of Ireland
   Copy at SUNY SB Box 28, 29, 30

The Seven Sages   SEVE SAGE
   Copy of drafts from white vellum notebook. See
   Miscellany: DIAR JOUR (Partial List...#545).
      Location of original unknown
      Copy at SUNY SB Box 88

   TMs. See Books: WIND STAI MA.
      National Library of Ireland
      Copy at SUNY SB Box 6

The Shadowy Waters   SHAD WATE
   TMsS and two AMsS, corrected but undated.
      The Huntington Library

   Some 55 items: AMs, TMs, notebooks, and other
   material relating to the play (some in Berg, others
   in Rare Books and Manuscripts).
      New York Public Library

   AMs fragment (15 lines), beginning "Fomor, or powers
   of darkness and barreness," with reference to children,
   the gods, and the dead (Berg lists under "Fomor..."
   and not as part of SHAD WATE).
      New York Public Library

   TMs of "new passages" for the stage version, with
   comments on how they will affect the play, enclosed
   in letter to FAY WILL GE.
      University of Kansas

   AMs of various sections in small white notebook.
   See Miscellany: DIAR JOUR (Partial List...#548).
      Yeats, Senator Michael

   Revisions in copy of POEM SECO 09 (item 2401).
      Yeats, Anne

   TMsS, with corrections and revisions (18 pp; MS Eng
   821.3).
      Harvard University

AMs drafts; also page proofs of POEM 1899 06 and
incomplete page proofs of ON BAIL ST and SHAD WATE;
drafts; TMs of acting version, revised (Ms 30467,
30017, 8762, 13565). TMs of note, with comments and
corrections, used as a basis for a later edition (Ms
13571).
    National Library of Ireland
    Copy at SUNY SB Box 4, 15, 16

TMs, with revisions (Ms 21506).
    National Library of Ireland

See also Books: PLAY IRIS 11.

She Turns the Dolls' Faces to the Wall   SHE TURN DO
   TMs with variant readings.
   University of Reading Library

See also Poems: UPON DYIN LA.

She Who Dwelt Among the Sycamores   SHE WHO DW
   AMs draft (1 p).
   National Library of Ireland
   Copy at SUNY SB Box 7

AMs draft in letter to HINK KATH TY.
   The Huntington Library

Shepherd and Goatherd   SHEP GOAT
   AMs (Ms 13587).
   National Library of Ireland
   Copy at SUNY SB Box 5

The Singing Head and the Lady   SING HEAD LA
   See Plays: FULL MOON MA and Books: SING HEAD 34.

Sixteen Dead Men   SIXT DEAD ME
   AMs, AMsS, dated Dec. 17, [1917] (Ms 13588).
   National Library of Ireland
   Copy at SUNY SB Box 3

TMs (original and carbon) with additions and
corrections (Za Dial).
   Yale University

Solomon and the Witch   SOLO WITC
   Revisions in copy of LATE POEM 22.
      Yeats, Anne

TMs (original and carbon) with additions and corrections.

AMs (Ms 13588).
    National Library of Ireland
    Copy at SUNY SB   Box 3

Solomon to Sheba   SOLO SHEB
    AMs; fragments of lines used in SOLO SHEB and LIVI BEAU
    (16 lines; Ms 13587).
        National Library of Ireland
        Copy at SUNY SB

A Song   SONG
    Copy of WILD SWAN 19 inscribed (to no one) with the
    lines, "O who could have foretold That the heart grows
    old."
        University of London Library

A Song from 'The Player Queen'   SONG PLAY QU
    AMs (Ms 13586).
        National Library of Ireland
        Copy at SUNY SB   Box 4

Song of the Faeries   SONG FAER
    No Ms located.

The Song of the Happy Shepherd   SONG HAPP SH
    Copy of SOME ESSA 05 with line, "Words alone are
    certain good," signed by Eglinton, with a note by WBY
    about Eglinton (EGLI JOHN; 1p. M271. 905S. copy 1).
        Yale University

    Page proofs with revision in WAND OISI 89.
        University of Texas at Austin

The Song of the Old Mother   SONG OLD MO
    AMs in small white notebook. See Miscellany: DIAR JOUR
    (Partial List...#548).
        Yeats, Senator Michael

A Song of the Rosy Cross   SONG ROSY CR
    AMs, untitled, dated November 18 [1891] (Ms 30318).
        National Library of Ireland
        Copy at SUNY SB   Box 8

Poems

>　　AMs entitled "A Ryme of the Rosy Cross" in small white
>　　notebook. See Miscellany: DIAR JOUR (Partial
>　　List...#548).
>　　　　Yeats, Senator Michael

The Song of Wandering Aengus　　　　　　　　　　SONG WAND AE
>　　Note about the poem in WIND REED 99, dated March, 1904.
>　　New York Public Library
>
>　　AMsS, with corrections, dated 1916 April 14.
>　　University of Texas at Austin
>
>　　TMs, with corrections. See also Books: WIND REED 99.
>　　New York Public Library

Songs from Deirdre I, II, III　　　　　　　　　　SONG DEIR 1
>　　See DEIR.

The Sorrow of Love　　　　　　　　　　　　　　　　SORR LOVE
>　　Two AMs, both of second stanza only, with revisions and
>　　deletions. One is inscribed to GREG LADY, in her copy
>　　of POEM 04 with her pencilled note: "altered in 1924";
>　　another in her copy of POEM 95 (I:21, 22).
>　　　　Emory University
>
>　　AMsS; fair copy, under title of "The Sorrow of the
>　　World."
>　　　　Queen's University (Canada)
>
>　　Photostat of AMsS, beginning "The quarrel of the
>　　sparrows in the eaves."
>　　University of Texas at Austin

Spilt Milk　　　　　　　　　　　　　　　　　　　　SPIL MILK
>　　AMs; three drafts in Other Authors: ERDM HIST 24
>　　(item 638).
>　　　　Yeats, Anne
>
>　　TMs (Ms 30378); AMs. See Books: WIND STAI MA.
>　　National Library of Ireland
>　　Copy at SUNY SB   Box 6

Spinning Song　　　　　　　　　　　　　　　　　　SPIN SONG
>　　AMsS, with revisions and deletions (I:5).
>　　　　Emory University

Two AMsS, one dated Oct. 9, 1901. See also Plays: DIAR GRAN.
    New York Public Library

The Spirit Medium   SPIR MEDI
    AMs (7 pp; Ms 13593).
        National Library of Ireland
        Copy at SUNY SB   Box 4

The Spur   SPUR
    TMs, with the note: "Proof for New Poem Lust and Rage" (Ms 13593).
        National Library of Ireland
        Copy at SUNY SB   Box 4

The Stare's Nest by My Window   STAR NEST MY
    AMs; copy with revisions and deletions, dated 14 July 1922, inscribed to GREG LADY, in copy of SEVE POEM 22 (I:23).
        Emory University

    AMs (Ms 13589).
        National Library of Ireland
        Copy at SUNY SB   Box 5

    See also Poems: MEDI TIME CI.

The Statesman's Holiday   STAT HOLI
    AMs (3 pp); two TMs and one carbon, with corrections (Ms 13593).
        National Library of Ireland
        Copy at SUNY SB   Box 27

    Two TMs with revisions, many by WBY, some in another hand, under title of "Avalon" (bMS Eng 338.12 [5-15]).
        Harvard University

    Copy in corrected page proofs (Add. MS 55881).
    See Books: ON BOIL 39.
        British Library

Statistics   STAT ISTI CS
   Copy of drafts and fair copy from white vellum notebook. See Miscellany: DAIR JOUR (Partial List...#545).
        Location of original unknown
        Copy at SUNY SB   Box 88

Poems 313

    TMs. See Books: WIND STAI MA.
       National Library of Ireland
       Copy at SUNY SB   Box 6

    AMs (Ms 30378, 13590).
       National Library of Ireland
       Copy at SUNY SB   Box 6

The Statues   STAT UES
    AMs (8 pp) and five carbon copies with corrections,
    originally entitled "Pythagorean Numbers" (Ms 13593).
       National Library of Ireland
       Copy at SUNY SB   Box 2

    TMs, with revisions, under title of "Pythagorean
    Numbers" (bMS Eng 338.12 [5-15]).
       Harvard University

A Stick of Incense   STIC INCE
    TMs (carbon) with opening word changed from "When"
    to "Whence."
       University of Texas at Austin

    AMs (Ms 13593).
       National Library of Ireland
       Copy at SUNY SB   Box 2

The Stolen Child   STOL CHIL
    Page proofs with revisions in WAND OISI 89.
       University of Texas at Austin

    AMs, fair copy (Ms 30478).
       National Library of Ireland
       Copy at SUNY SB   Box 1

    AMsS.
       Rosenbach Museum and Library

    AMs (Ms 4630-4649/4325).
       Trinity College Dublin

    AMs draft in letter to FRAS DR.
       University of California Los Angeles

Stream and Sun at Glendalough   STRE SUN GL
    TMs. See Books: WIND STAI MA.
       National Library of Ireland
       Copy at SUNY SB   Box 6

Copy of drafts and fair copy from white vellum notebook.
See Miscellany: DIAR JOUR (Partial List...#545).
   Location of original unknown
   Copy at SUNY SB   Box 88

Street Dancers   STRE DANC
   No Ms located.

Summer and Spring   SUMM SPRI
   AMs (2 pp; Ms 13589).
      National Library of Ireland
      Copy at SUNY SB   Box 5

A Summer Evening   SUMM EVEN
   AMs draft in letter to HINK KATH TY.
      The Huntington Library

Supernatural Songs   SUPE SONG
   See Miscellany: DIAR JOUR (Partial List...#351); see
   also titles of individual Poems.

Sweet Dancer   SWEE DANC
   AMs, TMs, and page proof (Ms 13593).
      National Library of Ireland
      Copy at SUNY SB   Box 3

Swift's Epitaph   SWIF EPIT
   Two AMs (Ms 13590, 21863).
      National Library of Ireland

   AMs. See Books: WIND STAI MA.
      National Library of Ireland
      Copy at SUNY SB   Box 6, 7

   AMs draft. See Miscellany: DIAR JOUR (Rapallo
   notebook D headed "Dublin August 1929"; Ms 13581).
      National Library of Ireland
      Copy at SUNY SB   Box 90

Symbols   SYMB
   AMs. See Books: WIND STAI MA. AMs in Miscellany:
   DIAR JOUR (Rapallo notebook finished June 1929;
   Ms 13580).
      National Library of Ireland
      Copy at SUNY SB   Box 6, 90

Poems   315

That the Night Come   THAT NIGH CO
   No Ms located.

There   THER
   AMs in Miscellany: DIAR JOUR (Partial List...#351).
      Yeats, Senator Michael
      Copy at SUNY SB   Box 4

There is a Queen in China   THER IS   QU
   See Poems: HIS PHOE.

These are the Clouds   THES ARE CL
   Copy of poem in page proofs for Books: UNPU MACM ED.
      National Library of Ireland
      Copy at SUNY SB   Box 5

Those Dancing Days are Gone   THOS DANC DA
   AMs, proof (Ms 13593). TMs, with correction of title
   (Ms 13591). AMs in Miscellany: DIAR JOUR (Rapallo
   notebook finished June 1929; Ms 13580).
      National Library of Ireland
      Copy at SUNY SB   Box 6, 90

Those Images   THOS IMAG
   AMs and TMs (Ms 13593).
      National Library of Ireland
      Copy at SUNY SB   Box 4

   AMsS (1 p); poem enclosed in letter. See Letters:
   HEAL EDIT SH (bMS Eng 338.12).
      Harvard University

A Thought from Propertius   THOU PROP
   TMs, typed by Ezra Pound with comments by him and
   sent to Harriet Monroe (Aug 1, 1917).
      University of Chicago

   Page proofs with corrections in WILD SWAN 17.
      University of Texas at Austin

   AMs, under title of "An Echo from Propertius" (Ms
   13587).
      National Library of Ireland
      Copy at SUNY SB   Box 5

The Three Beggars   THRE BEGG
    AMs (Ms 13586).
        National Library of Ireland
        Copy at SUNY SB   Box 4

The Three Bushes   THRE BUSH
    AMs of early version (Ms 30479). AMs (3 pp); TMs, with
    corrections; proof sheet with corrections (Ms 13593).
    AMs note (Ms 30773).
        National Library of Ireland
        Copy at SUNY SB   Box 3

    AMs note on poem, with music by Dulac for this and
    other poems (Partial List...#773).
        Yeats, Senator Michael

    TMs (carbon), enclosed in letter to WELL DORO.
        Meisei University

The Three Hermits   THRE HERM
    TMsS (2 pp), with corrections.
        Princeton University Library

    TMs, entitled "The Hermits."
        New York Public Library

Three Marching Songs   THRE MARC SO
    AMs (4 pp); TMs (2 copies; Ms 13593); draft in
    brown vellum notebook. See Miscellany: DIAR JOUR (Ms
    30547).
        National Library of Ireland
        Copy at SUNY SB   Box 2, 7, 87

The Three Monuments   THRE MONU
    AMs (11 pp; Ms 13589).
        National Library of Ireland
        Copy at SUNY SB   Box 5

Three Movements   THRE MOVE
    Copy of drafts from white vellum notebook. See
    Miscellany: DIAR JOUR (Partial List...#545).
        Location of original unknown
        Copy at SUNY SB   Box 88

    AMs (Ms 30378, 13590); TMs. See Books: WIND STAI MA.
        National Library of Ireland
        Copy at SUNY SB   Box 6

Three Songs to the One Burden   THRE SONG ON
 AMs (6 pp); three copies, all with corrections (Ms
 13593).
  National Library of Ireland
  Copy at SUNY SB Box 2

 AMs; very rough draft, almost completely scribbled
 over [bMS Eng 338.12 (5-15)].
  Harvard University

Three Songs to the Same Tune   THRE SONG SA
 TMsS with many revisions with a two-page fragment of
 an essay, beginning "In politics I have but one
 passion."
  University of Texas at Austin

 TMs with commentary.
  University of Chicago

 Copy of the SPECTATOR (23 February 1931), corrected in
 pencil, possibly by WBY, apparently for next printing
 (Ms 30004). AMs; draft of P.S. to the "Commentary on
 Three Songs" (VP p 835), with a draft of CHUR STAT,
 dated August 1938 (Ms 30521). AMs (Ms 13583). Draft
 in brown vellum notebooks. See Miscellany: DIAR JOUR
 (Ms 30546, 30547).
  National Library of Ireland
  Copy at SUNY SB Box 1, 4

 Extensive revisions in copy of FULL MOON MA; poems
 retitled "Three Revolutionary Songs" (item 2351).
  Yeats, Anne

 TMs (carbon), with ink corrections, divided into
 "Second Version" and "Third Version" (4 pp).
  Southern Illinois University

 Minor corrections in copy of KING GREA 35.
  New York Public Library

Three Things   THRE THIN
 AMs (Ms 13591).
  National Library of Ireland
  Copy at SUNY SB Box 6

AMs draft. See Miscellany: DIAR JOUR (Rapallo
notebook begun June...1929; Ms 13580).
    National Library of Ireland
    Copy at SUNY SB Box 90

Time and the Witch Vivien   TIME WITC VI
Manuscripts and revisions in copy of MOSA 86 ([1885];
MS3502/4).
    Trinity College Dublin

AMs; notebook with material under the title of "Vivien
and Time," dated 8 January 1884 (Ms 30460, 30357).
    National Library of Ireland
    Copy at SUNY SB Box 16

Page proofs with revisions in WAND OISI 89.
    University of Texas at Austin

See also Books: WAND OISI 99.

To a Child Dancing in the Wind   TO   CHIL DA
AMsS; fair copy on Coole Park stationery, under title
"To a Child Dancing on the Shore" (I:24).
    Emory University

TMsS, corrected, entitled "To a Child Dancing Upon the
Shore."
    University of Chicago

AMs (Ms 13586).
    National Library of Ireland
    Copy at SUNY SB Box 4

AMs; printing directions (Ms 30528).
    National Library of Ireland
    Copy at SUNY SB

To a Friend whose Work has come to Nothing   TO   FRIE WH
Fair copy in COLL WORK 08, vol. 6.
    New York Public Library

Note on the poem, inscribed to GREG LADY in her copy of
RESP POEM 14: "This poem is to Lady Gregory though she
thought it was for Hugh Lane" (I:25).
    Emory University

Poems 319

AMs draft in "red notebook...from Maud Gonne."
See Miscellany: DIAR JOUR (Ms 30358).
National Library of Ireland
Copy at SUNY SB   Box 88

To a Poet, who would have me Praise certain
Bad Poets, Imitators of His and Mine   TO   POET WH
TMs (Ms 13583).
National Library of Ireland
Copy at SUNY SB

To a Shade   TO   SHAD
AMs draft in "red notebook...from Maud Gonne."
See Miscellany: DIAR JOUR (Ms 30358).
National Library of Ireland
Copy at SUNY SB   Box 88

One TMsS (MS 7001/1729).
Trinity College Dublin

See also Books: SELE POEM 21.

To a Squirrel at Kyle-na-no   TO   SQUI KY
AMs, dated 1912 (Ms 13587).
National Library of Ireland
Copy at SUNY SB   Box 6

TMs, typed by Ezra Pound with comments by him and sent
to Harriet Monroe (Aug 1, 1917).
University of Chicago

To a Wealthy Man who promised a Second
Subscription to the Dublin Municipal Gallery
if it were proved the People wanted Pictures   TO   WEAL MA
TMs, with corrections.
New York Public Library

AMs, dated Dec. 25, 1912 and TMs with corrections
(Ms 13586).
National Library of Ireland
Copy at SUNY SB   Box 4

One AMs and one TMs, with revisions, entitled "To a
Friend who promises a bigger subscription than his
first to Dublin Municipal Gallery."
University of Texas at Austin

TMsS, entitled "To a friend who promises a bigger subscription than his first to Dublin Municipal Gallery" (1912; MS 7001/1728).
    Trinity College Dublin

To a Young Beauty   TO   YOUN BE
    Revisions in copy of LATE POEM 22.
        Yeats, Anne

    TMs (carbon).
        Yale University

To a Young Girl   TO   YOUN GI
    AMs (Ms 13587).
        National Library of Ireland
        Copy at SUNY SB   Box 5

    AMs draft in "red notebook...from Maud Gonne."
    See Miscellany: DIAR JOUR (Ms 30358).
        National Library of Ireland
        Copy at SUNY SB   Box 88

To An Isle In the Water   TO   ISLE WA
    AMsS, dated 1888.
        University of Tulsa

    AMs, with one revision.
        University of Delaware Library

To Be Carved on Stone at Thoor Ballylee   TO   BE   CA
    AMs (Ms 13588).
        National Library of Ireland
        Copy at SUNY SB   Box 3

To Dorothy Wellesley   TO   DORO WE
    AMs; TMs, initialed, with corrections, entitled "To a Friend" (Ms 13593).
        National Library of Ireland
        Copy at SUNY SB   Box 3

    TMs (carbon) entitled "To D. W.," and AMs of "correction in 'To D W,'" enclosed in letter to WELL DORO.
        Meisei University

To Garret or Cellar a wheel I send   TO   GARR CE
    No Ms located.

Poems

To his Heart, bidding it have no Fear   TO HEAR BI
  Copy of issue of THE SAVOY (Sept-Dec 1896), with
  corrections (item 1849).
    Yeats, Anne

  AMsS.
    Kenyon College Library

  AMs; fair copy in copy of POEM 95 belonging to GREG
  LADY (I:26).
    Emory University

  TMs, with revisions, entitled "To my heart, bidding it
  have no fear." See also Books: WIND REED 99.
    New York Public Library

  See also Poems, Unpublished: IMPE HEAR GI.

To Ireland in the Coming Times   TO IREL CO
  Copy of poem in page proofs for Books: SELE POEM 29.
    National Library of Ireland
    Copy at SUNY SB Box 5

To Some I Have Talked with by the Fire   TO SOME I
  Page proofs with corrections in POET WORK 06.
    New York Public Library

  AMs in small white notebook. See Miscellany:
  DIAR JOUR (Partial List...#548).
    Yeats, Senator Michael

To the Rose upon the Rood of Time   TO ROSE RO
  Page proofs with corrections in POET WORK 06.
    New York Public Library

  One AMs (Ms 30419).
    National Library of Ireland
    Copy at SUNY SB Box 5

  Copy of WIND REED 99 inscribed to QUIN JOHN, with
  short passage from poem, dated March 1904.
    Wake Forest University Library

  Copy of IDEA GOOD 04 inscribed (to no one) with two
  lines, beginning "To find in all poor foolish things,"
  dated May 1904.
    Mills College Library

Copies of IN SEVE 03 and of WAND OISI 89 inscribed (to
no one) with two lines, beginning "To find in all poor
foolish things."
    University of Texas at Austin

Tom at Cruachan   TOM   CRUA
    Copy of drafts from white vellum notebook. See
    Miscellany: DIAR JOUR (Partial List...#545).
        Location of original unknown
        Copy at SUNY SB   Box 88

    AMs; TMs, entitled "Tom at Crockham," dated July
    1931, with corrections (1 p; Ms 13591).
        National Library of Ireland
        Copy at SUNY SB   Box 6

Tom O'Roughley   TOM   O'RO
    Fair copy, dated Oct 1918 (Ashley B. 4678).
        British Library

    Bookplate of MOOR STUR inscribed with lines beginning
    "For wisdom is a butterfly."
        University of London Library

    Copy of COUN CATH 29 inscribed (to no one) with the
    line "'An aimless joy is a pure joy' W B Yeats July 28
    1932" (item 2335).
        Yeats, Anne

    Copy of WIND STAI 29 inscribed to OSHI SHOT, with the
    lines "Wisdom is a butterfly And not a gloomy bird of
    prey" (item 2447).
        Yeats, Anne

    Copy of POEM WILL 93 inscribed (to no one) with the
    lines, "For wisdom is a butterfly And not a gloomy
    bird of prey," dated May 5 1925 (item 208).
        Yeats, Anne

    Copy of POEM 1899 06 inscribed (to no one) with lines
    beginning "For wisdom is a butterfly."
        University of London Library

    Advance copy of WILD SWAN 19 inscribed with two lines,
    beginning "And wisdom is a butterfly."
        Colby College Library

Copy of TWO PLAY 19 inscribed (to no one) with the
line "An aimless joy is a pure joy."
    Emory University

Copy of WIND STAI inscribed (to no one) with the line
"An aimless joy is a pure joy" (PR5904 T9 cop. 2).
    Yeats Tower

Copy of POEM 12 with the line, "An aimless joy is a
pure joy" inscribed on bookplate of MOOR STUR (item
2402a).
    Yeats, Anne

Copy of REVE CHIL 16 inscribed (to no one) with the
line, "An aimless joy is a pure joy," dated Dec. 1925.
    University of London Library

Copy of WIND REED 99 inscribed (to no one) with the
line "An aimless joy is a pure joy."
    Indiana University

Copy of POEM 12 inscribed (to no one) with the line
"An aimless joy is a pure joy."
    University of Kansas

Copy of POEM 95 inscribed (to no one) with the line
"An aimless joy is a pure joy."
    University of Texas at Austin

Tom the Lunatic   TOM   LUNA
    AMs and TMs, dated July 1931 (Ms 13591).
    National Library of Ireland
    Copy at SUNY SB   Box 6

    Copy of drafts from white vellum notebook. See
    Miscellany: DIAR JOUR (Partial List...#548).
        Location of original unknown
        Copy at SUNY SB   Box 88

Towards Break of Day   TOWA BREA DA
    AMs, with revisions (Ms 13588).
    National Library of Ireland
    Copy at SUNY SB   Box 3

    TMs (original and carbon) with additions and
    corrections (Za Dial).
        Yale University

The Tower   TOWE
    AMs, partly in hand of Lady Gregory, partly in hand of
    WBY.
        New York Public Library

    TMs and AMsS; poem (lines 81-104 missing) and notes (3
    pp); two typed copies, signed; proof draft with
    corrections (Ms 13589). See also Miscellany: DIAR JOUR
    (red looseleaf notebook; Ms 30373).
        National Library of Ireland
        Copy at SUNY SB   Box 5, 88

    AMs; copy with revisions and deletions; 25 lines of the
    opening to the last section, with final eight lines
    crossed out (I:27).
        Emory University

    Copy of OCTO BLAS 27, inscribed to HEAL JAME, dated
    1938, noting that the poem "describes my own old
    Tower...or rather its neighborhood. Mrs. French lived
    a couple of miles off in the eighteenth century."
        Stanford University

The Travail of Passion   TRAV PASS
    AMs in small white notebook. See Miscellany: DIAR JOUR
    (Partial List...#548).
        Yeats, Senator Michael

The Two Kings   TWO KING
    AMs and TMs, with corrections; AMs (Ms 13586, 30517).
        National Library of Ireland
        Copy at SUNY SB   Box 7

    AMs (10 pp), dated Jan. 8, 1912.
        New York Public Library

Two Songs From a Play   TWO SONG PL
    AMs. See Miscellany: DIAR JOUR (Ms 13589).
        National Library of Ireland
        Copy at SUNY SB   Box 5

    Fair copy in LATE POEM 22 (book inscribed to GREG
    LADY).
        New York Public Library

Poems   325

>   AMsS, with one correction, dated May 1925, with note
>   indicating that it is sung before and after the
>   performance of the play RESU.
>> New York Public Library

Two Songs of a Fool   TWO   SONG FO
>   AMs (2 pp; Ms 13587).
>> National Library of Ireland
>> Copy at SUNY SB   Box 6

Two Songs Rewritten for the Tune's Sake   TWO   SONG RE
>   AMs from POT BROT (1935) in Miscellany: DIAR JOUR
>   (Partial List...#351).
>> Yeats, Senator Michael
>> Copy at SUNY SB   Box 90

>   AMs (1 p) inscribed on separate sheet to F.R. Higgins
>   (HIGG FRED).
>> New York Public Library

The Two Titans   TWO   TITA
>   No Ms located.

The Two Trees   TWO   TREE
>   Exercise book containing drafts (Ms 30473).
>> National Library of Ireland
>> Copy at SUNY SB   Box 5

Two Years Later   TWO   YEAR LA
>   AMs (Ms 13586).
>> National Library of Ireland
>> Copy at SUNY SB   Box 4

>   AMs draft in "red notebook...from Maud Gonne."
>   See Miscellany: DIAR JOUR (Ms 30358).
>> National Library of Ireland
>> Copy at SUNY SB

The Unappeasable Host   UNAP HOST
>   Copy of poem in page proofs for Books: UNPU MACM ED.
>> National Library of Ireland
>> Copy at SUNY SB   Box 28, 29, 30

Under Ben Bulben   UNDE BEN BU
>   AMs (13 pp), three carbons with corrections, and AMs of
>   Epitaph (4 lines; Ms 13593).
>> National Library of Ireland
>> Copy at SUNY SB   Box 2

TMs under title of "His Convictions," with one change in line four ("when they set" to "spoke and set All").
University of Texas at Austin

Last four lines inscribed in NEW POEM 38, with variant punctuation and line:
> Draw rein; draw breath;
> Cast a cold eye
> Upon life, upon death.
> Horseman pass by [no end punctuation]

Berlind, Bruce

Under Saturn   UNDE SATU
AMs (Ms 13588).
National Library of Ireland
Copy at SUNY SB Box 3

TMs (original and carbon) with additions and corrections (Za Dial).
Yale University

Under the Moon   UNDE MOON
Page proofs with corrections in POET WORK 06. Two TMs: one signed; another, with corrections, unsigned.
New York Public Library

Revisions in POEM SECO 09 (item 2401) and in SELE POEM 21 (item 2417).
Yeats, Anne

Proof sheets with corrections (Ms 13584).
National Library of Ireland
Copy at SUNY SB Box 1

Under the Round Tower   UNDE ROUN TO
No Ms located.

Upon a Dying Lady   UPON DYIN LA
TMs with variant readings of CERT ARTI BR, HER COUR AG, HER COUR TE, and SHE TURN DO (MS288).
University of Reading Library

AMs and TMs with corrections of all the individual
poems, dated 1912-13 (Ms 13587).
   National Library of Ireland
   Copy at SUNY SB   Box 6

TMs and carbon (4 pp each), both with corrections in
several poems, including CERT ART BR (under title of
"We Bring Her Dolls and Drawings"), SHE TURN DO,
HER COUR AG, and HER FRIE BR (under title of
"Christmas Tree").
   New York Public Library

Revisions in copy of SELE POEM 21.
   Yeats, Anne

Copy of WILD SWAN 17 inscribed to HEAL JAME, dated
July 1938, with comments: "The poems headed 'To a
dying Lady' are about Mabel Beardsley, the sister of
the artist. She died of cancer. ...She was an heroic
person. She always managed to seem well...I did not
see her at the very end."
   Stanford University

Upon a House shaken by the Land Agitation   UPON HOUS SH
   TMs, revised (Ms 21872).
   National Library of Ireland

   Fair copy in COLL WORK 08, vol. 1.
   New York Public Library

Vacillation   VACI
   Change in the text included in letter to YEAT GEOR.
      Yeats, Senator Michael
      Copy at SUNY SB

   Copy of DRAM PERS 36 inscribed (to no one) with
   the lines "'Animate the trivial days and ram them
   with the sun' W B Yeats" (item 2342).
      Yeats, Anne

   Copy of drafts from white vellum notebook. See
   Miscellany: DIAR JOUR (Partial List...#545).
      Location of original unknown
      Copy at SUNY SB   Box 88

TMs, and AMs draft of fragment. See Books: WIND STAI MA.
    National Library of Ireland
    Copy at SUNY SB Box 6

The Valley of the Black Pig   VALL BLAC PI
AMs; fair copy of POEM 95 belonging to GREG LADY (I:28).
    Emory University

AMs in small white notebook. See Miscellany: DIAR JOUR (Partial List...#548).
    Yeats, Senator Michael

Two TMs with revisions. See also Books: WIND REED 99.
    New York Public Library

Veronica's Napkin   VERO NAPK
AMs. See Books: WIND STAI MA.
    National Library of Ireland
    Copy at SUNY SB Box 6

AMs draft. See Miscellany: DIAR JOUR (Rapallo notebook D headed "Dublin August 1929"; Ms 13581).
    National Library of Ireland
    Copy at SUNY SB Box 90

The Wanderings of Oisin   WAND OISI
AMs, notebook (Partial List...#353).
    Yeats, Senator Michael
    Copy at SUNY SB Box 90

Page proofs with corrections in POET WORK 06.
    New York Public Library

AMs notebook; AMs version of Part I, Books I-III; fragment, beginning "Enter a fawn holding a shell" (6 pp; Ms 3726).
    National Library of Ireland
    Copy at SUNY SB Box 88

AMs notes on WAND OISI and CROS (Ms 13583).
    National Library of Ireland
    Copy at SUNY SB Box 7

Inscribed copy of WAND OISI 89 with a few corrections in title poem and in ANAS VIJA.
    Providence Public Library

Poems

The Well and the Tree WELL TREE
    No Ms located.

What Magic Drum WHAT MAGI DR
    TMs (Ms 30178).
    National Library of Ireland
    Copy at SUNY SB

What Then? WHAT THEN
    AMs; TMs, with corrections (Ms 13593).
    National Library of Ireland
    Copy at SUNY SB   Box 3

What Was Lost WHAT WAS LO
    AMs; TMs (Ms 13593).
    National Library of Ireland
    Copy at SUNY SB   Box 4

The Wheel WHEE
    AMs; AMsS, dated Sept. 13, 1921 (Ms 13589).
    National Library of Ireland
    Copy at SUNY SB   Box 5

When Helen Lived WHEN HELE LI
    Page proofs with revisions in RESP POEM 14.
    New York Public Library

    AMs (Ms 13586); AMs draft in "red notebook...from Maud Gonne." See Miscellany: DIAR JOUR (Ms 30358).
    National Library of Ireland
    Copy at SUNY SB   Box 4, 88

When You Are Old WHEN YOU OL
    Copy of poem in page proofs for Books: UNPU MACM ED.
    National Library of Ireland
    Copy at SUNY SB   Box 5

    AMs draft in letter to HINK KATH TY.
        The Huntington Library

When You Are Sad WHEN YOU SA
    AMsS.
        University of Virginia

    AMs draft in letter to HINK KATH TY.
        The Huntington Library

Whence Had They Come					WHEN HAD TH
   TMs (1 p; Ms 30167).
      National Library of Ireland
      Copy at SUNY SB

Where my Books Go					WHER MY BO
   No Ms located.

While I, from that reed-throated whisperer		WHIL I RE
   AMs and proof sheet, with corrections by WBY and Pound
   (I:31).
      Emory University

   Proof sheet.
      University of Chicago

   Page proofs with revisions in RESP POEM 14.
      New York Public Library

   Printed copy, with "Notoriety (suggested by a recent
   magazine article)" in WBY's hand at the top; signed at
   the end of the poem (Autograph file).
      Harvard University

The White Birds					WHIT BIRD
   No Ms located.

Who Goes with Fergus?				WHO GOES FE
   No Ms located.

Why does my Heart beat so?			WHY DOES MY
   No Ms located.

Why does your Heart beat thus?			WHY DOES YO
   No Ms located.

Why Should Not Old Men Be Mad?			WHY SHOU NO
   AMs; two TMs and one carbon, with corrections (Ms
   13593).
      National Library of Ireland
      Copy at SUNY SB   Box 27

   TMs (carbon) with revisions (bMS Eng 338.12 [5-15]).
      Harvard University

   Copy in corrected page proofs (Add. MS 55881).
   See Books: ON BOIL.
      British Library

"Why is it," Queen Edain Said.　　　　　　　WHY IS IT
　　See Poems: QUEE EDAI.

Why should the Heart take Fright　　　　　WHY SHOU HE
　　No Ms located.

The Wicked Hawthorn Tree　　　　　　　　　WICK HAWT TR
　　No Ms located.

The Wild Old Wicked Man　　　　　　　　　　WILD OLD WI
　　AMs and TMs with corrections (6 pp; Ms 13593).
　　　　National Library of Ireland
　　　　Copy at SUNY SB   Box 4

　　TMs (carbon), with revisions.
　　　　University of Texas at Austin

　　AMs, early version (Ms 21874).
　　See also Books: UNPU SCRI ED (Ms 13593).
　　　　National Library of Ireland
　　　　Copy at SUNY SB

The Wild Swans at Coole　　　　　　　　　　WILD SWAN CO
　　AMsS; notes dated Oct. 11 1918 and Oct. 24 1918
　　(Ms 13587).
　　　　National Library of Ireland
　　　　Copy at SUNY SB   Box 5

　　Cuala hand-colored print (no. 50) with lines from poem,
　　inscribed to PROK FRED.
　　　　Wesleyan University

　　AMs with revisions, dated October 1918.
　　　　University of Texas at Austin

　　Fair copy, dated July 13, 1917, in COLL WORK 08,
　　vol. 8, with AN about the poem; another AMs.
　　　　New York Public Library

　　Revisions in copy of SELE POEM 21 (item 2417).
　　　　Yeats, Anne

Wisdom　　　　　　　　　　　　　　　　　　　WISD
　　AMS; TMs, under title of "True Faith" (1 p; Ms 13589).
　　　　National Library of Ireland
　　　　Copy at SUNY SB   Box 5

Wisdom and Dreams   WISD DREA
   AMs in small white notebook. See Miscellany:
   DIAR JOUR (Partial List...#548).
      Yeats, Senator Michael

The Witch   WITC
   AMs (Ms 13586).
      National Library of Ireland
      Copy at SUNY SB Box 4

   AMs draft in "red notebook...from Maud Gonne."
   See Miscellany: DIAR JOUR (Ms 30358).
      National Library of Ireland
      Copy at SUNY SB Box 88

The Withering of the Boughs   WITH BOUG
   Proof sheets with corrections (Ms 13584).
      National Library of Ireland
      Copy at SUNY SB Box 1

   Page proofs with corrections in POET WORK 06; galley
   proofs with revisions in POEM 1899 06; one AMsS,
   dated July 30, 1900; one TMsS, with corrections.
      New York Public Library

   Copy of LAND HEAR 03 inscribed to COAT FLOR EA with
   two lines beginning "No boughs have withered."
      Indiana University

   Copy of POEM 99 inscribed to COAT FLOR EA, with some
   mistakes and corrections, beginning "No boughs have
   withered."
      Wake Forest University Library

   Copy of DEIR 07 inscribed (to no one) with line
   (slightly varied): "the boughs are withered because I
   have told them my dreams," dated Dec 1 1905.
      State University of New York at Albany

A Woman Homer Sung   WOMA HOME SU
   AMsS.
      University of Texas at Austin

A Woman Young and Old   WOMA YOUN OL
   TMsS (17 lines), dated Mar. 1928; TMs and AMs of
   drafts, with revisions (Ms 21860, 13582, 13589).
      National Library of Ireland

TMs of the ten poems with corrections; TMs and carbon of the "Notes," beginning "I am of Ireland," on the symbolic use of sun and light with earth and darkness (Ms 13592).
    National Library of Ireland
    Copy at SUNY SB Box 7

AMs of CONS; AMs and TMs of HER VISI WO; AMs of CHOS; AMs and TMs of PART; TMs note on DIAL SELF SO, FIRS CONF, CHOS, and PART; TMsS of LAST CONF under title of "Last Memories," dated August 1926; another under title of "A Woman's Song"; TMs of FROM ANTI, with corrections and note, not in WBY's hand, indicating "corrections by Ezra Pound" (Ms 13592).
    National Library of Ireland
    Copy at SUNY SB Box 7

See also Books: WIND STAI 33.

A Woman's Beauty is like a white frail Bird   WOMA BEAU IS
    No Ms located.

Words   WORD
    No Ms located.

Words for Music Perhaps   WORD MUSI PE
Drafts of various poems, including those with the "Cracked Mary" titles. See Miscellany: DIAR JOUR (Rapallo notebooks; Ms 13580, 13581).
    National Library of Ireland
    Copy at SUNY SB Box 90

AMs and corrections of "Note" (Ms 13591, 30441, 30802).
    National Library of Ireland
    Copy at SUNY SB Box 6

See also Poems: TOM LUNA, TOM CRUA, and DELP ORAC.

Young Man's Song   YOUN MAN' SO
TMs (Ms 13591); AMs in Miscellany: DIAR JOUR (Rapallo notebook finished June 1929; Ms 13580).
    National Library of Ireland
    Copy at SUNY SB Box 6, 90

Youth and Age   YOUT AGE
AMs (1 p; Ms 13589).
    National Library of Ireland
    Copy at SUNY SB Box 5

Poems, Unpublished

This section includes poetic material not listed in the Poems section above, that is, not published in Allt's VARIORUM EDITION or Finneran's POEMS OF W.B. YEATS: A NEW EDITION. The listing notes if an individual item has been published elsewhere. Most early (up to 1895) manuscripts listed here will be published in George Bornstein's W.B. YEATS: THE EARLY POETRY (vol. 2) in the Cornell Yeats series.

All day you flitted before me   ALL DAY YO
   Published. See Bibliography: Ellmann, IDENTITY.
   AMs; poem beginning "All day you flitted before me Moving like Artemis"; includes the lines beginning "Portrayed before his eyes," listed separately under PORT BE EY (Partial List...#351).
      Yeats, Senator Michael
      Copy at SUNY SB   Box 90

All night there have been ghosts about us   ALL NIGH TH
   AMs; poem, beginning "All night there have been ghosts about us" (Ms 30358).
      National Library of Ireland
      Copy at SUNY SB

All our Europe that for so long   ALL OUR EU
   AMs; poem beginning "All our Europe that for so long" (3 lines; Ms 13593).
      National Library of Ireland
      Copy at SUNY SB   Box 8

Am I a fool or a wise man?   AM   I   FO
   Published. See Bibliography: Parrish, YEATS ANNUAL 6.
   AMs; poem beginning "Am I a fool or a wise man And if a fool what other can," related to the Solomon and Sheba poems (Ms 13587).
      National Library of Ireland
      Copy at SUNY SB

Among the sighing foam and roses hang   AMON SIGH FO
    TMs, beginning "Among the sighing foam and roses hang"
    (Ms 13583).
        National Library of Ireland
        Copy at SUNY SB

And ceased I saw the sea lines citron glare   AND CEAS I
    AMs, beginning "And ceased I saw the sea lines [lions?]
    citron glare" (4 lines).
        National Library of Ireland
        Copy at SUNY SB   Box 8

And clamour whether of voice or hoof   AND CLAM WH
    AMs; with the line "And clamour whether of voice or
    hoof" (Ms 13583).
        National Library of Ireland
        Copy at SUNY SB

An[d] I will call   AND I WI
    AMs; beginning "An I will call search and find"
    (Ms 12161).
        National Library of Ireland
        Copy at SUNY SB   Box 8

And thy daughter will warm   AND THY DA
    Ms (fragment) of poem, beginning "And thy daughter will
    warm" (1 p; Ms 30822).
        National Library of Ireland
        Copy at SUNY SB   Box 8

And wherever around   AND WHER AR
    AMs, beginning "And wherever around" (13 lines).
        National Library of Ireland
        Copy at SUNY SB   Box 8

Art Without Imitation   ART IMIT
    AMs; fragment (10 lines) entitled "Art Without
    Imitation," beginning "Old Mathematics plied the shears
    He has the fragments in a bag" (Ms 30510).
        National Library of Ireland
        Copy at SUNY SB   Box 8

As know all workers for the poor   AS KNOW AL
    AMs, beginning "As know all workers for the poor" (18
    lines).
        National Library of Ireland
        Copy at SUNY SB   Box 8

Poems, Unpublished 337

Awake in a world of ecstasy AWAK WORL EC
   AMsS; fragments referring to "those who did not
   understand Shelley's thought" with some lines of
   poetry, including "Awake in a world of ecstasy."
      New York Public Library

A barren valley there I found encompassed BARR VALL TH
   AMs; fragment of poem, beginning "A barren valley there
   I found encompassed" (1 p; Ms 12161).
      National Library of Ireland
      Copy at SUNY SB Box 8

Because the moon had reached her fifteenth night BECA MOON HA
   AMs, beginning "Because the moon...had reached her
   fifteenth night" (13 lines).
      National Library of Ireland
      Copy at SUNY SB Box 8

Behold the man--behold his brow of care BEHO MAN BE
   AMs, beginning "Behold the man--behold his brow of
   care," dated March 8 1884 (1 p; Ms 30347).
      National Library of Ireland
      Copy at SUNY SB Box 8

Being in a half BEIN HALF
   AMs, beginning "Being [ ] in a half...Everything must
   wear" (4 lines; Ms 13583).
      National Library of Ireland

Being was not at these times BEIN WAS NO
   Ms (fragment) of poem, beginning "Being was not at
   these times nor yet non being" (2 pp; Ms 30821).
      National Library of Ireland
      Copy at SUNY SB

Billy Boy BILL BOY
   AMs draft of poem "Billy Boy," beginning "At first we
   seemed a married pair That on the feathers lay" (12
   lines); may be a variant of a folk song (Ms 12593).
      National Library of Ireland
      Copy at SUNY SB Box 8

But an art BUT ART
   AMs, beginning "But [an art?]" with reference to King
   Rolf [Roth?] (14 lines).
      National Library of Ireland
      Copy at SUNY SB Box 8

By the emperor's command　　　　　　　　　　　　BY　EMPE CO
　　AMs, beginning "By the emperor's command, a foreign
　　story teller" (Ms 13583).
　　　　National Library of Ireland
　　　　Copy at SUNY SB　Box 8

Child's Play　　　　　　　　　　　　　　　　　CHIL PLAY
　　AMs, beginning "I know a merry thicket It was never
　　spoilt by man's care" (Ms 12161).
　　　　National Library of Ireland
　　　　Copy at SUNY SB　Box 8

Come hither hither hither water folk　　　　　COME HITH HI
　　AMs (fragment), beginning "Come hither hither hither
　　water folk Come all ye elemental populace" (2 pp; Ms
　　30834).
　　　　National Library of Ireland
　　　　Copy at SUNY SB

Concerning Lane　　　　　　　　　　　　　　　CONC LANE
　　AMs; draft of stanza, entitled "Concerning Lane," with
　　the line "The anguish of the bird and (demon?) meet in
　　this cry" (1 p). See also Miscellany: DIAR JOUR (Ms
　　13577).
　　　　National Library of Ireland
　　　　Copy at SUNY SB　Box 88

Crazy Jane and the King　　　　　　　　　　　CRAZ JANE KI
　　Published. See Bibliography: Finneran, ICARBS.
　　AMs copy on back flyleaf of copy of LATE POEM 22
　　belonging to GREG LADY.
　　　　New York Public Library

　　TMs, originally entitled "Cracked Mary's Vision,"
　　intended for WORD MUSI PE, with corrections.
　　　　Southern Illinois University

　　Several draft versions, one under title of "Cracked
　　Mary," in Rapallo notebook [C], ca 1929. See
　　Miscellany: DIAR JOUR (Ms 13580).
　　　　National Library of Ireland
　　　　Copy at SUNY SB　Box 90

　　AMs, in Lady Gregory's hand, of this poem: three
　　eight-line stanzas beginning "Yesternight I saw in
　　a vision," dated Aug. 1929 (Ms 21861).
　　　　National Library of Ireland

Poems, Unpublished   339

The deer he followed alone   DEER HE   FO
    AMs, beginning "The deer [?] he followed alone"
    (4 lines).
        National Library of Ireland
        Copy at SUNY SB   Box 8

The Dell   DELL
    AMs fragment, beginning "All the best that in this
    country dwell" (1 p; Ms 12161).
        National Library of Ireland
        Copy at SUNY SB   Box 8

The dew comes dropping   DEW   COME DR
    AMs, beginning "The dew comes dropping O'er elm and
    willow And soft without stopping As tear on pillow"
    (1 p; Ms 30572).
        National Library of Ireland
        Copy at SUNY SB

A double moon or more ago   DOUB MOON MO
    Published. See Bibliography: Wade, LETTERS.
    AMs of early unpublished poem, beginning "A double
    moon or more ago" (Ms 30338).
        National Library of Ireland
        Copy at SUNY SB   Box 8

A flower has blossomed   FLOW HAS   BL
    Published. See Bibliography: Wade, LETTERS; Ellmann, MAN
    AND MASKS; Kelly, LETTERS.
    AMs on back of pencil draft of letter to CRON MARY;
    a poem beginning "A flower has blossomed, the world
    heart core" (Ms 30439).
        National Library of Ireland
        Copy at SUNY SB   Box 8

For all the stars were diminished   FOR   ALL ST
    AMs, beginning "For all the stars were diminished"
    (Ms 13583).
        National Library of Ireland
        Copy at SUNY SB   Box 8

For clapping hands of all men's love   FOR   CLAP HA
    AMs fragment of poem, beginning "For clapping hands of
    all men's love" (Ms 30823).
        National Library of Ireland
        Copy at SUNY SB   Box 8

Fully alone will I choose FULL ALON WI
   AMs draft, beginning "Fully alone will I choose Yes I
   have chosen my share" (Ms 30417).
      National Library of Ireland
      Copy at SUNY SB

Garden of Eden GARD EDEN
   Copy of AMs; several versions (one entitled "Youthful
   Innocence") of a quatrain, beginning "The phantom
   impropriety" from white vellum notebook. See
   Miscellany: DIAR JOUR (Partial List...#545).
      Location of original unknown
      Copy at SUNY SB Box 88

God loves the road of ghost & gleam GOD LOVE RO
   AMs in small white notebook. See Miscellany: DIAR JOUR
   (Partial List...#548).
      Yeats, Senator Michael

Half asleep as the train came in HALF ASLE AS
   AMs, beginning "Half asleep as the train came in Bound,
   idle and empty of mind and gaze" (3 pp; Ms 30382).
      National Library of Ireland
      Copy at SUNY SB

Half in articulo HALF ARTI
   AMs fragment, beginning "Half in articulo, I go to and
   fro In mind confused," on back of letter to WBY from
   A.P. Watt (17 Nov 1936; Ms 30836).
      National Library of Ireland
      Copy at SUNY SB

He who bids the white plains of the pole HE WHO BI
   Published. See Bibliography: Ellmann, MAN AND MASKS.
   AMs, beginning "He who bids the white plains of the
   pole From his brooding warm years be apart" (Ms
   30318).
      National Library of Ireland
      Copy at SUNY SB Box 8

Heart on sleeve is handsome wear HEAR SLEE IS
   AMs, beginning "Heart on sleeve is handsome wear" (four
   lines; Ms 13583).
      National Library of Ireland
      Copy at SUNY SB Box 8

Poems, Unpublished

Here I am   HERE I   AM
    AMs, beginning "Here I am" (Ms 13583).
        National Library of Ireland
        Copy at SUNY SB Box 8

Here comes Mrs. Phillamore   HERE COME MR
    Quatrain entitled "Here Comes Mrs. Phillamore,"
    beginning "I learned to think in a man's way
    And Women's toys forget" (Ms 30891). AMs in Miscellany:
    DIAR JOUR (Rapallo notebook finished June 1929; Ms
    13580).
        National Library of Ireland
        Copy at SUNY SB Box 90

Hills of Mourne   HILL MOUR
    AMs and TMs, entitled "Hills of Mourne," beginning
    "Come on to the hills of Mourne, Come on, come on my
    dear," possibly a version of a folk song (Ms 30508).
        National Library of Ireland
        Copy at SUNY SB Box 8

Hushed in a vale in Dajestan   HUSH VALE DA
    AMs; draft beginning "Hushed in a vale in Dajestan
    I lay alone and lead was in my side" (20 lines;
    Ms 30459).
        National Library of Ireland
        Copy at SUNY SB Box 8

I heard a rose on the brim   I   HEAR RO
    AMs; draft, beginning "I heard a rose on the brim
    Of the moss in the woodways dim" (2 pp; Ms 30458).
        National Library of Ireland
        Copy at SUNY SB Box 8

I know a merry thicket   I   KNOW ME
    See Poems, Unpublished: CHIL PLAY.

I know of no love but my Lord's
    AMs, much revised and less legible than most, with
    reference to a Lord and Lady, and the lines "Sing to me
    my lord a song...gallant knights...who fight."
        University of Arizona Library

I once had peace among   I   ONCE HA
   AMs; fragment of poem, beginning "I once had peace
   among" (1 p; Ms 30835).
          National Library of Ireland
          Copy at SUNY SB

I sat upon a high gnarled root   I   SAT UP
   AMs, beginning "I sat upon a high gnarled root Counting
   the songs of sap and fruit (2 pp; Ms 12161).
          National Library of Ireland
          Copy at SUNY SB   Box 8

I sing of Pan and his piping sweet   I   SING PA
   Three fragments, one beginning "I sing of Pan and his
   piping sweet" (3 pp; Ms 12161).
          National Library of Ireland
          Copy at SUNY SB   Box 8

I stood in the tower window   I   STOO TO
   AMs, beginning "I stood in the tower window To find
   who stood below" (Ms 13583).
          National Library of Ireland
          Copy at SUNY SB   Box 8

I tire of seeing always the same face   I   TIRE SE
   AMs fragment, beginning "I tire of seeing always the
   same face On shields that hang upon mens shoulders,"
   possibly related to SHAD WATE (1 p; Ms 30837).
          National Library of Ireland
          Copy at SUNY SB

I will not in grey hours retake   I   WILL NO
   AMs, beginning "I will not in grey hours retake The
   gift I gave in hours of light" (1 p; Ms 12161).
          National Library of Ireland
          Copy at SUNY SB   Box 8

   AMs in small white notebook. See Miscellany:
   DIAR JOUR (Partial List...#548, 496).
          Yeats, Senator Michael

If the melancholy music of the spheres   IF   MELA MU
   AMs; fragment, beginning "If the melancholy music of
   the spheres Ever be perplexing to his mortal ears" (10
   lines; Ms 30446).
          National Library of Ireland
          Copy at SUNY SB

Poems, Unpublished

Images   IMAG
   Published. See Bibliography: Ellmann, MAN AND MASKS.
   TMs with corrections, of poem, beginning "On Abiegnos'
   side a multitude Restored by drinking that miraculous
   wine" (42 lines; Ms 30434).
         National Library of Ireland
         Copy at SUNY SB Box 8

Imagination's Bride   IMAG BRID
   See Unpublished Poems: TWO FAVO CE.

In a primrose glade   IN   PRIM GL
   AMs fragment, beginning "In a primrose glade,
   well beloved" (1 p; Ms 12161).
         National Library of Ireland
         Copy at SUNY SB Box 8

In the heart of the wood love straying   IN   HEAR WO
   AMs; fragment, beginning "In the heart of the
   wood love straying Where the leaf with the wren is
   playing" (9 pp; Ms 30455).
         National Library of Ireland
         Copy at SUNY SB

Keep far off dancing feet   KEEP FAR OF
   AMs; fragment drafts, one beginning "Keep far off
   dancing feet, I am of those who die," perhaps related
   to AT HAWK WE (5 pp; Ms 30182).
         National Library of Ireland
         Copy at SUNY SB

Knowledge and Wisdom   KNOW WISD
   Published. See Bibliography: Ellmann, MAN AND MASKS.
   AMs, beginning "The Hermit stays at home for he Dances
   out eternity" (8 lines; Ms 13583).
         National Library of Ireland
         Copy at SUNY SB Box 8

Lancelot Switchback   LANC SWIT
   AMs and TMs entitled "Poem of Lancelot Switchback," of
   three stanzas, beginning "Lay down, lay down that
   leather thong and I will lay down mine." Middle stanza
   is a variant of part of the unpublished poem "Billy Boy"
   (BILL BOY). TN by Mrs. Yeats says "the poem was written
   to shock Dorothy Wellesley, which it did" (Ms 30508).
         National Library of Ireland
         Copy at SUNY SB Box 8

A little puritan in Sunday best　　　　　　　　LITT PURI SU
   AMs fragment, beginning "A little Puritan in Sunday
   best"; that line is cancelled, and fragment continues:
   "Mong meadows of sweet grain and musing kine" (8
   lines; Ms 30454).
      National Library of Ireland
      Copy at SUNY SB　Box 8

Look at the white birds　　　　　　　　　　　LOOK WHIT BI
   AMs, beginning "Look at the white birds" (Ms 13583).
      National Library of Ireland
      Copy at SUNY SB　Box 8

The Loud Years Come　　　　　　　　　　　　LOUD YEAR CO
   See Unpublished Poems: THOU LOUD YE.

Low hums the wind　　　　　　　　　　　　　LOW　HUMS WI
   AMs; Spenserian stanzas numbered 27, 28, 29 and 30 of a
   poem; 28 beginning "Low hums the wind and as the smoky
   rings　Fall ring on ring from kindling watch fires
   heart" (2 pp; Ms 30440).　See also Poems, Unpublished:
   SANS SANS SA.
      National Library of Ireland
      Copy at SUNY SB

The Magpie　　　　　　　　　　　　　　　　　　MAGP
   AMsS draft, beginning "Over the heath has the magpie
   flown　Over the hazel cover" (four 8-line stanzas; Ms
   30449).
      National Library of Ireland
      Copy at SUNY SB　Box 8

May time be very kind to thee　　　　　　　MAY　TIME BE
   AMs; inscription for a Christmas card, beginning "May
   time be very kind to thee　Through solitary bower" (Ms
   12161).
      National Library of Ireland
      Copy at SUNY SB　Box 8

Mong meadows of sweet grain　　　　　　　　MONG MEAD SW
   See Poems, Unpublished: LITT PURI SU.

The moon that shone last night　　　　　　　MOON SHON LA
   AMs fragment, beginning "The moon that shone last
   night...Shall grow as white" (1 p; Ms 12161).
      National Library of Ireland
      Copy at SUNY SB　Box 8

Poems, Unpublished   345

My intellect is sain   MY   INTE IS
    AMs, beginning "My intellect is sain [sane?]" (4 lines).
        National Library of Ireland
        Copy at SUNY SB   Box 8

My song thou knowest   MY   SONG TH
    AMs; five lines, beginning "My song thou knowest of a
    dreaming castle" (1 p; Ms 31042).
        National Library of Ireland
        Copy at SUNY SB   Box 8

No daughter of the iron times   NO   DAUG IR
    See Poems, Unpublished: TO SIST CR.

No not now for that fray   NO   NOT NO
    AMs, beginning "No not now for that fray" (2 lines).
        National Library of Ireland
        Copy at SUNY SB   Box 8

O what a tedious herald was the death   O   WHAT TE
    AMs; fragment of a poem or play, beginning "O what a
    tedious herald was the death" (1 p; Ms 30825).
        National Library of Ireland
        Copy at SUNY SB

The Old Grey Man   OLD   GREY MA
    AMs, beginning "Sudden as I sat in a wood An old grey
    bard by me stood" (Ms 12161).
        National Library of Ireland
        Copy at SUNY SB   Box 8

Old and older by many a winter   OLD   OLD MA
    AMs draft with revisions, beginning "Old and older by
    many a winter" (1 p; Ms 12161).
        National Library of Ireland
        Copy at SUNY SB   Box 8

An Old and Solitary One   OLD   SOLI ON
   Published. See Bibliography: Ellmann, MAN AND MASKS.
    AMs fragment of a poem, beginning "They say I'm proud
    and solitary, yes proud" (2 pp; Ms 30826).
        National Library of Ireland
        Copy at SUNY SB   Box 8

On a Child's Death   ON   CHIL DE
    Published. See Bibliography: Schuchard, YEATS ANNUAL 3.
    AMs of poem beginning "You shadowy armies of the dead,"
    in small white notebook. See Miscellany: DIAR JOUR
    (Partial List...#548).
        Yeats, Senator Michael

    Copy of poem, not in WBY's hand. See Miscellany: DIAR
    JOUR (Partial List...#496).
        Yeats, Senator Michael
        Copy at SUNY SB Box 6

    AMsS; 16-line poem, dated 1893 September 5, on death of
    Maud Gonne's son George, in copy of POEM 99 inscribed
    to GREG LADY (I:15).
        Emory University

Once God had stored his peace away in books   ONCE GOD   HA
    AMs, beginning "Once God had stored his peace away in
    books" (1 p).
        National Library of Ireland
        Copy at SUNY SB Box 8

Once I followed a ring dove   ONCE I   FO
    AMs; 14 lines, beginning "Once I followed a ring dove
    From the hill through the wooded past" (Ms 30452).
        National Library of Ireland
        Copy at SUNY SB

Once, a meteor's fickle flair   ONCE METE FI
    AMs, beginning "Once, a meteor's fickle flair,"
    possibly a draft of part of the unpublished poem PROT
    LEAP (1 p; Ms 30346).
        National Library of Ireland
        Copy at SUNY SB Box 8

Only the dead have wisdom   ONLY DEAD HA
    Copy of AMs drafts of poem (partially illegible), with
    the refrain "Only the dead have wisdom"; from a white
    vellum notebook. See Miscellany: DIAR JOUR (Partial
    List...#545).
        Location of original unknown
        Copy at SUNY SB Box 88

Poems, Unpublished

The Outlaw's Bridal   OUTL BRID
    AMs; fragment, entitled "The Outlaw's Bridal,"
    beginning "Dost thou not fear an outlaw's mournful love
    To be always with him, young lowland's daughter,"
    ending with part of FAER SONG (6 pp; Ms 30456).
        National Library of Ireland
        Copy at SUNY SB   Box 8

Pathway   PATH
    See Poems, Unpublished: YOUR PATH.

Poem of Launcelot Switchback   POEM LAUN SW
    See Poems, Unpublished: LANC SWIT.

The politician used to be   POLI USED BE
    Poem, beginning "The politician used to be A happy sort
    of skipping flea" (Ms 30358).
        National Library of Ireland
        Copy at SUNY SB

Portrayed before his eyes   PORT BEFO HI
  Published. See Bibliography: Ellmann, IDENTITY; and
  Gould, YEATS ANNUAL 6.
    AMs; draft of poem, beginning "Portrayed before his eyes
    Implacably lipped" and ending "All gyres be still"
    (1 p; 3 stanzas; Ms 30189).
        National Library of Ireland
        Copy at SUNY SB   Box 8

    See also Poems, Unpublished: ALL DAY YO.

Priest of Pan   PRIE PAN
    AMs, beginning "If the melancholy music of the spheres"
    (2 pp; Ms 30446).
        National Library of Ireland
        Copy at SUNY SB   Box 8

The Protestants' Leap   PROT LEAP
  Published. See Bibliography: Kelly, YEATS: AN ANNUAL
  (1984).
    AMs; three drafts of poem, also called "The Cromwellian
    Speaks," "Loquiter the Cromwellian," and "Lug-na-Gall"
    (Ms 30340). See also Miscellany: DIAR JOUR (Partial
    List...#353).
        National Library of Ireland
        Copy at SUNY SB   Box 7, 88

Copy of poem under title of "The Cromwellian Speaks."
See Miscellany: DIAR JOUR (AMsS; notebook, 10 Ashfield
Terrace; Partial List...#353).
    Yeats, Senator Michael
    Copy at SUNY SB   Box 88

The Queen and the Jester   QUEE JEST
  Published. See Bibliography: Londraville, ARIEL.
    AMs (3 pp).
        Londraville, Richard

Re-engraved time after time   REEN TIME TI
  Signed eight-line stanza, dated Oct. 1901, in POEM WILL
  93, beginning "Re-engraved time after time, Ever in
  their youthful prime" (Ip.Y34.C893p).
        Yale University

The red blood and our laden heavy heart   RED BLOO OU
  Published. See Bibliography: O'Shea, CATALOG.
    Draft of poem inserted into back of RESP OTHE 16,
    beginning "The red blood and our laden heavy heart"
    (item 2412d).
        Yeats, Anne

The riddle is half mastered   RIDD IS   HA
  AMs draft, beginning "The riddle is half mastered." See
  Miscellany: DIAR JOUR (red notebook...from Maud Gonne;
  Ms 30358).
        National Library of Ireland
        Copy at SUNY SB   Box 88

Sansloy-Sansfoy-Sansjoy   SANS SANS SA
  AMs; three Spenserian stanzas; one begins "Tis of a
  vision heard and seen In a garden by the sea"
  (Ms 30440).
        National Library of Ireland
        Copy at SUNY SB

She has us by the throat   SHE HAS US
  Poem, beginning "She has us by the throat She'll
  make and end of us" (Ms 3920).
        National Library of Ireland
        Copy at SUNY SB

Poems, Unpublished

The Song of Heffernan the Blind   SONG HEFF BL
  Published. See Bibliography: Nash, YEATS ANNUAL 4; and
  Schuchard, YEATS ANNUAL 3.
    AMsS; four-line poem based on a prose translation from
    the Gaelic by Douglas Hyde, in copy of POEM 99,
    inscribed to GREG LADY (I:20).
        Emory University

Sonnet I   SONN I
  AMs with title only: "Sonnet I" (Ms 12161).
    National Library of Ireland
    Copy at SUNY SB Box 8

A soul of the fountains spoke me a word   SOUL FOUN SP
  AMs fragment, beginning "A soul of the fountains spoke
  me a word" (2 pp; Ms 30832).
    National Library of Ireland
    Copy at SUNY SB Box 8

Spirit of the Sea   SPIR SEA
  AMs (fragment) of a poem, beginning "Far off in green
  sky meadows dawn's glistening" (10 lines; Ms 30831).
    National Library of Ireland
    Copy at SUNY SB Box 8

  See also Plays: UNPU SEA SP.

Sunrise   SUNR
  AMs fragment, beginning "The young leaves spring, the
  cattle low" (2 pp; Ms 12161).
    National Library of Ireland
    Copy at SUNY SB Box 8

Take up your rifle   TAKE UP   RI
  AMs, beginning "Take up your rifle" (Ms 13583).
    National Library of Ireland
    Copy at SUNY SB Box 8

The tall men   TALL MEN
  AMs, beginning "The tall men the court men" (1 p; Ms
  13583).
    National Library of Ireland
    Copy at SUNY SB Box 8

Tethra before whose windy throne   TETH WHOS WI
    AMs fragment of poem, beginning "Tethra before whose
    windy throne" (4 pp; Ms 30824).
        National Library of Ireland
        Copy at SUNY SB

Then up spring up before me on the saddle   THEN UP   SP
    AMs, beginning "Then up spring up before me on the
    saddle" (4 pp).
        National Library of Ireland
        Copy at SUNY SB   Box 8

There is a flowery sunny dotted glade   THER IS   FL
   Published. See Bibliography: O'Shea, CATALOG.
    AMs; draft of seven-line poem, beginning "There is a
    flowery sunny dotted glade," written in THE WORKS OF
    ALFRED TENNYSON (item 2115).
        Yeats, Anne

There is no man   THER IS   NO
    AMs, beginning "There is no man but may   Meet
    suddenly face to face" (Ms 13583).
        National Library of Ireland
        Copy at SUNY SB

There lived a man of wealth   THER LIVE MA
    AMs; draft of poem, beginning "There lived a man of
    wealth and lust and pride   Where the green sandals of
    the stars imprint" (1 p; Ms 30441).
        National Library of Ireland
        Copy at SUNY SB   Box 8

They mingle with the briar   THEY MING BR
    AMs draft of poem, beginning "They mingle with
    the briar" (1 p; Ms 12161).
        National Library of Ireland
        Copy at SUNY SB   Box 8

This lake washeth around the ruby strand   THIS LAKE WA
    AMs, beginning "This lake washeth around the ruby
    strand" (Ms 12161).
        National Library of Ireland
        Copy at SUNY SB   Box 8

Poems, Unpublished   351

This man is murdered   THIS MAN   IS
   AMs, beginning "This man is murdered" (1 p).
      National Library of Ireland
      Copy at SUNY SB   Box 8

Though leagues asunder   THOU LEAG AS
   Three-line poem inscribed in copy of BOOK IRIS 95
   belonging to SMIT PAME, who did a sketch of him:
   "Though leagues asunder our opinions tend, We are one
   in heart with you as Ireland's friend; There are but
   two great parties in the end." Probably written for the
   occasion.
      Emory University

Though loud years come and loud years go   THOU LOUD YE
   Published. See Bibliography: Schuchard, YEATS ANNUAL 3.
   AMs, beginning "Though loud years come and loud years
   go" (4 lines).
      National Library of Ireland
      Copy at SUNY SB   Box 8

      AMs in small white notebook. See Miscellany:
      DIAR JOUR (Partial List...#548).
         Yeats, Senator Michael

      AMsS; four-line untitled poem beginning "The loud years
      come, the loud years go," accompanying an inscribed
      dedication to Lady Gregory of WIND REED 99, dated 1899
      April 14 (I:30).
         Emory University

Thus ignorant of your features   THUS IGNO FE
   AMs fragment of poem, beginning "Thus ignorant of your
   features" on Coole Park stationery (1 p; Ms 30828).
      National Library of Ireland
      Copy at SUNY SB   Box 8

To Maud Gonne   TO   MAUD GO
   Published. See Bibliography: Ellmann, MAN AND MASKS.
   Eight-line poem, beginning "We poets labour all our days
   To make a little beauty be, But vanquished by a woman's
   gaze And the unlabouring stars are we" (related to HE
   TELL PE) inscribed to MACB MAUD GO in copy of JOHN SHER
   91, dated September 1st, 1891.
      University of Texas at Austin

To Moorhead, Blind   TO   MOOR BL
    TMs with corrections, beginning "It takes us all our
    time with all our eyes To learn to know, since
    knowledge comes from sight" (1 p; Ms 30198).
            National Library of Ireland
            Copy at SUNY SB   Box 8

To a Sister of the Cross of the Rose   TO   SIST CR
    Published. See Bibliography: Ellmann, MAN AND MASKS, and
    Bornstein, YEATS ANNUAL 7.
        AMs, beginning "No daughter of the Iron Times, The Holy
    Future summons you," dated August 1891 (Ms 30318).
            National Library of Ireland
            Copy at SUNY SB   Box 8

    AMs, beginning "White daughter of the Iron Time A
    mystic morning cries to you," in small white notebook.
    See Miscellany: DIAR JOUR (Partial List...#548).
            Yeats, Senator Michael

    Copy of AMs beginning "White daughter of the Iron
    time," not in WBY's hand. See Miscellany: DIAR JOUR
    (Partial List...#496).
            Yeats, Senator Michael
            Copy at SUNY SB   Box 6

Tower wind beaten grim   TOWE WIND BE
    AMs fragment, beginning "Tower wind beaten grim" (1 p;
    Ms 12161).
            National Library of Ireland
            Copy at SUNY SB   Box 8

Twilight--Loch an Eilan   TWIL LOCH AN
    AMs; four quatrains, beginning "The placid water
    undisturbed sleeps: In all the air no sound, save one
    owl's cry." Possibly in WBY's hand, but probably not
    by him.
            University of Texas at Austin

The Two Favorites of the Celestial Bodies   TWO   FAVO CE
    AMs, beginning "Imagination's bride Having thrown aside
    The skin of the wild beast" (Ms 13580, 13583).
            National Library of Ireland
            Copy at SUNY SB   Box 8

Poems, Unpublished   353

Two names all day   TWO   NAME AL
   AMs, beginning "Two names all day have run in my ear
   Parnell's name and Synge's"   (Ms 13583).
      National Library of Ireland
      Copy at SUNY SB   Box 8

Unpublished Unidentified Material   UNPU UNID MA
   AMs; numerous fragments: a few lines or phrases,
   scribbled at random on scraps of paper, often partly
   illegible, with no clear identity (Ms 13580, 30159,
   30182).
      National Library of Ireland
      Copy at SUNY SB

   AMs; drafts of fragments of poems, written in small
   three-hole looseleaf notebook; probably late poems
   (Ms 30416).
      National Library of Ireland
      Copy at SUNY SB

Veiled voices and the questions dark   VEIL VOIC QU
   AMs fragment of a poem, beginning "The veiled voices
   and the questions dark," with crossed out title, "A
   Rime Democratic" (Ms 30829).
      National Library of Ireland
      Copy at SUNY SB   Box 8

The Watch-Fire   WATC FIRE
   Published. See Bibliography: O'Shea, CATALOG.
   Poem (printed), inserted at half title page of COLL
   WORK 08, vol. 2, beginning "This song unto all who
   would gather together" (item 2326).
      Yeats, Anne

We heard the thrushes by the shore of the sea   WE   HEAR TH
   AMs, beginning "We heard the thrushes by the shore of
   the sea" (Ms 13583).
      National Library of Ireland
      Copy at SUNY SB

What is the explanation of it all?   WHAT IS   EX
   Published. See Bibliography: Gould, YEATS ANNUAL 5.
   AMsS, in hand of Edith Shackleton Heald, of four-line
   poem, beginning "What is the explanation of it all?
   What does it look like to a learned man?" Dated
   "Oxford. May 8. 1938."
      Gould, Warwick

When Constantine's descendant ruled the world   WHEN CONS DE
   AMs draft of a poem, possibly related to BYZA,
   beginning "When Constantine's descendant ruled the
   world" (2 pp; Ms 30183).
          National Library of Ireland
          Copy at SUNY SB

When I have wrapped the wolf hide   WHEN I   HA
   AMs fragment of poem, beginning "When I have wrapped
   the wolf hide round my face" (14 lines, 4 crossed out;
   Ms 30827).
          National Library of Ireland
          Copy at SUNY SB

When to its end   WHEN TO   IT
   Published. See Bibliography: Ellmann, MAN AND MASKS.
   AMs fragment of a poem, beginning "When two [to?] its
   end o'er ripened July nears" (4 pp; Ms 30830).
          National Library of Ireland
          Copy at SUNY SB   Box 8

Where thy white waters   WHER THY   WH
   AMs, beginning "Where thy white waters" (4 lines).
          National Library of Ireland
          Copy at SUNY SB   Box 8

Wherever in the wastes of wrinkling sand   WHER WAST WR
   Published. See Bibliography: Kelly, LETTERS.
   AMs draft of poem (probably WBY's) in letter to HINK
   KATH TY.
          The Huntington Library

The world is but a strange romance   WORL IS   ST
   AMs, beginning "The world is but a strange romance
   The end is lost by woeful chance" (Ms 12161).
          National Library of Ireland
          Copy at SUNY SB   Box 8

You are Eternal O Mother Eri   YOU   ARE ET
   AMs in small white notebook. See Miscellany: DIAR JOUR
   (Partial List...#548).
          Yeats, Senator Michael

You are my good   YOU   ARE GO
   AMs, beginning "You are my good, my [beauty]" (1 p).
          National Library of Ireland
          Copy at SUNY SB   Box 8

Poems, Unpublished 355

Your Pathway   YOUR PATH
  Published. See Bibliography: Ellmann, MAN AND MASKS.
  AMs beginning "Archangels were I God should go,"
  dated August 5, 1891. The last two lines are
  used in HE WISH CL (Ms 30318).
     National Library of Ireland
     Copy at SUNY SB   Box 8

Youthful Innocence   YOUT INNO
  See Poems, Unpublished: GARD EDEN.

Prose

This section includes prose, primarily essays and stories
published in periodicals and pamphlets; prose material that
seems to have been intended for publication is also listed
here under an "Unpublished: ..." heading; random prose
pieces that seem not intended for publication are listed
in the Miscellany section.

The Ainu   AINU
   (Wade 1893)
      Two AMs (Ms 12148, 30127).
         National Library of Ireland
         Copy at SUNY SB   Box 19

Art and Ideas   ART IDEA
   (Wade 1914)
      TMs, corrected; also AMs and TMs (Ms 30270, 30471).
         National Library of Ireland
         Copy at SUNY SB   Box 20

Althea Gyles   ALTH GYLE
   (Wade 298)
      AMs; paragraph from Stopford Brooke's A TREASURY OF
      IRISH POETRY IN THE ENGLISH TONGUE (p. 475), beginning
      "Miss Althea Gyles may come to be one of the most
      important of the little group of Irish poets."
         New York Public Library

Away   AWAY
   (Wade 1902)
      Five TMs and AMs, some with corrections and revisions,
      one dated Aug. 9, 1909 (93 pp).
         New York Public Library

A Biographical Fragment   BIOG FRAG
   (Wade 1923)
      TMs (original and carbon) with corrections for the
      DIAL, July 1923 (Za Dial).
         Yale University

By the Roadside   BY   ROAD
   (Wade 1901)
   One clipping of article, with corrections in WBY's
   hand; one TMs with corrections in Lady Gregory's hand.
      New York Public Library

The Censorship and St. Thomas Aquinas   CENS ST.T AQ
   (Wade 1928)
      TMsS of version A (4 pp) and B (4 pp); TMsS (5 pp)
      (Ms 30170, 30867). See also Miscellany: DIAR JOUR
      (Ms 13578).
         National Library of Ireland
         Copy at SUNY SB   Box 19, 90

Compulsory Gaelic: A Dialogue   COMP GAEL
   (Wade 1924)
      AMs (Ms 30412).
         National Library of Ireland
         Copy at SUNY SB   Box 17

Costello the Proud   COST PROU
   (Wade 21, 295)
      AMs, dated August 1895; later appeared in SECR ROSE 97
      (Ms 30369).
         National Library of Ireland
         Copy at SUNY SB   Box 31

Dublin Fanaticism   DUBL FANA
   (Wade 1913)
      TMs (3 pp; Ms 30174).
         National Library of Ireland
         Copy at SUNY SB

Dust hath closed Helen's eye   DUST HATH CL
   (Wade 1899)
      AMs; draft of conclusion to this essay (later published
      in CELT TWIL 02), beginning "Long the light was seen
      streaming up to heaven from the roof of the tower," with
      references to Mary Hynes and Raftery (20 lines).
         New York Public Library

Emmet the Apostle of Irish Liberty   EMME APOS IR
      See Speeches: EMME APOS IR.

The Folly of Argument   FOLL ARGU
   (Wade 1911)
      TMs with corrections, entitled "Casual Meditations."
         The Huntington Library

Prose

The Great Blasket   GREA BLAS
   (Wade 1933)
   AMs; draft of a review of Maurice O'Sullivan's TWENTY
   YEARS A-GROWING, beginning "Aroon was John Synge's
   first choice" (4 pp; Ms 30511).
      National Library of Ireland
      Copy at SUNY SB   Box 20

How Writers Work: WBY on the Future of Poetry   HOW WRIT WO
   TMs with revisions (first printed in EVERYMAN, 25 June
   1931).
      University of Texas at Austin

Hugh Lane's Pictures   HUGH LANE PI
   (Wade 1916)
   Galley proofs with corrections.
      New York Public Library

I Became an Author   I   BECA AU
   (Wade 1938)
   TMs fragment (5 pp; Ms 30554); AMs, with revisions
   (9pp; Ms 30266); TMs, with corrections, entitled, "How
   I Began" (with "My first writings" crossed out),
   beginning "How did I begin to write? I have nothing to
   say" (6 pp; Ms 30790).
      National Library of Ireland
      Copy at SUNY SB   Box 20

Introductions   INTR
   For introductions to books written or edited by WBY,
   see title under Books. For introductions to books by
   other writers, see author and title under Other
   Authors.

Ireland Bewitched   IREL BEWI
   (Wade 1899)
   Page proof, incomplete, with corrections; title changed
   to "Witchcraft and Biddy Early."
      New York Public Library

Ireland, 1921-1931   IREL 1921
   (Wade 1932)
   One TMs; AMs and two TMsS (3 pp; Ms 30100, 30520).
      National Library of Ireland
      Copy at SUNY SB   Box 20

The Irish Censorship   IRIS CENS
   (Wade 1928)
      Copy of AMs of notes related to the essay, in white
      vellum notebook; also an AMs. See Miscellany: DIAR
      JOUR (Partial List...#545 and Ms 13578).
         Location of original unknown
         Copy at SUNY SB   Box 88, 90

      TMsS ([Version A] 6 pp, [Version B] 8 pp). Also a
      [Version C] under title of "A Protest against the Irish
      censorship" (9 pp; Ms 30105, 30116). See also
      Miscellany: DIAR JOUR (Partial List...#545).
         National Library of Ireland
         Copy at SUNY SB   Box 20

Irish Witch Doctors   IRIS WITC DO
   (Wade 1900)
      AMs, with typed pasteovers (46 pp).
         New York Public Library

J.M. Synge and the Ireland of His Time   J.M. SYNG IR
   (Wade 1911)
      AMs, dated Sept. 16, 1910 (42 pp).
         New York Public Library

      See also Books: SYNG IREL 11.

John Eglinton and Spiritual Art   JOHN EGLI SP
   (Wade 1898)
      AMs (10 pp) and TMs (8 pp), beginning "John Eglinton
      misunderstands the issue" (Ms 30301).
         National Library of Ireland
         Copy at SUNY SB   Box 20

      TMs; incomplete draft (3 pp) tipped in at the end of
      EGLI LITE 99 (I:39).
         Emory University

John Shawe-Taylor   JOHN SHAW TA
   (Wade 1911)
      AMs fragment (1 p); TMs with corrections, entitled
      "Captain Shaw Taylor."
         New York Public Library

The King's Visit   KING VISI
   (Wade 1903)
      TMs with corrections, entitled "The new peace in
      Ireland and the king's visit."
         New York Public Library

Prose

Leo Africanus   LEO AFRI
   See Miscellany: OCCU.

Literature and the Living Voice   LITE LIVI VO
   (Wade 1906)
   AMs; incomplete draft of essay, beginning "One Sunday in Summer, a few years ago, I went to the little village of Killeenan," (22 pp; listed in Berg as "[Raftery] incomplete holograph draft of essay"). Also published in SAMHAIN 1906.
      New York Public Library

The Literary Movement in Ireland   LITE MOVE IR
   (Wade 1899)
   Two TMs (19 pp, 23 pp) with corrections and additions; also an AMs, dated Nov. 9, 1900, of "A Postscript."
      New York Public Library

   TMs, with revisions (16 pp).
      Colby College Library

Louis Lambert   LOUI LAMB
   (Wade 1934)
   Corrected pages; TMs, incomplete, with corrections; TMs, entitled "A Note on Louis Lambert" (Ms 30152, 30432, 30054).
      National Library of Ireland
      Copy at SUNY SB   Box 20

   Copy of an AMs insert for the essay, in white vellum notebook. See Miscellany: DIAR JOUR (Partial List...#545).
      Location of original unknown
      Copy at SUNY SB   Box 88

   TMs, with corrections, entitled "A Note on Louis Lambert" (11 pp).
      Southern Illinois University

The Mandukya Upanishad   MAND UPAN
   Two AMs (Ms 30505, 30507). See also Books: ESSA W.B. 37.
      National Library of Ireland
      Copy at SUNY SB

The Message of the Folk-Lorist   MESS FOLK LO
   (Wade 1893)
   AMs (7 pp; Ms 30093). Copy of article from THE SPEAKER, with corrections (Ms 12148).
      National Library of Ireland
      Copy at SUNY SB   Box 20

Michael Clancy, the Great Ghoul, and Death   MICH CLAN GR
   (Wade 1893)
      Copy of THE OLD COUNTRY (Christmas Annual) with this
      story inscribed to GREG LADY, dated 19 October 1897
      (AY14 05 Dec. 1893).
            Emory University

Michael Field's Sight and Song   MICH FIEL SI
   (Wade 1892)
      AMs draft of a review of Michael Field's SIGHT AND SONG
      (Ms 30136).
            National Library of Ireland
            Copy at SUNY SB   Box 20

Modern Poetry   MODE POET
      See Speeches: MODE POET.

More Memories   MORE MEMO
   (Wade 1922)
      TMs (original and carbon) with corrections, for article
      in DIAL (Za Dial).
            Yale University

My Friend's Book   MY   FRIE BO
   (Wade 1932)
      Uncorrected TMs (7 pp) and AMs (12 pp) (Ms 30115,
      30518).
            National Library of Ireland
            Copy at SUNY SB   Box 20

The Need for Audacity of Thought   NEED AUDA TH
   (Wade 1926)
      TMsS and AMs of various parts, with corrections (13 pp;
      Ms 30194).
            National Library of Ireland
            Copy at SUNY SB   Box 20

      Two copies: one AMs, with corrections, initialed (3
      pp); one TMsS, with corrections and a note (8 pp).
            Southern Illinois University

      TMs (carbon) and galley proofs, with corrections (Za
      Dial).
            Yale University

Prose 363

Old Gaelic Love Songs   OLD GAEL LO
   (Wade 1893)
      AMs; review of D. Hyde's LOVE SONGS, under title of
      "Old Irish Love Songs" (5 pp; Ms 30176).
         National Library of Ireland
         Copy at SUNY SB Box 20

Parnell   PARN
   (Wade 1938)
      TMs and AMs (Ms 30394, 30497).
         National Library of Ireland
         Copy at SUNY SB Box 20

A People's Theatre   PEOP THEA
   (Wade 1919)
      Two TMs and a carbon TMs (Ms 30195, 30294).
         National Library of Ireland
         Copy at SUNY SB Box 20

      Pencilled notes on the back flyleaves and cover of
      SELE POEM 21, referring to "People Theatre," possibly
      related to a late broadcast (item 2417a).
         Yeats, Anne

      AMs, with corrections, dated Oct 22; later used as
      Preface to PLAY CONT 23.
         The Huntington Library

Poetry and Tradition   POET TRAD
   (See Wade 82)
      AMs (Ms 30383).
         National Library of Ireland
         Copy at SUNY SB Box 19

      See also POET IREL 08.

Prefaces   PREF
      For prefaces to books written or edited by WBY, see
      title under Books. For prefaces to books by other
      authors, see author and title under Other Authors.

Prometheus Unbound   PROM UNBO
   (Wade 1933)
      TMs and AMs (Ms 30033, 30512).
         National Library of Ireland
         Copy at SUNY SB Box 20

The Rose of Shadow   ROSE SHAD
   (Wade 21, 1894)
   AMs fragment (Ms 30463).
      National Library of Ireland
      Copy at SUNY SB

Samhain: 1904   SAMH 1904
   (Wade 230)
   Copy inscribed to "Miss Monsell from W B Yeats"
   (MONS MISS).
      University of Texas at Austin

Samhain: 1905   SAMH 1905
   (Wade 233)
   TMsS with corrections (1 p).
      New York Public Library

      Copy inscribed to QUIN JOHN, dated Nov. 1905.
         University of Victoria

Samhain: 1906   SAMH 1906
   See Prose: LITE LIVI VO.

Samhain: 1908. First Principles   SAMH 1908 FI
   (Wade 241, 1908)
   Galley proofs with WBY's and Lady Gregory's
   corrections.
      New York Public Library

Samhain: 1909   SAMH 1909
   Title page and paragraphs with corrections, possibly
   intended as copy for a later edition.
      New York Public Library

Samhain: 1910   SAMH 1910
   See Miscellany: THEA MATE (Ms 13068).

Swedenborg, Mediums and the Desolate Places   SWED MEDI DE
   (Wade 312)
   TMs, dated Oct. 14, 1914.
      New York Public Library

   TMs, AMs draft (fragment), and corrected galley proofs;
   two TMsS (Ms 30271, 30276, 30623). Also TMs and AMs in
   notebook and folders (Ms 13575).
      National Library of Ireland
      Copy at SUNY SB   Box 31

      See also Miscellany: FOLK MYTH LE (Ms 13575).

Prose   365

Symbolism in Painting   SYMB PAIN
   (Wade 255)
   Copy of HORT BOOK 98 inscribed to GREG LADY, with
   revisions in Introduction used as basis for this
   essay as it appeared in IDEA GOOD 03 (NC1115 H7).
      Emory University

The Theatre of Beauty   THEA BEAU
   (Wade 1911)
      TMs draft (Ms 30608).
         National Library of Ireland
         Copy at SUNY SB   Box 18

      See also Speeches: THEA BEAU.

Thomas Davis   THOM DAVI
   (Wade 1915; see also Wade 208)
      Two TMs; AMs draft (incomplete); AMs prose fragment
      (2 pp; Ms 30603, 30494, 30849, 30867).
         National Library of Ireland
         Copy at SUNY SB   Box 20

      See also Speeches: THOM DAVI LE.

To All Artists and Writers   TO   ALL   AR
   (Wade 1924)
      AMs under the signatures of H. Stuart and Cecil Salkeld,
      with note by WBY describing it as a "Manifest for Stuart"
      (Ms 30278).
         National Library of Ireland
         Copy at SUNY SB   Box 20

The Tragic Theatre   TRAG THEA
   (Wade 1910)
      TMs with corrections, dated Aug., 1910 (13 pp); later
      used as Preface for PLAY IRIS 11.
         New York Public Library

The Tribes of the Danu   TRIB DANU
   (Wade 1897)
      Two incomplete TMs with corrections (21 pp; 13 pp).
         New York Public Library

Unpublished: Agnes Tobin Translation   UNPU AGNE TO
   According to a note, probably by George Yeats, this is
   a revision of two pages of an Agnes Tobin translation,
   beginning "May these my spirit--did not faint shadows
   fall about you? Therefore on our golden day" (Ms
   30050).
       National Library of Ireland
       Copy at SUNY SB Box 25

Unpublished: All but an empty room   UNPU ALL EM
   AMs with revisions, beginning "An all but empty room"
   (may be stage directions; 17 lines).
       New York Public Library

Unpublished: Anglo Ireland, a conversation   UNPU ANGL IR
   AMs, entitled "Anglo Ireland, a conversation,"
   with a dialogue between "W B Yeats" and "Owen Ahern,"
   and a reference to Mary Hynes (6 pp; Ms 30103).
       National Library of Ireland
       Copy at SUNY SB Box 17

Unpublished: Chicago schools   UNPU CHIC SC
   AMs, in hand of Lady Gregory, initialled by WBY;
   written for CHICAGO DAILY NEWS, urging schools to teach
   the legends and poems of Ireland, dated 1903 (1 p).
       New York Public Library

Unpublished: Contempt for idealism   UNPU CONT ID
   AMs fragment (1 p), referring to a "contempt for
   idealism and memories which served neither church nor
   party."
       New York Public Library

Unpublished: Death of Lady Gregory   UNPU DEAT LA
   Copy of unpublished essay, dated June 19, 1932, in white
   vellum notebook. See Miscellany: DIAR JOUR (Partial
   List...#545).
       Location of original unknown
       Copy at SUNY SB Box 88

Unpublished: Feud   UNPU FEUD
   AMs; early prose story entitled "The Feud" (7 pp; Ms
   30406).
       National Library of Ireland
       Copy at SUNY SB Box 17

Prose   367

Unpublished: Gonne, Maud   UNPU GONN MA
   AMs; notes, possibly for a press release, beginning
   "Miss Maud Gonne since her return to France," about
   a lecture tour.
        Harvard University

Unpublished: I have read your examination   UNPU I   HA
   AMs; fragments (10 pp) of a conversation between Aherne
   and Robartes, beginning "I have read your examination,
   Carlyle," dated June 1920 (Ms 30525).
        National Library of Ireland

Unpublished: I press that thought   UNPU I   PR
   TMs beginning "I press that thought upon the cellars
   and garrets," intended for but not used in WHEE BUTT 34
   and marked "to be used in some new Diary" (Ms 30865).
        National Library of Ireland

Unpublished: I wrote this   UNPU I   WR
   AMs fragment, beginning "I wrote this and other dance
   plays for performance in private houses," possibly a
   program note.
        National Library of Ireland

Unpublished: Irish Dramatic Movement   UNPU IRIS DR
   AMs, subtitled "An open letter to the students of a
   California School," beginning "Nearly twenty years ago"
   (28 pp; Ms 30365).
        National Library of Ireland
        Copy at SUNY SB   Box 20

Unpublished: Lady Gregory's "Doctor in Spite
of Himself"   UNPU LADY GR
   AMs, with a reference to Lady Gregory's adaptation of
   "The Doctor in Spite of Himself" (3 pp; Ms 30056).
        National Library of Ireland
        Copy at SUNY SB   Box 135

Unpublished: Modern Ireland   UNPU MODE IR
   Copy of an AMs draft of essay, or possibly a speech for
   an American tour (over 40 pp), in white vellum
   notebook. See Miscellany: DIAR JOUR (Partial
   List...#545).
        Location of original unknown
        Copy at SUNY SB   Box 88

Unpublished: Modern Poetry   UNPU MODE PO
   TMs fragment with corrections in Lady Gregory's hand,
   with the words "of the musician for its own purposes,"
   referring to modern poetry (1 p).
      New York Public Library

Unpublished: Political Situation in the 1920's   UNPU POLI SI
   AMs; fragment about the political situation in the
   1920's (5 pp; Ms 30444).
      National Library of Ireland

Unpublished: Politics are the forge   UNPU POLI AR
   AMs fragments, beginning "Politics are the forge in
   which the nations are made" (1 p).
      New York Public Library

Unpublished: The Revival of Irish Literature   UNPU REVI IR
   AMs, beginning "In the last century [Imen--i.e.
   Irishmen?] spoke gaelic and had poets in plenty," with
   references to Hyde and Gaelic speech (14 pp; MS Eng
   821.1).
      Harvard University

Unpublished: Sacred grove   UNPU SACR GR
   AMs fragment (1 p) referring to a "sacred grove or
   cave" for the muses.
      New York Public Library

Unpublished: Shelley's thought   UNPU SHEL TH
   AMs; fragments referring to "those who did not
   understand Shelley's thought" with some lines of
   poetry, including "Awake in a world of ecstasy" (1 p).
   See also Poems, Unpublished: AWAK WORL EC.
      New York Public Library

Unpublished: Tribute to Miss Horniman   UNPU TRIB MI
   TMs with corrections of a "Tribute to Miss Horniman,"
   beginning "some time in 1902 or 3 I spoke from the
   stage," possibly an obituary (two copies; Ms 30282).
      National Library of Ireland
      Copy at SUNY SB   Box 20

Unpublished: Younger Generation   UNPU YOUN GE
   TMs (two copies, one 4 pp, one 3 pp) with a few
   revisions, of essay entitled "The Younger Generation,"
   beginning "I had been looking over the proof sheets of
   this book." A note in another hand indicates that
   Ellmann identified this as an account of an interview
   with Joyce (Ms 30311). See also Prose: YOUN GENE.
      National Library of Ireland

Unpublished: Unidentified Prose   UNPU UNID PR
  Numerous prose fragments: AMs mentioning Berkeley and
  Lady Gregory (Ms 30842); TMs beginning, "Dr. Hyde once
  told a public meeting" (Ms 30840); TMs beginning,
  "Someone has informed me that we stand at the verge of
  our Hellenistic age" (Ms 30845); TMs, with cancelled
  date of April 1931, reading in part "plunging into the
  immensity of God" Ms 30846); TMs reading "beyond the
  circle of the student's lamp (Ms 30847); TMs reading
  "it is the monument to Parnell" (Ms 30848); AMs
  mentioning Wilde and Shaw (Ms 30850); AMs reading
  "Christians have in visions communion with Christ"
  (Ms 30852); AMs about "the reality of the beautiful
  shape" (Ms 30853); AMs mentioning Mr. Burke and Mr.
  Grey (Ms 30854).
      National Library of Ireland
      Copy at SUNY SB   Box 40, 41

William Blake and His Illustrations
to the Divine Comedy   WILL BLAK IL
  (Wade 1896)
    AMs (27 pp).
      Harvard University

  Issue of the SAVOY (Sept-Dec 1896) with corrections
  that appear in later editions (item 1849).
      Yeats, Anne

  See also Poems: SECR ROSE and TO HEAR BI.

Wizards and Witches in Irish Folk-Lore   WIZA WITC IR
  TMs and corrected galley proofs (Ms 30276, 30041).
      National Library of Ireland
      Copy at SUNY SB   Box 31

  See also Other: GREG VISI 20.

Speeches

This section lists material related to WBY's numerous talks and lectures, including radio broadcasts, arranged by title, or location, or an "Unidentified: ..." heading for untitled material.

The Abbey Subsidy   ABBE SUBS
    Two TMs (one with corrections), beginning "I have come before you tonight to thank the government," dated 8 Aug. 1925 (3 pp each; Ms 30173, 30558).
        National Library of Ireland
        Copy at SUNY SB   Box 18

Aberdeen Lecture   ABER LECT
    Notes for a lecture at Aberdeen in 1906, beginning "The age of print."
        Wellesley College Library

All the Popular Arts have been Degraded   ALL POPU AR
    TMs of lecture notes, beginning "First; rise of a half educated class"; other lecture notes entitled "The Degradation of Popular Art" (10 pp; Ms 30163, 30632).
        National Library of Ireland
        Copy at SUNY SB   Box 18

American Tour Lectures   AMER TOUR LE
    AMs list of poems to be read for 1920 USA tour, with TMs copies of poems, including BALL FATH GI, IRIS AIRM FO, SEPT 1913, and others (Ms 30624).
        National Library of Ireland
        Copy at SUNY SB   Box 18

    Notes for several lectures: TMs, beginning "I cannot tell you what a pleasure," headed New York, 1903 (33 pp; Ms 30627); AMs, miscellaneous notes (3 pp); TMs, beginning "I asked Mrs. Fowler to invite" (Dec 19 1913; 17 pp; Ms 30627).
        National Library of Ireland
        Copy at SUNY SB   Box 18

Lecture, beginning "When I stand up to lecture about books and poetry being exclusively reserved for the leisure class of people"; one complete copy (15 pp), one incomplete copy; headed New York, 1903-4 (12 pp; Ms 30118).
    National Library of Ireland
    Copy at SUNY SB   Box 18

Notes for lecture, beginning "When I stand up to lecture" with reference to Hallam (in Rare Books and Ms).
    New York Public Library

Notes for lecture in Washington D.C. with reference to "Commercial Play...makeup...morals of Oisin and Patrick" (Ms 30620).
    National Library of Ireland
    Copy at SUNY SB   Box 18

Lecture (headed New York, 1903-4), beginning "I was very glad to accept when you invited me," about the need for theatre to forget the props and return to the power of oration, with corrections (8 pp; Ms 30118).
    National Library of Ireland
    Copy at SUNY SB   Box 18

Notes for lecture, beginning "I was very glad to accept when you invited me" with a reference to Victor Hugo (in Rare Books and Ms).
    New York Public Library

AMs notes, beginning "Topical, make up, moral, emotion," on stationery from Pennsylvania College for Women (3 pp; Ms 30640).
    National Library of Ireland
    Copy at SUNY SB   Box 18

AMs, on stationery of the ship "New Zealand," probably notes for a lecture on Irish literature, referring to Hyde's THE LOVE SONGS OF CONNAUGHT and to John Eglinton (3 pp; Ms 30099).
    National Library of Ireland
    Copy at SUNY SB   Box 18

AMs notes for lecture, beginning "Music Earth
Knowledge," referring to "saint...language of
primitive people... ecstasy...beauty," on
stationery of University Club, Pittsburgh
(5 pp; Ms 30630).
    National Library of Ireland
    Copy at SUNY SB Box 18

Notes for lecture, beginning "Before we begin
considering what sort of theatre we want"
(in Rare Books and Ms).
    New York Public Library

See also Speeches: EMME APOS IR and THEA BEAU.

Belfast Broadcasts   BELF BROA
  See Speeches: READ POEM, OEDI KING and ST. PATR NI.

Birmingham Lecture   BIRM LECT
  Fragmented notes for lecture in Birmingham, beginning
  "Every man has one lecture," with the questions, "What
  is a good play? What is a bad play?" (Ms 30619).
    National Library of Ireland
    Copy at SUNY SB Box 18

Blake Lecture   BLAK LECT
  AMs notes, dated 1919, evidently not used (Ms 30622).
    National Library of Ireland
    Copy at SUNY SB

Burlington House Lectures   BURL HOUS LE
  Series of lectures given at Burlington House in March
  1910, and at other times under various titles. TMs and
  AMs (not in WBY's hand) with stenographic reports of
  lectures, entitled "The Theatre," "Contemporary Irish
  Theatre," and "Friends of My Youth" (82 pp; Ms 30589).
  Other related titles and topics: lecture notes
  entitled "Synge and the Ireland of his Time," with
  headings of "America," "Old Burlington Street," and
  "Wales" (26 pp; Ms 30621); other sets of lecture notes
  for "Friends of My Youth" (4 pp; Ms 30635), "Theatre
  Old Burlington St," and "Theatre" (14 pp; Ms 30637).
    National Library of Ireland
    Copy at SUNY SB Box 18

Page of brief notes, entitled "Lectures 1910," and a
list, "March 7. Theatre...March 9. Contemporary
Poetry...March 11. J.M. Synge & the Dialect...Old
Burlington" (1 p).
    New York Public Library

See also Speeches: AMER TOUR LE and RHYM CLUB LE.

Congratulations from the RSL to the RDS   CONG RSL RD
A speech of congratulations from the Royal Society of
Literature to the Royal Dublin Society on the occasion
of the Bi-Centenary Celebration, beginning "I am here
as a representative of the Royal Society," dated August
2 1924 (2 pp; Ms 30097).
    National Library of Ireland
    Copy at SUNY SB   Box 18

Contemporary Lyric Poets   CONT LYRI PO
AMs lecture notes (5 pp; Ms 30634).
    National Library of Ireland
    Copy at SUNY SB   Box 18

A Defence of the Abbey Theatre   DEFE ABBE TH
TMsS, beginning "Mr. Reddin complains that the Abbey
Theater" (8 pp; Ms 30097).
    National Library of Ireland
    Copy at SUNY SB   Box 18

Divorce Speech   DIVO SPEE
Three TMsS with several versions, dated June 10, 1925
(22 pp; Ms 30080).
    National Library of Ireland
    Copy at SUNY SB   Box 18

Dreams and Ghosts   DREA GHOS
AMs lecture notes (4 pp; Ms 30629).
    National Library of Ireland
    Copy at SUNY SB   Box 18

Emmet the Apostle of Irish Liberty   EMME APOS IR
TMs (carbon; 26 pp) with corrections, of speech
delivered at the New York Academy of Music, to
Clan-Na-Gael on February 28, 1904.
    New York Public Library

Friends of my Youth   FRIE YOUT
See Speeches: BURL HOUS LE.

Speeches

In Memory of Thomas William Lyster   IN   MEMO TH
   Text of speech (2 pp) given by WBY in honor of service
   of Lyster to the National Library of Ireland, and list
   of subscribers to memorial unveiled March 27, 1926, in
   the NLI (1 p).
      Southern Illinois University

In the Poet's Parlour   IN   POET PA
  Broadcast (Wade 10), April 22 1937.
   TMs of broadcast of April 22 1937, beginning "When we
   were in" (7 pp).
      National Library of Ireland
      Copy at SUNY SB   Box 23

In the Poets' Pub   IN   POET PU
  Broadcast (Wade 9), April 2 1937.
   AMs and TMs of radio broadcast (April 2, 1937; Ms
   30310, 30580).
      National Library of Ireland
      Copy at SUNY SB   Box 23

Interview with Deirdre MacDonagh   INTE DEIR MA
   TMs of radio interview, with discussion of Lane
   pictures and Tate Gallery (5 pp; Ms 30571).
      National Library of Ireland
      Copy at SUNY SB   Box 23

Irish Literary Movement   IRIS LITE MO
  Broadcast (Wade #12)
   TMs of interview with Deirdre MacDonagh (different from
   above), beginning with her question, "Mr. Yeats, how
   did the Irish Literary Movement begin?" and his answer,
   "If you had lived at the time you would know that
   something had to be done" (on verso of text for "My Own
   Poetry" broadcast; Ms 30590); another TMs of same
   interview (7pp; Ms 30397).
      National Library of Ireland
      Copy at SUNY SB   Box 23

The Lane Pictures   LANE PICT
   One TMs with revisions, of a Senate Speech, beginning,
   "It will be within the memory" (12 pp; Ms 30429).
      National Library of Ireland
      Copy at SUNY SB   Box 18

Manchester Lecture   MANC LECT
   TMs of lecture given in Manchester (note in another
   hand suggests it was a lecture by Fay) with corrections
   in WBY's hand, beginning "It is pleasant coming to
   Manchester," about the reception of a travelling Irish
   theatre company (9 pp; Ms 13572).
      National Library of Ireland
      Copy at SUNY SB   Box 136

Modern Ireland   MODE IREL
   See Prose: UNPU MODE IR.

Modern Poetry   MODE POET
   Broadcast (Wade #7), Oct 11 1936.
   AMs fragment (Oct 1936; 7 pp; Ms 30386); another AMs
   fragment (Ms 30327).
      National Library of Ireland
      Copy at SUNY SB   Box 23

My Own Poetry   MY OWN PO
   Broadcast (Wade #11), July 3 1937.
   TMs (9 pp) and AMs draft with copies of poems to read.
   Has notes on back of interview with Deirdre MacDonagh
   (Ms 30590). See Speeches: IRIS LITE MO.
      National Library of Ireland
      Copy at SUNY SB   Box 23

My Own Poetry Again   MY OWN AG
   Broadcast (Wade #12), October 29 1937.
   Corrected TMs (marked "My own copy" in WBY's hand) of
   broadcast by BBC, 29 October 1937 (Ms 30320).
      National Library of Ireland
      Copy at SUNY SB   Box 23

Necessity for Manhood   NECE MANH
   Ms in the hand of Annie Horniman, beginning "I had
   lately, for the sake of a speech I have to the
   Clan-na-Gael in New York, to read through the life of
   Emmett," entitled "Necessity for Manhood," with the
   note, "shortly after 1st AM. lecture tour" (5 pp; Ms
   30609).
      National Library of Ireland
      Copy at SUNY SB   Box 135

Speeches

Oedipus the King   OEDI KING
   Broadcast (Wade #1), Sept 8 1931.
   TMsS, TMs, and TMsS carbon with corrections of a speech
   "to be broadcasted from Belfast September 8" (Ms
   30109).
       National Library of Ireland
       Copy at SUNY SB   Box 23

Poems About Women   POEM WOME
   Broadcast (Wade #3), April 10 [1932].
   TMsS and AMs notes from Broadcast, beginning "I asked a
   great friend, a very old woman, what I should read
   tonight. She said, Read them poems about women," with
   poems to read, and a discussion of how he came to write
   these poems (13 pp; Ms 30117).
       National Library of Ireland
       Copy at SUNY SB   Box 23

Poetry New and Old   POET NEW OL
   TMs lecture notes, with corrections, beginning "Poetry
   is the flower of life" (Ms 30617; 4 pp).
       National Library of Ireland
       Copy at SUNY SB   Box 18

Polignac Prize Speech   POLI PRIZ SP
   (Wade 308)
   Ms, headed by WBY, "Speech awarding the Polignac
   Prize" (1913; Ms 30180).
       National Library of Ireland
       Copy at SUNY SB

Reading of Poems   READ POEM
   Broadcast (Wade #2), Sept 8 1931.
   Incomplete TMs, with corrections, of broadcast,
   beginning "I am going to read" (7 pp).
       National Library of Ireland
       Copy at SUNY SB   Box 23

Rhymer's Club Lecture   RHYM CLUB LE
   AMs (9 pp) and TMs (14 pp) of notes, with reference to
   "academic form...Abstract Morality (Wordsworth,
   Tennyson)...rhetoric" (Ms 30607). Probably a version
   of the "Friends of My Youth" speech. See Speeches:
   BURL HOUS LE.
       National Library of Ireland
       Copy at SUNY SB   Box 18

Rome Lecture   ROME LECT
   TMsS, with corrections, of 1935 lecture in Rome about
   the Irish theatre, beginning "I am about to describe
   the rise and achievement of a small dingy, impecunious
   theatre" (8 pp; Ms 30113); TMs (carbon) of parts of
   same lecture (12 pp; Ms 30796).
        National Library of Ireland
        Copy at SUNY SB   Box 18

St. Patrick's Night   ST. PATR NI
   Broadcast (Wade #4), March 17 1934.
   Two TMs of the reading and poems, with corrections.
   Poems include SONG OLD MO, FAER SONG, FIDD DOON, FISH
   (5 pp; Ms 30249).
        National Library of Ireland
        Copy at SUNY SB   Box 23

   TMs draft, beginning "When I was a young man" (Mar
   17 1934; Ms 31091).
        National Library of Ireland
        Copy at SUNY SB   Box 23

Stockholm Banquet Speech   STOC BANQ SP
   Drafts of speech given at banquet in Stockholm, Royal
   Academy of Sweden, Dec 1923. TMs, with corrections,
   beginning "I have been all my working life" (2 pp);
   AMs, beginning "She was a" (2 pp); AMs fragment (14
   pp); AMs, beginning "Draft, Speech for Sweden Academy"
   (1 p); TMs, beginning "I have chosen as my theme"
   (Dec 13 1923; 17 pp; Ms 30611).
        National Library of Ireland
        Copy at SUNY SB   Box 18, 26

   See also Books: BOUN SWED 25.

Synge and the Ireland of his Time   SYNG IREL TI
   See Speeches: BURL HOUS LE.

Tailteann Banquet Speech   TAIL BANQ SP
   TMsS, headed "Speech for Tailteann banquet," dated
   August 2 1924, beginning "In our long struggle for
   National independence" (4 pp; Ms 30097).
        National Library of Ireland
        Copy at SUNY SB   Box 18

Theatre of Beauty   THEA BEAU
   Incomplete TMs (two drafts) with autograph corrections
   by WBY and someone else, and note by WBY: "Report of a
   lecture...revised at Stone Cottage, December 1913" (20
   pp; Ms 30052); TMs draft entitled "Theatre of Beauty,"
   but differing from the above drafts, beginning "All
   over Europe just now" (5 pp; Ms 30608); TMs (two sets
   of lecture notes, one on University of Toronto
   stationery), beginning "All over Europe just now" (14
   pp; Ms 30631).
         National Library of Ireland
         Copy at SUNY SB   Box 18

   TMsS of lecture, marked "Version of 'The Theatre of
   Beauty,'" beginning "Before we begin considering what
   sort of theatre we want," about the need for the
   theatre to satisfy the audience; headed New York,
   1903-4 (11 pp; Ms 30118).
         National Library of Ireland
         Copy at SUNY SB   Box 18

   See also Speeches: AMER TOUR LE and UNID WRIT AU.

Thomas Davis Lecture   THOM DAVI LE
   TMs, beginning "I think we are all glad" (4 pp; Ms
   31100); TMs entitled "Thomas Davis," with a different
   text, beginning "Fifteen or twenty years ago" (8 pp; Ms
   30037).
         National Library of Ireland
         Copy at SUNY SB   Box 18

   See also Prose: THOM DAVI.

Unidentified: Compulsory Education   UNID COMP ED
   TMsS (carbon) of "Speech on November 30, 1925,"
   beginning "Perhaps there are some here, one or two,"
   about the Government's introducing a compulsory
   education bill (9 pp; Ms 30162).
         National Library of Ireland
         Copy at SUNY SB   Box 18

Unidentified: A Glass of Beer   UNID GLAS BE
   AMs; fragment of notes for a radio broadcast with
   reference to Stephens's "A Glass of Beer" and to a
   "Malachy" (3 pp; Ms 30392). Wade Broadcast #8
   mentions Stephens.
         National Library of Ireland
         Copy at SUNY SB   Box 23

Unidentified: Home Rule   UNID HOME RU
    TMs, with corrections, beginning "I have a profound
    belief in the Irish mind," in support of Home Rule
    (5 pp; Ms 30095).
        National Library of Ireland
        Copy at SUNY SB   Box 18

Unidentified: Ideal Drama   UNID IDEA DR
    AMs summary of a lecture (Ms 30470).
        National Library of Ireland
        Copy at SUNY SB   Box 18

Unidentified: Irish Folklore   UNID IRIS FO
    TMs, with corrections, beginning "I address you tonight
    with some little timidity" on the subject of Irish
    folklore (10 pp; Ms 30610).
        National Library of Ireland
        Copy at SUNY SB   Box 18

Unidentified: Lecture Notes   UNID LECT NO
    Lecture notes, with no indication of time or place,
    mentioning items such as "symbols...myths...new light
    and shade...characters...morale...Macpherson...old
    house...language movements," probably from American
    tours (14 pp; Ms 30641).
        National Library of Ireland
        Copy at SUNY SB   Box 18

Unidentified: Mysticism   UNID MYST
    AMs lecture notes on mysticism, beginning "My personal
    consciousness" (7 pp).
        National Library of Ireland
        Copy at SUNY SB   Box 18

Unidentified: A New Unionist Party   UNID NEW UN
    TMs, with corrections, beginning "The need for a new
    party" (4 pp).
        National Library of Ireland
        Copy at SUNY SB   Box 18

Unidentfied: Poetics   UNID POET
    AMs, beginning "We our poets have one theme in common"
    (4 pp; Ms 30397).
        National Library of Ireland
        Copy at SUNY SB   Box 18

Speeches

Unidentified: Theatre Speeches   UNID THEA SP
   TMs (two carbon copies) of speech, beginning "The
   resolution that is before this meeting asks the
   parties to the present industrial dispute" regarding
   loss of revenues to the Theatre as well as society and
   need for settlement of dispute between Press of Dublin
   and Unionist Press (2 pp each; Ms 30615).
        National Library of Ireland
        Copy at SUNY SB   Box 18

   AMs; fragment beginning "Every man has one lecture,
   with the questions "What is a good play &, what is a
   bad play"   (4 pp; Ms 30619).
        National Library of Ireland
        Copy at SUNY SB   Box 18

Unidentified: Three Shafts   UNID THRE SH
   AMs (7 pp), entitled "Three Shafts"; first page (the
   middle of notes, perhaps for a lecture) reads "and
   through a sympathetic Movement Society itself has so
   split into abstracting qualities," and ending "any
   prophet or evangelist who will break for us at last
   the three black shafts of death" (Ms 30333).
        National Library of Ireland
        Copy at SUNY SB   Box 130

Unidentified: Writer and Audience   UNID WRIT AU
   AMs, on the relation of the writer to his audience,
   with reference to d'Annunzio and Claudel, perhaps a
   draft of the THEA BEAU lecture (Ms 30053).
        National Library of Ireland
        Copy at SUNY SB

Younger Generation   YOUN GENE
   AMs, entitled "Younger Generation," with corrections,
   of outline of poetry readings (2 pp); TMs of poems, and
   "A Letter to Mrs. Pearse" (11 pp; Ms 30612).
        National Library of Ireland
        Copy at SUNY SB   Box 18, 20

   See also Prose: UNPU YOUN GE.

LIBRARIES AND OTHER OWNERS

Libraries and Other Owners

This section includes names and addresses of libraries and individuals holding manuscripts of W.B. Yeats. Holdings are listed by QUICK title and arranged by type. Restrictions (other than the usual ones given in the preface to this CENSUS) are noted, as are published guides to specific collections.

Amherst College Library
Special Collections
Amherst, MA 01002
USA

   Letters:
      MEIK ALEX
      MORT DAVI
      O'DO

Archivae Provincia Hibernia
Milltown Park, Ranelagh Road
Dublin, Ireland

   Letters:
      RUSS FATH MA

Belfast City Libraries
Belfast BT1 1EA
Northern Ireland

   Letters:
      CRON DR. J.
      RYAN MR.

Berlind, Bruce
Department of English
Colgate University
Hamilton, NY 13346
USA

   Books: Poems:
      NEW   POEM 38   UNDE BEN BU
   Inscriptions:
      UNKN RECI

Bibliotheque de l'Arsenal
Department des Arts du Spectacle
Le Conservateur en Chef
1, rue de Sully
Paris 75004
France

  Letters:
    CRAI EDWA GO

Bibliotheque Literaire Jacques Doucet
10 Place du Pantheon
Paris 75005
France

  Letters:
    MALL STEP

Birmingham Reference Library
Chamberlain Square
Birmingham B3 3HQ
England

  Letters:
    BULL A.H.

Bodleian Library
Keeper of Western Manuscripts
Broad Street
Oxford OX1 3BG
England
  See Bibliography: "Wordsworth to Robert Evans...An Exhibition."

  Inscriptions:
    UNKN RECI
  Letters:

BRID MRS. RO	GRIG MISS EM
BRID ROBE	MASE JOHN
CROO WILL MO	MORR MAY
DOBE BERT	MURR GILB
ERVI ST. JO	OWLE F.C.
FISH H.A.	RICK CHAR
GORE ELIZ	UNKN CORR
GRIE H.J.	

Boston College

Boston College
Burns Library
Special Collections
Chestnut Hill, MA 02167
USA

   Books:
      CELT TWIL 05
      POEM   99
   Letters:
      DAY F.H.
      MEYN ALIC

   Inscriptions:
      MEYN ALIC
      SMIT J.
   Poems:
      DAWN
      MEMO
      ON   BEIN AS

Boston Public Library
Curator of Manuscripts
P.O. Box 286
Boston, MA 02117
USA

   Books:
      CELT TWIL 93
   Letters:
      COOM AMAN KE
      EMER FLOR FE
      WILS JOHN GI

   Inscriptions:
      UNKN RECI

Boston University
Mugar Library
Special Collections
771 Commonwealth Avenue
Boston, MA 02215
USA

   Books:
      WHEE BUTT 34
   Miscellany:
      IRIS ACAD MA
   Plays:
      PURG

   Letters:
      CHAK AMIY
      GOGA OLIV ST
      JACO JOSE BO
      MCCA PATR
      O'CO FRAN

Brandeis University Library
Special Collections
415 South Street
Waltham, MA 02254
USA

   Letters:
      LEGA RICH

British Library
Great Russell Street
London WC1B 3DG
England
    Manuscripts accessible to scholars only, upon
    application.
    See Bibliography: Blake-Hill, Philip V. "The Macmillan
    Archive."

  Books:
      ON   BOIL 39
      UNPU MACM ED
      WIND STAI 33
  Letters:

ARCH WILL	MOOR STUR
BAGN ENID	MORR MAY
BELL C.C.	PYPE J.S.
BOUG RUTL	RHYS ERNE
CAMP MRS. B.	RICK CHAR
DRYH NORA	SHAN CHAR
DUFF ARTH	SHAW GEOR B.
ELLI P.D.	SHOR CLEM
FITZ MISS	SHOR MRS. DO
GOSS EDMU	SPEY EDWA
MACM COMP	THRI HERB
MONR ALID	WALK EMER

  Poems:

CRAZ JANE MO	STAT HOLI
EAST 1916	TOM O'RO
HIS DREA	WHY SHOU NO

Brown University
John Carter Brown Library
Manuscripts Division
Box 1894
Providence, RI 02912
USA

Books:	Inscriptions:
PLAY IRIS 11	UNKN RECI
Letters:	
ACAD EDIT	SPAR HENR
COTT JAME	UNKN CORR
FROS WILL H.	WALK EMER
SHER PHIL	YEAT ELIZ

Bucknell University
Ellen Clarke Bertrand Library
Special Collections
Lewisburg, PA 17837
USA

   Letters:
       DUNN MR   WALK EMER
       FRAN RENE   WARD JAME
       GOGA OLIV ST   YEAT ELIZ
       MACD NORM
   Miscellany:
       MISC

Cambridge University Library
Keeper of Manuscripts
Cambridge CB3 9DR
England

   Letters:
       BENS A.C.
       GOSS LADY

Case Western Reserve University Library
Special Collections
11161 East Boulevard
Cleveland, OH 44106
USA

   Letters:
       MCCA PATR

The Catholic Univeristy of America Library
Archivist
Washington, DC 20064
USA
    Manuscripts accessible to scholars only.

   Letters:
       SHAH THOM

Churchill College
Archives Centre
Cambridge
England CB3 0DS

   Letters:
       LYTT EDIT

Clark University
Goddard Library
Rare Books Librarian
Worchester, MA 01610
USA

   Inscriptions: Miscellany:
      DODD LORI HO   PHOT

Colby College Library
Special Collections
Waterville, ME 04901
USA
   See Bibliography: Abbot, Cheryl and J. Fraser
   Cocks, III. JAMES AUGUSTINE HEALY COLLECTION.

   Books: Inscriptions:
      COUN KATH 92   HEAL JAME
      JOHN SHER 91   HINK KATH TY
      KING THRE 04   MATH MRMS
      REVE CHIL 15   UNKN RECI
      WILD SWAN 19
   Letters: Poems:
      ARTH CHES   LIFT WHIT KN
      DIGG DUDL   TOM O'RO
      GOGA OLIV ST   Prose:
      LAUR THOM WE   LITE MOVE IR
      MASE JOHN
      MORR MAY
      RUSS GEOR
      SASS SIEG
      SMIT T.R.

College of the Holy Cross
Dinand Library
Rare Book Librarian
Worcester, MA 01610
USA

   Letters:
      GUIN LOUI IM
   Poems:
      ON   BEIN AS

Columbia University
Butler Library
Rare Book and Manuscript Library
535 W. 114 Street
New York, NY 10027
USA
   Manuscripts accessible to scholars only.

  Books:
    FOUR PLAY 21

  Letters:
    BELM ELEA RO
    DUNC ELLE DO
    MASE JOHN

Connecticut College
Charles E. Shain Library
Special Collections
New London, CT 06320
USA
   Manuscripts accessible to scholars only.

  Letters:
    MATH ELKI

Cornell University
Olin Library
Rare Books Librarian
Ithaca, NY 14853
USA
   See Bibliography: Marcus, Philip L. "Catalogue
   of Yeats Manuscripts" and Scholes, Robert Edward.
   THE CORNELL JOYCE COLLECTION.

  Letters:
    CRAN MRS. RO
    CRAN ROLA
    JOYC JAME

    LEWI P.   WY
    POUN EZRA
    UNKN CORR

Crawford, William
237 E. 72 Street
New York, NY 10021
USA

  Books:
    AUTO REVE 26
  Letters:
    ASQU LADY

  Inscriptions:
    HARR FRAN

Dalhousie University Library
Halifax, Nova Scotia B3H 4H8
Canada

    Poem:
        PITY LOVE

Dorset County Museum
Dorchester DT1 1XJ
England

    Letters:
        HARD THOM

Dublin City Libraries
The Gilbert Library
Pearse Street
Dublin, Ireland

    Books: Inscriptions:
        DISC VOLU 07   COLL MARG
        GOLD HELM 08   UNKN RECI
        RESP POEM 14

Emory University
Robert W. Woodruff Library
Head of Special Collections
Atlanta, GA 30322
USA
    See Bibliography: Schuchard, Ronald W. "The Yeats-
    Lady Gregory Collection."

    Books:
        BELT   00   POEM   04
        BOOK IRIS 95   POEM BALL 88
        CAT MOON 24   POEM TRAN 09
        CELT TWIL 93   POET WORK 06
        COUN CATH 99   RESP OTHE 16
        COUN CATH 12   RESP POEM 14
        DEAT SYNG 28   REVE CHIL 15
        FOUR PLAY 21   SELE LOVE 13
        FOUR YEAR 21   SELE POEM 29
        IDEA GOOD 03   SEVE POEM 22
        JOHN SHER 91   SING HEAD 34
        LAND HEAR 94   SYNG IREL 11
        LAND HEAR 12   TABL LAW 97
        LAST POEM 39   TWO PLAY 19
        PACK EZRA 29   UNIC STAR 08
        POEM   95   WHER THER 02
        POEM   99   WIND REED 99

Emory University

Inscriptions:
- GREG LADY
- KIND MARG MA
- SMIT PAME
- TUCK MRS.
- UNKN RECI

Miscellany:
- MISC

Other Authors:
- EGLI LITE 04
- GOET GOET 88
- GREG GODS 04
- GREG SEVE 09
- HORT BOOK 98
- SYNG POEM 09

Poems:
- ALL SOUL NI
- ALL THIN CA
- APPO
- AT   GALW RA
- BLOO BOND
- BROW PENN
- FOR ANNE GR
- FRIE
- HAPP TOWN
- HE   HEAR CR
- HE   TELL PE
- IN   MEMO MA
- INTO TWIL
- LOVE TELL RO
- MAID QUIE

Poems, Unpublished:
- ON   CHIL DE
- SONG HEFF BL
- THOU LEAG AS
- THOU LOUD YE

Letters:
- BALL MRS. FR
- BLAN HENR ME
- GORM ERIC
- GOUG MRS
- GREG LADY
- GWYN STEP
- JACK HOLB
- LANG ROSA
- SOLO DR. B.

Plays:
- AT   HAWK WE
- CATH HOUL
- COUN CATH
- DEIR
- HOUR GLAS
- ONLY JEAL EM
- POT BROT
- UNIC STAR

- O   DO   NO
- OLD MEMO
- QUEE EDAI
- RAGG WOOD
- RED HANR SO
- SORR LOVE
- SPIN SONG
- STAR NEST MY
- TO   CHIL DA
- TO   FRIE WH
- TO   HEAR BI
- TOM O'RO
- TOWE
- VALL BLAC PI
- WHIL I   RE

Prose:
- JOHN EGLI SP
- MICH CLAN GR
- SYMB PAIN

Eton School Library
The Timbralls, Eton College
Windsor, Berkshire SL4 6H
England
   Manuscripts accessible to scholars only.

Poems:
- HE   WISH CL

Finneran, Richard
Department of Engish
University of Tennessee
Knoxville, TN 37996
USA

   Books: Inscriptions:
      TEN   PRIN 37   STEP JAME

Fiskin, Jeffrey
c/o Jess S. Morgan & Company, Inc.
6420 Wilshire Boulevard   19th Floor
Los Angeles, CA 90048
USA
    Access by appointment only.

   Books: Inscriptions:
      IN   SEVE 03   UNKN RECI
   Poems:
      FOLL BEIN CO
      PLAY ASK   BL

Fitzwilliam Museum
Trumpington St.
Cambridge CB2 1RB
England
    Manuscripts accessible by application and
    recommendation only.

   Inscriptions: Letters:
      LAMB MRS. EN   LINN MR.
   Plays:
      DEIR

Gould, Warwick
Royal Holloway and Bedford New College
Egham Hill, Egham
Surrey TW20 0EX
England
    See Bibliography: Gould, YEATS ANNUAL 5.

   Poems, Unpublished:
      WHAT IS   EX

Hamilton College Library

Hamilton College Library
Curator Special Collections
Clinton, NY 13323
USA
    Manuscripts accessible to scholars only.

   Letters:
      POUN EZRA

Harper, George
407 Plantation Road
Tallahassee, FL 32303
USA

   Books:
      EIGH POEM 16
      POEM   95
      REVE CHIL 16
   Other Authors:
      HINK MIDD 16

   Inscriptions:
      ALLE CHAR DE
      HORT WILL
      UNKN RECI
   Poems:
      PARN FUNE

Harvard University
Houghton Library
Manuscript Department
Cambridge, MA 02138
USA

   Books:
      DEIR   07
      DRAM PERS 35
      HERN EGG 38
      HOUR GLAS 04
      HOUR GLAS 14
      IN   SEVE 03
      LETT NEW 34
      POEM   99
      RESP POEM 14
      REVE CHIL 15
      SYNG IREL 11
   Letters:
      BLAK WARR BA
      BULL A.H.
      BYNN WITT
      CLAR AUST
      DAVR HENR
      DUNC ELLE DO
      FAY WILL GE
      FITT WILL B.
      GOGA OLIV ST

   Inscriptions:
      O'CO FRAN
      PEAB JOSE PR
      UNKN RECI

      GRAV ALFR PE
      GWYN STEP
      HEAL EDIT SH
      HINK HENR
      HINK KATH TY
      HORT WILL TH
      JAME HENR
      LEVE GEOR GR
      LIST MISS E.

Letters (continued):
    LOWE AMY
    MARK CONS
    MOOR ISAB
    MOSH THOM BI
    O'BR EDWA JO
    O'LE ELLE
    O'LE JOHN
    PARK D.
    PAYN IDEN
    REYN HORA
    ROBE GEOR
    ROBI CORI
    ROLL THOM WI
    ROTH WILL
    RUSS GEOR
    SCHR WILL LA
    SMIT MRS. TR
    STEP JAME
    TAGO RABI
    UNKN CORR
Miscellany:
    IRIS ACAD MA
Other Authors:
    TAGO POST 14
Plays:
    CALV
    COUN CATH
    DIAR GRAN
    DREA BONE
    KING THRE
    LAND HEAR DE
    ON   BAIL ST
    ONLY JEAL EM
    WORD WIND PA
Poems:
    CRAZ JANE MO
    EGO DOMI TU
    HOUN VOIC
    LONG LEGG FL
    MODE LAUR
    NEVE GIVE AL
    PARD OLD FA
    RIBH DENO PA
    SHAD WATE
    STAT HOLI
    STAT UES
    THRE SONG ON
    WHIL I   RE
    WHY SHOU NO
Prose:
    UNPU GONN MA
    UNPU REVI IR
    WILL BLAK IL

Higginson Family Museum
2 Glamorgan Ave. Apt. 1002
Scarborough M1P 2M8
Ontario, Canada

Letters:
    HIGG T.W.

The Historical Society of Pennsylvania
Curator of Manuscripts and Archives
1300 Locust St.
Philadelphia, PA 19107
USA
    Manuscripts accessible by application only.
    See Bibliography: GUIDE TO THE MANUSCRIPT
    COLLECTIONS.

Poems:
    MOOD

The Huntington Library
Curator, Literary Manuscripts
1151 Oxford Road
San Marino, CA 91108
USA
    Manuscripts accessible by application only.
    See Bibliography: GUIDE TO LITERARY MANUSCRIPTS
    and Schulz, H.C. "English Literary Manuscripts."

Books:
    PLAY CONT 23
    POEM   99
    POET IREL 08
Letters:
    GOSS PHIL
    HILL EDWI
    HINK KATH TY
    MACH IGNA
    ORME MR.
    ROBE WALF
    SCHE ALEX
    YEAT LILY
Prose:
    FOLL ARGU
    PEOP THEA
Poems, Unpublished:
    WHER WAST WR

Inscriptions:
    YOUN ELLA

Miscellany:
    QUOT PARA MA
Poems:
    CRAD SONG
    EAST 1916
    FAIR DOCT
    IN   CHUR
    SHAD WATE
    SUMM EVE
    WHEN YOU OL
    WHEN YOU SA

India Office Library and Records
197 Blackfriars Road
London SE1 8NG
England

    Letters:
        GIBS MR.
        MCMA MR.

Indiana University
The Lilly Library
Curator of Manuscripts
Bloomington, IN 47405
USA

    Books:
        BOOK IRIS 00
        COLL POEM 33
        CUTT AGAT 12
        GREE HELM 12

Books (continued):
   KING THRE 04
   LAND HEAR 03
   LAND HEAR 94
   LAND HEAR 12
   LAND HEAR 25
   SELE POEM 29
   SING HEAD 34
   UNIC STAR 08
   WAND OISI 89
   WHER THER 02
   WIND REED 99
Letters:
   DUBL MAGA ED
   FRED MISS
   GUTH MR.
   JACK SCHU B.
   KOEH THOM
   PLOM WILL C.
   POUN DORO
   POUN EZRA
   ROBI LENN
   RUSS GEOR
   SHAK OLIV
   STAR JAME
   WADE ALLA

Inscriptions:
   COAT FLOR EA
   DICK MABE
   FODE GWYN
   PROK FRED
   REES J.   RO
   ROBI LENN
   SAND CAST SC
   TAGE PHIL
   TURN W.J.
   UNKN RECI
   WADE ALLA
Miscellany:
   DOCU
Other Authors:
   GREG CASE 26
Poems:
   HE   WISH CL
   TOM O'RO
   WITH BOUG

John Rylands University Library
Oxford Road
Manchester   M13 9PP
England

Letters:
   HINK KATH TY   HUTC THOM
   HORN MISS AN   SCOT C.P.

Kain, Richard M.
1400 Willow, No. 1206
Louisville, KY 40204
USA

Letters:
   DUNN MR.   KNOL LADY
   HUNT VIOL   MAGE WILL KI
   KEEB LILL MC   THOR MR.

Kenyon College

Kenyon College Library
Librarian
Gambier, OH 43022
USA
    See Bibliography: Kenyon College Library. "The Charles Riker Collection of William Butler Yeats."

Books:
    HOUR GLAS 14
    JOHN SHER 91
    NINE POEM 14
    SPEE TWO 31

Letters:
    CART MR.
    HONE JOSE M.
    LERI ISAA ES
    MATT SEYM FR
    MORR LADY OT
    O'DO D.J.
    ROSS MARI
    UNKN CORR
    WAIT MISS

Inscriptions:
    MORR LADY OT
    WALS JAME P.

Miscellany:
    MISC

Poems:
    GLOV CLOA
    HE   REPR CU
    TO   HEAR BI

King's College Library
Modern Archivist
Cambridge CB2 1ST
England
    Manuscripts accessible to scholars only

Letters:
    BROO RUPE
    FORS E.M.
    KING GERT

The King's School Library
Canterbury
Kent CT1 2ES
England

Poems:
    ISLA STAT

Library of Congress
Washington, D.C. 20540
USA

Letters:
    YOUN ELLA

Londraville, Richard
6 Harrington Court
Potsdam, NY 13676
USA
    See Bibliography: Londraville, Richard. "The Manuscript of 'The Queen and the Jester.'"

  Poems, Unpublished:
    QUEE JEST

Martin, Walter
Chimera Books and Records
405 Kipling Street
Palo Alto, CA 94301
USA

  Letters:
    STEA W.F.

McGill University
McLennan Library
Rare Books and Special Collections
3459 McTavish St.
Montreal H3A 1Y1
Quebec, Canada

  Letters:
    UNKN CORR

McMaster University
Mills Memorial Library
Research Collections
1280 Main Street West
Hamilton L8S 4L6
Ontario, Canada

  Letters:
    ALLG SARA
    COUL JOHN
    FARR MR.

Meisei University Library
Librarian
337 Hodokubo, Hino-shi
Tokyo 191
Japan

Letters:
    ROBI LENN
    TRAV SMIT DO
    WELL DORO

Poems:
    COME GATH RO
    LADY SECO SO
    LONG LEGG FL
    MODE LAUR
    POLI
    SPUR
    STAT UES
    THRE BUSH
    TO   DORT WE
    UNDE BEN BU

Mills College Library
Special Collections
5000 MacArthur Blvd.
Oakland, CA 94613
USA
    Manuscripts accessible to scholars only.

Books:
    IDEA GOOD 04
    LATE POEM 26
Letters:
    BEND ALBE
    BLAI MR
    GARN PORT
    UNKN CORR

Inscriptions:
    BEND ALBE
    UNKN RECI
Poems:
    LAKE ISLE IN
    TO   ROSE RO

National Library of Ireland
Dublin 2, Ireland

The National Library of Ireland has more original manuscripts of W.B. Yeats than any other location. Copies of many of the manuscripts--those in the 13,000 and 30,000 series--are now on microfiche and individuals can expect to use the photocopies. NLI also has copies of other originals, including many still in the possession of Senator Michael Yeats, although the copies are not as thoroughly catalogued as those at SUNY SB. This CENSUS indicates, in the descriptions of individual manuscripts, if a copy is available at SUNY SB.

See Bibliography: Hayes, MANUSCRIPT SOURCES, for NLI holdings, though NLI has many manuscripts not listed in Hayes.

Books:
```
AUTO REVE 26              PLAY PROS 22
AUTO REVE 27              POEM      27
BISH BERK 31              POEM 1899 06
BOUN SWED 25              POET WRIT 13
BROA      35              POET WORK 06
BROA      37              RESP POEM 14
CAT  MOON 24              REVE CHIL 15
CATH HOOL 02              SECR ROSE 97
CELT TWIL 93              SELE POEM 29
CELT TWIL 12              STOR MICH 31
COUN KATH 92              TABL LAW  97
CUTT AGAT 12              TABL LAW  04
DEAT SYNG 28              TEN  PRIN 37
DISC VOLU 07              TOWE      28
DRAM PERS 36              TREM VEIL 22
EARL POEM 25              UNPU MACM ED
ESSA      24              UNPU ROSY CR
ESSA W.B. 37              UNPU SCRI ED
ESTR      26              UNPU SPEC BI
FOUR YEAR 21              UNPU YE   PL
HERN OTHE 38              VISI      37
IF   I    40              VISI MATE
IN   SEVE 03              WHEE BUTT 34
LAST POEM 39              WILD SWAN 17
MICH ROBA 20              WIND REED 99
NEW  POEM 38              WIND STAI 33
OCTO BLAS 27              WIND STAI MA
ON   BOIL 39              WORD MUSI 32
OXFO BOOK 36              WORD WIND 34
PACK EZRA 29              WORK WILL 93
PAGE DIAR 30           Inscriptions:
PER  AMIC 18              GREG LADY
PLAY CONT 23
```

Letters:

ABBE	THEA	BO	GREG	ROBE	
ALLG	SARA		GWYN	DENI	
BAIL	WILL	F.	GWYN	STEP	
BARN	GEOR		HALL	AGNE	
BARR	WILL		HARM	EDWA	
BEST	R.I.		HARR		
BIRR	AUGU		HARR	FRED	
BLYT	ERNE		HAYS	MR.	
BRET	GEOR		HEAL	EDIT	SH
BRID	ROBE		HEAL	JAME	
BROW			HIGG	FRED	
BULL	A.H.		HINK	KATH	TY
CLIF	HARR		HOLL	JOSE	
CLIN	BADD	V.	HONE	JOSE	M.
COLT	MR.		HORN	MISS	AN
CONA	JAME		JACO	MISS	
CONN	NORR		JOHN	FRED	
COOP	MRS.	ED	KINK	EUGE	
COSG	WILL	T.	LAMB	MAUR	
CRON	MARY		LANE	HUGH	
DARR	FLOR	LE	LAW	MR.	
DAS	MR.		LEWI	P.	WY
DE	BLAG	EA	LIST	MISS	E.
DE	VALE	EA	LITT	MR.	
DILL	JOHN	MI	LOND	LADY	
DOLA	M.J.		LONG	PRIN	PR
DOYL	MISS	C.	LYST	JANE	R.
DUFF	CHAR	GA	LYST	T.W.	
DULA			LYTT	EDIT	
DULA	EDMU		MACB	MAUD	GO
DUNC	ELLE	DO	MACD	SIR	AN
DUNC	JAME		MACD	THOM	
ELLI	EDWI	J.	MACK	STEP	
ELLI	MRS.		MACM	COMP	
EMER	FLOR	FA	MACM	MR.	
ERVI	ST.	JO	MARK	CONS	
FAGA	MR		MART	EDWA	
FAY	FRAN		MCDO	THOM	
FAY	MRS.		MCEL	J.J.	
FAY	WILL	GE	MCMA	MR.	
FROH	CHAR		MONC	NUGE	
GARV	MAIR		MOOR	DAVI	F.
GIBB	MONK		MOOR	GEOR	
GOGA	OLIV	ST	MOOR	STUR	
GRAV	ALFR	PE	MORE	AUGU	
GREG	LADY		MURP	DIAN	
GREG	MR.		NATI	BANK	
GREG	MRS.	MA	NOYE	ALFR	

Letters (continued):
 O'BR EDWA
 O'BR GEOR
 O'CA SEAN
 O'CO FRAN
 O'CO JOHN
 O'DO FRED
 O'HI MRS. KE
 O'LE JOHN
 O'SU SEUM
 ORPE R.C.
 OXFO UNIV
 PALM HERB E.
 PLUN COUN
 PLUN HORA CU
 POEL WILL
 POWE
 PURO SHRI SW
 PURS SARA
 QUIN JOHN
 RAE J.A.
 RAFE MR.
 REDM JOHN
 RHYS GRAC
 ROBE GEOR
 ROTH WILL
 ROYA IRIS AC
 RUSS GEOR
 SCRO MR.
 SHAK MEMO
Miscellany:
 DIAR JOUR
 DOCU
 FOLK MYTH LE
 LANE MATE
 LIST S
 MISC
 OCCU
 QUOT PARA MA
 REVI CHIN SH
 REVI MAC NU
 REVI MACN PL
 REVI MISC
 REVI RED PE
 REVI SHIE PL
 THEA MATE

 SHAW GEOR B.
 SHAW T.E.
 SHAW TAYL JO
 SHIN MRS.
 SIGE GEOR
 SIMP DR. RO
 SIR JOHN
 STOK MARG
 STUR FRAN P.
 SWAN F.C.
 SYNG JOHN
 TAGO RABI
 THRI HERB
 TURN W.J.
 UNKN CORR
 UNWI T. FI
 VAUG
 VERN
 WADE ALLA
 WAGG MR. E.
 WAGS W.H.
 WATK VERN
 WATT A.P.
 WELL DORO
 WILL GEOR
 WILS MR.
 WING SHEI
 YEAT ANNE
 YEAT LILY
Other Authors:
 DUNS SELE 12
 FENO CERT 16
 GOGA OFFE 23
 GREG COUN YO
 GREG IDEA 01
 GREG TRAV 09
 GREG VISI 20
 HAMS HOLY 34
 MERR MIDN ND
 PATA APHO 38
 RUDD LEMO 36
 SWAM INDI 32
 SWAM TEN 37
 TAGO POST 14
 VILL AXEL 25
 WELL SELE 36
 WILD COMP 23

National Library of Ireland   405

Plays: Poems:
   AT   HAWK WE   ACRE GRAS
   CALV   ADAM CURS
   CAT MOON   AFTE LONG SI
   CATH HOUL   AGAI WITC
   COUN CATH   ALL SOUL NI
   DEAT CUCH   ALTE SONG SE
   DEIR   AMON SCHO CH
   DIAR GRAN   ANAS VIJA
   DREA BONE   ANCE HOUS
   FULL MOON MA   APPA
   GREE HELM   APPO
   HERN EGG   ARE YOU CO
   HOUR GLAS   ARRO
   KING GREA CL   AT   ALGE ME
   KING THRE   BALL FATH O'
   LAND HEAR DE   BALL FOXH
   ON   BAIL ST   BALL MIND
   ONLY JEAL EM   BEAU LOFT TH
   PLAY QUEE   BEFO WORL WA
   POT BROT   BEGG BEGG CR
   PURG   BLAC TOWE
   RESU   BLOO MOON
   SOPH KING OE   BROK DREA
   SOPH OEDI CO   BRON HEAD
   UNIC STAR   BROW PENN
   UNPU BISH MO   BYZA
   UNPU BLIN   CAT MOON
   UNPU CHAI PA   CHAM FIRS SO
   UNPU COUN YO   CHAM SECO SO
   UNPU CYPR   CHOS
   UNPU DAGG ST   CHUR STAT
   UNPU DOOR LA   CIRC ANIM DE
   UNPU EPIC FO   COAT
   UNPU GIDD DA   COLD HEAV
   UNPU GIRL GO   COLL BONE HA
   UNPU ISLA FA   COLO MART
   UNPU LAYI FO   COLO PRAI
   UNPU LOVE 'S   COME GATH RO
   UNPU OLD MA   COME RIDE RI
   UNPU PETE SH   CONS
   UNPU POET AC   COOL PARK 19
   UNPU ROVE LO   COOL PARK BA
   UNPU SANS EY   CRAZ GIRL
   UNPU SEA SP   CRAZ JANE BI
   UNPU STAR RO   CRAZ JANE DA
   UNPU VILL EL   CRAZ JANE GO
   WHER THER IS   CRAZ JANE GR
   WORD WIND PA   CRAZ JANE JA

Poems (continued):
CRAZ JANE MO
CRAZ JANE RE
CRAZ JANE TA
CRAZ MOON
CROS
CUCH COMF
CURS CROM
DANC CRUA CR
DAWN
DEAT
DEDI
DEEP SWOR VO
DELP ORAC PL
DEMO BEAS
DIAL SELF SO
DOLL
DOUB VISI MI
DREA DEAT
DRUN MAN' PR
EAST 1916
EGO DOMI TU
EMPT CUP
END DAY
EPHE
EVER VOIC
FAER SONG
FALL LEAV
FALL MAJE
FATH CHIL
FIRS CONF
FIRS LOVE
FISH ERMA N
FOLL BEIN CO
FOR ANNE GR
FRIE
FRIE ILLN
FRIE YOUT
FROM ANTI
FROM OEDI CO
GHOS ROGE CA
GIFT HARU AL
GIRL SONG JS
GIRL SONG WS
GRAT UNKN IN
GREA DAY
GREY ROCK
GYRE
HAPP TOWN

HARL SANG BE
HAWK
HE HAS LO
HE TELL PE
HE WISH CL
HER ANXI
HER DREA
HER PRAI
HER TRIU
HER VISI WO
HERO GIRL FO
HIGH TALK
HIS BARG
HIS CONF
HIS MEMO
HIS PHOE
HIS WILD
HOUN VOIC
HOUR DAWN
HUMA DIGN
I AM IR
I WAS GO
IMAG PAST LI
IMIT JAPA
IN DRAW RO
IN MEMO AL
IN MEMO EV
IN MEMO MA
IN SEVE WO
IN TARA HA
INTO TWIL
IRIS AIRM FO
ISLA STAT
JOHN KINS LA
KANV HIMS
LADY FIRS SO
LADY THIR SO
LAKE ISLE IN
LAKE ISLE IN
LAPI LAZU
LAST CONF
LEAD CROW
LEDA SWAN
LIFE
LIFT WHIT KN
LINE WRIT DE
LIVI BEAT
LONG LEGG FL

National Library of Ireland

Poems (continued):
  LOVE DEAT
  LOVE LONE
  LOVE RS   SO
  LOVE SPEA HE
  LULL
  MAD MIST SN
  MAGI
  MAN ECHO
  MAN YOUN OL
  MASK
  MEDI OLD FI
  MEDI TIME CI
  MEET
  MEMO
  MEMO YOUT
  MEN IMPR YE
  MERM
  MERU
  MICH ROBA DA
  MODE LAUR
  MOHI CHAT
  MOOD
  MOSA
  MOTH GOD
  MOUN TOMB
  MUNI GALL RE
  MY   DESC
  MY   HOUS
  MY   TABL
  NATI
  NEW FACE
  NEWS DELP OR
  NINE CENT AF
  NINE HUND NI
  NOTH THAT HE
  O'RA
  OIL BLOO
  OLD AGE QU
  OLD MEMO
  OLD MEN AD
  OLD STON CR
  OLD TOM AG
  ON   BEIN AS
  ON   PICT BL
  ON   POLI PR
  ON   THOS TH
  ON   WOMA
  OWEN AHER DA

  PARD OLD FA
  PARN
  PARN FUNE
  PART
  PAUD
  PEOP
  PHAN SHIP
  PHAS MOON
  PILG
  PLAY ASK BL
  POET OWEN HA
  POLI
  PRAY GOIN MY
  PRAY MY   DA
  PRAY MY   SO
  PRES
  QUAR OLD AG
  QUAT APHO
  REAL
  RED HANR SO
  REMO INTE SP
  REPR
  RESU THOU
  RIBH ECST
  ROAD DOOR
  ROGE CASE
  ROSE TREE
  RUNN PARA
  SAD SHEP
  SAIL BYZA
  SAIN HUNC
  SCHO
  SECO COMI
  SECR OLD
  SEEK
  SEPT 1913
  SEVE PATE SE
  SEVE SAGE
  SHAD WATE
  SHE WHO DW
  SHEP GOAT
  SIXT DEAD ME
  SOLO SHEB
  SOLO WITC
  SONG PLAY QU
  SONG ROSY CR
  SPIL MILK
  SPIR MEDI

Poems (continued):
- SPUR
- STAR NEST MY
- STAT HOLI
- STAT ISTI CS
- STAT UES
- STIC INCE
- STOL CHIL
- STRE SUN GL
- SUMM SPRI
- SWEE DANC
- SWIF EPIT
- SYMB
- THES ARE CL
- THOS DANC DA
- THOS IMAG
- THOU PROP
- THRE BEGG
- THRE BUSH
- THRE MARC SO
- THRE MONU
- THRE MOVE
- THRE SONG ON
- THRE SONG SA
- THRE THIN
- TIME WITC VI
- TO BE CA
- TO CHIL DA
- TO DORT WE
- TO FRIE WH
- TO IREL CO
- TO POET WH
- TO ROSE RO
- TO SHAD
- TO SQUI KY
- TO WEAL MA
- TO YOUN GI
- TOM CRUA
- TOM LUNA
- TOWA BREA DA
- TOWE
- TWO KING
- TWO SONG FO
- TWO SONG PL
- TWO TREE
- TWO YEAR LA
- UNAP HOST
- UNDE BEN BU
- UNDE MOON
- UNDE SATU
- UPON DYIN LA
- UPON HOUS SH
- VACI
- VERO NAPK
- WAND OISI
- WHAT MAGI DR
- WHAT THEN
- WHAT WAS LO
- WHEE
- WHEN HAD TH
- WHEN HELE LI
- WHEN YOU AR
- WHY SHOU NO
- WILD OLD WI
- WILD SWAN CO
- WISD
- WITC
- WITH BOUG
- WOMA YOUN OL
- WORD MUSI PE
- YOUN MAN' SO
- YOUT AGE

Poems, Unpublished:
- ALL NIGH TH
- ALL OUR EU
- AM I FO
- AMON SIGH FO
- AND CEAS I
- AND CLAM WH
- AND I WI
- AND THY DA
- AND WHER AR
- ART IMIT
- AS KNOW AL
- BARR VALL TH
- BECA MOON RE
- BEHO MAN BE
- BEIN HALF
- BEIN WAS NO
- BILL BOY
- BUT ART
- BY EMPE CO
- CHIL PLAY
- COME HITH HI
- CONC LANE
- CYPR

Poems, Unpublished (continued):

CRAZ JANE KI
DEER HE FO
DELL
DEW COME DR
DOUB MOON MO
FLOW HAS BL
FOR ALL ST
FOR CLAP HA
FULL ALON WI
HALF ARTI
HALF ASLE AS
HE WHO BI
HEAR SLEE HA
HERE COME MR
HERE I AM
HILL MOUR
HUSH VALE DA
I HEAR RO
I ONCE HA
I SAT UP
I SING PA
I STOO TO
I TIRE SE
I WILL NO
IF MELA MU
IMAG
IMAG BRID
IN HEAR WO
IN PRIM GL
KEEP FAR OF
KNOW WISD
LANC SWIT
LITT PURI SU
LOOK WHIT BI
LOW HUMS WI
MAGP
MAY TIME BE
MONG MEAD SW
MOON SHON CA
MY INTE IS
MY SONG TH
NO NOT NO
O WHAT TE
OLD GREY MA

OLD OLD MA
OLD SOLI ON
ONCE GOD HA
ONCE I FO
ONCE METE FI
OUTL BRID
PATH
POEM LAUN SW
POLI USED BE
PORT BEFO HI
PRIE PAN
PROT LEAP
RIDD IS HA
SANS SANS SA
SHE HAS US
SONN I
SOUL FOUN SP
SPIR SEA
SUNR
TAKE UP RI
TALL MEN
TETH WHOS WI
THEN UP SP
THER IS NO
THER LIVE MA
THEY MING BR
THIS LAKE WA
THIS MAN IS
THOU LOUD YE
THUS IGNO FE
TO MOOR BL
TO SIST CR
TOWE WIND BE
TWO FAVO CE
TWO NAME AL
UNPU UNID MA
VEIL VOIC QU
WE HEAR TH
WHEN CONS DE
WHEN I HA
WHEN TO IT
WHER THY WH
WORL IS ST
YOU ARE GO
YOUR PATH

Prose:
- AINU
- ART IDEA
- CENS ST.T AQ
- COMP GAEL
- COST PROU
- DUBL FANA
- GREA BLAS
- I BECA AU
- IREL 1921 31
- IRIS CENS
- JOHN EGLI SP
- LOUI LAMB
- MAND UPAN
- MESS FOLK LO
- MICH FIEL SI
- MODE POET
- MY FRIE BO
- NEED AUDA TH
- OLD GAEL LO
- PARN
- PEOP THEA
- POET TRAD
- PROM UNBO
- ROSE SHAD
- SWED MEDI DE
- SYNG COLL 33
- THEA BEAU
- THOM DAVI
- TO ALL AR
- UNPU AGNE TO
- UNPU ANGL IR
- UNPU FEUD
- UNPU I HA
- UNPU I PR
- UNPU I WR
- UNPU IRIS DR
- UNPU LADY GR
- UNPU POLI SI
- UNPU TRIB MI
- UNPU UNID PR
- UNPU YOUN GE
- WIZA WITC IR

Speeches:
- ABBE SUBS
- ALL POPU AR
- AMER TOUR LE
- BIRM LECT
- BLAK LECT
- BURL HOUS LE
- CONG RSL RD
- CONT LYRI PO
- DEFE ABBE TH
- DIVO SPEE
- DREA GHOS
- EMME APOS IR
- FRIE YOUT
- IN POET PA
- IN POET PU
- INTE DEIR MA
- LANE PICT
- MANC LECT
- MODE POET
- MY OWN AG
- MY OWN PO
- OEDI KING
- POEM WOME
- POET NEW OL
- POLI PRIZ SP
- READ POEM
- RHYM CLUB LE
- ROME LECT
- ST. PATR NI
- STEP GLAS BE
- STOC BANQ SP
- SYNG IREL TI
- TAIL BANQ SP
- THEA BEAU
- THOM DAVI LE
- UNID COMP ED
- UNID GLAS BE
- UNID HOME RU
- UNID IDEA DR
- UNID IRIS FO
- UNID LECT NO
- UNID MYST
- UNID NEW UN
- UNID POET
- UNID THEA SP
- UNID THRE SH
- UNID WRIT AU
- YOUN GENE

National Library of Scotland
George IV Bridge
Edinburgh EH1 1EW
Scotland

Letters:
    BLAC SONS WI   PURV JOHN
    GRAH R.B. CU   RAFF MARC AN
    GRIE H.J.   SHAR WILL
    HALD RICH BU   SHOR CLEM

New York Public Library
Rare Books and MSS Division
Fifth Avenue and 42 Street
New York, NY 10018
USA
    See Bibliography: Mattson, Francis O. "The John Quinn
    Memorial Collection"; NYPL. DICTIONARY CATALOGUE OF THE BERG
    COLLECTION; Simmonds, Harvey. "John Quinn: An Exhibition."

Books:
    AUGU BOOK 27   KING THRE 04
    AUTO REVE 26   KING THRE 05
    BOUN SWED 25   LAND HEAR 94
    CAT MOON 24   LAND HEAR 03
    CATH HOOL 02   LATE POEM 22
    CELT TWIL 12   MOSA   86
    COLL WORK 08   ON   BAIL 05
    COUN CATH 12   PLAY CONT 23
    COUN KATH 92   PLAY IRIS 11
    CUTT AGAT 12   PLAY PROS 22
    DEIR   07   POEM   95
    DEIR   11   POEM 1899 06
    EARL POEM 25   POEM SPEN 06
    EAST   16   POEM WRIT 13
    EIGH POEM 16   POET IREL 08
    ESSA   24   POET WORK 06
    FAIR FOLK 88   POET WORK 07
    GOLD HELM 08   RESP POEM 14
    GREE HELM 10   SECR ROSE 97
    GREE HELM 11   SELE POET 13
    GREE HELM 12   SHAD WATE 01
    HOUR CATH 04   SHAD WATE 07
    HOUR CATH 05   STOR RED 04
    HOUR GLAS 07   STOR RED 13
    IDEA GOOD 03   SYNG IREL 11
    IN   SEVE 03   TABL LAW 14
    KING BAIL 04   TREM VEIL 22
    KING GREA 35   WHER THER 02
    KING THRE 04   WHER THER 03
    KING THRE 05   WILD SWAN 17
    LAND HEAR 94   WILD SWAN 19

Books (continued):
  WIND REED 99
  WIND REED 03
                          WORK WILL 93
Inscriptions:
  BERE J.C.   HOWE W.T.
  BOYD ERNE   JOHN LION
  BULL A.H.   O'LE JOHN
  COLU PADR   QUIN JOHN
  FAY WILL   SHAR WILL
  GREG LADY   SPAR A.
  HIGG FRED   STOK BRAM
  HINK KATH TY   YEAT JACK
Letters:
  ALLG SARA   MAIR GEOR
  BAIL WILL F.   MARS EDWA
  BEEC STEL CA   MCCO DUGA S.
  BOTT GORD   METH CO.
  BROW   MONR HARO
  CAMP MRS. JO   MOON RIA
  COLU PADR   MOOR DAVI F.
  DOON RUPE   MOOR GEOR
  DUNC JAME   MURR THOM
  DUNS LADY   NATI EDIT
  DUNS LORD   NICO WILL R.
  EMER FLOR FA   O'CA SEAN
  FAY FRAN   O'DO D.J.
  FORD FORD MA   O'LE ELLE
  FOST JEAN   O'LE JOHN
  FREE JOUR ED   QUIN JOHN
  FREU FRAN   ROBE MICH
  GOOD EDWA   ROBI LENN
  GOSS EDMU   SEAL BRYE WA
  GREG LADY   SHOR CLEM
  GWYN STEP   SHOR MRS. DO
  HAMI MISS   STEP JAME
  HEND W.A.   SYMO ARTH
  HOLR CHAR   TIME EDIT
  HORN MISS AN   UNKN CORR
  HOWE W.T.   WALK MARY
  HUNT VIOL   WATT A.P.
  HYDE DOUG   WOLF HUMB
  JACK ARTH   YEAT ELIZ
  JACO MISS   YEAT JOHN
  KEIR THOM J.   YOUN MISS
  MAGE WILL KI

New York Public Library

Miscellany:
  DIAR JOUR
  DOCU
  IRIS ACAD MA
  LANE MATE
  MISC
  PHOT
  QUOT PARA MA
  REVI MACN PL
  THEA MATE

Plays:
  AT   HAWK WE
  CATH HOUL
  COUN CATH
  DEIR
  DIAR GRAN
  HOUR GLAS
  KING THRE
  LAND HEAR DE

Poems:
  ADAM CURS
  ALL THIN CA
  ANAS VIJA
  APPO
  ARRO
  AT   GALW RA
  BAIL AILL
  BALL FATH GI
  BALL MIND
  BLES
  BROK DREA
  CAP BELL
  CERT ARTI BR
  COAT
  COOL PARK BA
  CRAD SONG
  CUCH FIGH SE
  DAWN
  DEDI BOOK ST
  DREA DEAT
  DRIN SONG
  EAST 1916
  EGO DOMI TU
  END DAY
  FERG DRUI
  FIDD DOON
  FISH
  FISH ERMA N

Other Authors:
  CARL STOR 89
  GREG CUCH 02
  GREG GODS 04
  GREG IDEA 01
  HYDE LOVE 04
  SHEL SELE 66
  TAGO GITA 12
  WELL SELE 36

  ON   BAIL ST
  ONLY JEAL EM
  RESU
  UNIC STAR
  UNPU HE   IS
  UNPU OPEN CE
  UNPU YOU HA
  WHER THER IS

  GREY ROCK
  HAPP TOWN
  HAWK
  HE   GIVE HI
  HE   HEAR CR
  HE   MOUR CH
  HE   REME FO
  HE   TELL PE
  HE   TELL VA
  HE   THIN HI
  HE   THIN TH
  HE   WISH CL
  HE   WISH HI
  HER FRIE BR
  HER PRAI
  HIS PHOE
  HOST SIDH
  HOUR DAWN
  IN   FIRE
  IN   MEMO MA
  IN   SEVE WO
  INDI GOD
  IRIS AIRM FO
  LINE WRIT DE
  LOVE ASKS FO
  LOVE MOUR LO
  LOVE PLEA HI
  LOVE SPEA HE

Poems (continued):
    LOVE TELL RO
    MAID QUIE
    MAN WHO DR
    MEMO
    NEVE GIVE AL
    NEW FACE
    O   DO   NO
    OLD AGE QU
    OLD MEMO
    OLD MEN AD
    ON   THOS TH
    ON   WOMA
    PARD OLD FA
    PEA COCK
    PEOP
    POET HIS BE
    POET PLEA EL
    PRAY MY   DA
    PRES
    QUEE EDAI
    RAGG WOOD
    RED HANR SO
    RIBH TOMB BA
    ROSE PEAC
    ROSE TREE
    SEPT 1913
    SHAD WATE
    SHE TURN DO
    SONG WAND AE
    SPIN SONG
    THRE HERM
    THRE SONG SA
    TO   FRIE WH
    TO   HEAR BI
    TO   ROSE RO
    TO   SOME I
    TO   WEAL MA
    TOWE
    TWO KING
    TWO SONG PL
    TWO SONG RE
    UNDE MOON
    UPON DYIN LA
    UPON HOUS SH
    VALL BLAC PI
    WAND OISI
    WHEN HELE LI
    WHIL I   RE
    WILD SWAN CO
    WITH BOUG
Poems, Unpublished:
    AWAK WORL EC
    CRAZ JANE KI
Prose:
    ALTH GYLE
    AWAY
    BY   ROAD
    DUST HATH CL
    HUGH LANE PI
    IREL BEWI
    IRIS WITC DO
    J.M. SYNG IR
    JOHN SHAW TA
    KING VISI
    LITE LIVI VO
    LITE MOVE IR
    POET TRAD
    SAMH 1905
    SAMH 1908 FI
    SAMH 1909
    SWED MEDI DE
    TRAG THEA
    TRIB DANU
    UNPU ALL EM
    UNPU CHIC SC
    UNPU CONT ID
    UNPU MODE PO
    UNPU POLI AR
    UNPU SACR GR
    UNPU SHEL TH
Speeches:
    AMER TOUR LE
    EMME APOS IR
    UNID THEA SP

New York University
Fales Library
70 Washingon Square South
New York, NY 10012
USA
    Manuscripts accessible to scholars only.

Letters:
    ALLG SARA   ROBI ELIZ
    CAMP MRS. PA   SHER MR.
    LEGA RICH   THRI HERB
    MACD THOM   UNKN CORR
    MEYN WILF   WILS MR.
    PALM HERB E.   WRIG MR.

Newberry Library
Special Collections
60 West Walton Street
Chicago, IL 60610
USA

Books: Inscriptions:
    POEM BALL 90   JOHN LION
Letters:
    BELL EDWA PR
    STON MELV

Northwestern University Library
Special Collections Department
Evanston, IL 60208
USA

Books: Inscriptions:
    KING GREA 34   NIC SHIU MA
    SHAD WATE 00   WALK MARY
Letters:
    DAVR HENR   MCCA PATR
    GONN ISEU   MINC MR.
    GREG LADY   RUSS GEOR
    HONE JOSE M.   UNKN CORR
    LYND ROBE   WALK MARY
    MARK CONS   WILK MARG
Other Authors: Plays:
    NIET AS   01   CATH HOUL
    VIRG AENI

416   Libraries and Other Owners

Occidental College Library
Librarian
Los Angeles, CA 90041
USA

   Inscriptions: Miscellany:
      PHEL JAME   PHOT

Ohio State University
Main Library
Curator, Special Collections
Columbus, OH 43210
USA

   Books: Inscriptions:
      COUN KATH 92   UNKN RECI
   Poems:
      ROSE WORL

Pennsylvania State University Library
Special Collections
University Park, PA 16802
USA

   Books: Inscriptions:
      EIGH POEM 16   UNKN RECI
   Letters: Miscellany:
      ARND MRS.   IRIS ACAD MA
      EMER FLOR FA
      HORN
      PORT MR.
      UNKN CORR

Pierpont Morgan Library
Curator of Manuscripts
26 East 36 Street
New York, NY 10016
USA
      See Bibliography: Klinkenborg, Verlyn. BRITISH
      LITERARY MANUSCRIPTS.

   Books: Inscriptions:
      FOUR YEAR 21   DULA EDMU
      UNIC STAR 08   HENL W.E.
      VISI   25   MOOR GEOR
      WAND OISI 89   MORR LADY OT
      WIND REED 99

Pierpont Morgan Library

Letters:
    CHEW PROF SA
    GUIN LOUI IM
    HUGH RICH
    HUTC THOM
    KNIG W.A.
    LINA CARL
    MAGE WILL KI
    MCDO MR.
    MORR LADY OT
    O'BR REVE HE
    YEAT JOHN

Miscellany:
    OCCU
Poems:
    HE HEAR CR
    HE THIN TH
    LOVE MOUR LO

Plunkett Foundation for Cooperative Studies
31 Giles Street
Oxford OX1 3LF
England

Letters:
    PLUN HORA CU

Princeton University Library
Curator of Manuscripts
Princeton, NJ 08544
USA
    Manuscripts accessible to scholars only.
    See Bibliography: Wickenheiser, Robert J. "The Robert H. Taylor Collection."

Books:
    CATH HOOL 02
    CELT TWIL 93
    COUN CATH 12
    HOUR GLAS 14
    PLAY PROS 22
    POEM   95
    POEM 1899 06
    SECR ROSE 97
    SELE POET 13
    SHAD WATE 00
    TOWE   28
    UNPU SCRI ED
    WAND OISI 89
    WHER THER 03

Inscriptions:
    BROW MAUR
    GARN EDWA
    MACB MAUD GO
    MASE JOHN
    MEIK MRS.
    POLL GEOR
    RADF E
    REID FORR
    ROBI LENN
    SHAK OLIV
    SHAW GEOR BE

Letters:
    BEAR MABE
    BEAR MRS.
    BERT MR.
    BRIG MARY CH
    BROP JOHN
    CORR MADA GH
    CUMM HUBE M.
    GOGA OLIV ST
    HINK KATH TY
    HUGH RICH
    JACK HOLB
    MATH ELKI
    OXFO UNIV PR
    RAY MR.
    SCRI
    SPIC SIMS TH
    SUTH DUCH
    SYMO ARTH
    TORR RIDG
    UNKN CORR
    WILL GEOR
    YEAT ELIZ
Other Authors:
    SWAM INDI 32
Plays:
    LAND HEAR DE
Poems:
    GREY ROCK
    OLD MEMO
    THRE HERM

Providence Public Library
Special Collections
150 Empire St.
Providence, RI 02903
USA

Books:
    WAND OISI 89
Poems:
    ANAS VIJA
    WAND OISI

Inscriptions:
    WILL A.M.

Queen's University
Archives Assistant
Kingston K7L 3N6
Ontario, Canada
    See Bibliography: MacKenzie, Norman. "The Monk Gibbon Papers."

Letters:
    GIBB MONK

Poems:
    SORR LOVE

Regent's College
British Theatre Association
Inner Circle, Regent's Park
London NW1
England

Letters:
    ARCH WILL

Rosenbach Museum and Library
Curator of Literature
2010 Delancey Pl.
Philadelphia, PA 19103
USA

    Poems:
        LAKE ISLE IN
        NEVE GIVE AL
        STOL CHIL

The Royal Literary Fund
Secretary
144 Temple Chambers
London EC4Y 0DT
England

    Letters:
        ROBE ARTH LL
        UNKN CORR

Royal Society of Literature
1 Hyde Park Gardens
London W2 2LT
England

    Letters:
        SECR ROYA SO

Scripps College
Denison Library
Librarian
Claremont, CA 91711
USA

    Letters:
        DAVR HENR

Shakespeare Birthplace Trust
Guild Street
Stratfod-upon-Avon CV37 6QW
England

    Books:
        JOHN SHER 91

Sligo County Library
County Librarian
The Courthouse, Teeling Street
Sligo
Ireland

   Books:
      STOR RED 04
      STOR RED 27

   Letters:
      FALL GABR
      GOGA OLIV ST
      MANN ETHE
      MCGU NORA
      SIBE CHAR E.

   Poems:
      EAST 1916
      ROGE CASE

   Inscriptions:
      GREG LADY
      HINK KATH TY
      UNKN RECI

   Miscellany:
      MISC

   Other Authors:
      CARL STOR 89
      EGLI SOME 05

Smith, Simon Nowell
7 Beaumont Rd, Headington Quarry
Oxford OX3 8J
England

   Books:
      BOOK RHYM 92
      GREE HELM 12
      KING GREA 34
      NEW POEM 38
      POEM   95
      SECO BOOK 94
      WILD SWAN 17
      WIND REED 99

   Poems:
      MODE LAUR
      PARD OLD FA

   Inscriptions:
      DUCA EVA
      MASE JOHN
      ROSE EDWA
      SYMO ARTH
      UNKN RECI
      WELL DORO

Somerville College Library
Oxford
England

   Letters:
      WITH PERC

Southern Illinois University
Morris Library
Special Collections
Carbondale, IL 62901
USA
    See Bibliography: [Jackson, Thomas J.].   THE IRISH COLLECTION.

Books:
   DRAM PERS 35
   VISI MATE
Letters:
   BULL A.H.
   COLV WARN
   CONN NORR
   DAY F.H.
   DOWD EDWA
   EVAN EDWA
   FAGA MR
   HAYE DR. CA
   HOLL MISS
   HORN MISS AN
   JONE JENN IN
   JOYC JAME
   LANE HUGH
   LANG FRED
   MACK STEP
   MAGE WILL KI
   MARR MR.
   MATH ELKI
   MAUD MARY
   MCCA PATR
   MONR HARR
   MORR LADY OT
   MUNR MISS
   MURP DIAN
   NEED MR.
   NEVI HENR WO
   O'DO D.J.
   PALM HERB E.
   POLL DR.
   POND JAME
   RAWL MR.
   ROBI LENN
   SMIT MRS. TR
   SPIC SIMS TH
   STUA MR.
   UNKN CORR
   WATK VERN
   WILS MRS.
Other Authors:
   HAMS HOLY 34
Miscellany:
   LIST S
   PHOT
   QUOT PARA MA
   REVI CRIM TR
Plays:
   HOUR GLAS
   KING GREA CL
   ONLY JEAL EM
   SOPH KING OE
Poems:
   PARN FUNE
   THRE SONG SA
Poems, Unpublished:
   CRAZ JANE KI
Prose:
   LOUI LAMB
   NEED AUDA TH
Speeches:
   IN   MEMO TH

Sparrow, John
Beechwood House, Iffley Turn
Oxford OX4 4H
England

Books:
    DISC VOLU 07
    RESP POEM 14

Inscriptions:
    MACB MAUD GO

Stanford University
Green Library
Manuscripts Librarian
Stanford, CA 94305
USA

Books:
    BOUN SWED 25
    CAT MOON 24
    DEAT SYNG 28
    DISC VOLU 07
    DRAM PERS 35
    ESSA W.B. 37
    ESTR   26
    FOUR YEAR 21
    GREE HELM 10
    HOUR GLAS 14
    IN   SEVE 03
    KING GREA 34
    MICH ROBA 20
    NEW POEM 38
    OCTO BLAS 27
    PACK EZRA 29
    POEM WRIT 13
    POET IREL 08
    RESP POEM 14
    REVE CHIL 15
    SEVE POEM 22
    SPEE TWO 31
    STOR RED 04
    SYNG IREL 11
    TWO PLAY 19
    WILD SWAN 17
    WIND REED 99
    WORD MUSI 32
    WORD WIND 34

Inscriptions:
    HEAL JAME
    QUIN JOHN
    ROBI LENN
Letters:
    BOUR M.
    BOYD ERNE
    GOGA OLIV ST
    GREG LADY
    HEAL JAME
    KINK EUGE
    RUSS GEOR
    UNKN CORR
Other Authors:
    ALLI SIXT 05
    DOWD WOMA 13
    DUNS SELE 12
    EGLI SOME 05
    FENO CERT 16
    FLOW LOVE 25
    GOGA OFFE 23
    GOGA WILD 30
    GREG COOL 31
    GREG KILT 18
    HIGG ARAB 33
    HINK TWEN 07
    HYDE LOVE 04
    JOHN TWEN 04
    MASE JOHN 15
    MOOR LYRI 29

Stanford University

Other Authors (continued):
    O'CO LORD 38
    O'CO WILD 32
    PARN POEM 27
    ROBI LITT 28
    ROSS PILG 33
    RUSS BY   06
    SYNG POEM 09
    TAGO POST 14
    YEAT EARL 23
    YEAT FURT 20
    YEAT PASS 17

Poems:
    COAT
    LIFT WHIT KN
    NINE HUND NI
    POET OWEN HA
    POLI
    TOWE
    UPON DYIN LA

State Library of New South Wales
Mitchell Library
Mitchell Librarian
Macquarie Street
Sydney, N.S.W. 2000
Australia
    Manuscripts accessible to scholars by application only.
    Copies not available.

  Letters:
    STEP A.G.

State Library of Victoria
Manuscripts Librarian
328 Swanston Street
Melbourne, Victoria 3000
Australia

  Letters:
    STEV HILD A.

State University of New York at Albany
University Libraries
Special Collections
Albany, NY 12222
USA

  Books:
    DEIR   07
  Letters:
    GARD FRED

  Inscriptions:
                        UNKN RECI
  Poems:
                        WITH BOUG

State University of New York at Buffalo
University Libraries
Poetry & Rare Books Collection
420 Capen Hall
Buffalo, NY 14260
USA
    Manuscripts accessible to scholars only.

Books:
    MOSA   86
    SECR ROSE 97

Inscriptions:
    UNKN RECI
    VEAS MISS

Letters:
    BULL A.H.
    FRED MISS
    GOGA OLIV ST
    GREG FRED J.
    GRIG GEOF
    GWYN STEP
    HAGG H.RI SI
    HONE JOSE M.

    KENN W.S.
    LIST MISS E.
    MATH ELKI
    O'DO PAID
    PALM BARO
    UNKN CORR
    WOLL MAUR

State University of New York at Stony Brook
Frank Melville, Jr. Memorial Library
Department of Special Collections
Stony Brook, NY 11794
USA

SUNY SB has no original manuscripts, but has an extensive collection of copies, known as the W.B. Yeats Microfilmed Manuscripts Collection (MC 294). The collection includes microfilms (arranged by reel and frame numbers), bound photocopies in microfilm sequence, and photocopies arranged and described by series, shelved in boxes and folders. Most of the originals of these manuscripts are at the National Library of Ireland, though some originals are in the possession of Senator Michael Yeats, some in other libraries, and some in unknown locations. Although the processing of the collection at Stony Brook is not finished, a Finding Aid with a listing of the holdings and an index is available. In this CENSUS, a note at the end of the description in the "Manuscripts" section indicates if there is a "Copy at SUNY SB," and includes a box number if one is available.
    See Bibliography: Allen, "The Yeats Tapes."

Svenska Akademiens Nobelbibliotek
4 Borshuset
Stockholm S-1112
Sweden

   Letters:
      KARL ERIC

Syracuse University
George Arents Research Library
Manuscript Librarian
Syracuse, NY 13244
USA
   Manuscripts accessible to scholars only.

   Letters:
      BRIS ARTH

Tate Gallery Archive
Millbank
London SW1P 4RG
England

   Letters:
      GAUN WILL

Theosophical Society Archives
R. Radmini
Adyar, Madras
India

   Letters:
      COUS JAME H.

Trent University
Bata Library
University Archivist
Peterborough K9J 7B8
Ontario, Canada

   Letters:
      CURT MR.
      DELU ALFR
      KING RICH AS

Trinity College Dublin
Library
College St.
Dublin 2
Ireland

Manuscripts accessible to scholars only.
See Bibliography: Dougan, R.O. W.B. YEATS:
MANUSCRIPTS AND PRINTED BOOKS EXHIBITED.

Books:
    CELT TWIL 93
    COLL POEM 33
    CUTT AGAT 19
    GREE HELM 12
    IDEA GOOD 03
    JOHN SHER 91
    KING BAIL 04
    MOSA   86
    REPR IRIS 91

Inscriptions:
    YEAT ELIZ
    YEAT JOHN
    YEAT LILY
    YEAT MICH

Letters:
    BODK THOM
    CHIL MARY AL
    CLEM CYRI
    DAVI MICH
    FRAS DR.
    GILL THOM PA
    LANE HUGH
    LECK W.E.
    MACG THOM
    MAHA J.P.
    MARS EDWA
    O'SU SEUM
    SYNG JOHN
    WHIT ELIZ
    WHIT H.O.

Other Authors:
    EGLI LITE 99
    SAGE PIPE 03
    VERN NOVE 29

Poems:
    ISLA STAT
    MOSA
    STOL CHIL
    TIME WITC VI
    TO   SHAD
    TO   WEAL MA

Trinity College Library
Cambridge CB2 1TJ
England

Letters:
    MYER MRS. E.
    TREV R.C.

Tulane University
Howard-Tilton Memorial Library
Head
New Orleans, LA 70118
USA

   Letters:
      DUNN MR

   Poems:
      CRAD SONG

University College Dublin
Main Library
Special Collections Librarian
Belfield
Dublin 4
Ireland

   Books:
      CATH HOOL 02
   Letters:
      BLYT ERNE
      CURR CONS P.
      FAY WILL GE
      LAIR HELE
      O'BR R.   BA
      UNKN CORR

   Inscriptions:
      LAIR HELE
   Miscellany:
      OCCU

University of Aberdeen
King's College
Aberdeen AB9 2UB
Scotland

   Letters:
      ABER JEAN WA

University of Arizona Library
Special Collections
Tucson, AZ 85721
USA

   Poems, Unpublished:
      I   KNOW NO

University of British Columbia
Main Library
Special Collections
1956 Main Mall
Vancouver V6T 1W5
British Columbia, Canada

   Books:
      LAND HEAR 94

   Inscriptions:
      MARK CONS

University of California Berkeley
The Bancroft Library
Librarian
Berkeley, CA 94720
USA

Books:
  COUN KATH 92
Letters:
  BLAN HENR ME
  DICK MABE
  GOGA OLIV ST

Inscriptions:
  UNKN RECI

  MATH ELKI
  NEYL JOHN FR
  O'FA SEAN

University of California Los Angeles
William Andrews Clark Memorial Library
2520 Cimarron St. West Adams
Los Angeles, CA 90018
USA
  Manuscripts accessible to scholars only.

Books:
  MOSA   86
  WILD SWAN 19
Letters:
  ALDI BRIG
  ALDI RICH
  BRIT VERA MA
  BULL A.H.
  DOWD EDWA
  FRAS DR.
  GWYN STEP
  JACK HOLB
Other Authors:
  GREG IDEA 01

Inscriptions:
  CARM MISS
  POLL HENR

  MILL ALIC
  O'DO D.J.
  SHAN CHAR
  SINC MR.
  STEP JAME
  SUTH DUCH
  UNKN CORR
  WALK EMER
Poems:
  LOVE ASKS FO
  STOL CHIL

University of California San Diego
Central University Library
Special Collections Librarian
La Jolla, CA 92093
USA

Books:
  GOLD HELM 08
Letters:
  WEBE WILL

Inscriptions:
  UNKN RECI

University of Chicago
Joseph Regenstein Library
Manuscripts Specialist
1100 East 57th Street
Chicago, IL 60637
USA
   Manuscripts accessible to scholars only.

Letters:
   MONR HARR
   POUN EZRA
   ZABE MORT

Plays:
   FULL MOON MA
   ONLY JEAL EM

Poems:
   BALL MIND
   CONJ
   DAWN
   EGO DOMI TU
   FALL MAJE
   FISH ERMA N
   FOUR AGES MA
   GREY ROCK
   HE   SHE
   HER PRAI
   HIS PHOE
   LINE WRIT DE
   MEMO
   MEMO YOUT
   MERU
   MOUN TOMB

   NEED EYE
   ON   BEIN AS
   ON   WOMA
   PEOP
   PRAY MY   DA
   REAL
   RIBH CONS CH
   RIBH DENO PA
   RIBH TOMB BA
   SCHO
   THOU PROP
   THRE SONG SA
   TO   CHIL DA
   TO   SQUI KY
   WHIL I   RE

University of Delaware Library
Special Collections Librarian
Newark, DE 19717
USA

Books:
   AUTO REVE 27
   PLAY CONT 23

Inscriptions:
   ROBI LENN
   UNKN RECI

Letters:
    BLUN WILF
    FIEL MICH
    FODE GWYN
    GREG LADY
    HAMS SHRI
    MART HARV
    O'DO FRAN
    O'LE JOHN
    PALM HERB E.
    PURO SHRI SW
    RADI HERM
    RHYS ERNE
    RIDI LAUR
    THOM MR.
Poems:
    ALL THIN CA
    TO   ISLE WA

University of Glasgow Library
Hillhead St.
Glasgow G12 8QE
Scotland

Letters:
    DIXO W. MA
    MACC D.S.

University of Illinois at Urbana
Rare Book and Special Collections Library
Administrator
1408 W. Gregory
Urbana, IL 61801
USA

Letters:
    ALLI HELE
    STUR FRAN PE

University of Kansas
Kenneth Spencer Research Library
Librarian
Lawrence, KA 66045
USA
    See Bibliography: Black, Hester M. W.B. YEATS: A
    CATALOG ON AN EXHIBITION and Kansas University
    Libraries. A GUIDE TO THE COLLECTION.

Books:
    BELT   00
    BOOK IRIS 95
    COLL WORK 08
    HOUR GLAS 07
    PLAY PROS 24
    POEM   12
    POEM WRIT 13
    WAND OISI 89
    WORK WILL 93

University of Kansas

Inscriptions:
    FREN RHON
    GREG LADY
    GRIF MONT
    HOLL NORA
    HORN MISS AN
    MACB MAUD GO

Letters:
    ALDI RICH
    BULL A.H.
    FAY WILL GE
    GONN ISEU
    HEND W.A.
    HUTC THOM
    LIST MISS E.
    MACL E.R.
    MILL ALIC
    O'GR STAN
    O'HE PATR
    POEL WILL
    RHYS ERNE
    SALT DR.
    SETT MISS
    ST. LAWR MR
    STUA FRAN
    USSH ARLA
    WALK A.B.
    WHEL

    MACG T.
    MORR LADY OT
    UNKN RECI
    YEAT ELIZ
    YEAT LILY

Other Authors:
    ARNO POEM 00
    HINK MIRA 95
    MOOR MAXI ND
    O'KE CAIT 15
    PALG CHIL 98
    WARD GEOR 94
    WHIT POET 86

Plays:
    COUN CATH

Poems:
    SHAD WATE
    TOM O'RO

University of Leeds
The Brotherton Library
Sub-Librarian
Leeds
England
    Manuscripts accessible to scholars only.
    See Bibliography: Gosse, Sir Edmund. A CATALOGUE
    OF THE GOSSE COLLECTION.

Letters:
    CLOD EDWA
    GOSS EDMU
    HINK KATH TY
    MATH ELKI

    RATC DORO UN
    SHOR CLEM
    UNKN CORR

University of Liverpool
Sydney Jones Library
University Librarian
PO Box 123
Liverpool
England

    Letters:
        BIRR AUGU

University of London Library
Senate House, Malet Street
London WC1E 7HP
England
    See Bibliography: Baker, Pamela M. and Helen M. Young "W.B. Yeats Material."

Books:		Inscriptions:		
COLL POEM 33		MOOR STUR		
COUN CATH 12		UNKN RECI		
CUTT AGAT 19		Letters:		
FOUR PLAY 21		DUCK GERA		
GREE HELM 12		EMER FLOR FA		
PER AMIC 18		MOOR STUR		
POEM 01		Miscellany:		
POEM 1899 06		PHOT		
RESP OTHE 16		Other Authors:		
REVE CHIL 16		VILL AXEL 25		
TREM VEIL 22				
WILD SWAN 19				
Poems:				
DOUB VISI MI		PARD OLD FA		
EGO DOMI TU		PLAY ASK BL		
HOUR DAWN		SONG		
MEDI TIME WA		TOM O'RO		

University of Louisville
Ekstrom Library
Deptartment of Rare Books & Special Collections
Louisville, KY 40292
USA

Books:		Inscriptions:		
CELT TWIL 93		AHER KATH		
LATE POEM 22		UNKN RECI		
PLAY CONT 24		VYNN NORA		
PLAY PROS 22		YEAT ELIZ		
Letters:		Poems:		
GOUG MRS.		PARD OLD FA		
GREG LADY		PRAY MY DA		

University of Massachusetts Amherst
University Library
Special Collections
Amherst, MA 01003
USA

Books: Inscriptions:
    POEM   22   UNKN RECI
Poems:
    FERG DRUI

University of Notre Dame
Memorial Library
Notre Dame, IN 46556
USA
    See Bibliography: Masin, Anton C. (ed). CATALOGUE
    OF AN EXHIBIT.

Inscriptions: Letters:
    UNKN RECI   O'DO CHAR
Poems:
    LAKE ISLE IN

University of Reading Library
Keeper of Archives
P.O. Box 223
Reading, Berkshire RG6 2AE
England
    See Bibliography: Fletcher, Ian. "The Ellis-Yeats-Blake
    Manuscript Cluster"; James, Elizabeth Ingli. "The
    University of Reading Collections."

Books: Inscriptions:
    CELT TWIL 93   ELLI EDWI J.
    COUN KATH 92   ELLI MRS.
    HOUR CATH 04   GREG LADY
    POEM   95   UNKN RECI
    POEM WILL 93
    UNPU SPEC BI
    WAND OISI 89
    WORD WIND 34
    WORK WILL 93
Letters:
    BULL A.H.   HORT WILL TH
    CHAT WIND LT   KEYN GEOF
    ELLI EDWI J.   MACM COMP
    ELLI MRS.   MATH ELKI
    FAY   FRAN   UNKN CORR

Other Authors:
    BLAK MARR HE
Plays:
    WORD WIND PA

Poems:
    CERT ARTI BR
    HER COUR AG
    HER COUR TE
    SHE TURN DO
    UPON DYIN LA

University of Texas at Austin
Harry Ransom Humanities Research Center
P. O. Drawer 7219
Austin, TX 78713
USA
    See Bibliography: Adams, Hazard. "The William Butler
    Yeats Collection" and Finneran "A Note on the Scribner
    Archive."

Books:
    AUTO REVE 26
    AUTO REVE 27
    BOOK IRIS 95
    BOOK RHYM 92
    BOUN SWED 25
    CELT TWIL 93
    CELT TWIL 02
    COLL POEM 33
    COLL WORK 08
    COUN CATH 12
    COUN KATH 92
    CUTT AGAT 12
    CUTT AGAT 19
    DEIR   07
    DRAM PERS 36
    EARL POEM 25
    EIGH POEM 16
    ESSA   24
    ESSA W.B. 37
    ESTR   26
    FAIR FOLK 88
    FOUR PLAY 21
    GREE HELM 10
    HERN EGG 38
    HOUR CATH 04
    HOUR GLAS 03
    HOUR GLAS 14
    IDEA GOOD 03
    IN   SEVE 03

    JOHN SHER 91
    KING BAIL 04
    KING THRE 04
    LAKE ISLE 24
    LAND HEAR 94
    LATE POEM 22
    MICH ROBA 20
    MOSA   86
    NINE POEM 14
    NINE POEM 18
    OCTO BLAS 27
    OXFO BOOK 36
    PER AMIC 18
    PLAY CONT 23
    PLAY IRIS 11
    PLAY PROS 22
    POEM   95
    POEM   01
    POEM   04
    POEM SECO 09
    POEM WRIT 13
    POET IREL 08
    REPR IRIS 91
    RESP POEM 14
    REVE CHIL 15
    REVE CHIL 16
    SECR ROSE 97
    SELE LOVE 13
    SELE POET 13

University of Texas at Austin 435

Books (continued):
    SHAD WATE 00
    SHAD WATE 07
    SING HEAD 34
    STOR MICH 31
    STOR RED 04
    TABL LAW 97
    TABL LAW 04
    TABL LAW 14
    TOWE 28
    TWO PLAY 19
    UNPU SCRI ED
    VISI 25
    VISI 37
    VISI MATE
    WAND OISI 89
    WHEE BUTT 34
    WHER THER 03
    WILD SWAN 17
    WILD SWAN 19
    WIND REED 99
    WIND STAI 29
    WIND STAI 33
    WIND STAI MA
    WORD MUSI 32

Inscriptions:
    BEEC THOM
    BLUN EDMU HE
    BOGG TOM
    COCK SYDN
    DAVI LILI
    DRIN JOHN
    DUGG ELIZ
    DULA EDMU
    DULA HELE
    EMER FLOR FA
    FAY WILL
    GONN ISEU
    GOSS EDMU
    HAYW JOHN
    HEAL JAME
    HENL W.E.
    KING RICH
    LINL LAUR
    MACB MAUD GO
    MANN ETHE
    MARK T.
    MARR RAYM
    MATT HILD
    MORR LADY OT
    MOYN THOM KI
    NETT MRS. J.
    O'LE ELLE
    POLL GEOR
    POLL HENR
    PROK FRED
    QUIN JOHN
    ROBI LENN
    ROTH WILL
    RUSS GEOR
    SHAK OLIV
    SHAR WILL
    STUA FRAN IS
    SWET LYAL
    SYMO ARTH
    TODH JOHN
    UNKN RECI
    VIEL FRAN
    WELL CARO
    YEAT JACK
    YEAT JOHN
    YEAT LILY

Letters:
    ACAD EDIT
    ARMS WILS R.
    BAIL WILL F.
    BAX CLIF
    BEAR MABE
    BEAU MISS HE
    BIGG FRAN J.
    BLUN EDMU C.
    BLUN WILF
    BROP JOHN
    BROW
    BULL A.H.
    CAMP MRS. PA
    CART
    CHAM MARI C.
    CHES NORA
    CHES WILF H.
    CHUR RICH

Inscriptions (continued):

CLEM	CYRI		MORG	LOUI	
COCK	SYDN		MORR	GEOR	E.
COFF	GEOR		MORR	LADY	OT
CONN	NORR		MORR	PHIL	
COUS	JAME	H.	MURR	JOHN	
DAY	F.H.		O'CA	SEAN	
DRYH	NORA		O'CO	MISS	MO
DULA	EDMU		O'DO	D.J.	
DULA	HELE		O'LE	JOHN	
DUNC	ELLE	DO	O'NE	MAIR	
DUNN	MR		PAYN	LEON	W.
EMER	FLOR	FA	PEN		
ERVI	ST.	JO	POEL	WILL	
FODE	GWYN		PROK	FRED	
GARN	EDWA		RATT	R.F.	
GARV	JAME	L.	RAY	MR.	
GONN	ISEU		REAR		
GREG	LADY		REDM	MISS	
GUIN	JOHN		RICH	GRAN	
GWYN	STEP		RIDI	LAUR	
HACK			ROBI	LENN	
HARR	FRAN		ROSS	MARI	
HAYW	JOHN		RUFF	WALT	
HEAL	EDIT	SH	RUMM	WALT	MO
HEND	W.A.		RUSS	GEOR	
HIGG	FRED		SCOT	ROLF	
HINK	KATH	TY	SCRI		
HONE	JOSE	M.	SHAK	OLIV	
HORT	WILL	TH	SHAN	CHAR	
KEEB	LILL	MC	SHAW	GEOR	B.
KING	FRED	A.	SHOR	CLEM	
KING	RICH	AS	SIDG	FRAN	
LANG	FRED		SITW	DAME	ED
LAUR	THOM	WE	SMIT		
LEFA	MRS.		SQUI	JOHN	
LEGA	RICH		STAR	JAME	
MACB	MAUD	GO	STON	MISS	
MACD	THOM		STRO	L.A.	
MACK	GRAH		STUA	FRAN	
MASE	CONS		SYMO	ARTH	
MASE	JOHN		UNKN	CORR	
MATH	ELKI		UNWI	T.	FI
MCCA	PATR		WELL	DORO	
MEO	MRS.	CR	WHEL		
MEYN	WILF		WILS	RATH	
MILL	ALIC		WRIG	MRS.	
MONR	HARO		YEAT	JOHN	
MOOR	STUR		YOUN	STAR	

University of Texas at Austin

Miscellany:
  MISC
  OCCU
  PHOT
  REVI GOMB

Plays:
  AT   HAWK WE
  COUN CATH
  DIAR GRAN
  DREA BONE

Poems:
  AMON SCHO CH
  ANAS VIJA
  AT   GREY RO
  BALL EARL PA
  BROK DREA
  COUN CATH PA
  DAWN
  DOWN SALL GA
  EGO DOMI TU
  EPHE
  FAER SONG
  FISH ERMA N
  HER COUR AG
  HER COUR TE
  HIS PHOE
  IN   MEMO MA
  INDI GOD
  JOHN KINS LA
  KANV HIMS
  LAKE ISLE IN
  LINE WRIT DE
  MADN KING GO

Poems, Unpublished:
  TO   MAUD GO
  TWIL LOCH AN

Other Authors:
  LINL OUT 16
  RAPH ASTR ND
  STUA PIGE 32
  TAGO GITA 12

  FULL MOON MA
  HOUR GLAS
  LAND HEAR DE
  SOPH OEDI CO

  NEVE GIVE AL
  ON   THOS TH
  PEOP
  PHAN SHIP
  QUAT APHO
  ROGE CASE
  SONG HAPP SH
  SONG WAND AE
  SORR LOVE
  STIC INCE
  STOL CHIL
  THOU PROP
  THRE SONG SA
  TIME WITC VI
  TO   ROSE RO
  TO   WEAL MA
  TOM O'RO
  UNDE BEN BU
  WILD OLD WI
  WILD SWAN CO
  WOMA HOME SU
  WOMA YOUN OL

Prose:
  HOW WRIT WO
  SAMH 1904

University of Toronto
Thomas Fisher Rare Book Library
Toronto M5S 1A5
Ontario, Canada

Books:
  POEM   95
  SECO BOOK 94

Inscriptions:
  PAYE JAME VI
  UNKN RECI

        Letters: Poems:
            DELU ALFR   LAKE ISLE IN
            MAVO JAME   OIL BLOO
            PAYE JAME B.
            WETH J.E.

University of Tulsa
McFarlin Library
Curator of Library Manuscripts
Tulsa, OK 74104
USA
        Manuscripts accessible to scholars only.

    Books:
        REVE CHIL 15
    Letters: Other Authors:
        FERG LADY   MILT POET 35
        LINC   Poems:
        NEVI HENR WO   DOWN SALL GA
        O'FA SEAN   NEWS DELP OR
        RUSS GEOR   TO   ISLE WA
        UNKN CORR
        WILS MR.

University of Vermont
Bailey-Howe Library
Curator of Manuscripts
Burlington, VT 05405
USA

    Letters:
        MASE JOHN

University of Victoria
McPherson Library
Special Collections
Victoria V8W 3H5
British Columbia, Canada

    Books: Inscriptions:
        AUTO REVE 26   EATO NOLA
        BOOK IRIS 95   FODE GWYN
        CELT TWIL 93   O'LE JOHN
                                              QUIN JOHN
                                              UNKN RECI
    Letters: Other Authors:
        LEVE A.J.   EGLI LITE 04
        READ HERB   JOHN SHAD
        UNKN CORR
    Prose:

University of Virginia
Alderman Library
Charlottesville, VA 22903
USA

   Inscriptions:
      TRAN EDIT B.
      UNKN RECI
   Poems:
      WHEN YOU   SA

   Letters:
      HARR CLIF

Wake Forest University Library
Librarian
Winston-Salem, NC 27109
USA

   Books:
      CELT TWIL 94
      IRIS FAIR 95
      NINE POEM 18
      POEM   99
      WIND REED 99
   Letters:
      FAGA MR
      GIBS WILF
      HARD W.G.
      RUSS GEOR
      WATS LADY
      WILS DAVI

   Inscriptions:
      COAT FLOR EA
      GONN ISEU
      QUIN JOHN

   Other Authors:
      GREG GODS 04
      TREA IRIS 00
   Poems:
      TO   ROSE RO
      WITH BOUG

Washington State University
The Libraries
Special Collections
Pullman, WA 99164
USA

   Books:
      KING BAIL 04
      POEM   13
      STOR RED 04
   Letters:
      GRIG MRS.

   Inscriptions:
      UNKN RECI
      WOLL MISS

Washington University Libraries
Special Collections
Campus Box 1061
St Louis, MO 63130
USA

   Plays:
      DIAR GRAN

Wellcome Institute for History of Medicine
Contemporary Medical Archives Centre
Assistant Archivist
183 Euston Road
London NW1 2BP
England

   Letters:
      BLAC DR.
      EUGE SOCI

Wellesley College Library
Special Collections
Wellesley, MA 02181
USA

Books:		Inscriptions:		
CELT TWIL 12		BATE KATH		
IN SEVE 03		UNKN RECI		
JOHN SHER 91				
POET WORK 06				
POET WORK 12				
REVE CHIL 16				
SING HEAD 34				
SYNG IREL 11				
WILD SWAN 19				
Letters:				
BATE KATH LE		KLEE RITA SU		
BROW TOM		MATT MR.		
GAWS JOHN		MCDE MARY SC		
GREG LADY		REES J.		RO
HALL MRS. LO		REES MRS. J.		
HENL W.E.		WOOD MRS.		
HONE JOSE M.				
Speeches:				
ABER LECT				

Wertheim, Stanley
180 Cabrini Blvd.
New York, NY 10033
USA

  Books: Inscriptions:
     RESP OTHE 16   GREG LADY

Wesleyan University
Olin Memorial Library
Special Collections
Middletown, CT 06457
USA
    See Bibliography: Durkan, Michael J. W.B.
    YEATS. A CATAOGUE.

  Books: Inscriptions:
     MICH ROBA 20   DULA EDMU
     NEW POEM 38   LANE HUGH
     POEM WRIT 13   PROK FRED
     SING HEAD 34   Letters:
     STOR MICH 31   PETE MR.
  Miscellany: Poems:
     MISC   LOVE TELL RO
                                         PAUD
                                         WILD SWAN CO

West Sussex Record Office
County Hall
Chichester
West Sussex PO19 1RN
England

  Letters:
     BLUN WILF
     UNWI JANE CO

Westfield College
Caroline Skeel Library
Librarian
Kidderpore Avenue
Hampstead NW3 7ST
England

  Letters:
     LYTT LADY KA

Yale University
Beinecke Library
New Haven, CT 06520
USA
    See Bibliography: Gallup, Donald. "Ezra Pound...The Catalogue of an Exhibition."

Books:
    AUTO REVE 26
    BOUN SWED 25
    CELT TWIL 93
    COUN KATH 92
    DEAT SYNG 28
    DISC VOLU 07
    EAST 16
    FOUR YEAR 21
    HOUR GLAS 04
    JOHN SHER 91
    KING THRE 04
    LAND HEAR 94
    MICH ROBA 20
    POEM 95
    POEM WILL 93
    RESP OTHE 16
    RESP POEM 14
    SOME ESSA 05
    SYNG IREL 11
    TABL LAW 97

Inscriptions:
    BOYD ERNE
    RUSS FATH
    SHAK OLIV
    UNKN RECI
    YOUN JAME CA

Letters:
    ALMA TADE MI
    DIAL
    DIRC W.H.
    DRIN JOHN
    FORD JULI
    HODG RALP
    JOYC JAME
    LEGA RICH
    MATH ELKI
    MOON MRS.
    O'CO JOHN
    OWEN MARY
    PHEL WILL LY
    POUN EZRA
    SHEI FRAN J.
    SQUI JOHN
    STEA W.F.
    THAY SCOF
    UNIV CAIR
    UNKN CORR
    WELL JAME R.
    WHAR MRS.
    YEAT JOHN

Miscellany:
    MISC
    PHOT

Other Authors:
    ALLI SIXT 05
    FENO CERT 16
    GREG CUCH 02
    GREG POET 03
    HORT BOOK 98

Plays:
    CAT MOON
    COUN CATH
    HOUR GLAS
    ONLY JEAL EM
    PLAY QUEE

Yale University

   Poems:
      AMON SCHO CH
      DEMO BEAS
      DOUB VISI MI
      EAST 1916
      FERG DRUI
      FRIE THAT HA
      GIFT HARU AL
      HE   WISH CL
      IN   MEMO MA
      LEDA SWAN
      MEDI TIME CI
      MICH ROBA DA
   Poems, Unpublished:
      REEN TIME TI
      NINE HUND NI
      ON   BEIN AS
      OWEN AHER DA
      PHAS MOON
      REME
      ROSE TREE
      SECO COMI
      SIXT DEAD ME
      SONG HAPP SH
      TO   YOUN BE
      TOWA BREA DA
      UNDE SATU
   Prose:
      BIOG FRAG
      MORE MEMO
      NEED AUDA TH

Yeats Tower
Curator
Ballylee
Ireland

   Books:
      WIND STAI 33
   Poems:
      TOM   O'RO

   Inscriptions:
      UNKN RECI

Yeats, Anne
Dalkey
Dublin
Ireland
   See Bibliography: O'Shea.   DESCRIPTIVE CATALOG.

   Books:
      AUTO REVE 26
      BOOK IRIS 95
      CELT TWIL 93
      COLL POEM 33
      COLL WORK 08
      COUN CATH 12
      COUN CATH 29
      CUTT AGAT 12
      DEIR   07
      DEIR   11
      DRAM PERS 36
      EARL POEM 25
      EIGH POEM 16
      GREE HELM 12
      HERN EGG 38
      HOUR CATH 04
      HOUR CATH 05
      HOUR GLAS 04
      HOUR GLAS 07
      IRIS FAIR 92
      LATE POEM 22
      OXFO BOOK 36
      PER AMIC 18
      PLAY IRIS 11

Books (continued):
```
    PLAY PROS 22
    POEM      22
    POEM      29
    POEM 1899 06
    POEM SECO 09
    POEM WILL 93
    RESP OTHE 16
    SELE POEM 21
    SELE POET 13
    SHAD WATE 00
    SHAD WATE 07
    STOR RED  14
    TABL LAW  97
    TOWE      28
    TREM VEIL 22
    VISI      25
    VISI      37
    WHEE BUTT 34
    WILD SWAN 19
    WIND REED 99
    WIND STAI 29
    WIND STAI 33
    WORK WILL 93
```
Plays:
```
    CATH HOUL
    COUN CATH
    DEIR
    FULL MOON MA
    HOUR GLAS
    KING THRE
    ON   BAIL ST
    POT  BROT
    RESU
    SOPH KING OE
```
Poems:
```
    ADAM CURS
    ARRO
    AT   GALW RA
    BAIL AILL
    BALL FATH O'
    BEAU LOFT TH
    COLD HEAV
    DOUB VISI MI
    FOLL BEIN CO
    GREY ROCK
    LIVI BEAT
    LOVE RS   SO
```

Inscriptions:
```
    GRIG MISS
    HORN MISS AN
    JOHN LION
    MOOR STUR
    OSHI SHOT
    PRIC FRAN
    SATO JUNZ
    TUCK MRS.
    UNKN RECI
    VANK HILD
    YEAT ANNE
    YEAT GEOR
    YEAT JOHN
    YEAT LILY
```
Letters:
```
    UNWI T.   FI
```
Other Authors:
```
    BLUN SONN 75
    ERDM HIST 24
    GREG CUCH 02
    GREG THRE 23
    PHIL PAUL 30
    WELL POEM 34
    YEAT SLIG 30
```

```
    MY   TABL
    NEED EYE
    NEW  FACE
    OLD  AGE  QU
    OLD  MEMO
    PARD OLD  FA
    PRAY MY   SO
    RAGG WOOD
    SCHO
    SECR ROSE
    SHAD WATE
    SOLO WITC
```

Yeats, Anne

Poems (continued):
    SPIL MILK
    THRE SONG SA
    TO   HEAR BI
    TO   YOUN BE
    TOM O'RO
    UNDE MOON
    UPON DYIN LA
    VACI
    WILD SWAN CO

Poems, Unpublished:
    RED BLOO LA
    THER IS   FL
    WATC FIRE
Prose:
    PEOP THEA
    WILL BLAK IL

Yeats, Senator Michael
Dalkey, Co. Dublin
Ireland
    Accessible only by prior arrangement.

Books:
    AUTO REVE 27
    COLL POEM 33
    VISI MATE
    WIND REED 99
Letters:
    MACB MAUD GO
    POLL GEOR
    SHAK OLIV
    WALK MARY
    YEAT ANNE
    YEAT ELIZ
    YEAT GEOR
    YEAT JOHN
    YEAT LILY
    YEAT MICH
Poems:
    AMON SCHO CH
    CAT MOON
    COUN CATH PA
    EMPT CUP
    EVER VOIC
    FIRS LOVE
    FROM OEDI CO
    GLOV CLOA
    HE   BIDS HI
    HE   GIVE HI
    HE   TELL PE
    HEAR WOMA
    HOST AIR
    HOST SIDH

Inscriptions:
    YEAT MICH

Miscellany:
    DIAR JOUR
    DOCU
    MISC
    OCCU
Plays:
    UNPU LOVE DE

    LOVE ASKS FO
    LOVE SPEA HE
    LOVE TELL RO
    MAID QUIE
    MERU
    MOOD
    OUT SIGH IS
    POET HIS BE
    POET PLEA EL
    RED HANR SO
    RIBH ECST
    SHAD WATE
    SONG OLD MO
    SONG ROSY CR

Poems (continued):
   THER
   THRE BUSH
   TO   SOME I
   TRAV PASS
   TWO SONG RE
   VACI
   VALL BLAC PI
   WAND OISI
   WISD DREA

Poems, Unpublished:
   ALL DAY YO
   GOD LOVE RO
   I   WILL NO
   IMPE HEAR GI
   ON   CHIL DE
   PROT LEAP
   THOU LOUD YE
   WHIT DAUG IR
   YOU ARE ET

APPENDIX

Alternate and Variant Titles of Poems

Over the years, WBY used many alternate and variant titles for his poems. Often, the same poem appeared with a different title; occasionally, different poems appeared with the same title. In the CENSUS, published poems are listed under their titles from Allt's VARIORUM or Finneran's NEW EDITION, with the alternate or variant titles noted in the description of the manuscript.

The following list, compiled with help from George Bornstein and Peggy McMullen, is based not only on titles appearing in manuscripts, but also in Wade's BIBLIOGRAPHY, in Allt's VARIORUM EDITION, and in other sources; it thus includes some titles for which there is no direct manuscript authority, and no description in this CENSUS.

The full title and description of those listed can be found by using the QUICK title and the index of manuscripts.

Aedh Gives his Beloved Certain Rhymes	HE GIVE HI
Aedh Hears the Cry of the Sedge	HE HEAR CR
Aedh Laments the Loss of Love	LOVE MOUR LO
Aedh Pleads with the Elemental Powers	POET PLEA EL
Aedh Tells of a Valley Full of Lovers	HE TELL VA
Aedh Tells of the Perfect Beauty	HE TELL PE
Aedh Tells of the Rose in his Heart	LOVE TELL RO
Aedh Thinks of those who have Spoken Evil of his Beloved	HE THIN TH
Aedh Wishes for the Cloths of Heaven	HE WISH CL
Aedh Wishes His Beloved Were Dead	HE WISH HI
Aiofe's Lover	GREY ROCK
Aodh pleads with the Elemental Powers	POET PLEA EL
Aodh to Dectira I	HE HEAR CR
Aodh to Dectira II	LOVE MOUR LO
Aodh to Dectira III	HE THIN TH
Aodh to Dectora	HE WISH BE
Aodh to Dectora: Three Poems	HE HEAR CR
	HE THIN TH
	LOVE MOUR LO
Aodh to Dectora with certain rhymes	HE GIVE BE

Apologia Addressed to Ireland in the Coming Days	TO IRE CO
At Barcelona	CRAZ GIRL
At Last	RESU THOU
Avalon	STAT HOLI
Ballad of the Old Foxhunter, The	BALL FOXH
Ballad of the Three Bushes, The	THRE BUSH
Black Centaur, The	ON PICT BL
Breasal the Fisherman	FISH
Bressel the Fisherman	FISH
Breaking Day	PART
Bronze Bust, The	BRON HEAD
Celtic Twilight, The	INTO TWIL
Chambermaid's Song, The	CHAM FIRS SO
Child's Song	TO SQUI KY
Christmas Tree	HER FRIE BR
Civil War	MEDI TIME CI
Coat on a Coathanger. A	APPA
Cloths of Heaven, The	HE WISH CL
Come All Parnellites	COME GATH RO
Coole 1932	COOL PARK BA
Cradle Song, A	UNAP HOST
Cracked Mary's Vision	CRAZ JANE KI
Crazy Cromwell	CURS CROM
Crazy Jane and the Dancers	CRAZ JANE GR
Crevice by my Window, The	STAR NEST WI
Cromwellian Speaks, The	PROT LEAP
Crowded Cross, A	NEED EYE
Cuchulain Dead	CUCH COMF
Cuchulain, the Girl, and the Fool	HERO GIRL FO
Dancer at Cruachan and Ocris, The	DANC CRUA CR
Dancer, The	DANC CRUA CR
Dark Horses, The	HE BID HI
Death of Cuchulain, The	CUCH FIGH SE
Dedication of 'Irish Tales'	DEDI BOOK IR
Desire of Man and of Woman, The	HE MOUR CH
Distraction	ALL THIN CA
Dream of a Blessed Spirit, A	COUN CATH PA
Dream of the valley of lovers, A	HE TELL VA
Dying Lady, The	UPON DYIN LA
Echo from Propertius, An	THOU PROP
Entrance of Deirdre, The	QUEE EDAI
Epilogue to the Island of Statues, An	SONG HAPP SH
Epitaph, An	DREA DEAT
Faery Host, The	HOST SIDH
Father Gilligan	BALL FATH GI
Father O'Hart	BALL FATH O'
Fisher Aodh, The	FISH
Fisherman, The	FISH

Folk of the Air, The	HOST	AIR	
Forty Years Later	THRE	SONG	SA
Friend, A	LOVE	MOUR	LO
Galway Races	AT	GALW	RA
Glove in the Cloak, The	GLOV	CLOA	
Hanrahan Laments because of His Wanderings	MAID	QUIE	
Hanrahan Reproves the Curlew	HE	REPR	CU
Hanrahan Speaks to the Lovers of His Songs in Coming Days	LOVE	SPEA	HE
Hanrahan the Red Upon his Wanderings	MAID	QUIE	
He brings her dolls and drawings	CERT	ARTI	BR
Heart Replies, The	OWEN	AHER	DA
His Convictions	UNDE	BEN	BU
Host, The	HOST	SIDH	
Hosting of the children of Danu, The	HOST	SIDH	
How goes the weather?	O'RA		
I dreamed they laid her	HE	WISH	HI
I knew a Phoenix	HIS	PHOE	
In a Drawing Room	QUAT	APHO	
In Memoriam	MOUR	THEN	ON
In Memory	IN	MEMO	AL
Indian Song, An	INDI	LOVE	
Irish Legend, An	MAD	KING	GO
Jealousy	ANAS	VIJA	
Kanva the Indian on God	INDI	GOD	
Kathleen	COUN	KATH	PA
King Goll	MAD	KING	GO
Lady of Tuneful Guile, The	ISLA	STAT	
Lady to Chambermaid, The	LADY	THIR	SO
Lady to her Chambermaid, The	LADY	SECO	SO
Lady's Song	LADY	FIRS	SO
Last Memories	LAST	CONF	
Legend of the Phantom Ship, A	PHAN	SHIP	
Letter to the Delphic Oracle, A	NEWS	DELP	OR
Loquiter the Cromwellian	PROT	LEAP	
Love and the Bird	MEMO	YOUT	
Lover to his heart, The	IMPE	HEAR	GI
Lug-na-Gall	PROT	LEAP	
Lust and Rage	SPUR		
Lover Speaks, The	OWEN	AHER	DA
Mad Song, A	SONG	WAND	AE
Marriage Ode, A	MODE	LAUR	
Mary Virgin	MOTH	GOD	
Michael Robartes Asks Forgiveness because of his Many Moods	LOVE	ASKS	FO
Michael Robartes bids his Beloved be at Peace	HE	BIDS	BE
Michael Robartes remembers Forgotten Beauty	HE	REME	FO

Michael Robartes to his Beloved II	LOVE ASK FO
Michael Robartes to his Beloved III	HE REME FO
Miserrimus	SAD SHEP
Mongan Laments the Change That Has Come upon Him and His Beloved	HE MOUR CH
Mongan Thinks of His Past Greatness	HE THIN HI
Morning	PART
Mystical Prayer to the Masters of the Elements	POET PLEA EL
New Ireland	SEPT 1912
O sweet everlasting voices be still	EVER VOIC
Oisin and the Islands of Youth	WAND OISI
Old Friends	LOVE PLEA FR
Old Pensioner, The	LAME OLD PE
Old Poem Re-written, An	DEDI BOOK ST
Old Song Re-sung, An	DOWN SALL GA
On Being Asked to write a war poem	ON BEIN AS
On the death of an Irish air-man who joined early in the war	IRIS AIRM FO
One and the Dancer, The	DANC CRUA CR
O'Sullivan Rua to the Curlew	HE REPR CU
O'Sullivan Rua to the Secret Rose	SECR ROSE
O'Sullivan the Red to Mary Lavell	POET BELO
O'Sullivan the Red upon his Wanderings	MAID QUIE
Out of the Old Days	TO HEAR BI
Parnellite at Parnell's Funeral, A	PARN FUNE
Peace of the Rose	ROSE PEAC
Perfect Beauty, The	HE TELL PE
Phoenix, The	PEOP
Poet, The	BROK DREA
Poet Pleads with His Friend for Old Friends, The	POET PLEA HI
Praise of Deirdre, The	QUEE EDAI
Priest of Coloony, The	BALL FATH O'
Procession, The	HIGH TALK
Pythagorian Numbers	STAT
Reason for Keeping Silent, A	ON BEIN AS
Ribh Prefers an Older Theology	RIBH DENO PA
Road, The	ROAD DOOR
Rosa Mundi	ROSE WORL
Rose in my Heart, The	LOVE TELL RO
Rider of the North	HAPP TOWN
Salutation, A	HE TELL PE
Second Song, The	THRE SONG SA
Shadowy Horses, The	HE BID BE
Silk, Sword, and Town	DIAL SELF SO
Soldier Takes Pride, The	THRE SONG SA
Solitary Fairy, The	FAIR PEDA
Somebody at Parnell's Funeral	PARN FUNE

Song (COUN KATH)	CRAD SONG
Song of Mongan	HE THIN PA
Song of the Old Fisherman, The	MEDI OLD FI
Song of the Old Man, The	OLD MEN AD
Song of the Rose and the Cross	SONG ROSY CR
Song of Sunset, A	LIFE
Stolen Bride, The	HOST AIR
Sullivan the Red upon his Wandering	MAID QUIE
Summing Up, The	MERU
There Is a Queen in China	QUEE EDAI
They Went forth to the Battle	ROSE BATT
Things that come again, The	NINE HUND NI
Thoor Ballylea	MEDI TIME CI
Thorn Tree, The	HER PRAI
Thoughts Upon the Present State of the World	NINE HUND NI
Three Marching Songs	THRE SONG SA
Three Revolutionary Songs	THRE SONG SA
Three Songs for a Woman	LAST CONF
	HER VISI WO
	PART
To a friend who asked me to sign on his manifesto to the neutral nations	ON BEIN AS
To DW	TO DORO WE
To Eva Gore-Booth	IN MEMO EV
To the Tune of "O'Donnell Abu"	PARN FUNE
Toward Byzantium	SAIL BYZA
Travelling Man Sings, The	COME RIDE
True Faith, The	WISD
Twilight of Forgiveness, The	LOVE ASKS FO
Two Love Poems	HE BIDS BE
Two Poems by O'Sullivan the Red concerning Mary Lavell	POET HIS BE
	HE TELL PE
Two Poems Concerning Peasant Visionaries	UNAP HOST
	VALL BLAC PI
Two Love Poems	TRAV PASS
Under the Moon	POET BELO
What Other Spur?	SPUR
"Why is it," Queen Edain said	QUEE EDAI
Windle-straws [two poems]	
1) O'Sullivan Rua to the Curlew	HE REPR CU
1) Hanrahan Reproves the Curlew, and	HE REPR CU
2) Out of the Old Days	UNAP HOST
Woman's Song, A	LAST CONF
Yang and Ying	LOVE SONG
Young Country Man Sings, The	FIRS LOVE
Your Pathway	HE WISH CL

453

BIBLIOGRAPHY

Bibliography

The bibliography lists works directly related to manuscripts: reference works; descriptions of exhibits, collections, and holdings; works that include previously unpublished poems; and works cited in this CENSUS. Some works contain references to or descriptions of manuscripts not listed in this CENSUS, since the location of the manuscripts is unknown.

Abbott, Cheryl and J. Fraser Cocks, III. JAMES AUGUSTINE HEALY COLLECTION OF NINETEENTH AND TWENTIETH CENTURY IRISH LITERATURE. Waterville, Maine: Colby College, 1978.

Adams, Hazard. "The William Butler Yeats Collection at Texas." LIBRARY CHRONICLE OF THE UNIVERSITY OF TEXAS 6:1 (Spring 1957): 33-38.

Allen, James Lovic. "The Yeats Tapes." IRISH LITERARY SUPPLEMENT, 2:2 (October, 1983): 17, 19.
    On the SUNY SB microfilm collection; comments still relevant.

Allt, Peter and Russell K. Alspach, eds. THE VARIORUM EDITION OF THE POEMS OF W.B. YEATS. New York: Macmillan, 1957.

Alspach, Russell K., ed. THE VARIORUM EDITION OF THE PLAYS OF W.B. YEATS. New York: Macmillan, 1966.

Ash, Lee and Denis Lorenz. SUBJECT COLLECTIONS: A GUIDE TO SPECIAL BOOK COLLECTIONS AND SUBJECT EMPHASES AS REPORTED BY UNIVERSITY, COLLEGE, PUBLIC, AND SPECIAL LIBRARIES IN THE UNITED STATES AND CANADA. 3rd edition. New York: Bowker, 1967: 1216-1217.

Baker, Pamela M. and Helen M. Young. "W.B. Yeats Material in the University of London Library." YEATS ANNUAL 4 (1986): 175-180.

Black, Hester M. W.B. Yeats: A CATALOG OF AN EXHIBITION FROM THE P.S. O'HEGARTY COLLECTION IN THE UNIVERSITY OF KANSAS LIBRARY (1958).

Blake-Hill, Philip V. "The Macmillan Archive." BRITISH MUSEUM QUARTERLY 36:3-4 (Autumn 1972): 74-80.

Bornstein, George and Warwick Gould. "'To a Sister of the Cross & the Rose': An Unpublished Early Poem." YEATS ANNUAL 7 (1987): 179-183.
    Has discussion and text of the manuscript poem TO SIST CR.

Dougan, R.O. W.B. YEATS: MANUSCRIPTS AND PRINTED BOOKS EXHIBITED IN THE LIBRARY OF TRINITY COLLEGE, DUBLIN, 1956. Dublin: Friends of the Library of Trinity College, 1956.

Durkan, Michael J. W.B. YEATS 1865-1965: A CATALOGUE OF HIS WORKS AND ASSOCIATED ITEMS IN OLIN LIBRARY, WESLEYAN UNIVERSITY. Middletown: Dulmer Press (1965).

Ellman, Richard. THE IDENTITY OF YEATS. New York: Oxford, 1954.
    Has copies of several previously unpublished poems: ALL DAY YO, KNOW WISD, PORT BEFO HI.

_____. YEATS: THE MAN AND THE MASKS. New York: Macmillan, 1948.
    Has copies of a number of previously unpublished poems: HE WHO BI, FLOW HAS BL, IMAG, IMPE HEAR GI, KNOW WISD, OLD SOLI ON, TO MAUD GO, TO SIST CR, WHEN TO IT, YOUR PATH.

Elmore, C.R. ENGLISH LITERARY MANUSCRIPTS IN VICTORIA INSTITUTIONAL LIBRARIES. Melbourne: 1978.

Finneran, Richard J. ANGLO-IRISH LITERATURE: A REVIEW OF RESEARCH. New York: MLA, 1976; and A SUPPLEMENT... New York: MLA, 1983.

_____. "The Composition and Final Text of 'Crazy Jane on the King.'" ICARBS 4:2 (1984): 227-32.

_____. EDITING YEATS'S POEMS. London: Macmillan, 1983.

_____. "A Note on the Scribner Archive at the Humanities Research Center." YEATS 2 (1984): 227-32.

_____. ed. W.B. YEATS: THE POEMS, A NEW EDITION. New York: Macmillan, 1983.

Fletcher, Ian, "The Ellis--Yeats--Blake Manuscript Cluster." THE BOOK COLLECTOR 21 (1972): 72-94.

Gallup, Donald. "Ezra Pound (1885-1972): The Catalogue of an Exhibition in the Beinecke Library, 30 October-31 December 1975." THE YALE UNIVERSITY LIBRARY GAZETTE 50 (January 1976): 135-163.
    Includes brief descriptions of letters from WBY not listed in this CENSUS.

Gilbert, R.A. "Magical Manuscripts: an Introduction to the Archives of the Hermetic Order of the Golden Dawn." YEATS ANNUAL 5 (1987): 163-177.
    Has descriptions and some reproductions of occult material, including letters, from private collections.

Gordon, Donald James and Ian Fletcher. W.B. YEATS: IMAGES OF A POET. Manchester: University of Manchester, 1961.
    Refers to a few manuscripts not listed in this CENSUS.

Gordon, R.S. UNION LIST OF MANUSCRIPTS IN CANADIAN REPOSITORIES. Ottowa: Public Archives of Canada, 1975.

Gosse, Sir Edmund. A CATALOGUE OF THE GOSSE CORRESPONDENCE IN THE BROTHERTON COLLECTION. Leeds: University of Leeds, 1950.

Gould, Warwick. "'Portrayed before his eyes': an abandoned late poem." YEATS ANNUAL 6 (1988): 214-221.
    Has text of PORT BEFO EY.

_____. "'What is the explanation of it all?': Yeats's 'little poem about nothing,'" YEATS ANNUAL 5 (1987): 212-213.
    Includes discussion and copy of the manuscript poem (WHAT IS EX).

GUIDE TO LITERARY MANUSCRIPTS IN THE HUNTINGTON LIBRARY.
[San Marino]: Huntington Library, 1979.

GUIDE TO THE MANUSCRIPT COLLECTIONS OF THE HISTORICAL SOCIETY
OF PENNSYLVANIA. Philadelphia: The Historical Society
of Pennsylvania, 1949.

Harvard University Library. DIRECTORY OF ARCHIVES AND
MANUSCRIPT REPOSITORIES AT HARVARD UNIVERSITY AND
RADCLIFFE COLLEGE. Cambridge: Harvard University
Library, 1983.

Hayes, Richard J. MANUSCRIPT SOURCES FOR THE HISTORY OF
IRISH CIVILIZATION. Boston: Hall, 1965; and SUPPLEMENT.

Hodges, Figgis and Co., Ltd. WILLIAM BUTLER YEATS: 13 JUNE
1865-13 JUNE 1965. Dublin: Dolmen Press, 1965.

JACK B. YEATS AND HIS FAMILY. Sligo: Sligo County
Library/Museum, 1971.

[Jackson, Thomas J.] THE IRISH COLLECTION: RARE BOOK ROOM,
MORRIS LIBRARY. Carbondale: Southern Illinois
University, [1970].

James, Elizabeth Ingli. "The University of Reading
Collections." YEATS ANNUAL 3 (1985): 167-172.

Jochum, K.P.S. W.B. YEATS: A CLASSIFIED BIBLIOGRAPHY OF
CRITICISM. Urbana: University of Illinois Press, c1978.

Kain, Richard M. "The Curran Library." EIRE-IRELAND 7:4
(Winter 1972): 135-6.

Kansas University Libraries. A GUIDE TO THE COLLECTION.
Lawrence, Kansas: University of Kansas Libraries, 1964.

Kelly, John. "Aesthete Among the Athletes: Yeats's
Contributions to THE GAEL." YEATS: AN ANNUAL OF
CRITICAL AND TEXTUAL CRITICISM 2 (1984): 75-143.
    Includes discussion and text of "The Protestant's
Leap" (PROT LEAP).

_____, ed. THE COLLECTED LETTERS OF W.B. YEATS, vol. I.
Oxford: Clarendon, 1986.
    Includes copies of "A flower has blossomed" (FLOW
HAS BL) and "Wherever in the wastes of wrinkling sands"
(WHER WAST WR).

Bibliography

Kenyon College Library. "The Charles Riker Collection of William Butler Yeats." KENYON COLLEGE LIBRARY ACQUISITIONS BULLETIN #83 (Feb 1959): 1-6; #109 (Nov 1961): 1-4.

Klinkenborg, Verlyn. BRITISH LITERARY MANUSCRIPTS (SERIES II FROM 1800 -1914). New York: Pierpont Morgan Library and Dover, c1981.
    Has photocopy of "Aodh to Dectora" and list of holdings of Pierpont Morgan Library.

Lester, DeeGee. IRISH RESEARCH: A GUIDE TO COLLECTIONS IN NORTH AMERICA, IRELAND, AND GREAT BRITAIN. New York: Greenwood, 1987.

Londraville, Richard. "The Manuscript of 'The Queen and the Jester." ARIEL: A REVIEW OF INTERNATIONAL ENGLISH LITERATURE, 3 (1972): 67-68.

MacKenzie, Norman. "The Monk Gibbon Papers." CANADIAN JOURNAL OF IRISH STUDIES, 1-2 (Dec 1983): 5-24. [Queens U, Kingston, Canada].

Marcus, Philip L. "Catalogue of Yeats Manuscripts in the Olin Library, Cornell University." In Robert O'Driscoll and Lorna Reynolds, YEATS AND THE THEATRE (Macmillan of Canada, 1975): 281-284.

Masin, Anton C. CATALOGUE OF AN EXHIBIT OF SELECTIONS ON WILLIAM BUTLER YEATS. Memorial Library, University of Notre Dame, May-September, 1980.

Mattson, Francis O. "The John Quinn Memorial Collection: An Inventory and Index." BULLETIN OF THE NEW YORK PUBLIC LIBRARY 78 (Winter 1975): 145-230.

Myers, Andrew B. "Exhibitions in Retrospect: The Indomitable Irishry." GAZETTE OF THE GROLIER CLUB (October 1966): 4-37.
    Has descriptions of numerous manuscripts, letters, and books with inscriptions not listed in this CENSUS including POEM BALL 88 inscribed to May Morris, BOOK RHYM 92 to Maud Gonne, TABL LAW 97 to E.A. Boyd, Brooke's TREASURY OF IRISH POETRY (1900) to Quinn, and others (present locations unknown).

Naito, Shiro. YEATS AND ZEN. Kyoto: Yamaguchi, 1984.
Reprints two letters from WBY to Daisetz Suzuki and
Kazumi Yano.

Nash, Nancy Rutkowski. "Yeats and Heffernan the Blind,"
YEATS ANNUAL 4 (1986): 201-206.
Includes text and discussion of a manuscript poem
(SONG HEFF BL).

National Gallery of Ireland. W.B. YEATS: A CENTENARY
EXHIBITION. Dublin: Dolmen Press, 1965.

NATIONAL UNION CATALOG OF MANUSCRIPT COLLECTIONS.
Washington: Library of Congress, 1959-85.

New York Public Library. DICTIONARY CATALOG OF THE ALBERT A.
AND HENRY W. BERG COLLECTION OF ENGLISH AND AMERICAN
LITERATURE, Vols. IV, V, and SUPPLEMENT. Boston: Hall,
1969-1975..

Newcastle-upon-Tyne. WILLIAM BUTLER YEATS, 1865-1939:
CATALOGUE OF AN EXHIBITION, 13TH-22ND MAY 1965.
[Newcastle-upon-Tyne, 1965].
Exhibition was based on "a small private
collection" that included a copy of CUTT AGAT 19
inscribed to "Miss Marsh," dated April 20 1919.

Niland, Nora. JACK B. YEATS AND HIS FAMILY, 1971.

_____. "The Yeats Memorial Museum, Sligo." IRISH BOOK,
2:3-4 (Autumn 1963): 122-26.

O'Shea, Edward. A DESCRIPTIVE CATALOG OF W.B. YEATS'S
LIBRARY. New York: Garland, 1985.
Major items are noted at the appropriate place in
this CENSUS, but the CATALOG includes many items with
marginalia and markings not noted here. Has several
previously unpublished poems: RED BLOO OU, THER IS FL,
WATC FIRE.

_____. "The 1920's Catalogue of W.B. Yeats's Library,"
YEATS ANNUAL 4 (1986): 279-290.

Oshima, Shotaro. YEATS AND JAPAN. [Tokyo]: Hokuseido, 1965.
Has photocopies of signed, autograph Poems (NINE
CENT AF, SYMB, WHEE, YOUT AGE, latter with variant
lines); and of three ALS (one to Oshima, one to
Frederick Langbridge, one to "Dear Sir" (location
of originals unknown).

Bibliography

Parrish, Stephen. "A New Solomon and Sheba Poem." YEATS ANNUAL 6 (1988): 211-213. Published text of poem beginning "Am I a fool or a wise man" (AM I FO).

PARTIAL LIST OF MANUSCRIPTS IN THE COLLECTION OF SENATOR MICHAEL B. YEATS. Compiled June 1978 and July 1981, by Curtis Bradford, Mary Fitzgerald, Richard Finneran and others.
    Though many of these manuscripts are now at NLI, with copies available at SUNY SB, this mimeographed (and often photocopied) list is the basis for the NLI 30,000 series and of some descriptions in this CENSUS. Copies of the list can be found at NLI, SUNY SB, and other research libraries.

Scholes, Robert Edward. THE CORNELL JOYCE COLLECTION: A CATALOGUE. Ithaca: Cornell Universtiy Press, 1961.

Schuchard, Ronald W. "The Lady Gregory-Yeats Collection at Emory University." YEATS ANNUAL 3 (1985): 153-166.
    Includes texts of the unpublished poems "The loud years come (THOU LOUD YE) and SONG HEFF BL.

_____. "Yeats's 'On a Child's Death': A Critical Note." YEATS ANNUAL 3 (1985): 190-192.
    Includes copy and discussion of this previously unpublished poem (ON CHIL DE).

Schulz, H.C. "English Literary Manuscripts in the Huntington Library." HUNTINGTON LIBRARY QUARTERLY, 31:3 (May 1968): 251-302.

Simmonds, Harvey. "John Quinn: An Exhibition to Mark the Gift of the John Quinn Memorial Collection." BULLETIN OF THE NEW YORK PUBLIC LIBRARY, 72:9 (Nov 1968): 569-583.

Sligo County Museum and Art Gallery: YEATS EXHIBITION. Mitsukoshi Department Store, Tokyo. Oct 1979.

Van de Kamp, Peter G.W. "Some Notes on the Literary Estate of Pamela Hinkson." YEATS ANNUAL 4 (1986): 181-186.

Wade, Allen. A BIBLIOGRAPHY OF THE WRITINGS OF W.B. YEATS, 3RD EDITION. London: Hart Davis, 1968.

_____. THE LETTERS OF W.B. YEATS. New York: Macmillan, 1955.
    Has copies of a few previously unpublished poems, including DOUB MOON MO and FLOW HAS BLOS.

Wickenheiser, Robert J. "The Robert H. Taylor Collection."
   THE PRINCETON UNIVERSITY LIBRARY CHRONICLE, 33 (Winter-
   Spring 1977): 211, 221.

Yeats Society of Japan. CATALOGUE OF THE CENTENARY
   EXHIBITION OF THE BIRTH OF WILLIAM BUTLER YEATS,
   19 MAY-21 MAY 1966. Tokyo: Waseda University, 1966.

INDEXES

Libraries and Other Owners

Alphabetical Index

Amherst College Library	385
Archivae Provincia Hibernia	385
Belfast City Libraries	385
Berlind, Bruce	385
Bibliotheque de l'Arsenal	386
Bibliotheque Literaire Jacques Doucet	386
Birmingham Reference Library	386
Bodleian Library	386
Boston College	387
Boston Public Library	387
Boston University	387
Brandeis University Library	387
British Library	388
Brown University	388
Bucknell University	389
Cambridge University Library	389
Case Western Reserve University Library	389
The Catholic University of America	389
Churchill College	389
Clark University	390
Colby College Library	390
College of the Holy Cross	390
Columbia University	391
Connecticut College	391
Cornell University	391
Crawford, William	391
Dalhousie University Library	392
Dorset County Museum	392
Dublin City Libraries	392
Emory University	392
Eton School Library	393
Finneran, Richard	394
Fiskin, Jeffrey	394
Fitzwilliam Museum	394
Glasgow University Library	430
Gould, Warwick	394

Hamilton College Library	395
Harper, George	395
Harvard University	395
Higginson Family Museum	396
The Historical Society of Pennsylvania	396
The Huntington Library	397
India Office Library and Records	397
Indiana University	397
John Rylands University Library	398
Kain, Richard M.	398
Kenyon College Library	399
King's College Library	399
The King's School Library	399
Library of Congress	399
Londraville, Richard	400
Martin, Walter	400
McGill University	400
McMaster University	400
Meisei University Library	401
Mills College Library	401
National Library of Ireland	402
National Library of Scotland	411
New York Public Library	411
New York University	415
Newberry Library	415
Northwestern University Library	415
Occidental College Library	416
Ohio State University	416
Pennsylvania State University Library	416
Pierpont Morgan Library	416
Plunkett Foundation for Cooperative Studies	417
Princeton University Library	417
Providence Public Library	418
Queen's University (Canada)	418
Regent's College	418
Rosenbach Museum and Library	419
The Royal Literary Fund	419
Royal Society of Literature	419
Scripps College	419
Shakespeare Birthplace Trust	419
Sligo County Library	420
Smith, Simon Nowell	420
Somerville College Library	420
Southern Illinois University	421
Sparrow, John	422
Stanford University	422
State Library of New South Wales	423
State Library of Victoria	423
State University of New York at Albany	423
State University of New York at Buffalo	424

Alphabetical Index 469

State University of New York at Stony Brook	424
Svenska Akademiens Nobelbibliotek	425
Syracuse University	425
Tate Gallery Archive	425
Theosophical Society Archives	425
Trent University	425
Trinity College Dublin	426
Trinity College Library (Cambridge, England)	426
Tulane University	427
University College Dublin	427
University of Aberdeen	427
University of Arizona Library	427
University of British Columbia	427
University of California Berkeley	428
University of California Los Angeles	428
University of California San Diego	428
University of Chicago	429
University of Delaware Library	429
University of Glasgow Library	430
University of Illinois at Urbana	430
University of Kansas	430
University of Leeds	431
University of Liverpool	432
University of London Library	432
University of Louisville	432
University of Massachusetts Amherst	433
University of Notre Dame	433
University of Reading Library	433
University of Texas at Austin	434
University of Toronto	437
University of Tulsa	438
University of Vermont	438
University of Victoria	438
University of Virginia	439
Wake Forest University Library	439
Washington State University	439
Washington University Libraries (St. Louis)	440
Wellcome Institute for History of Medicine	440
Wellesley College Library	440
Wertheim, Stanley	441
Wesleyan University	441
West Sussex Record Office	441
Westfield College	441
Yale University	442
Yeats Tower	443
Yeats, Anne	443
Yeats, Senator Michael	445

Libraries and Other Owners

Geographical Index

Australia
- Melbourne, Victoria — State Library of Victoria — 423
- Sydney, N.S.W. — State Library of New South Wales — 423

Canada
- Halifax, Nova Scotia — Dalhousie University — 392
- Hamilton, Ontario — McMaster University — 400
- Kingston, Ontario — Queen's University — 418
- Montreal, Quebec — McGill University — 400
- Peterborough, Ontario — Trent University — 425
- Scarborough, Ontario — Higginson Family Museum — 396
- Toronto, Ontario — University of Toronto — 437
- Vancouver, B.C. — University of British Columbia — 427
- Victoria, B.C. — University of Victoria — 438

France
- Paris — Bibliotheque Literaire Jacques Doucet — 386
- Bibliotheque de l'Arsenal — 386

Great Britain
  England
  - Birmingham — Birmingham Reference Library — 386
  - Cambridge — Cambridge University Library — 389
    - Churchill College — 389
    - Fitzwilliam Museum — 394
    - King's College Library — 399
    - Trinity College Library — 426
  - Canterbury — The King's School Library — 399
  - Chichester — West Sussex Record Office — 441
  - Dorchester — Dorset County Museum — 392
  - Egham, Surrey — Gould, Warwick — 394
  - Hampstead — Westfield College — 441
  - Leeds — University of Leeds — 431
  - Liverpool — University of Liverpool — 432

London	British Library	388
	India Office Library and Records	397
	Regent's College	418
	Royal Society of Literature	419
	Tate Gallery Archive	425
	The Royal Literary Fund	419
	University of London Library	432
	Wellcome Institute for the History of Medicine	440
Manchester	John Rylands University	398
Oxford	Bodleian Library	386
	Plunkett Foundation for Cooperative Studies	417
	Smith, Simon Nowell	420
	Somerville College Library	420
	Sparrow, John	422
Reading	University of Reading	433
Stratford-upon-Avon	Shakespeare Birthplace Trust	419
Windsor, Berkshire	Eton School Library	393

Northern Ireland
| Belfast | Belfast City Libraries | 385 |

Scotland
Aberdeen	University of Aberdeen	427
Edinburgh	National Library of Scotland	411
Glasgow	University of Glasgow	430

India
| Madras | Theosophical Society Archives | 425 |

Ireland
Ballylee	Yeats Tower	443
Dalkey, Co. Dublin	Yeats, Anne	443
	Yeats, Senator Michael	445
Dublin	Archivae Provincia Hibernia	385
	Dublin City Libraries	392
	National Library of Ireland	402
	Trinity College Dublin	426
	University College Dublin	427
Sligo	Sligo County Library	420

Japan
| Tokyo | Meisei University Library | 401 |

Sweden
| Stockholm | Svenska Akademiens Nobelbibliotek | 425 |

Geographical Index

United States of America
Arizona
  Tucson   University of Arizona   427
California
  Berkeley   University of CA Berkeley   428
  Claremont   Scripps College   419
  La Jolla   University of CA San Diego 428
  Los Angeles   Fiskin, Jeffrey   394
                             Occidental College Library 416
                             University of CA Los Angeles 428
  Oakland   Mills College Library   401
  Palo Alto   Martin, Walter   400
  San Marino   The Huntington Library   397
  Stanford   Stanford University   422
Connecticut
  Middletown   Wesleyan University   441
  New Haven   Yale University   442
  New London   Connecticut College   391
District of Columbia
                             Library of Congress   399
                             The Catholic University
                               of America   389
Delaware
  Newark   University of Delaware   429
Florida
  Tallahassee   Harper, George   395
Georgia
  Atlanta   Emory University   392
Illinois
  Carbondale   Southern Illinois University 421
  Chicago   Newberry Library   415
                             University of Chicago   429
  Evanston   Northwestern University   415
  Urbana   University of Illinois   430
Indiana
  Bloomington   Indiana University   397
  Notre Dame   University of Notre Dame   433
Kansas
  Lawrence   University of Kansas   430
Kentucky
  Louisville   Kain, Richard M.   398
                             University of Louisville   432
Louisiana
  New Orleans   Tulane University   427
Massachusetts
  Amherst   Amherst College Library   385
                             University of MA Amherst   433
  Boston   Boston Public Library   387
                             Boston University   387
  Cambridge   Harvard University   395

Chestnut Hill	Boston College	387
Waltham	Brandeis University Library	387
Wellesley	Wellesley College Library	440
Worcester	College of the Holy Cross	390
	Clark University	390
Maine		
Waterville	Colby College Library	390
Missouri		
St. Louis	Washington University	440
North Carolina		
Winston-Salem	Wake Forest University	439
New Jersey		
Princeton	Princeton University Library	417
New York		
Albany	State University of New York	
	(SUNY) at Albany	423
Buffalo	SUNY at Buffalo	424
Clinton	Hamilton College Library	395
Hamilton	Berlind, Bruce	385
Ithaca	Cornell University	391
New York	Columbia University	391
	Crawford, William	391
	New York Public Library	411
	New York University	415
	Pierpont Morgan Library	416
	Wertheim, Stanley	441
Potsdam	Londraville, Richard	400
Stony Brook	SUNY at Stony Brook	424
Syracuse	Syracuse University	425
Ohio		
Cleveland	Case Western Reserve	
	University Library	389
Columbus	Ohio State University	416
Gambier	Kenyon College Library	399
Oklahoma		
Tulsa	University of Tulsa	438
Pennsylvania		
Lewisburg	Bucknell University	389
Philadelphia	Rosenbach Museum and Library	419
	The Historical Society	
	of Pennsylvania	396
University Park	Pennsylvania State	
	University Library	416
Rhode Island		
Providence	Brown University	388
	Providence Public Library	418
Tennessee		
Knoxville	Finneran, Richard	394
Texas		
Austin	University of Texas	434

Geographical Index

Virginia
  Charlottesville   University of Virginia   439
Vermont
  Burlington   University of Vermont   438
Washington
  Pullman   Washington State University 439
  Washington, D.C.   See District of Columbia.

Index of Manuscripts

Manuscripts

This index lists manuscripts by title, and individuals (recipients of letters and inscriptions; authors of other books) by name; it includes as well the QUICK title, the type (or genre), and the page number of the initial entry.

A.E. See RUSS GEOR.		Letter	159
Abbey Subsidy, The	ABBE SUBS	Speech	371
Abbey Theatre See also THEA MATE.		Miscellany	202
Abbey Theatre Board	ABBE THEA BO	Letter	99
Aberdeen Lecture	ABER LECT	Speech	371
Aberdein, Jeanie Watson	ABER JEAN WA	Letter	99
Academy Editor	ACAD EDIT	Letter	99
Accursed who brings to light of day	ACCU WHO BR	Poem	243
Acre of Grass, An	ACRE GRAS	Poem	243
Adam's Curse	ADAM CURS	Poem	243
After Long Silence	AFTE LONG SI	Poem	243
Against Unworthy Praise	AGAI UNWO PR	Poem	244
Against Witchcraft	AGAI WITC	Poem	244
Ahern, Katharine	AHER KATH	Inscription	73
Ainu, The	AINU	Prose	357
Aldington, Brigit	ALDI BRIG	Letter	99
Aldington, Richard	ALDI RICH	Letter	99
All day you flitted before me	ALL DAY YO	Poem, Unpu.	335
All night there have been ghosts about us	ALL NIGH TH	Poem, Unpu.	335
All our Europe that for so long	ALL OUR EU	Poem, Unpu.	335
All Souls' Night	ALL SOUL NI	Poem	244
All the Popular Arts have been degraded	ALL THIN CA	Poem	244
All Things can Tempt Me	ALL POPU AR	Speech	371
Allen, Charles Dexter	ALLE CHAR DE	Inscription	73
Allgood, Sara (Sally)	ALLG SARA	Letter	99
Allingham, Helen	ALLI HELE	Letter	100
Allingham, William: SIXTEEN POEMS	ALLI SIXT 05	Other	205
Alma-Tadema, Miss Laurence	ALMA TADE MI	Letter	100

Alternative Song for the Severed Head in 'The King of the Great Clock Tower'	ALTE SONG SE	Poem		244
Althea Gyles	ALTH GYLE	Prose		357
Am I a fool or a wise man	AM I FO	Poem, Unpu.		335
American Tour Lectures	AMER TOUR LE	Speech		371
Among School Children	AMON SCHO CH	Poem		244
Among the sighing foam and roses hang	AMON SIGH FO	Poem, Unpu.		336
An[d] I will call	AND I WI	Poem, Unpu.		336
Anashuya and Vijaya	ANAS VIJA	Poem		245
Ancestral Houses	ANCE HOUS	Poem		245
And ceased I saw the sea lines citron glare	AND CEAS I	Poem, Unpu.		336
And clamour whether of voice or hoof	AND CLAM WH	Poem, Unpu.		336
And thy daughter will warm	AND THY DA	Poem, Unpu.		336
And wherever around...	AND WHER AR	Poem, Unpu.		336
Anglo Ireland See UNPU ANGL IR.		Prose		366
Another Song of a Fool	ANOT SONG FO	Poem		245
Apparitions, The	APPA	Poem		245
Appointment, An	APPO	Poem		246
Archer, William	ARCH WILL	Letter		100
Are You Content?	ARE YOU CO	Poem		246
Armsby-Wilson, R.	ARMS WILS R.	Letter		100
Arndt, Mrs.	ARND MRS.	Letter		100
Arnold, Matthew: POEMS	ARNO POEM OO	Other		205
Arrow, The	ARRO	Poem		246
Art Without Imitation	ART IMIT	Poem, Unpu.		336
Art and Ideas	ART IDEA	Prose		357
Arthur, Chester	ARTH CHES	Letter		100
As know all workers for the poor	AS KNOW AL	Poem, Unpu.		336
Asquith, Lady	ASQU LADY	Letter		100
At Algeciras--A Meditation upon Death	AT ALGE ME	Poem		246
At Galway Races	AT GALW RA	Poem		246
At the Abbey Theatre	AT ABBE TH	Poem		247
At the Grey Round of the Hill	AT GREY RO	Poem		247
At the Hawk's Well	AT HAWK WE	Play		223
Augustan Books of English Poetry: W.B. Yeats, The	AUGU BOOK 27	Book		3
Autobiographies: Reveries over Childhood and Youth and the Trembling of the Veil	AUTO REVE 26	Book		3
Autobiographies: Reveries over Childhood and Youth and the Trembling of the Veil	AUTO REVE 27	Book		4
Awake in a world of ecstasy	AWAK WORL EC	Poem, Unpu.		337

Index

Away	AWAY	Prose	357
Bagnold, Enid	BAGN ENID	Letter	100
Baile and Aillinn	BAIL AILL	Poem	247
Bailey, William F.	BAIL WILL F.	Letter	101
Baker, Gladys	BAKE GLAD	Inscription	73
Ball, Mrs. [Frances]	BALL MRS. FR	Letter	101
Ballad of Earl Paul, The	BALL EARL PA	Poem	247
Ballad of Father Gilligan, The	BALL FATH GI	Poem	247
Ballad of Father O'Hart, The	BALL FATH O'	Poem	247
Ballad of Moll Magee, The	BALL MOLL MA	Poem	247
Ballad of the Foxhunter, The	BALL FOXH	Poem	248
Balloon of the Mind, The	BALL MIND	Poem	248
Barnes, George	BARN GEOR	Letter	101
Barren valley there I found encompassed, A	BARR VALL TH	Poem, Unpu.	337
Barry, William	BARR WILL	Letter	101
Bates, Katharine Lee	BATE KATH LE	Letter	101
Bates, Katherine	BATE KATH	Inscription	73
Battle, Mary See FOLK MYTH LE.		Miscellany	189
Bax, Clifford	BAX CLIF	Letter	101
Beardsley, Mabel	BEAR MABE	Letter	101
Beardsley, Mrs.	BEAR MRS.	Letter	101
Beauclerk, Miss	BEAU MISS HE	Letter	101
Beautiful Lofty Things	BEAU LOFT TH	Poem	248
Because the moon had reached her fifteenth night	BECA MOON HA	Poem, Unpu.	337
Beech, Stella Campbell	BEEC STEL CA	Letter	102
Beecham, Thomas	BEEC THOM	Inscription	73
Before the World Was Made	BEFO WORL WA	Poem	248
Beggar to Beggar Cried	BEGG BEGG CR	Poem	248
Behold the man- behold his brow of care	BEHO MAN BE	Poem, Unpu.	337
Being in a half	BEIN HALF	Poem, Unpu.	337
Being was not at these times	BEIN WAS NO	Poem, Unpu.	337
Belfast Broadcast	BELF BROA	Speech	373
Bell, C.C.	BELL C.C.	Letter	102
Bell, Edward Price	BELL EDWA PR	Letter	102
Belmont, Eleanor Robson	BELM ELEA RO	Letter	102
Beltaine	BELT 00	Book	4
Bender, Albert	BEND ALBE	Inscription	74
Bender, Albert	BEND ALBE	Letter	102
Benson, A.C.	BENS A.C.	Letter	102
Beresford, J. Cooke (Tommy the Song)	BERE J.C.	Inscription	74
Bertram, Mr.	BERT MR.	Letter	102
Best, R.I.	BEST R.I.	Letter	102
Biggar, Francis J.	BIGG FRAN J.	Letter	102
Billy Boy	BILL BOY	Poem, Unpu.	337
Biographical Fragment, A	BIOG FRAG	Prose	357
Birmingham Lecture	BIRM LECT	Speech	373

Birrell, Augustine	BIRR AUGU	Letter	102
Bishop and the Monk, The See UNPU BISH MO.		Play	238
Bishop Berkeley	BISH BERK 31	Book	4
Black Tower, The	BLAC TOWE	Poem	248
Blacker, Dr.	BLAC DR.	Letter	103
Blackwood & Sons, William	BLAC SONS WI	Letter	103
Blair, Mr.	BLAI MR.	Letter	103
Blake Lecture	BLAK LECT	Speech	373
Blake, Warren Barton	BLAK WARR BA	Letter	103
Blake, William See WORK WILL 93.		Book	71
Bland, Henry Mead	BLAN HENR ME	Letter	103
Blessed, The	BLES	Poem	249
Blood and the Moon	BLOO MOON	Poem	249
Blood Bond, The	BLOO BOND	Poem	249
Blunden, Edmund and Helen	BLUN EDMU HE	Inscription	74
Blunden, Edmund C.	BLUN EDMU C.	Letter	103
Blunden, Edmund: SONNETS AND SONGS	BLUN SONN 75	Other	205
Blunt, Wilfrid	BLUN WILF	Letter	103
Blythe, Ernest	BLYT ERNE	Letter	103
Bodkin, Thomas	BODK THOM	Letter	104
Boggs, Tom	BOGG TOM	Inscription	74
Book of Irish Verse, A	BOOK IRIS 00	Book	5
Book of Irish Verse, A	BOOK IRIS 95	Book	5
Book of the Rhymers' Club, The	BOOK RHYM 92	Book	5
Booth, Miss Gore	BOOT MISS GO	Letter	104
Bottomley, Gordon	BOTT GORD	Letter	104
Boughton, Rutland	BOUG RUTL	Letter	104
Bounty of Sweden, The	BOUN SWED 25	Book	6
Bourgeois, M.	BOUR M.	Letter	104
Boyd, Ernest	BOYD ERNE	Inscription	74
Boyd, Ernest	BOYD ERNE	Letter	104
Boylan, Josephine	BOYL JOSE	Letter	104
Bradley, Katherine	BRAD KATH	Letter	104
Bravest from the gods but ask	BRAV FROM GO	Poem	249
Brett [George]	BRET GEOR	Letter	104
Bridges, Mrs. Robert	BRID MRS. RO	Letter	105
Bridges, Robert	BRID ROBE	Letter	105
Bright, Mary Chavelita	BRIG MARY CH	Letter	105
Brisbane, Arthur	BRIS ARTH	Letter	105
Brittain, Vera Mary	BRIT VERA MA	Letter	105
Broadsides	BROA 35	Book	6
Broadsides	BROA 37	Book	6
Broken Dreams	BROK DREA	Poem	249
Bronze Head, A	BRON HEAD	Poem	250
Brooke, Rupert	BROO RUPE	Letter	105
Brophy, John	BROP JOHN	Letter	105
Brown Penny	BROW PENN	Poem	250
Brown, Tom	BROW TOM	Letter	105

Index 481

Browne	BROW	Letter	105
Browne, Maurice	BROW MAUR	Inscription	74
Bryers, Mr. See SEAL BRYE WA.		Letter	161
Bullen, A.H.	BULL A.H.	Letter	106
Bullen, A.H.	BULL A.H.	Inscription	74
Burlington House Lectures	BURL HOUS LE	Speech	373
But an art	BUT ART	Poem, Unpu.	337
By the Roadside	BY ROAD	Prose	358
By the emperor's command	BY EMPE CO	Poem, Unpu.	338
Bynner, Witter	BYNN WITT	Letter	106
Byzantium	BYZA	Poem	250
Calvary	CALV	Play	223
Campbell, Mrs. B.	CAMP MRS. B.	Letter	106
Campbell, Mrs. Joseph	CAMP MRS. JO	Letter	106
Campbell, Mrs. Patrick	CAMP MRS. PA	Letter	107
Cap and Bells, The	CAP BELL	Poem	250
Carleton, William: STORIES FROM CARLETON	CARL STOR 89	Other	206
Carmichael, Miss	CARM MISS	Inscription	74
Carter, Mr.	CART MR.	Letter	107
Carton	CART	Letter	107
Cat and the Moon and Certain Poems	CAT MOON 24	Book	7
Cat and the Moon, The	CAT MOON	Play	224
Cat and the Moon, The	CAT MOON	Poem	251
Cathleen Ni Houlihan	CATH HOUL	Play	224
Cathleen ni Hoolihan	CATH HOOL 02	Book	7
Celtic Twilight, The	CELT TWIL 93	Book	8
Celtic Twilight, The	CELT TWIL 94	Book	9
Celtic Twilight, The	CELT TWIL 02	Book	9
Celtic Twilight, The	CELT TWIL 05	Book	9
Celtic Twilight, The	CELT TWIL 12	Book	9
Censorship and St. Thomas Aquinas	CENS ST.T AQ	Prose	358
Certain Artists Bring Her Dolls and Drawings	CERT ARTI BR	Poem	251
Chakravarty, Amiya	CHAK AMIY	Letter	107
Chambermaid's First Song, The	CHAM FIRS SO	Poem	251
Chambermaid's Second Song, The	CHAM SECO SO	Poem	251
Chambers, Maria C.	CHAM MARI C.	Letter	107
Chatto & Windus Ltd.	CHAT WIND LT	Letter	107
Chesson, Nora	CHES NORA	Letter	107
Chesson, Wilfrid H.	CHES WILF H.	Letter	107
Chew, Prof. Samuel C.	CHEW PROF SA	Letter	107
Child's Play	CHIL PLAY	Poem, Unpu.	338
Childers, Mary Alden	CHIL MARY AL	Letter	107
Choice, The	CHOI	Poem	251
Chosen	CHOS	Poem	251
Church and State	CHUR STAT	Poem	251
Church, Richard	CHUR RICH	Letter	107

Circus Animal's Desertion, The	CIRC ANIM DE	Poem	251
Clarke, Austin	CLAR AUST	Letter	108
Clemens, Cyril	CLEM CYRI	Letter	108
Clifton, [Harry]	CLIF HARR	Letter	108
Clinton-Baddeley, V.C.	CLIN BADD V.	Letter	108
Cloak, the Boat, and the Shoes	CLOA BOAT SH	Poem	251
Clodd, Edward	CLOD EDWA	Letter	108
Coat, A	COAT	Poem	252
Coates, Florence Earle	COAT FLOR EA	Inscription	74
Cockerell, Sydney	COCK SYDN	Letter	108
Cockerell, Sydney	COCK SYDN	Inscription	75
Coffey, [George]	COFF GEOR	Letter	108
Cold Heaven, The	COLD HEAV	Poem	252
Collar-Bone of a Hare, The	COLL BONE HA	Poem	252
Collected Poems, The	COLL POEM 33	Book	9
Collected Works in Verse and Prose 8 vols	COLL WORK 08	Book	10
Collinson, Margaret	COLL MARG	Inscription	75
Colonel Martin	COLO MART	Poem	252
Colonus' Praise	COLO PRAI	Poem	252
Colton, Mr.	COLT MR.	Letter	108
Colum, Padraic	COLU PADR	Letter	108
Colum, Padraic	COLU PADR	Inscription	75
Colville, Warner	COLV WARN	Letter	108
Come Gather Round me, Parnellites	COME GATH RO	Poem	252
Come hither hither hither water folk	COME HITH HI	Poem, Unpu.	338
Come ride and ride to the garden	COME RIDE RI	Poem	253
Coming of Wisdom with Time, The	COMI WISD TI	Poem	253
Compulsory Education See UNPU COMP ED.		Speech	379
Compulsory Gaelic	COMP GAEL	Prose	358
Conant, [James]	CONA JAME	Letter	108
Concerning Lane	CONC LANE	Poem, Unpu.	338
Congratulations from the RSL to the RDS	CONG RSL RD	Speech	374
Conjunctions	CONJ	Poem	253
Connell, Norreys	CONN NORR	Letter	109
Consolation	CONS	Poem	253
Contemporary Lyric Poets	CONT LYRI PO	Speech	374
Coole Edition See UNPU MACM ED.		Book	59
Coole Park, 1929	COOL PARK 19	Poem	253
Coole Park and Ballylee, 1931	COOL PARK BA	Poem	254
Coomaraswamy, Amanda Kentish	COOM AMAN KE	Letter	109
Cooper, Mrs. [Edith]	COOP MRS. ED	Letter	109
Corri, Madame Ghita	CORR MADA GH	Letter	109
Cosgrave, William T.	COSG WILL T.	Letter	109
Costello the Proud	COST PROU	Prose	358
Cotton, James	COTT JAME	Letter	109

Index

Coulter, John	COUL JOHN	Letter	109
Countess Cathleen in Paradise	COUN CATH PA	Poem	254
Countess Cathleen, The	COUN CATH	Play	225
Countess Cathleen, The	COUN CATH 99	Book	10
Countess Cathleen, The	COUN CATH 12	Book	10
Countess Cathleen, The	COUN CATH 29	Book	11
Countess Kathleen, The	COUN KATH 92	Book	11
Country of the Young See UNPU COUN YO.		Play	238
Cousins, James H.	COUS JAME H.	Letter	109
Cradle Song, A	CRAD SONG	Poem	254
Craig, Edward Gordon	CRAI EDWA GO	Letter	110
Crangle, Mrs. Roland	CRAN MRS. RO	Letter	110
Crangle, Roland	CRAN ROLA	Letter	110
Crazed Girl, A	CRAZ GIRL	Poem	254
Crazed Moon, The	CRAZ MOON	Poem	254
Crazy Jane and Jack the Journeyman	CRAZ JANE JA	Poem	254
Crazy Jane and the Bishop	CRAZ JANE BI	Poem	255
Crazy Jane and the King	CRAZ JANE KI	Poem, Unpu.	338
Crazy Jane Grown Old Looks at the Dancers	CRAZ JANE GR	Poem	255
Crazy Jane on God	CRAZ JANE GO	Poem	255
Crazy Jane on the Day of Judgement	CRAZ JANE DA	Poem	255
Crazy Jane on the Mountain	CRAZ JANE MO	Poem	256
Crazy Jane Reproved	CRAZ JANE RE	Poem	256
Crazy Jane Talks With the Bishop	CRAZ JANE TA	Poem	256
Cronan, Mary	CRON MARY	Letter	110
Crone, Dr. J.S.	CRON DR. J.	Letter	110
Crook, William Montgomery	CROO WILL MO	Letter	110
Crossways	CROS	Poem	256
Cuchulain Comforted	CUCH COMF	Poem	256
Cuchulain's Fight with the Sea	CUCH FIGH SE	Poem	256
Cummings, Hubertis M.	CUMM HUBE M.	Letter	110
Curran, Constantine P.	CURR CONS P.	Letter	110
Curse of Cromwell, The	CURS CROM	Poem	257
Curtis, Mr.	CURT MR.	Letter	110
Cutting of an Agate, The	CUTT AGAT 12	Book	12
Cutting of an Agate, The	CUTT AGAT 19	Book	13
Cyprian See UNPU CYPR.		Play	238
Danaan Quicken Tree, The	DANA QUIC TR	Poem	257
Dancer at Cruachan and Cro-Patrick	DANC CRUA CR	Poem	257
Darragh, Florence Leticia	DARR FLOR LE	Letter	110
Das, Mr.	DAS MR.	Letter	110
Davidson, Lilian	DAVI LILI	Inscription	75
Davitt, Michael	DAVI MICH	Letter	111
Davray, Henry	DAVR HENR	Letter	111

Dawn, The	DAWN	Poem	257
Dawn-Song, A	DAWN SONG	Poem	258
Day, F. H.	DAY F.H.	Letter	111
De Blaghd, Earndn See BLYT ERNE.		Letter	103
De Valera, Eamon	DE VALE EA	Letter	111
Death	DEAT	Poem	258
Death of Cuchulain, The	DEAT CUCH	Play	226
Death of Lady Gregory See UNPU DEAT LA.		Prose	366
Death of Hare, The	DEAT HARE	Poem	258
Death of Synge and Other Passages	DEAT SYNG 28	Book	13
Dedication	DEDI	Poem	258
Dedication to a Book of Stories selected from the Irish Novelists	DEDI BOOK ST	Poem	258
Deep-Sworn Vow, A	DEEP SWOR VO	Poem	258
Deer he followed alone, The	DEER HE FO	Poem, Unpu.	339
Defence of the Abbey Theatre, A	DEFE ABBE TH	Speech	374
Deirdre	DEIR 07	Book	13
Deirdre	DEIR 11	Book	14
Deirdre	DEIR	Play	226
Dell, The	DELL	Poem, Unpu.	339
Delphic Oracle upon Plotinus, The	DELP ORAC PL	Poem	258
DeLury, Alfred	DELU ALFR	Letter	111
Demon and Beast	DEMO BEAS	Poem	259
Dew comes dropping, The	DEW COME DR	Poem, Unpu.	339
Dial	DIAL	Letter	111
Dialogue of Self and Soul, A	DIAL SELF SO	Poem	259
Diaries and Journals	DIAR JOUR	Miscellany	181
Diarmuid and Grania	DIAR GRAN	Play	228
Dickinson, Mabel	DICK MABE	Letter	112
Dickinson, Mabel	DICK MABE	Inscription	75
Digges, Dudley	DIGG DUDL	Letter	112
Dillon, John and Miles	DILL JOHN MI	Letter	112
Dircks, W.H.	DIRC W.H.	Letter	112
Discoveries: A Volume of Essays	DISC VOLU 07	Book	14
Divorce Speech	DIVO SPEE	Speech	374
Dixon, W. Macneile	DIXO W. MA	Letter	112
Dobell, Bertram	DOBE BERT	Letter	112
Documents	DOCU	Miscellany	187
Dodd, Loring Holmes	DODD LORI HO	Inscription	75
Dolan, M.J.	DOLA M.J.	Letter	112
Dolls, The	DOLL	Poem	259
Doone, Rupert	DOON RUPE	Letter	112
Double moon or more ago, A	DOUB MOON MO	Poem, Unpu.	339
Double Vision of Michael Robartes, The	DOUB VISI MI	Poem	259
Dowden, Edward	DOWD EDWA	Letter	112

Index

Dowden, Edward: A WOMAN'S RELIQUARY	DOWD WOMA 13	Other	206
Down by the Salley Gardens	DOWN SALL GA	Poem	260
Doyle, Miss C.M.	DOYL MISS C.	Letter	112
Dramatis Personae	DRAM PERS 35	Book	15
Dramatis Personae	DRAM PERS 36	Book	15
Dream of Death, A	DREA DEAT	Poem	260
Dreaming of the Bones, The	DREA BONE	Play	228
Dreams and Ghosts	DREA GHOS	Speech	374
Drinking Song, A	DRIN SONG	Poem	260
Drinkwater, John	DRIN JOHN	Inscription	75
Drinkwater, John	DRIN JOHN	Letter	112
Drunken Man's Praise of Sobriety, A	DRUN MAN' PR	Poem	260
Dryhurst, Norah	DRYH NORA	Letter	113
Dublin Fanaticism	DUBL FANA	Prose	358
Dublin Magazine Editor	DUBL MAGA ED	Letter	113
Ducat, Eva	DUCA EVA	Inscription	75
Duckworth, Gerald	DUCK GERA	Letter	113
Duff, Arthur	DUFF ARTH	Letter	113
Duffy, Charles Gavan	DUFF CHAR GA	Letter	113
Duggan, Elizabeth	DUGG ELIZ	Inscription	75
Dulac, Edmund	DULA EDMU	Inscription	76
Dulac, Edmund	DULA EDMU	Letter	113
Dulac, Helen	DULA HELE	Inscription	76
Dulac, Helen	DULA HELE	Letter	113
Dulanty	DULA	Letter	113
Duncan, Ellen Douglas	DUNC ELLE DO	Letter	114
Duncan, James	DUNC JAME	Letter	114
Dunn, Mr.	DUNN MR.	Letter	114
Dunsany, Lady	DUNS LADY	Letter	114
Dunsany, Lord	DUNS LORD	Letter	114
Dunsany, Lord Edward: SELECTIONS FROM THE WRITINGS OF LORD DUNSANY	DUNS SELE 12	Other	206
Dust hath closed Helen's eye	DUST HATH CL	Prose	358
Early Poems and Stories (London)	EARL POEM 25	Book	15
Early Poems and Stories (New York)	EARL POEM 25	Book	16
Easter 1916	EAST 16	Book	16
Easter 1916	EAST 1916	Poem	260
Eaton, Nolan	EATO NOLA	Inscription	76
Editor	EDIT	Letter	115
Eglinton, John: LITERARY IDEALS IN IRELAND	EGLI LITE 99	Other	206
Eglinton, John: SOME ESSAYS AND PASSAGES	EGLI SOME 05	Other	207
See also SOME ESSA 05.		Book	52
Ego Dominus Tuus	EGO DOMI TU	Poem	261

Eight Poems	EIGH	POEM 16	Book	16
Ellis, Edwin J.	ELLI	EDWI J.	Inscription	76
Ellis, Edwin J.	ELLI	EDWI J.	Letter	115
Ellis, Mrs.	ELLI	MRS.	Letter	115
Ellis, Mrs.	ELLI	MRS.	Inscription	76
Ellis, P.D.	ELLI	P.D.	Letter	115
Emery, Florence Farr	EMER	FLOR FA	Letter	115
Emery, Florence Farr	EMER	FLOR FA	Inscription	76
Emmet the Apostle of Irish Liberty	EMME	APOS IR	Speech	374
Empty Cup, The	EMPT	CUP	Poem	261
End of Day, The	END	DAY	Poem	261
Entrance of Deirdre, The	ENTR	DEIR	Poem	262
Ephemera	EPHE		Poem	262
Epic of the Forest See UNPU EPIC FORE.			Play	239
Erdman, Johann Eduard: A HISTORY OF PHILOSOPHY	ERDM	HIST 24	Other	207
Ervine, St. John	ERVI	ST. JO	Letter	116
Essays	ESSA	24	Book	17
Essays by W.B. Yeats, 1931 to 1936	ESSA	W.B. 37	Book	17
Estrangement	ESTR	26	Book	18
Eugenics Society	EUGE	SOCI	Letter	116
Evans, Edward	EVAN	EDWA	Letter	116
Everlasting Voices, The	EVER	VOIC	Poem	262
Faery Song, A	FAER	SONG	Poem	262
Fagan, Mr.	FAGA	MR.	Letter	116
Fairy and Folk Tales of the Irish Peasantry	FAIR	FOLK 88	Book	18
Fairy Doctor, The	FAIR	DOCT	Poem	262
Fairy Pedant, The	FAIR	PEDA	Poem	262
Fallen Majesty	FALL	MAJE	Poem	262
Falling of the Leaves, The	FALL	LEAV	Poem	263
Fallon, Gabriel	FALL	GABR	Letter	116
Farr, Florence See EMER FARR FA			Letter	115
Farrell, Mr.	FARR	MR.	Letter	116
Fascination of What's Difficult, The	FASC	WHAT DI	Poem	263
Father and Child	FATH	CHIL	Poem	263
Fay, Frank	FAY	FRAN	Letter	117
Fay, Mrs.	FAY	MRS.	Letter	117
Fay, William	FAY	WILL	Inscription	77
Fay, William	FAY	WILL	Letter	117
Fenollosa, Ernest: CERTAIN NOBLE PLAYS OF JAPAN	FENO	CERT 16	Other	207
Fergus and the Druid	FERG	DRUI	Poem	263
Fergusson, Lady	FERG	LADY	Letter	117
Ffrench, Rhona	FFRE	RHON	Inscription	77

Index 487

Fiddler of Dooney, The	FIDD DOON	Poem	263
Field, Michael	FIEL MICH	Letter	117
Fighting the Waves See ONLY JEAL EM.		Play	233
First Confession, A	FIRS CONF	Poem	263
First Love	FIRS LOVE	Poem	263
Fish, The	FISH	Poem	264
Fisher, H.A.L.	FISH H.A.	Letter	118
Fisherman, The	FISH ERMA N	Poem	264
Fitts, [William B.]	FITT WILL B.	Letter	118
Fitzgerald, Miss	FITZ MISS	Letter	118
Flower has blossomed, A	FLOW HAS BL	Poem, Unpu.	339
Flower, Robin: LOVE'S BITTERSWEET: TRANSLATIONS FROM THE IRISH POETS OF THE SIXTEENTH AND SEVENTEENTH CENTURIES	FLOW LOVE 25	Other	207
Foden, Gwyneth	FODE GWYN	Inscription	77
Foden, Gwyneth	FODE GWYN	Letter	118
Folklore, Myth, and Legend	FOLK MYTH LE	Miscellany	188
Folly of Argument, The	FOLL ARGU	Prose	358
Folly of Being Comforted, The	FOLL BEIN CO	Poem	264
For all the stars were diminished	FOR ALL ST	Poem, Unpu.	339
For Anne Gregory	FOR ANNE GR	Poem	264
For clapping hands of all men's love	FOR CLAP HA	Poem, Unpu.	339
Ford, Ford Madox	FORD FORD MA	Letter	118
Ford, Julia	FORD JULI	Letter	118
Forster, E.M.	FORS E.M.	Letter	118
Foster, Jeanne	FOST JEAN	Letter	118
Four Ages of Man, The	FOUR AGES MA	Poem	264
Four Plays for Dancers	FOUR PLAY 21	Book	18
Four Years	FOUR YEAR 21	Book	19
Fragments	FRAG	Poem	264
Francis, Rene	FRAN RENE	Letter	118
Fraser, Dr.	FRAS DR.	Letter	118
Fredman, Miss	FRED MISS	Letter	119
Freemans Journal Editor	FREE JOUR ED	Letter	119
Freund, Frank	FREU FRAN	Letter	119
Friends	FRIE	Poem	265
Friend's Illness, A	FRIE ILLN	Poem	265
Friends of His Youth, The	FRIE YOUT	Poem	265
Friends of my Youth See BURL HOUS LE.		Speech	373
Friends that have it I do wrong, The	FRIE THAT HA	Poem	265
Frohman, Charles	FROH CHAR	Letter	119
From 'Oedipus at Colonus'	FROM OEDI CO	Poem	265

From the 'Antigone'	FROM ANTI	Poem	265
Frost, William H.	FROS WILL H.	Letter	119
Full moody is my love and sad See GIRL SONG JS.		Poem	266
Full Moon in March, A	FULL MOON MA	Play	229
Fully alone will I choose	FULL ALON WI	Poem, Unpu.	340
Garden of Eden	GARD EDEN	Poem, Unpu.	340
Gardner, Fredrick	GARD FRED	Letter	119
Garnett, Edward	GARN EDWA	Inscription	77
Garnett, Edward	GARN EDWA	Letter	119
Garnett, Porter	GARN PORT	Letter	119
Garvey, Maire	GARV MAIR	Letter	119
Garvin, James L.	GARV JAME L.	Letter	119
Gaunt, William	GAUN WILL	Letter	120
Gawsworth, John	GAWS JOHN	Letter	120
Ghost of Roger Casement, The	GHOS ROGE CA	Poem	266
Gibbon, Monk	GIBB MONK	Letter	120
Gibson, Mr.	GIBS MR.	Letter	120
Gibson, Wilfrid	GIBS WILF	Letter	120
Gift of Harun Al-Rashid, The	GIFT HARU AL	Poem	266
Gill, Thomas Patrick	GILL THOM PA	Letter	120
Girl's Song (from JOHN SHER 12)	GIRL SONG JS	Poem	266
Girl's Song (from WIND STAI 33)	GIRL SONG WS	Poem	266
Glove and the Cloak, The	GLOV CLOA	Poem	266
God loves the road of ghost & gleam	GOD LOVE RO	Poem, Unpu.	340
Goethe, Johann W.: GOETHE'S BOYHOOD	GOET GOET 88	Other	208
Gogarty, Oliver St. John	GOGA OLIV ST	Letter	120
Gogarty, Oliver St. John: AN OFFERING OF SWANS	GOGA OFFE 23	Other	208
Gogarty, Oliver St. John: WILD APPLES	GOGA WILD 30	Other	208
Golden Helmet, The	GOLD HELM 08	Book	19
Golden Helmet, The	GOLD HELM	Play	229
Gonne, Iseult	GONN ISEU	Inscription	77
Gonne, Iseult (Stuart)	GONN ISEU	Letter	121
Gonne, Maud See MACB MAUD GO.		Inscription	82
Goodman, Edward	GOOD EDWA	Letter	121
Gorell, Elizabeth	GORE ELIZ	Letter	121
Gorman, Eric	GORM ERIC	Letter	121
Gosse, Edmund	GOSS EDMU	Letter	121
Gosse, Edmund	GOSS EDMU	Inscription	78
Gosse, Lady	GOSS LADY	Letter	122
Gosse, Phillip	GOSS PHIL	Letter	122
Gough, Mrs.	GOUG MRS.	Letter	122
Graham, R.B. Cunningham	GRAH R.B. CU	Letter	122
Gratitude to the Unknown Instructors	GRAT UNKN IN	Poem	267

Index

Graves, Alfred Perceval	GRAV ALFR PE	Letter	122
Great Blasket, The	GREA BLAS	Prose	359
Great Day, The	GREA DAY	Poem	267
Green Helmet and Other Poems, The	GREE HELM 10	Book	20
Green Helmet and Other Poems, The	GREE HELM 11	Book	20
Green Helmet and Other Poems, The	GREE HELM 12	Book	20
Green Helmet, The	GREE HELM	Play	229
Gregg, Fredrick J.	GREG FRED J.	Letter	122
Gregory, Lady	GREG LADY	Letter	122
Gregory, Lady	GREG LADY	Inscription	78
Gregory, Mr.	GREG MR.	Letter	123
Gregory, Mrs. Margaret	GREG MRS. MA	Letter	123
Gregory, Robert	GREG ROBE	Inscription	79
Gregory, Robert	GREG ROBE	Letter	123
Gregory, Lady Augusta: CASE FOR THE RETURN OF SIR HUGH LANE'S PICTURES TO DUBLIN	GREG CASE 26	Other	208
Gregory, Lady Augusta: COOLE	GREG COOL 31	Other	208
Gregory, Lady Augusta: COUNTRY OF THE YOUNG	GREG COUN YO	Other	208
Gregory, Lady Augusta: CUCHULAIN OF MUIRTHEMNE	GREG CUCH 02	Other	209
Gregory, Lady Augusta: GODS AND FIGHTING MEN	GREG GODS 04	Other	209
Gregory, Lady Augusta: IDEALS IN IRELAND	GREG IDEA 01	Other	210
Gregory, Lady Augusta: POETS AND DREAMERS	GREG POET 03	Other	210
Gregory, Lady Augusta: SEVEN SHORT PLAYS	GREG SEVE 09	Other	210
Gregory, Lady Augusta: THE KILTARTAN POETRY BOOK	GREG KILT 18	Other	210
Gregory, Lady Augusta: THE TRAVELLING MAN	GREG TRAV 09	Other	211
Gregory, Lady Augusta: THREE LAST PLAYS	GREG THRE 23	Other	211
Gregory, Lady Augusta: VISIONS & BELIEFS IN THE WEST OF IRELAND	GREG VISI 20	Other	211
Grey Rock, The	GREY ROCK	Poem	267
Grierson, H.J.C.	GRIE H.J.	Letter	123
Griffin, Montagu	GRIF MONT	Inscription	79
Grigsby, Miss	GRIG MISS	Inscription	79
Grigsby, Miss [Emilie]	GRIG MISS EM	Letter	124
Grigson, Geoffrey	GRIG GEOF	Letter	124

Guinan, John	GUIN JOHN	Letter	124
Guiney, Louise Imogen	GUIN LOUI IM	Letter	124
Guthrie, Mr.	GUTH MR.	Letter	124
Gwynn, Denis	GWYN DENI	Letter	124
Gwynn, Stephen	GWYN STEP	Letter	124
Gyres, The	GYRE	Poem	267
Hackett	HACK	Letter	125
Haggard, Rider	HAGG RIDE	Letter	125
Haldane, Richard Burdon	HALD RICH BU	Letter	125
Half asleep as the train came in	HALF ASLE AS	Poem, Unpu.	340
Half in articulo	HALF ARTI	Poem, Unpu.	340
Hall, Agnes	HALL AGNE	Letter	125
Halle, Mrs. Louis	HALL MRS. LO	Letter	125
Hamilton, Miss	HAMI MISS	Letter	125
Hamsa, Shri	HAMS SHRI	Letter	125
Hamsa, Shri Bhagwan: THE HOLY MOUNTAIN	HAMS HOLY 34	Other	211
Happy Townland, The	HAPP TOWN	Poem	268
Harding, W.G.	HARD W.G.	Letter	125
Hardy, Thomas	HARD THOM	Letter	125
Harlot sang to the beggarman, The	HARL SANG BE	Poem	268
Harmsworth, Edward	HARM EDWA	Letter	125
Harp of Aengus, The	HARP AENG	Poem	268
Harris, Frank	HARR FRAN	Letter	126
Harris, Frank	HARR FRAN	Inscription	79
Harris, Fred	HARR FRED	Letter	126
Harrison	HARR	Letter	126
Harrison, Clifford	HARR CLIF	Letter	126
Hawk, The	HAWK	Poem	268
Hayes, Dr. Carlton	HAYE DR. CA	Letter	126
Hays, Mr.	HAYS MR.	Letter	126
Hayward, John	HAYW JOHN	Inscription	79
Hayward, John	HAYW JOHN	Letter	126
He and She	HE SHE	Poem	268
He bids his Beloved be at Peace	HE BIDS HI	Poem	268
He gives his Beloved certain Rhymes	HE GIVE HI	Poem	269
He has lost what may not be found	HE HAS LO	Poem	269
He hears the Cry of the Sedge	HE HEAR CR	Poem	269
He mourns for the Change that has come upon him and his Beloved, and longs for the End of the World	HE MOUR CH	Poem	269
He remembers Forgotten Beauty	HE REME FO	Poem	270
He Reproves the Curlew	HE REPR CU	Poem	270
He tells of a Valley full of Lovers	HE TELL VA	Poem	270

Index

He tells of the Perfect Beauty	HE TELL PE	Poem	270
He thinks of his Past Greatness when a Part of the Constellations of Heaven	HE THIN HI	Poem	271
He thinks of those who have Spoken Evil of his Beloved	HE THIN TH	Poem	271
He who bids the white plains of the pale	HE WHO BI	Poem, Unpu.	340
He wishes for the Cloths of Heaven	HE WISH CL	Poem	271
He wishes his Beloved were Dead	HE WISH HI	Poem	272
Heald, Edith Shackleton	HEAL EDIT SH	Letter	126
Healy, James	HEAL JAME	Inscription	80
Healy, James A.	HEAL JAME	Letter	127
Heart of the Woman, The	HEAR WOMA	Poem	272
Heart on sleeve is handsome wear	HEAR SLEE IS	Poem, Unpu.	340
Heart well worn upon the sleeve may be the best of sights	HEAR WELL WO	Poem	272
Henderson, W.A.	HEND W.A.	Letter	127
Henley, W.E.	HENL W.E.	Letter	127
Henley, W.E.	HENL W.E.	Inscription	80
Her Anxiety	HER ANXI	Poem	272
Her Courage	HER COUR AG	Poem	272
Her Courtesy	HER COUR TE	Poem	272
Her Dream	HER DREA	Poem	272
Her Friends Bring Her a Christmas Tree	HER FRIE BR	Poem	272
Her Praise	HER PRAI	Poem	273
Her Race	HER RACE	Poem	273
Her Triumph	HER TRIU	Poem	273
Her Vision in the Wood	HER VISI WO	Poem	273
Here I am	HERE I AM	Poem, Unpu.	341
Here comes Mrs. Phillamore	HERE COME MR	Poem, Unpu.	341
Herne's Egg, The	HERN EGG	Play	230
Herne's Egg: A Stage Play, The	HERN EGG 38	Book	21
Herne's Egg and Other Plays, The	HERN OTHE 38	Book	21
Hero, the Girl, and the Fool, The	HERO GIRL FO	Poem	273
Higgins, Fred	HIGG FRED	Inscription	80
Higgins, Frederick	HIGG FRED	Letter	127
Higgins, Frederick R.: ARABLE HOLDINGS	HIGG ARAB 33	Other	212
Higginson, T.W.	HIGG T.W.	Letter	127
High Talk	HIGH TALK	Poem	273
Hill, Edwin Bliss	HILL EDWI	Letter	128
Hills of Mourne	HILL MOUR	Poem, Unpu.	341
Hinkson, Henry Albert	HINK HENR	Letter	128
Hinkson, Katherine Tynan	HINK KATH TY	Letter	128

Hinkson, Katherine Tynan	HINK KATH TY	Inscription	80
Hinkson, Katherine Tynan: MIRACLE PLAYS	HINK MIRA 95	Other	212
Hinkson, Katherine Tynan: THE MIDDLE YEARS	HINK MIDD 16	Other	212
Hinkson, Katherine Tynan: TWENTY ONE POEMS	HINK TWEN 07	Other	212
His Bargain	HIS BARG	Poem	274
His Confidence	HIS CONF	Poem	274
His Dream	HIS DREA	Poem	274
His Memories	HIS MEMO	Poem	274
His Phoenix	HIS PHOE	Poem	274
His Wildness	HIS WILD	Poem	275
Hodgson, Ralph	HODG RALP	Letter	128
Holland, Miss	HOLL MISS	Letter	128
Holland, Nora	HOLL NORA	Inscription	81
Holloway, Joseph	HOLL JOSE	Letter	129
Holroyd, Charles	HOLR CHAR	Letter	129
Home Rule See UNID HOME RU.		Speech	380
Hone, Joseph M.	HONE JOSE M.	Letter	129
Horn	HORN	Letter	129
Horniman, Miss Annie	HORN MISS AN	Inscription	81
Horniman, Miss Annie	HORN MISS AN	Letter	129
Horton, William	HORT WILL	Inscription	81
Horton, William	HORT WILL	Letter	130
Horton, W.T.: A BOOK OF IMAGES	HORT BOOK 98	Other	212
Host of the Air, The	HOST AIR	Poem	275
Hosting of the Sidhe, The	HOST SIDH	Poem	275
Hound Voice	HOUN VOIC	Poem	275
Hour Glass: A Morality, The	HOUR GLAS 03	Book	21
Hour Glass and Other Plays, The	HOUR GLAS 04	Book	22
Hour-Glass, The	HOUR GLAS	Play	230
Hour-Glass, The, Cathleen ni Houlihan, The Pot of Broth,	HOUR CATH 04	Book	22
Hour Glass, The, Cathleen ni Houlihan, The Pot of Broth	HOUR CATH 05	Book	23
Hour Glass: A Morality, The	HOUR GLAS 07	Book	23
Hour Glass, The	HOUR GLAS 14	Book	23
Hour before Dawn, The	HOUR DAWN	Poem	275
How Ferencz Renyi Kept Silent	HOW FERE RE	Poem	275
How Writers Work: WBY on the Future of Poetry	HOW WRIT WO	Prose	359
Howe, W.T.	HOWE W.T.	Inscription	81
Howe, W.T.	HOWE W.T.	Letter	130
Huddon, Duddon and Daniel O'Leary	HUDD DUDD DA	Poem	276
Hugh Lane's Pictures	HUGH LANE PI	Prose	359
Hughes, Richard	HUGH RICH	Letter	130

Index   493

Human Dignity	HUMA DIGN	Poem	276
Hunt, Violet	HUNT VIOL	Letter	130
Hushed in a vale in Dajestan	HUSH VALE DA	Poem, Unpu.	341
Hutchinson, Thomas	HUTC THOM	Letter	130
Hyde, Douglas	HYDE DOUG	Letter	131
Hyde, Douglas: THE LOVE SONGS OF CONNAUGHT	HYDE LOVE 04	Other	213
I Am of Ireland	I AM IR	Poem	276
I Became an Author	I BECA AU	Prose	359
I heard a rose on the brim	I HEAR RO	Poem, Unpu.	341
I know a merry thicket See CHIL PLAY.		Poem, Unpu.	338
I know of no love but my Lord's	I KNOW NO	Poem, Unpu.	341
I once had peace among	I ONCE HA	Poem, Unpu.	342
I sat upon a high gnarled root	I SAT UP	Poem, Unpu.	342
I See phantoms of Hatred and of the Heart's Fullness and of the Coming Emptiness	I SEE PH	Poem	276
I sing of Pan and his piping sweet	I SING PA	Poem, Unpu.	342
I stood in the tower window	I STOO TO	Poem, Unpu.	342
I tire of seeing always the same face	I TIRE SE	Poem, Unpu.	342
I walked among the Seven Woods of Coole	I WALK SE	Poem	276
I was going the road one day	I WAS GO	Poem	276
I will not in grey hours retake	I WILL NO	Poem, Unpu.	342
Ideal Drama See UNID IDEA DR.		Speech	380
Ideas of Good and Evil	IDEA GOOD 03	Book	24
Ideas of Good and Evil	IDEA GOOD 04	Book	24
If I Were Four-and-twenty	IF I 40	Book	24
If the melancholy music of the spheres	IF MELA MU	Poem, Unpu.	342
Image from a Past Life, An	IMAG PAST LI	Poem	276
Images	IMAG	Poem, Unpu.	343
Imagination's Bride See TWO FAVO CE.		Poem, Unpu.	352
Imitated from the Japanese	IMIT JAPA	Poem	276
Impetuous heart be still	IMPE HEAR BE	Poem	277
In a Drawing-Room	IN DRAW RO	Poem	277
In a primrose glade	IN PRIM GL	Poem, Unpu.	343
In Church	IN CHUR	Poem	277
In Memory of Alfred Pollexfen	IN MEMO AL	Poem	277
In Memory of Eva Gore-Booth and Con Markiewicz	IN MEMO EV	Poem	277
In Memory of Major Robert Gregory	IN MEMO MA	Poem	278
In Memory of Thomas William Lyster	IN MEMO TH	Speech	375

Title	Code	Type	Page
In Tara's Halls	IN TARA HA	Poem	278
In the Firelight	IN FIRE	Poem	278
In the Poet's Parlor	IN POET PA	Speech	375
In the Poets' Pub	IN POET PU	Speech	375
In the Seven Woods	IN SEVE WO	Poem	279
In the Seven Woods (Dundrum)	IN SEVE 03	Book	25
In the Seven Woods (New York)	IN SEVE 03	Book	26
In the heart of the wood love straying	IN HEAR WO	Poem, Unpu.	343
Indian to His Love, The	INDI LOVE	Poem	279
Indian Upon God, The	INDI GOD	Poem	279
Interview with Deidre MacDonagh	INTE DEIR MA	Speech	375
Into the Twilight	INTO TWIL	Poem	279
Introductions See titles of individual works.			
Ireland Bewitched	IREL BEWI	Prose	359
Ireland, 1921-1931	IREL 1921	Prose	359
Irish Academy material	IRIS ACAD MA	Miscellany	189
Irish Airman Foresees His Death, An	IRIS AIRM FO	Poem	279
Irish Censorship, The	IRIS CENS	Prose	360
Irish Fairy and Folk Tales	IRIS FAIR 95	Book	26
Irish Fairy Tales	IRIS FAIR 92	Book	26
Irish Literary Movement	IRIS LITE MO	Speech	375
Irish Witch Doctors	IRIS WITC DO	Prose	360
Island of Statues, The	ISLA STAT	Poem	279
J.M. Synge and the Ireland of His Time	J.M. SYNG IR	Prose	360
Jackson, Arthur	JACK ARTH	Letter	131
Jackson, Holbrook	JACK HOLB	Letter	131
Jackson, Schuyler B.	JACK SCHU B.	Letter	131
Jacob, Miss	JACO MISS	Letter	131
Jacobson, Josephine Boylan	JACO JOSE BO	Letter	131
James, Henry	JAME HENR	Letter	131
John Eglinton and Spiritual Art	JOHN EGLI SP	Prose	360
John Kinsella's Lament for Mrs. Mary Moore	JOHN KINS LA	Poem	280
John Shawe-Taylor	JOHN SHAW TA	Prose	360
John Sherman and Dhoya	JOHN SHER 91	Book	26
Johnson, Fred	JOHN FRED	Letter	131
Johnson, Lionel	JOHN LION	Inscription	81
Johnson, Lionel: TWENTY ONE POEMS	JOHN TWEN 04	Other	213
Johnston, Denis: SHADOWDANCE	JOHN SHAD	Other	213
Jones, Jennie Ina	JONE JENN IN	Letter	132
Joyce, James	JOYC JAME	Letter	132
Kanva on Himself	KANV HIMS	Poem	280
Karlfeldt, Eric	KARL ERIC	Letter	132

Keeble, Lillah McCarthy	KEEB	LILL MC	Letter	132
Keep far off dancing feet	KEEP	FAR OF	Poem, Unpu.	343
Keller, Mr.	KELL	MR.	Letter	132
Kennedy, W.S.	KENN	W.S.	Letter	132
Keynes, Geoffrey	KEYN	GEOF	Letter	132
Kiernan, Thomas J.	KIER	THOM J.	Letter	132
Kinder, Margaret Martin	KIND	MARG MA	Inscription	82
King and No King	KING	NO KI	Poem	280
King of the Great Clock Tower, The	KING	GREA CL	Play	231
King of the Great Clock Tower, The	KING	GREA 34	Book	27
King of the Great Clock Tower, The	KING	GREA 35	Book	27
King's Threshold & On Baile's Strand, The	KING	BAIL 04	Book	28
King's Threshold, The	KING	THRE 04	Book	27
King's Threshold, The	KING	THRE 05	Book	28
King's Threshold, The	KING	THRE	Play	231
King's Visit, The	KING	VISI	Prose	360
King, Frederick A.	KING	FRED A.	Letter	132
King, Richard Ashe	KING	RICH AS	Inscription	82
King, Richard Ashe	KING	RICH AS	Letter	133
Kingston, Gertrude	KING	GERT	Letter	133
Kinkead, Eugene	KINK	EUGE	Letter	133
Kleeman, Rita Sulzbacher Halle	KLEE	RITA SU	Letter	133
Knight, W.A.	KNIG	W.A.	Letter	133
Knole, Lady	KNOL	LADY	Letter	133
Knowledge and Wisdom	KNOW	WISD	Poem, Unpu.	343
Koehler, Thomas	KOEH	THOM	Letter	133
Lady's First Song, The	LADY	FIRS SO	Poem	280
Lady's Second Song, The	LADY	SECO SO	Poem	280
Lady's Third Song, The	LADY	THIR SO	Poem	280
Laird, Helen	LAIR	HELE	Inscription	82
Laird, Helen	LAIR	HELE	Letter	133
Lake Isle of Innisfree, The	LAKE	ISLE IN	Poem	281
Lake Isle of Innisfree, The	LAKE	ISLE 24	Book	28
Lambert, Maurice	LAMB	MAUR	Letter	133
Lambert, Mrs. Enid	LAMB	MRS. EN	Inscription	82
Lamentation of the Old Pensioner, The	LAME	OLD PE	Poem	281
Lancelot Switchback	LANC	SWIT	Poem, Unpu.	343
Land of Heart's Desire, The	LAND	HEAR DE	Play	232
Land of Heart's Desire, The (London)	LAND	HEAR 94	Book	28
Land of Heart's Desire, The (Chicago)	LAND	HEAR 94	Book	29
Land of Heart's Desire, The (Bibelot)	LAND	HEAR 03	Book	29

Land of Heart's Desire, The (Mosher)	LAND HEAR 03	Book	29
Land of Heart's Desire, The	LAND HEAR 12	Book	30
Land of Heart's Desire.....The Countess Cathleen	LAND HEAR 25	Book	30
Lane, Hugh	LANE HUGH	Letter	133
Lane, Hugh	LANE HUGH	Inscription	82
Lane Material	LANE MATE	Miscellany	190
Lane Pictures, The	LANE PICT	Speech	375
Langbridge, Fred	LANG FRED	Letter	134
Langbridge, Rosamund	LANG ROSA	Letter	134
Lapis Lazuli	LAPI LAZU	Poem	281
Last Confession, A	LAST CONF	Poem	281
Last Poems and Two Plays	LAST POEM 39	Book	30
Later Poems	LATE POEM 22	Book	30
Later Poems	LATE POEM 24	Book	31
Later Poems	LATE POEM 26	Book	31
Laurie, Thomas Werner	LAUR THOM WE	Letter	134
Law, Mr.	LAW MR.	Letter	134
Le Fanu, Mrs.	LEFA MRS.	Letter	134
Leaders of the Crowd, The	LEAD CROW	Poem	281
Lecky, W.E.H.	LECK W.E.	Letter	135
Leda and the Swan	LEDA SWAN	Poem	282
LeGallienne, Richard	LEGA RICH	Letter	134
Legend, A	LEGE	Poem	282
Legends See FOLK MYTH LE.		Miscellany	188
Leo Africanus	LEO AFRI	Miscellany	196
Lerine, Isaac Esq.	LERI ISAA ES	Letter	135
Letters to the New Island	LETT NEW 34	Book	31
Leventhal, A.J.	LEVE A.J.	Letter	135
Leveson, George Granville []	LEVE GEOR GR	Letter	135
Lewis, P. Wyndham	LEWI P. WY	Letter	135
Life	LIFE	Poem	282
Lift Up the White Knee	LIFT WHIT KN	Poem	282
Linati, Carlo	LINA CARL	Letter	135
[Linc?]	LINC	Letter	135
Lines Written in Dejection	LINE WRIT DE	Poem	282
Linley, Laura	LINL LAUR	Inscription	82
Linley, Laura: OUT OF THE VORTEX	LINL OUT 16	Other	213
Linnell, Mr.	LINN MR.	Letter	135
Lister, Miss E.M.	LIST MISS E.	Letter	135
Lists	LIST	Miscellany	191
Literary Movement in Ireland, The	LITE MOVE IR	Prose	361
Literature and the Living Voice	LITE LIVI VO	Prose	361
Little, Mr.	LITT MR.	Letter	136
Little puritan in Sunday best, A	LITT PURI SU	Poem, Unpu.	344

Index

Living Beauty, The	LIVI BEAT	Poem	283
Londonderry, Lady	LOND LADY	Letter	136
Long-legged Fly	LONG LEGG FL	Poem	283
Longford Printing Press	LONG PRIN PR	Letter	136
Look at the white birds	LOOK WHIT BI	Poem, Unpu.	344
Loud Years Come, The See THOU LOUD YE.		Poem, Unpu.	351
Louis Lambert	LOUI LAMB	Prose	361
Love and Death	LOVE DEAT	Poem	283
Love Song	LOVE SONG	Poem	283
Lover asks Forgiveness because of his Many Moods	LOVE ASKS FO	Poem	283
Lover mourns for the Loss of Love	LOVE MOUR LO	Poem	284
Lover pleads with his Friend for Old Friends	LOVE PLEA HI	Poem	284
Lover speaks to the Hearers of his Songs in Coming Days	LOVE SPEA HE	Poem	284
Lover Tells of the Rose in his Heart	LOVE TELL RO	Poem	284
Lover's Quarrel Among the Fairies, A	LOVE QUAR FA	Poem	285
Lover's Song, The	LOVE RS SO	Poem	285
Love's Loneliness	LOVE LONE	Poem	283
Low hums the wind	LOW HUMS WI	Poem, Unpu.	344
Lowell, Amy	LOWE AMY	Letter	136
Lullaby	LULL	Poem	285
Lynd, [Robert]	LYND ROBE	Letter	136
Lyster, Jane R.	LYST JANE R.	Letter	136
Lyster, T.W.	LYST T.W.	Letter	136
Lyttelton, Edith	LYTT EDIT	Letter	136
Lyttelton, Lady Katherine	LYTT LADY KA	Letter	137
MacBride, Maud Gonne	MACB MAUD GO	Letter	137
MacBride, Maud Gonne	MACB MAUD GO	Inscription	82
MacColl, D.S.	MACC D.S.	Letter	137
MacDermott, Norman	MACD NORM	Letter	137
MacDonagh, Thomas	MACD THOM	Letter	137
MacDonald, Sir Anthony	MACD SIR AN	Letter	137
MacGreevy, T.	MACG T.	Inscription	83
MacGreevy, Thomas	MACG THOM	Letter	137
MacHugh, Ignatius	MACH IGNA	Letter	138
Mackenna, Stephen	MACK STEP	Letter	138
Mackintosh, Graham	MACK GRAH	Letter	138
Maclagan, [E.R.D.]	MACL E.R.	Letter	138
MacManus, Mr.	MACM MR.	Letter	138
Macmillan Company	MACM COMP	Letter	138
Macmillan Edition de Luxe See UNPU MACM ED.		Book	59
Macmillan, Frederick	MACM FRED	Letter	138

Macmillan, Harold	MACM HARO	Letter	138
Mad as the Mist and Snow	MAD MIST SN	Poem	285
Madness of King Goll, The	MADN KING GO	Poem	285
Magee, William Kirkpatrick	MAGE WILL KI	Letter	138
Magee, William: SOME ESSAYS AND PASSAGES See EGLI SOME 05.		Other	207
Magi, The	MAGI	Poem	285
Magpie, The	MAGP	Poem, Unpu.	344
Mahaffy, J.P.	MAHA J.P.	Letter	139
Maid Quiet	MAID QUIE	Poem	285
Mair, George	MAIR GEOR	Letter	139
Mallarme, Stephane	MALL STEP	Letter	139
Man and the Echo, The	MAN ECHO	Poem	286
Man Who Dreamed of Faeryland, The	MAN WHO DR	Poem	286
Man Young and Old	MAN YOUN OL	Poem	286
Manchester Lecture	MANC LECT	Speech	376
Mandukya Upanishad, The	MAND UPAN	Prose	361
See also ESSA W.B. 37.		Book	17
Mannin, Ethel	MANN ETHE	Letter	139
Mannin, Ethel	MANN ETHE	Inscription	83
Mark, Mr. See MACM COMP.		Letter	138
Mark, T.	MARK T.	Inscription	83
Markievicz, Constance	MARK CONS	Letter	139
Markiewicz, Constance	MARK CONS	Inscription	83
Marriott, Mr.	MARR MR.	Letter	140
Marriott, Raymond	MARR RAYM	Inscription	83
Marsh, Edward	MARS EDWA	Letter	140
Martin, Harvey	MART HARV	Letter	140
Martyn, Edward	MART EDWA	Letter	140
Masefield, Constance	MASE CONS	Letter	140
Masefield, John	MASE JOHN	Letter	140
Masefield, John	MASE JOHN	Inscription	84
Masefield, John: JOHN M. SYNGE: A FEW PERSONAL RECOLLECTIONS	MASE JOHN 15	Other	214
Mask, The	MASK	Poem	286
Mathers, Mr. and Mrs.	MATH MRMS	Inscription	84
Mathews, Elkin	MATH ELKI	Letter	140
Mattheson, Hilda	MATT HILD	Inscription	84
Matthews, Mr.	MATT MR.	Letter	141
Matthews, Seymour Freeman	MATT SEYM FR	Letter	141
Maude, Mary	MAUD MARY	Letter	141
Mavor, James	MAVO JAME	Letter	141
May time be very kind to thee	MAY TIME BE	Poem, Unpu.	344
McCartan, Patrick	MCCA PATR	Letter	141
McCarthy, Lillah See KEEB LILL MC.		Letter	132
McColl, Dugald S.	MCCO DUGA S.	Letter	142
McDermott, Mary Scudder	MCDE MARY SC	Letter	142

Index

McDonagh, Thomas	MCDO THOM	Letter	142
McDonald, Mr.	MCDO MR.	Letter	142
McElligott, J.J.	MCEL J.J.	Letter	142
McGuinness, Norah	MCGU NORA	Letter	142
McMahon, Mr.	MCMA MR.	Letter	142
McManus, Mr.	MCMA MR.	Letter	143
Meditation in Time of War, A	MEDI TIME WA	Poem	286
Meditation of the Old Fisherman, The	MEDI OLD FI	Poem	287
Meditations in Time of Civil War	MEDI TIME CI	Poem	287
Meeting	MEET	Poem	287
Meiklejohn, Alexander	MEIK ALEX	Letter	143
Meiklejohn, Mrs.	MEIK MRS.	Inscription	84
Memory	MEMO	Poem	287
Memory of Youth, A	MEMO YOUT	Poem	287
Men Improve With The Years	MEN IMPR YE	Poem	288
Meo, Mrs Craig (Elena)	MEO MRS. CR	Letter	143
Mermaid, The	MERM	Poem	288
Merriman, Brian: Midnight Court	MERR MIDN ND	Other	214
Meru	MERU	Poem	288
Message of the Folk-Lorist, The	MESS FOLK LO	Prose	361
Methuen and Co.	METH CO.	Letter	143
Meynell, Alice	MEYN ALIC	Letter	143
Meynell, Alice	MEYN ALIC	Inscription	84
Meynell, Wilfred	MEYN WILF	Letter	143
Michael Clancy, the Great Ghoul, and Death	MICH CLAN GR	Prose	362
Michael Field's Sight and Song	MICH FIEL SI	Prose	362
Michael Robartes and the Dancer	MICH ROBA DA	Poem	288
Michael Robartes and the Dancer	MICH ROBA 20	Book	31
Milligan, Alice	MILL ALIC	Letter	143
Milton, John: THE POETICAL WORKS	MILT POET 35	Other	214
Minchin, Mr.	MINC MR.	Letter	143
Miscellaneous	MISC	Miscellany	193
Model for the Laureate, A	MODE LAUR	Poem	288
Modern Ireland See UNPU MODE IR.		Prose	368
Modern Poetry	MODE POET	Speech	376
Mohini Chatterjee	MOHI CHAT	Poem	289
Monck, Nugent	MONC NUGE	Letter	144
Mong meadows of sweet grain	MONG MEAD SW	Poem, Unpu.	344
Monro, Alida	MONR ALID	Letter	144
Monro, Harold	MONR HARO	Letter	144
Monroe, Harriet	MONR HARR	Letter	144
Moods, The	MOOD	Poem	289
Moon, Mrs.	MOON MRS.	Letter	144
Moon that shone last night, The	MOON SHON LA	Poem, Unpu.	344

Mooney, Ria	MOON RIA	Letter	144
Moore, David F. (Solicitor)	MOOR DAVI F.	Letter	144
Moore, George	MOOR GEOR	Inscription	84
Moore, George	MOOR GEOR	Letter	144
Moore, George: LYRICS AND SATIRES	MOOR LYRI 29	Other	214
Moore, George: MAXIMS	MOOR MAXI ND	Other	214
Moore, Isabel	MOOR ISAB	Letter	145
Moore, Sturge	MOOR STUR	Inscription	84
Moore, Sturge	MOOR STUR	Letter	145
More Memories	MORE MEMO	Prose	362
Morel, Auguste	MORE AUGU	Letter	146
Morgan, Louise	MORG LOUI	Letter	146
Morrell, Lady Ottoline	MORR LADY OT	Letter	146
Morrell, Lady Ottoline	MORR LADY OT	Inscription	85
Morrell, Philip	MORR PHIL	Letter	146
Morris, May	MORR MAY	Letter	146
Morrison, George E.	MORR GEOR E.	Letter	146
Morton, David	MORT DAVI	Letter	146
Mosada	MOSA 86	Book	32
Mosada	MOSA	Poem	289
Mosher, Thomas Bird	MOSH THOM BI	Letter	146
Mother of God, The	MOTH GOD	Poem	289
Mountain Tomb, The	MOUN TOMB	Poem	290
Mourn--and Then Onward!	MOUR THEN ON	Poem	290
Moynan, Thomas King	MOYN THOM KI	Inscription	85
Municipal Gallery Revisited, The	MUNI GALL RE	Poem	290
Munroe, Miss	MUNR MISS	Letter	146
Murphy, Diana	MURP DIAN	Letter	146
Murray, Gilbert	MURR GILB	Letter	146
Murray, John	MURR JOHN	Letter	146
Murray, Thomas	MURR THOM	Letter	146
My Descendants	MY DESC	Poem	290
My Friend's Book	MY FRIE BO	Prose	362
My House	MY HOUS	Poem	290
My intellect is sain	MY INTE IS	Poem, Unpu.	345
My Own Poetry	MY OWN PO	Speech	376
My Own Poetry Again	MY OWN AG	Speech	376
My song thou knowest	MY SONG TH	Poem, Unpu.	345
My Table	MY TABL	Poem	290
Myers, Mrs. E.	MYER MRS. E.	Letter	147
Myths See FOLK MYTH LE.		Miscellany	188
National Bank	NATI BANK	Letter	147
Nationales Editor	NATI EDIT	Letter	147
Nativity, A	NATI	Poem	290
Necessity for Manhood	NECE MANH	Speech	376
Need for Audacity of Thought, The	NEED AUDA TH	Prose	362

Index

Needham, Mr.	NEED MR.	Letter	147
Needle's Eye, A	NEED EYE	Poem	290
Nettleship, Mrs. J.T.	NETT MRS. J.	Inscription	85
Never Give all the Heart	NEVE GIVE AL	Poem	291
Nevinson, [Henry Woodd]	NEVI HENR WO	Letter	147
New Faces, The	NEW FACE	Poem	291
New Poems	NEW POEM 38	Book	32
News for the Delphic Oracle	NEWS DELP OR	Poem	291
Neylan, John Francis	NEYL JOHN FR	Letter	147
Nic Shiubhlaigh, Maire See WALK MARY.		Inscription	94
Nicoll, William R.	NICO WILL R.	Letter	147
NIETZSCHE AS CRITIC, PHILOSOPHER AND PROPHET	NIET AS 01	Other	214
Nine Poems	NINE POEM 14	Book	33
Nine Poems	NINE POEM 18	Book	33
Nineteen Hundred and Nineteen	NINE HUND NI	Poem	292
Nineteenth Century and After, The	NINE CENT AF	Poem	292
No daughter of the iron times See TO SIST CR.		Poem, Unpu.	352
No not now for that fray	NO NOT NO	Poem, Unpu.	345
No Second Troy	NO SECO TR	Poem	292
Nothing That He Has Done	NOTH THAT HE	Poem	292
Noyes, Alfred	NOYE ALFR	Letter	147
O Do Not Love Too Long	O DO NO	Poem	293
O what a tedious herald was the death	O WHAT TE	Poem, Unpu.	345
O'Brien, Edward Joseph	O'BR EDWA JO	Letter	147
O'Brien, R. Barry	O'BR R. BA	Letter	147
O'Brien, Reverend Henry	O'BR REVE HE	Letter	148
O'Brien, [George]	O'BR GEOR	Letter	148
O'Casey, Sean	O'CA SEAN	Letter	148
O'Connell, John	O'CO JOHN	Letter	148
O'Connor, Frank	O'CO FRAN	Letter	148
O'Connor, Frank	O'CO FRAN	Inscription	85
O'Connor, Frank Llewelyn-Davis	O'CO MISS MO	Letter	148
O'Connor, Frank: LORDS AND COMMONS	O'CO LORD 38	Other	215
O'Connor, Frank: THE WILD BIRD'S NEST	O'CO WILD 32	Other	215
O'Connor, Miss Moya			
O'Donaghue, Paidh	O'DO PAID	Letter	148
O'Donahue	O'DO	Letter	149
O'Donnell, Charles	O'DO CHAR	Letter	149
O'Donnell, Frank	O'DO FRAN	Letter	149
O'Donoghue, D.J.	O'DO D.J.	Letter	149
O'Donovan, [Fred]	O'DO FRED	Letter	149
O'Donovan, Michael	O'DO MICH	Letter	149

O'Faolain, Sean	O'FA	SEAN	Letter	149
O'Grady, Standish	O'GR	STAN	Letter	150
O'Hegarty, Patrick	O'HE	PATR	Letter	150
O'Higgins, Mrs. Kevin	O'HI	MRS. KE	Letter	150
O'Kelly, Seumas: CAITLIN NI UALLACHAIN	O'KE	CAIT 05	Other	215
O'Leary, Ellen	O'LE	ELLE	Letter	150
O'Leary, Ellen	O'LE	ELLE	Inscription	86
O'Leary, John	O'LE	JOHN	Letter	150
O'Leary, John	O'LE	JOHN	Inscription	86
O'Neill, Maire	O'NE	MAIR	Letter	151
O'Rahilly, The	O'RA		Poem	296
O'Riordan, Conal	O'RI	CONA	Letter	151
O'Sullivan, Seumas	O'SU	SEUM	Letter	151
Occult	OCCU		Miscellany	196
October Blast	OCTO	BLAS 27	Book	34
Oedipus the King	OEDI	KING	Speech	377
Oil and Blood	OIL	BLOO	Poem	293
Old Age of Queen Maeve, The	OLD	AGE QU	Poem	293
Old and older by many a winter	OLD	OLD MA	Poem, Unpu.	345
Old and solitary one, An	OLD	SOLI ON	Poem, Unpu.	345
Old Gaelic Love Songs	OLD	GAEL LO	Prose	363
Old Grey Man, The	OLD	GREY MA	Poem, Unpu.	345
Old Memory	OLD	MEMO	Poem	293
Old Men Admiring Themselves in the water, The	OLD	MEN AD	Poem	294
Old Stone Cross, The	OLD	STON CR	Poem	294
Old Tom Again	OLD	TOM AG	Poem	294
On a Child's Death	ON	CHIL DE	Poem, Unpu.	346
On a Picture of a Black Centaur by Edmund Dulac	ON	PICT BL	Poem	294
On a Political Prisoner	ON	POLI PR	Poem	294
On Baile's Strand	ON	BAIL 05	Book	34
On Baile's Strand	ON	BAIL ST	Play	233
On Being Asked for a War Poem	ON	BEIN AS	Poem	295
On George Moore	ON	GEOR MO	Poem	295
On hearing that the Students of our New University have joined the Agitation against Immoral Literature	ON	HEAR TH	Poem	295
On Mr. Nettleship's Picture at the Royal Hibernian Academy	ON	MR. NE	Poem	295
On the Boiler	ON	BOIL 39	Book	34
On those that hated 'The Playboy of the Western World,' 1907	ON	THOS TH	Poem	296
On Woman	ON	WOMA	Poem	296
Once God had stored his peace away in books	ONCE	GOD HA	Poem, Unpu.	346

Index

Once I followed a ring dove	ONCE I FO	Poem, Unpu.	346
Once, a meteor's fickle flair	ONCE METE FI	Poem, Unpu.	346
Only Jealousy of Emer and Fighting the Waves	ONLY JEAL EM	Play	233
Only the dead have wisdom	ONLY DEAD HA	Poem, Unpu.	346
Ormerod, Mr.	ORME MR.	Letter	151
Orpen, R.C.	ORPE R.C.	Letter	151
Oshima, Shotaro	OSHI SHOT	Inscription	86
Out of sight is out of mind	OUT SIGH IS	Poem	296
Outlaw's Bridal, The	OUTL BRID	Poem, Unpu.	347
Owen Aherne and His Dancers	OWEN AHER DA	Poem	296
Owen, Mary	OWEN MARY	Letter	151
Owlett, F.C.	OWLE F.C.	Letter	151
Oxford Book of Modern Verse, The	OXFO BOOK 36	Book	34
Oxford University	OXFO UNIV	Letter	151
Oxford University Press	OXFO UNIV PR	Letter	151
PEN	PEN	Letter	151
Packet for Ezra Pound, A	PACK EZRA 29	Book	35
Pages from a Diary Written in 1930	PAGE DIAR 30	Book	35
Palgrave, Francis Turner: CHILDREN'S TREASURY OF LYRICAL POETRY	PALG CHIL 98	Other	215
Palmer, Herbert E.	PALM HERB E.	Letter	152
Palmstierna, Baron	PALM BARO	Letter	152
Pardon, Old Fathers	PARD OLD FA	Poem	297
Parkhill, D.	PARK D.	Letter	152
Parnell	PARN	Prose	363
Parnell	PARN	Poem	298
Parnell's Funeral	PARN FUNE	Poem	298
Parnell, Thomas: POEMS	PARN POEM 27	Other	215
Parting	PART	Poem	298
Patanjali, Shri Baghwan: APHORISMS OF YOGA	PATA APHO 38	Other	215
Pathway, The See YOUR PATH.		Poem, Unpu.	355
Paudeen	PAUD	Poem	298
Payen-Payne, James B. de Vincheles	PAYE JAME B.	Letter	152
Payen-Payne, James B. de Vincheles	PAYE JAME B.	Inscription	86
Payne, [Iden]	PAYN IDEN	Letter	152
Payne, Leonidas W.	PAYN LEON W.	Letter	152
Peabody, Josephine Preston	PEAB JOSE PR	Inscription	86
Peace	PEAC	Poem	299
Peacock, The	PEA COCK	Poem	299
People, The	PEOP	Poem	299
People's Theatre, A	PEOP THEA	Prose	363
Per Amica Silentia Lunae (London)	PER AMIC 18	Book	35

Per Amica Silentia Lunae (New York)	PER	AMIC 18	Book	36
Peters, Mr.	PETE	MR.	Letter	152
Phantom Ship, The	PHAN	SHIP	Poem	299
Phases of the Moon, The	PHAS	MOON	Poem	299
Phelan, James	PHEL	JAME	Inscription	86
Phelps, William Lyon	PHEL	WILL LY	Letter	152
Phillimore, Cecily: PAUL: THE CHRISTAIN	PHIL	PAUL 30	Other	216
Photographs	PHOT		Miscellany	197
Pilgrim, The	PILG		Poem	299
Pity of Love, The	PITY	LOVE	Poem	299
Player Queen, The	PLAY	QUEE	Play	234
Players ask for a Blessing on the Psalteries and on Themselves	PLAY	ASK BL	Poem	300
Plays and Controversies	PLAY	CONT 23	Book	36
Plays and Controversies	PLAY	CONT 24	Book	36
Plays for an Irish Theatre	PLAY	IRIS 11	Book	37
Plays in Prose and Verse	PLAY	PROS 22	Book	37
Plays in Prose and Verse	PLAY	PROS 24	Book	38
Plomer, William C.F.	PLOM	WILL C.	Letter	152
Plunkett, Count	PLUN	COUN	Letter	153
Plunkett, Horace Curzon	PLUN	HORA CU	Letter	153
Poel, William	POEL	WILL	Letter	153
Poem of Launcelot Switchback	POEM	LAUN SW	Poem, Unpu.	343
Poems	POEM	95	Book	38
Poems	POEM	99	Book	39
Poems	POEM	01	Book	40
Poems	POEM	04	Book	40
Poems	POEM	12	Book	40
Poems	POEM	13	Book	40
Poems	POEM	22	Book	40
Poems	POEM	27	Book	41
Poems	POEM	29	Book	41
Poems About Women	POEM	WOME	Speech	377
Poems and Ballads of Young Ireland	POEM	BALL 88	Book	42
Poems and Ballads of Young Ireland	POEM	BALL 90	Book	42
Poems and Translations by John Syunge	POEM	TRAN 09	Book	42
Poems of Spenser	POEM	SPEN 06	Book	42
Poems of William Blake, The	POEM	WILL 93	Book	42
Poems, 1899-1905	POEM	1899 06	Book	43
Poems Written in Discouragement	POEM	WRIT 13	Book	41
Poems: Second Series	POEM	SECO 09	Book	43

Index   505

Poet and the Actress, The			
See UNPU POET AC		Play	240
Poet Owen Hanrahan under a bush			
of May, The	POET OWEN HA	Poem	300
Poet pleads with the Elemental			
Powers	POET PLEA EL	Poem	300
Poet to his Beloved, A	POET HIS BE	Poem	300
Poetical Works of William B.			
Yeats	POET WORK 12	Book	44
Poetical Works. Vol. 1. Lyrical			
Poems	POET WORK 06	Book	43
Poetical Works. Vol. 2.			
Dramatical Poems	POET WORK 07	Book	44
Poetry and Ireland	POET IREL 08	Book	44
Poetry and Tradition	POET TRAD	Prose	363
Poetry New and Old	POET NEW OL	Speech	377
Polignac Prize Speech	POLI PRIZ SP	Speech	377
Politician used to be, The	POLI USED BE	Poem, Unpu.	347
Politics	POLI	Poem	301
Pollexfen, George	POLL GEOR	Letter	153
Pollexfen, George	POLL GEOR	Inscription	86
Pollexfen, Henrietta	POLL HENR	Inscription	86
Pollock, Dr.	POLL DR.	Letter	153
Pond, James	POND JAME	Letter	153
Porter, Mr.	PORT MR.	Letter	153
Portrayed before his eyes	PORT BEFO HI	Poem, Unpu.	347
Pot of Broth, The	POT BROT	Play	235
Pound, Dorothy	POUN DORO	Letter	153
Pound, Ezra	POUN EZRA	Letter	154
Power	POWE	Letter	154
Prayer for my Daughter, A	PRAY MY DA	Poem	301
Prayer for my Son, A	PRAY MY SO	Poem	301
Prayer for Old Age, A	PRAY OLD AG	Poem	301
Prayer on Going into my House, A	PRAY GOIN MY	Poem	301
Prefaces See titles of			
individual works.			
Presences	PRES	Poem	301
Price, Franklin	PRIC FRAN	Inscription	87
Priest and the Fairy, The	PRIE FAIR	Poem	302
Priest of Pan	PRIE PAN	Poem, Unpu.	347
Prokosch, Frederic	PROK FRED	Inscription	87
Prokosch, Frederick	PROK FRED	Letter	154
Prometheus Unbound	PROM UNBO	Prose	363
Protestants' Leap, The	PROT LEAP	Poem, Unpu.	347
Purgatory	PURG	Play	235
Purohit, Shri Swami	PURO SHRI SW	Letter	154
Purser, Sarah	PURS SARA	Letter	154
Purves, John	PURV JOHN	Letter	154
Pyper, J.S.	PYPE J.S.	Letter	154

Quarrel in Old Age	QUAR OLD AG	Poem	302
Quatrains and Aphorisms	QUAT APHO	Poem	302
Queen and the Jester, The	QUEE JEST	Poem, Unpu.	348
Queen Edaine	QUEE EDAI	Poem	302
Quinn, John	QUIN JOHN	Inscription	87
Quinn, John	QUIN JOHN	Letter	155
Quinn, Joseph	QUIN JOSE	Letter	155
Quoted and Paraphrased Material	QUOT PARA MA	Miscellany	198
RAPHAEL'S ASTRONOMICAL EPHEMERIS OF THE PLANETS	RAPH ASTR ND	Other	216
Radford, E.	RADF E	Inscription	88
Radin, Herman	RADI HERM	Letter	155
Rae, J.A.	RAE J.A.	Letter	155
Raferty, Mr.	RAFE MR.	Letter	155
Raffalovich, Marc-Andre	RAFF MARC AN	Letter	155
Ragged Wood, The	RAGG WOOD	Poem	303
Ratcliffe, Dorothy Una	RATC DORO UN	Letter	155
Rattray, R.F.	RATT R.F.	Letter	155
Rawley, Mr.	RAWL MR.	Letter	155
Ray, Mr.	RAY MR.	Letter	155
Re-engraved time after time	REEN TIME TI	Poem, Unpu.	348
Read, Herbert	READ HERB	Letter	156
Reading of Poems	READ POEM	Speech	377
Realists, The	REAL	Poem	303
Reardon	REAR	Letter	156
Reconciliation	RECO	Poem	303
Red blood and our laden heavy heart, The	RED BLOO OU	Poem, Unpu.	348
Red Hanrahan's Song about Ireland	RED HANR SO	Poem	303
Redman, Miss	REDM MISS	Letter	156
Redmond, John	REDM JOHN	Letter	156
Rees, J. Rogers	REES J. RO	Letter	156
Rees, J. Rogers	REES J. RO	Inscription	88
Rees, Mrs. J. Rogers	REES MRS.	Letter	156
Reid, Forrest	REID FORR	Inscription	89
Reith, Lord	REIT LORD	Letter	156
Remembrance	REME	Poem	303
Remorse for Intemperate Speech	REMO INTE SP	Poem	304
Representative Irish tales	REPR IRIS 91	Book	45
Reprisals	REPR	Poem	304
Responsibilities and Other Poems	RESP OTHE 16	Book	45
Responsibilities: Poems and a Play	RESP POEM 14	Book	45
Results of Thought, The	RESU THOU	Poem	304
Resurrection, The	RESU	Play	236
Reveries over Childhood and Youth	REVE CHIL 15	Book	47

Index

Reveries over Childhood and Youth	REVE CHIL 16	Book	48
Review of "A China Shop"	REVI CHIN SH	Miscellany	201
Review of "Crimson on the Tricolour"	REVI CRIM TR	Miscellany	201
Review of "Gombeenism"	REVI GOMB	Miscellany	201
Review of MacNamara's play	REVI MACN PL	Miscellany	201
Review of MacNutty's Play	REVI MAC NU	Miscellany	202
Review of Shiels's Play	REVI SHIE PL	Miscellany	202
Review of "The Red Petticoat"	REVI RED PE	Miscellany	201
Reviews, Miscellaneous	REVI MISC	Miscellany	202
Reynolds, Horace Mason	REYN HORA MA	Letter	156
Rhymer's Club Lecture	RHYM CLUB LE	Speech	377
Rhys, Ernest	RHYS ERNE	Letter	156
Rhys, Grace	RHYS GRAC	Letter	157
Ribh at the Tomb of Baile and Aillinn	RIBH TOMB BA	Poem	304
Ribh Considers Christian Love Insufficient	RIBH CONS CH	Poem	304
Ribh Denounces Patrick	RIBH DENO PA	Poem	304
Ribh in Ecstasy	RIBH ECST	Poem	305
Richards, Grant	RICH GRAN	Letter	157
Ricketts, Charles	RICK CHAR	Letter	157
Riddle is half mastered, The	RIDD IS HA	Poem, Unpu.	348
Riding, Laura	RIDI LAUR	Letter	157
Road at My Door, The	ROAD DOOR	Poem	305
Roberts, Arthur Llewelyn	ROBE ARTH LL	Letter	157
Roberts, George	ROBE GEOR	Letter	157
Roberts, Michael	ROBE MICH	Letter	157
Robertson, Walford	ROBE WALF	Letter	157
Robins, Elizabeth	ROBI ELIZ	Letter	158
Robinson, Corinne (Roosevelt)	ROBI CORI	Letter	158
Robinson, Lennox	ROBI LENN	Letter	158
Robinson, Lennox	ROBI LENN	Inscription	89
Robinson, Lennox: A LITTLE ANTHOLOGY OF MODERN IRISH VERSE	ROBI LITT 28	Other	216
Roger Casement	ROGE CASE	Poem	305
Rolleston, [Thomas William]	ROLL THOM WI	Letter	158
Rome Lecture	ROME LECT	Speech	378
Rose of Battle, The	ROSE BATT	Poem	305
Rose of Peace, The	ROSE PEAC	Poem	306
Rose of Shadow, The	ROSE SHAD	Prose	364
Rose of the World, The	ROSE WORL	Poem	306
Rose, Edward	ROSE EDWA	Inscription	89
Rose Tree, The	ROSE TREE	Poem	306
Rossi, Mario: PILGRIMAGE IN THE WEST	ROSS PILG 33	Other	216

Rossi, Mario	ROSS MARI	Letter	158
Rosy Cross, The See UNPU ROSY CR.		Book	60
Rothenstein, William	ROTH WILL	Letter	158
Rothenstein, William	ROTH WILL	Inscription	89
Royal Irish Academy	ROYA IRIS AC	Letter	158
Ruddock, Margot: THE LEMON TREE	RUDD LEMO 36	Other	216
Ruffort, Walter	RUFF WALT	Letter	159
Rummel, Walter Morse	RUMM WALT MO	Letter	159
Running to Paradise	RUNN PARA	Poem	306
Russel, Father	RUSS FATH	Inscription	89
Russell, Father Matthew	RUSS FATH MA	Letter	159
Russell, George	RUSS GEOR	Inscription	89
Russell, George	RUSS GEOR	Letter	159
Russell, George: BY STILL WATERS	RUSS BY 06	Other	217
Ryan, Mr.	RYAN MR.	Letter	160
Sad Shepherd, The	SAD SHEP	Poem	306
Sage, Michael: MRS. PIPER AND THE SOCIETY FOR PSYCHICAL RESEARCH	SAGE PIPE 03	Other	217
Sailing to Byzantium	SAIL BYZA	Poem	306
Saint and the Hunchback, The	SAIN HUNC	Poem	306
Salt, Dr.	SALT DR.	Letter	160
Samhain: 1904	SAMH 1904	Prose	364
Samhain: 1905	SAMH 1905	Prose	364
Samhain: 1906	SAMH 1906	Prose	364
Samhain: 1908. First Principles	SAMH 1908 FI	Prose	364
Samhain: 1909	SAMH 1909	Prose	364
Samhain: 1910 See THEA MATE.		Prose	203
Sandymount Castle School Library	SAND CAST SC	Inscription	90
Sansloy-Sansfoy-Sansjoy	SANS SANS SA	Poem, Unpu.	348
Sassoon, Siegfried	SASS SIEG	Letter	160
Sato, Junzo	SATO JUNZ	Inscription	90
Schepeler, Alexandria	SCHE ALEX	Letter	160
Scholars, The	SCHO	Poem	307
Schroeder, [William Lawrence]	SCHR WILL LA	Letter	160
Scott, C.P.	SCOT C.P.	Letter	160
Scott-James, Rolfe (Editor, London Mercury)	SCOT ROLF	Letter	160
Scribner	SCRI	Letter	160
Scribner Edition See UNPU SCRI ED.		Book	56
Scroope, Mr.	SCRO MR.	Letter	160
Sealy, Bryers, and Walker	SEAL BRYE WA	Letter	161
Second Book of the Rhymers' Club	SECO BOOK 94	Book	48
Second Coming, The	SECO COMI	Poem	307
Secret Rose, The	SECR ROSE 97	Book	48
Secret Rose, The	SECR ROSE	Poem	307
Secretary of Royal Society	SECR ROYA SO	Letter	161

Secrets of the Old, The	SECR OLD	Poem	307
Seeker, The	SEEK	Poem	307
Selected Poems	SELE POEM 21	Book	49
Selected Poems	SELE POEM 29	Book	49
Selection from the Love Poetry, A	SELE LOVE 13	Book	50
Selection from the Poetry, A	SELE POET 13	Book	50
September 1913	SEPT 1913	Poem	307
Settle, Miss	SETT MISS	Letter	161
Seven paters seven times	SEVE PATE SE	Poem	308
Seven Poems and a Fragment	SEVE POEM 22	Book	51
Seven Sages, The	SEVE SAGE	Poem	308
Shadowy Waters, The	SHAD WATE	Poem	308
Shadowy Waters, The	SHAD WATE 00	Book	51
Shadowy Waters, The	SHAD WATE 01	Book	51
Shadowy Waters, The	SHAD WATE 07	Book	52
Shahan, Thomas	SHAH THOM	Letter	161
Shakespear, Olivia	SHAK OLIV	Inscription	90
Shakespear, Olivia	SHAK OLIV	Letter	161
Shakespeare Memorial	SHAK MEMO	Letter	161
Shannon, Charles	SHAN CHAR	Letter	161
Sharp, William	SHAR WILL	Inscription	90
Sharp, William	SHAR WILL	Letter	162
Shaw, Charlotte	SHAW CHAR	Letter	162
Shaw, George B.	SHAW GEOR B.	Letter	162
Shaw, George Bernard	SHAW GEOR BE	Inscription	91
Shaw, T.E.	SHAW T.E.	Letter	162
Shaw-Taylor John	SHAW TAYL JO	Letter	162
See also JOHN SHAW TA.		Prose	360
She has us by the throat	SHE HAS US	Poem, Unpu.	348
She Turns the Dolls' Faces to the Wall	SHE TURN DO	Poem	309
She Who Dwelt Among the Sycamores	SHE WHO DW	Poem	309
Sheil, Frank J.	SHEI FRAN J.	Letter	162
Shelly, Percy Bysshe: SELECT WORKS	SHEL SELE 66	Other	217
Shepherd and Goatherd	SHEP GOAT	Poem	309
Sherman, Philip	SHER PHIL	Letter	162
Sherrard, Mr.	SHER MR.	Letter	162
Shine, Mrs.	SHIN MRS.	Letter	163
Shiubhaligh, Maire See WALK MARY.		Letter	174
Shorter, Clement	SHOR CLEM	Letter	163
Shorter, Mrs. Dora	SHOR MRS. DO	Letter	163
Siberry, Charles E.	SIBE CHAR E.	Letter	163
Sidgewick, Frank	SIDG FRAN	Letter	163
Sigerson, George	SIGE GEOR	Letter	163
Simpson, Dr. Robert	SIMP DR. RO	Letter	164

Simson, Theodore See SPIC SIMS TH.		Letter	165
Sinclair, Mr.	SINC MR.	Letter	164
Singing Head and the Lady, The	SING HEAD 34	Book	52
Singing Head and the Lady, The	SING HEAD LA	Poem	309
Sir John	SIR JOHN	Letter	164
Sitwell, Dame Edith	SITW DAME ED	Letter	164
Sixteen Dead Men	SIXT DEAD ME	Poem	309
Smith	SMIT	Letter	164
Smith, J.	SMIT J.	Inscription	91
Smith, Mrs. Travers	SMIT MRS. TR	Letter	164
Smith, Pamela	SMIT PAME	Inscription	91
Smith, T.R.	SMIT T.R.	Letter	164
Solomon and the Witch	SOLO WITC	Poem	309
Solomon to Sheba	SOLO SHEB	Poem	310
Solomons, Dr. B.	SOLO DR. B.	Letter	164
Some Essays and Passages by John Eglinton	SOME ESSA 05	Book	52
See also EGLI SOME 05.		Other	207
Song, A	SONG	Poem	310
Song from The Player Queen, A	SONG PLAY QU	Poem	310
Song of Heffernan the Blind, The	SONG HEFF BL	Poem, Unpu.	349
Song of the Faeries	SONG FAER	Poem	310
Song of the Happy Shepherd, The	SONG HAPP SH	Poem	310
Song of the Old Mother, The	SONG OLD MO	Poem	310
Song of the Rosy Cross, A	SONG ROSY CR	Poem	310
Song of Wandering Aengus, The	SONG WAND AE	Poem	311
Songs from Deirdre I, II, III	SONG DEIR 1	Play	226
Sonnet I	SONN I	Poem, Unpu.	349
Sophocles' King Oedipus	SOPH KING OE	Play	237
Sophocles' Oedipus at Colonus	SOPH OEDI CO	Play	237
Sorrow of Love, The	SORR LOVE	Poem	311
Soul of the fountains spoke me a word	SOUL FOUN SP	Poem, Unpu.	349
Spare, A.	SPAR A.	Inscription	91
Sparling, Henry H.	SPAR HENR H.	Letter	164
Speckled Bird, The See UNPU SPEC BI.		Book	60
Speech and Two Poems, A	SPEE TWO 31	Book	53
Speyer, Edward	SPEY EDWA	Letter	165
Spicer-Simson, Theodore	SPIC SIMS TH	Letter	165
Spilt Milk	SPIL MILK	Poem	311
Spinning Song	SPIN SONG	Poem	311
Spirit Medium, The	SPIR MEDI	Poem	312
Spirit of the Sea	SPIR SEA	Poem, Unpu.	349
Spur, The	SPUR	Poem	312
Squire, J.	SQUI J.	Inscription	91
Squire, John	SQUI JOHN	Letter	165
St. Lawrence, Mrs.	ST. LAWR MR	Letter	165

Index

St. Patrick's Night	ST. PATR NI	Speech	378
Stare's Nest by My Window, The	STAR NEST MY	Poem	312
Starkey, James	STAR JAME	Letter	165
Statesman's Holiday, The	STAT HOLI	Poem	312
Statistics	STAT ISTI CS	Poem	312
Statues, The	STAT UES	Poem	313
Stead, W.F.	STEA W.F.	Letter	165
Stephens, A.G.	STEP A.G.	Letter	165
Stephens, James	STEP JAME	Inscription	91
Stephens, James	STEP JAME	Letter	165
Steven, [Hilda A.]	STEV HILD A.	Letter	166
Stick of Incense, A	STIC INCE	Poem	313
Stockholm Banquet Speech	STOC BANQ SP	Speech	378
Stoker, Bram	STOK BRAM	Inscription	91
Stokes, Margaret	STOK MARG	Letter	166
Stolen Child, The	STOL CHIL	Poem	313
Stone, Melville	STON MELV	Letter	166
Stories of Michael Robartes and his Friends	STOR MICH 31	Book	53
Stone, Miss	STON MISS	Letter	166
Stories of Red Hanrahan	STOR RED 04	Book	54
Stories of Red Hanrahan	STOR RED 14	Book	54
Stories of Red Hanrahan and The Secret Rose	STOR RED 27	Book	55
Stories of Red Hanrahan: Secret Rose: Rosa Alchemica	STOR RED 13	Book	54
Stream and Sun at Glendalough	STRE SUN GL	Poem	313
Street Dancers	STRE DANC	Poem	314
Strong, L.A.G.	STRO L.A.	Letter	166
Stuart, Frances	STUA FRAN	Letter	166
Stuart, Francis and Iseult	STUA FRAN IS	Inscription	91
Stuart, Francis: PIGEON IRISH	STUA PIGE 32	Other	217
Stuart, Iseult See GONN ISEU.		Letter	121
Stuart, Mr.	STUA MR.	Letter	166
Sturm, Frank Pearce	STUR FRAN PE	Letter	166
Summer and Spring	SUMM SPRI	Poem	314
Summer Evening, A	SUMM EVEN	Poem	314
Sunrise	SUNR	Poem, Unpu.	349
Supernatural Songs	SUPE SONG	Poem	314
Sutherland, Duchess	SUTH DUCH	Letter	167
Swami, Shri Purohit: AN INDIAN MONK	SWAM INDI 32	Other	217
Swami, Shri Purohit: THE TEN PRINCIPAL UPANISHADS See TEN PRIN 37.		Book	56
Swanton, F.C.J.	SWAN F.C.	Letter	167
Swedenborg, Mediums and the Desolate Places	SWED MEDI DE	Prose	364
Sweet Dancer	SWEE DANC	Poem	314

Swete, Lyall	SWET LYAL	Inscription	92
Swift's Epitaph	SWIF EPIT	Poem	314
Symbolism in Painting	SYMB PAIN	Prose	365
Symbols	SYMB	Poem	314
Symons, Arthur	SYMO ARTH	Inscription	92
Symons, Arthur	SYMO ARTH	Letter	167
Synge and the Ireland of his Time	SYNG IREL 11	Book	55
Synge and the Ireland of his Time See BURL HOUS LE.		Speech	373
Synge, John	SYNG JOHN	Letter	167
Synge, John M.: COLLECTED PLAYS	SYNG COLL 23	Other	218
Synge, John M.: POEMS AND TRANSLATIONS	SYNG POEM 09	Other	218
Tables of the Law, The	TABL LAW 04	Book	56
Tables of the Law, The	TABL LAW 14	Book	56
Tables of the Law, The Adoration of the Magi	TABL LAW 97	Book	55
Tage, Philip	TAGE PHIL	Inscription	92
Tagore, Rabindranath	TAGO RABI	Letter	167
Tagore, Rabindranath: GITANJALI	TAGO GITA 12	Other	218
Tagore, Rabindranath: THE POST OFFICE	TAGO POST 14	Other	218
Tailteann Banquet Speech	TAIL BANQ SP	Speech	378
Take up your rifle	TAKE UP RI	Poem, Unpu.	349
Tall men, The	TALL MEN	Poem, Unpu.	349
Ten Principal Upanishads, The	TEN PRIN 37	Book	56
Tethra before whose windy throne	TETH WHOS WI	Poem, Unpu.	350
That the Night Come	THAT NIGH CO	Poem	315
Thayer, Scofield	THAY SCOF	Letter	167
Theatre Material	THEA MATE	Miscellany	202
Theatre of Beauty	THEA BEAU	Speech	379
Theatre of Beauty, The	THEA BEAU	Prose	365
Theatre Speeches See UNID THEA SP.		Speech	381
Then up spring up before me on the saddle	THEN UP SP	Poem, Unpu.	350
There	THER	Poem	315
There is a flowery sunny dotted glade	THER IS FL	Poem, Unpu.	350
There is no man but may meet	THER IS NO	Poem, Unpu.	350
There lived a man of wealth	THER LIVE MA	Poem, Unpu.	350
These are the Clouds	THES ARE CL	Poem	315
They mingle with the briar	THEY MING BR	Poem, Unpu.	350
This lake washeth around the ruby strand	THIS LAKE WA	Poem, Unpu.	350
This man is murdered	THIS MAN IS	Poem, Unpu.	351
Thomas Davis	THOM DAVI	Prose	365
Thomas Davis Lecture	THOM DAVI LE	Speech	379

Index

Thompson, Mr.	THOM MR.	Letter	167
Thorpe, Mr.	THOR MR.	Letter	168
Those Dancing Days are Gone	THOS DANC DA	Poem	315
Those Images	THOS IMAG	Poem	315
Though leagues asunder	THOU LEAG AS	Poem, Unpu.	351
Though loud years come and loud years go	THOU LOUD YE	Poem, Unpu.	351
Thought from Propertius, A	THOU PROP	Poem	315
Three Beggars, The	THRE BEGG	Poem	316
Three Bushes, The	THRE BUSH	Poem	316
Three Hermits, The	THRE HERM	Poem	316
Three Marching Songs	THRE MARC SO	Poem	316
Three Monuments, The	THRE MONU	Poem	316
Three Movements	THRE MOVE	Poem	316
Three Shafts See UNID THRE SH.		Speech	381
Three Songs to the One Burden	THRE SONG ON	Poem	317
Three Songs to the Same Tune	THRE SONG SA	Poem	317
Three Things	THRE THIN	Poem	317
Thring, Herbert	THRI HERB	Letter	168
Thus ignorant of your features	THUS IGNO FE	Poem, Unpu.	351
Time and the Witch Vivien	TIME WITC VI	Poem	318
Times Editor	TIME EDIT	Letter	168
To a Child Dancing in the Wind	TO CHIL DA	Poem	318
To a Friend whose Work has come to Nothing	TO FRIE WH	Poem	318
To a Poet, who would have me Praise certain bad Poets, Imitators of His and Mine	TO POET WH	Poem	319
To a Shade	TO SHAD	Poem	319
To a Sister of the Cross of the Rose	TO SIST CR	Poem, Unpu.	352
To a Squirrel at Kyle-na-no	TO SQUI KY	Poem	319
To a Wealthy Man who promised a Second Subscription to the Dublin Municipal Gallery if it were proved the People wanted Pictures	TO WEAL MA	Poem	319
To a Young Beauty	TO YOUN BE	Poem	320
To a Young Girl	TO YOUN GI	Poem	320
To All Artist and Writers	TO ALL AR	Prose	365
To An Isle In the Water	TO ISLE WA	Poem	320
To Be Carved on Stone at Thoor Ballylee	TO BE CA	Poem	320
To Dorothy Wellesley	TO DORO WE	Poem	320
To Garret or Cellar a wheel I send	TO GARR CE	Poem	320
To his Heart, bidding it have no fear	TO HEAR BI	Poem	321

To Ireland in the Coming Times	TO	IREL CO	Poem	321
To Maud Gonne	TO	MAUD GO	Poem, Unpu.	351
To Moorhead, Blind	TO	MOOR BL	Poem, Unpu.	352
To Some I Have Talked with by the Fire	TO	SOME I	Poem	321
To the Rose upon the Rood of Time	TO	ROSE RO	Poem	321
Todhunter, John	TODH	JOHN	Inscription	92
Tom at Cruachan	TOM	CRUA	Poem	322
Tom O'Roughley	TOM	O'RO	Poem	322
Tom the Lunatic	TOM	LUNA	Poem	323
Torrence, Ridgeley	TORR	RIDG	Letter	168
Towards Break of Day	TOWA	BREA DA	Poem	323
Tower, The	TOWE		Poem	324
Tower, The	TOWE	28	Book	56
Tower wind beaten grim	TOWE	WIND BE	Poem, Unpu.	352
Tragic Theatre, The	TRAG	THEA	Prose	365
Trantis, Edith B.	TRAN	EDIT B.	Inscription	92
Travail of Passion, The	TRAV	PASS	Poem	324
Travers-Smith, Dorothy	TRAV	SMIT DO	Letter	168
TREASURY OF IRISH POETRY IN THE ENGLISH TONGUE	TREA	IRIS 00	Other	219
Trembling of the Veil, The	TREM	VEIL 22	Book	57
Trevelyan, R.C.	TREV	R.C.	Letter	168
Tribes of the Danu, The	TRIB	DANU	Prose	365
Tucker, Mrs.	TUCK	MRS.	Inscription	92
Turner, W.J.	TURN	W.J.	Letter	168
Turner, W.J.	TURN	W.J.	Inscription	92
Twilight--Loch an Eilan	TWIL	LOCH AN	Poem, Unpu.	352
Two Favorites of the Celestial Bodies, The	TWO	FAVO CE	Poem, Unpu.	352
Two Kings, The	TWO	KING	Poem	324
Two names all day	TWO	NAME AL	Poem, Unpu.	353
Two Plays for Dancers	TWO	PLAY 19	Book	58
Two Songs From a Play	TWO	SONG PL	Poem	324
Two Songs of a Fool	TWO	SONG FO	Poem	325
Two Songs Rewritten for the Tune's Sake	TWO	SONG RE	Poem	325
Two Titans, The	TWO	TITA	Poem	325
Two Trees, The	TWO	TREE	Poem	325
Two Years Later	TWO	YEAR LA	Poem	325
Unappeasable Host, The	UNAP	HOST	Poem	325
Under Ben Bulben	UNDE	BEN BU	Poem	325
Under Saturn	UNDE	SATU	Poem	326
Under the Moon	UNDE	MOON	Poem	326
Under the Round Tower	UNDE	ROUN TO	Poem	326
Unicorn From the Stars, The	UNIC	STAR 08	Book	58

Index   515

Unicorn from the Stars, The	UNIC STAR	Play	237
Unidentified: A Glass of Beer	UNID GLAS BE	Speech	379
Unidentified: Compulsory Education	UNID COMP ED	Speech	379
Unidentified: Home Rule	UNID HOME RU	Speech	380
Unidentified: Ideal Drama	UNID IDEA DR	Speech	380
Unidentified: Irish Folklore	UNID IRIS FO	Speech	380
Unidentified: Lecture Notes	UNID LECT NO	Speech	380
Unidentified: Mysticism	UNID MYST	Speech	380
Unidentified: A New Unionist Party	UNID NEW UN	Speech	380
Unidentified: Poetics	UNID POET	Speech	380
Unidentified: Theatre Speech	UNID THEA SP	Speech	381
Unidentified: Three Shafts	UNID THRE SH	Speech	381
Unidentified: Writer and Audience	UNID WRIT AU	Speech	381
University of Cairo	UNIV CAIR	Letter	168
Unknown Correspondent	UNKN CORR	Letter	169
Unknown Recipient	UNKN RECI	Inscription	93
Unpublished Unidentified Material	UNPU UNID MA	Poem, Unpu.	353
Unpublished: Agnes Tobin Translation	UNPU AGNE TO	Prose	366
Unpublished: An all but an empty room	UNPU ALL EM	Prose	366
Unpublished: Anglo Ireland	UNPU ANGL IR	Prose	366
Unpublished: Bishop and the Monk	UNPU BISH MO	Play	238
Unpublished: Blindness, The See UNPU EPIC FO.		Play	239
Unpublished: Chairman and Parliamentary Party	UNPU CHAI PA	Play	238
Unpublished: Chicago schools	UNPU CHIC SC	Prose	366
Unpublished: Contempt for idealism	UNPU CONT ID	Prose	366
Unpublished: Country of the Young	UNPU COUN YO	Play	238
Unpublished: Cyprian	UNPU CYPR	Play	238
Unpublished: Dagger still in his Hand	UNPU DAGG ST	Play	238
Unpublished: Death of Lady Gregory	UNPU DEAT LA	Prose	366
Unpublished: Door of a Large House	UNPU DOOR LA	Play	239
Unpublished: Epic of the Forest	UNPU EPIC FO	Play	239
Unpublished: Feud	UNPU FEUD	Prose	366
Unpublished: Giddy day goes barefoot	UNPU GIDD DA	Play	239
Unpublished: Girl and Goatherd	UNPU GIRL GO	Play	239

Unpublished: Gonne, Maud	UNPU GONN MA	Prose	367
Unpublished: He is out [of?] his wits	UNPU HE IS	Play	239
Unpublished: I have read your examination	UNPU I HA	Prose	367
Unpublished: I press that thought	UNPU I PR	Prose	367
Unpublished: I wrote this	UNPU I WR	Prose	367
Unpublished: Irish Dramatic Movement	UNPU IRIS DR	Prose	367
Unpublished: Island Faeries at Evening	UNPU ISLA FA	Play	239
Unpublished: Lady Gregory's "Doctor in Spite of Himself"	UNPU LADY GR	Prose	367
Unpublished: Laying of the Foundations	UNPU LAYI FO	Play	240
Unpublished: Love and Death: A Tragedy	UNPU LOVE DE	Play	239
Unpublished: Love's Decay	UNPU LOVE 'S	Play	240
Unpublished: Macmillan Edition	UNPU MACM ED	Book	59
Unpublished: Modern Ireland	UNPU MODE IR	Prose	367
Unpublished: Modern Poetry	UNPU MODE PO	Prose	368
Unpublished: Old Man and Girl	UNPU OLD MA	Play	240
Unpublished: Opening Ceremony for the Masquers	UNPU OPEN CE	Play	240
Unpublished: Peter and the Shepherd	UNPU PETE SH	Play	240
Unpublished: Poet and the Actress, The	UNPU POET AC	Play	240
Unpublished: Political Situation in the 1920's	UNPU POLI SI	Prose	368
Unpublished: Politics are the forge	UNPU POLI AR	Prose	368
Unpublished: Revival of Irish Literature, The	UNPU REVI IR	Prose	368
Unpublished: Rosy Cross, The	UNPU ROSY CR	Book	60
Unpublished: Rover and the Lord of the Tower, The	UNPU ROVE LO	Play	240
Unpublished: Sacred Grove	UNPU SACR GR	Prose	368
Unpublished: Sans Eyes	UNPU SANS EY	Play	240
Unpublished: Scribner Edition	UNPU SCRI ED	Book	59
Unpublished: Sea Spirit	UNPU SEA SP	Play	241
Unpublished: Shelley's Thought	UNPU SHEL TH	Prose	368
Unpublished: Speckled Bird, The	UNPU SPEC BI	Book	60
Unpublished: Starving of Rothsay	UNPU STAR RO	Play	241
Unpublished: Village of the Elms, The See UNPU EPIC FO.		Play	239
Unpublished: Unidentified Prose	UNPU UNID PR	Prose	369

Index

Unpublished: Tribute to Miss Horniman	UNPU TRIB MI		Prose	368
Unpublished: Ye Pleiades	UNPU YE PL		Book	60
Unpublished: You have grey hair	UNPU YOU HA		Play	241
Unpublished: Younger Generation	UNPU YOUN GE		Prose	368
Unwin, Jane Cobden	UNWI JANE CO		Letter	172
Unwin, T. Fisher	UNWI T. FI		Letter	172
Upon a Dying Lady	UPON DYIN LA		Poem	326
Upon a House shaken by the Land Agitation	UPON HOUS SH		Poem	327
Ussher, Arland	USSH ARLA		Letter	173
Vacillation	VACI		Poem	327
Valley of the Black Pig, The	VALL BLAC PI		Poem	328
Van Krop, Hildo	VANK HILD		Inscription	94
Vaughan	VAUG		Letter	173
Veasey, Miss	VEAS MISS		Inscription	94
Veiled voices and the questions dark	VEIL VOIC QU		Poem, Unpu.	353
Vernandulaynstett	VERN		Letter	173
Verne, Jules: NOVELS	VERN NOVE	29	Other	219
Veronica's Napkin	VERO NAPK		Poem	328
Viele-Griffin, Francis	VIEL FRAN		Inscription	94
Villiers de L'Isle-Adam: AXEL	VILL AXEL	25	Other	219
Virgil: AENEID	VIRG AENE		Other	219
Vision, A	VISI	25	Book	60
Vision, A	VISI	37	Book	61
Vision Material	VISI MATE		Book	61
Vynne, Nora	VYNN NORA		Inscription	94
Wade, Allan	WADE ALLA		Inscription	94
Wade, Allan	WADE ALLA		Letter	173
Waggett, Mr. [E.S.]	WAGG MR. E.		Letter	173
Wagstaff, W.H.	WAGS W.H.		Letter	173
Waithman, Miss	WAIT MISS		Letter	173
Walker, Emery	WALK EMER		Letter	173
Walker, Mary	WALK MARY		Letter	174
Walker, Mary	WALK MARY		Inscription	94
Walkley, A.B.	WALK A.B.		Letter	174
Walsh, James P.	WALS JAME P.		Inscription	94
Wanderings of Oisin, The	WAND OISI	89	Book	62
Wanderings of Oisin, The	WAND OISI		Poem	328
Ward, James	WARD JAME		Letter	174
Wardrop, Marjory Scott: GEORGIAN FOLK TALES	WARD GEOR	94	Other	219
Watch-Fire, The	WATC FIRE		Poem, Unpu.	353
Watkins, Vernon	WATK VERN		Letter	174
Watson, Lady	WATS LADY		Letter	174
Watt, A.P.	WATT A.P.		Letter	174
Watt, Mr. See MACM COMP.			Letter	138
We heard the thrushes by the shore of the sea	WE HEAR TH		Poem, Unpu.	353

Weber, William	WEBE WILL	Letter	174
Well and the Tree, The	WELL TREE	Poem	329
Wellesley, Dorothy	WELL DORO	Inscription	94
Wellesley, Dorothy	WELL DORO	Letter	175
Wellesley, Dorothy: POEMS OF TEN YEARS	WELL POEM 34	Other	220
Wellesley, Dorothy: SELECTIONS FROM THE POEMS	WELL SELE 36	Other	220
Wells, Caroline	WELL CARO	Inscription	95
Wells, James R.	WELL JAME R.	Letter	175
Wetherell, J.E.	WETH J.E.	Letter	175
Wharton, Mrs.	WHAR MRS.	Letter	175
What is the explanation of it all?	WHAT IS EX	Poem, Unpu.	353
What Magic Drum	WHAT MAGI DR	Poem	329
What Then?	WHAT THEN	Poem	329
What Was Lost	WHAT WAS LO	Poem	329
Wheel, The	WHEE	Poem	329
Wheels and Butterflies	WHEE BUTT 34	Book	63
Whelan	WHEL	Letter	175
When Constantine's descendant ruled the world	WHEN CONS DE	Poem, Unpu.	354
When Helen Lived	WHEN HELE LI	Poem	329
When I have wrapped the wolf hide	WHEN I HA	Poem, Unpu.	354
When to its end	WHEN TO IT	Poem, Unpu.	354
When You are Old	WHEN YOU OL	Poem	329
When You Are Sad	WHEN YOU SA	Poem	329
Whence Had They Come	WHEN HAD TH	Poem	330
Where My Books Go	WHER MY BO	Poem	330
Where There Is Nothing	WHER THER IS	Play	241
Where There Is Nothing (Lane)	WHER THER 02	Book	65
Where There Is Nothing (Samhain)	WHER THER 02	Book	64
Where There Is Nothing (London)	WHER THER 03	Book	65
Where There Is Nothing (New York)	WHER THER 03	Book	65
Where thy white waters	WHER THY WH	Poem, Unpu.	354
Wherever in the wastes of wrinkling sand	WHER WAST WR	Poem, Unpu.	354
While I, from that reed-throated whisperer	WHIL I RE	Poem	330
White Birds, The	WHIT BIRD	Poem	330
White, Elizabeth	WHIT ELIZ	Letter	175
White, H.O.	WHIT H.O.	Letter	175
Whittier, John Greenleaf: THE POETICAL WORKS	WHIT POET 86	Other	220
Who Goes with Fergus	WHO GOES FE	Poem	330
Why does my Heart beat so?	WHY DOES MY	Poem	330

Index

Why does your Heart beat thus?	WHY DOES YO	Poem	330
Why is it," Queen Edain Said. See QUEE EDAI.	WHY IS IT	Poem Poem	331 302
Why Should Not Old Men Be Mad?	WHY SHOU NO	Poem	330
Why should the Heart take Fright	WHY SHOU HE	Poem	331
Wicked Hawthorn Tree, The	WICK HAWT TR	Poem	331
Wild Old Wicked Man, The	WILD OLD WI	Poem	331
Wild Swans at Coole, Other Verses and a Play in Verse	WILD SWAN 17	Book	66
Wild Swans at Coole (London), The	WILD SWAN 19	Book	66
Wild Swans at Coole (New York), The	WILD SWAN 19	Book	67
Wild Swans at Coole, The	WILD SWAN CO	Poem	331
Wilde, Oscar: THE COMPLETE WORKS OF OSCAR WILDE	WILD COMP 23	Other	220
Wilkinson, Marguerit	WILK MARG	Letter	176
William Blake and His Illustrations to the Divine Comedy	WILL BLAK IL	Prose	369
Williams, A.M.	WILL A.M.	Inscription	95
Williamson, George	WILL GEOR	Letter	176
Wilson, David	WILS DAVI	Letter	176
Wilson, John Gideon	WILS JOHN GI	Letter	176
Wilson, Mr.	WILS MR.	Letter	176
Wilson, Mrs.	WILS MRS.	Letter	176
Wilson, Rathmell	WILS RATH	Letter	176
Wind Among the Reeds, The	WIND REED 99	Book	67
Wind Among the Reeds, The	WIND REED 03	Book	69
Winding Stair Material	WIND STAI MA	Book	70
Winding Stair, The (Fountain)	WIND STAI 29	Book	69
Winding Stair, The (Gaige)	WIND STAI 29	Book	69
Winding Stair, The	WIND STAI 33	Book	69
Wingfield, Sheila	WING SHEI	Letter	176
Wisdom	WISD	Poem	331
Wisdom and Dreams	WISD DREA	Poem	332
Witch, The	WITC	Poem	332
Withering of the Boughs, The	WITH BOUG	Poem	332
Withers, Percy	WITH PERC	Letter	176
Wizards and Witches in Irish Folklore	WIZA WITC IR	Prose	369
Wolfe, Humbert	WOLF HUMB	Letter	177
Wolley, Miss	WOLL MISS	Inscription	95
Wollman, Maurice	WOLL MAUR	Letter	177
Woman Homer Sung, A	WOMA HOME SU	Poem	332
Woman Young and Old, A	WOMA YOUN OL	Poem	332
Woman's beauty is like a white frail Bird, A	WOMA BEAU IS	Poem	333

Wood, Mrs.	WOOD MRS.	Letter	177
Words	WORD	Poem	333
Words for Music Perhaps	WORD MUSI PE	Poem	333
Words for Music Perhaps and Other Poems	WORD MUSI 32	Book	71
Words Upon the Window-Pane, The	WORD WIND PA	Play	241
Words upon the Window Pane, The	WORD WIND 34	Book	71
Works of William Blake, The	WORK WILL 93	Book	71
World is but a strange romance, The	WORL IS ST	Poem, Unpu.	354
Wright, Mr.	WRIG MR.	Letter	177
Wright, Mrs.	WRIG MRS.	Letter	177
Writer and Audience See UNID WRIT AU.		Speech	381
Ye Pleiades See UNPU YE PLEI.		Book	60
Yeats, Anne	YEAT ANNE	Inscription	95
Yeats, Anne	YEAT ANNE	Letter	177
Yeats, Elizabeth	YEAT ELIZ	Inscription	95
Yeats, Elizabeth	YEAT ELIZ	Letter	177
Yeats, George	YEAT GEOR	Letter	178
Yeats, George	YEAT GEOR	Inscription	96
Yeats, Jack	YEAT JACK	Inscription	97
Yeats, Jack: SLIGO	YEAT SLIG 30	Other	220
Yeats, John Butler	YEAT JOHN BU	Inscription	97
Yeats, John Butler	YEAT JOHN BU	Letter	178
Yeats, John Butler: EARLY MEMORIES	YEAT EARL 23	Other	221
Yeats, John Butler: FURTHER LETTERS OF JOHN BUTLER YEATS	YEAT FURT 20	Other	221
Yeats, John Butler: PASSAGES FROM THE LETTERS	YEAT PASS 17	Other	221
Yeats, Lily	YEAT LILY	Letter	178
Yeats, Lily	YEAT LILY	Inscription	97
Yeats, Michael	YEAT MICH	Letter	178
Yeats, Michael	YEAT MICH	Inscription	98
You are Eternal O Mother Eri	YOU ARE ET	Poem, Unpu.	354
You are my good	YOU ARE GO	Poem, Unpu.	354
Young Man's Song	YOUN MAN' SO	Poem	333
Young, Ella	YOUN ELLA	Inscription	98
Young, Ella	YOUN ELLA	Letter	178
Young, James Carleton	YOUN JAME CA	Inscription	98
Young, Miss	YOUN MISS	Letter	179
Young, Stark	YOUN STAR	Letter	179
Younger Generation	YOUN GENE	Speech	381
Your Pathway	YOUR PATH	Poem, Unpu.	355
Youth and Age	YOUT AGE	Poem	333
Youthful Innocence See GARD EDEN.		Poem, Unpu.	340
Zabel, Morton	ZABE MORT	Letter	179

For Product Safety Concerns and Information please contact our EU representative GPSR@taylorandfrancis.com
Taylor & Francis Verlag GmbH, Kaufingerstraße 24, 80331 München, Germany

www.ingramcontent.com/pod-product-compliance
Lightning Source LLC
Chambersburg PA
CBHW071133300426
44113CB00009B/962